The A L A Glossary

The A L A Glossary
of Library and Information Science

Heartsill Young, Editor

with the assistance of

Terry Belanger
John B. Corbin
Rose Mary Magrill
Fred M. Peterson
Diana M. Thomas
Andrew G. Torok
Blanche Woolls

**AMERICAN
LIBRARY
ASSOCIATION**
Chicago 1983

Designed by Ellen Pettengell

Composed by Western Publishing Company
   in Times Roman on Information
   International Inc. videocomp
   typesetter

Printed on 50-pound Antique Glatfelter,
   a pH-neutral stock, by
   Malloy Lithographing, Inc.

Bound in B-grade Holliston linen cloth
   by John H. Dekker & Sons

Library of Congress Cataloging in Publication Data
Main entry under title:

The ALA glossary of library and information science.

   1. Library science—Dictionaries.   2. Information
science—Dictionaries.   I. Young, Heartsill,
1917–   .   II. Belanger, Terry.   III. Title:
A.L.A. glossary of library and information science.
Z1006.A48   1982   020′.3   82-18512
ISBN 0-8389-0371-1

Contents

v

Foreword

The idea of revising the *A.L.A. Glossary of Library Terms* was considered from the moment of publication in 1943, the first edition being viewed as tentative. Preliminary work was implemented by the Editorial Committee of ALA, which took two polls of the field to learn whether a revision was needed. The results of these polls, one in 1951 and the other in 1954, were inconclusive. With the passage of time, the answer became evident. Librarianship began to move in several distinct directions at one time, and the number of new terms being absorbed from other fields made the need for a new edition beyond dispute. In 1975 the Publishing Committee of the ALA accepted a staff plan for revising the work.

Because of the diverse sources of new terms, the essence of the plan was to call upon experts in the different specialties of library and information science to write definitions. The work of these specialists would be coordinated by a chairperson who would compile the terms to be defined, examine the definitions submitted, and make them stylistically consistent. J. Phillip Immroth accepted the chair in 1976. After his untimely death in 1977, Heartsill Young began the work anew. He assembled a group of seven subject specialists to compose definitions in their fields and supervised the compilation of the GLOSSARY to its completion in 1983.

The terms and definitions included in the GLOSSARY are utilitarian, reflecting as they do the current practices of libraries and related information agencies in the United States. While the definitions do not have the official endorsement of the American Library Association, the Publishing Committee approves them as a contribution toward the development of standard terminology, or a set of terms, which will enable librarians and other information scientists better to communicate with each other and with specialists in related fields.

JOHN Y. COLE
Chair, ALA
Publishing Committee
1982–83

Acknowledgments

The editor gratefully acknowledges the contributions to the GLOSSARY of the following persons, who served as consultants to the Contributing Advisers, reviewed definitions within their fields, or, in some instances, contributed definitions:

John P. Baker	Olivia M. A. Madison
Adele R. Chwalek	Stephen H. Roberts
Katherine T. Emerson	Nina J. Root
Donald P. Hammer	Elizabeth W. Stone
Janet Swan Hill	Samuel A. Streit
Herbert H. Hoffman	Don R. Swanson
Nancy R. John	Stephen Torok, Sr.
Mel Kavin	Dudley A. Weiss
Mary L. Larsgaard	Ronald E. Wyllys

Contributors

Editor

Heartsill Young, Associate Professor, Graduate School of Library and Information Science, University of Texas at Austin

Contributing Advisers

Fred M. Peterson, University Librarian, Illinois State University
Administration, Buildings and Equipment, Public Services

Rose Mary Magrill, Professor, School of Library and Information Sciences, North Texas State University
Technical Services

Terry Belanger, Assistant Dean, School of Library Service, Columbia University
Bibliography, Manuscripts, Rare Books, Archives, Conservation

Diana M. Thomas, Associate Professor, Graduate School of Library and Information Science, University of California, Los Angeles
Printing, Publishing, Bookbinding

John B. Corbin, Assistant Director for Administration and Systems, University of Houston Libraries
Information Science

Blanche Woolls, Professor, School of Library and Information Science, University of Pittsburgh
Educational Technology

Andrew G. Torok, Associate Professor, Department of Library Science, Northern Illinois University
Reprography

Introduction

The purpose of this GLOSSARY is to bring together, in one place, the definitions of terms that relate to the provision of access to recorded information by libraries and similar information agencies, individually and collectively, and to the functions and activities performed by those agencies.

More specifically, the GLOSSARY includes definitions of terms related to the production, reproduction, collection, organization, storage, retrieval, use, and conservation of documents, and to the organization, administration, and delivery of services by libraries, media centers, and related information agencies. It also includes terms used in research in those functional areas.

Terms included in the GLOSSARY are drawn not only from library and information science, but also from printing and publishing, including paper, typography, composition, and binding; graphic arts, including photography; computer science; telecommunications; reprography, including micrographics; educational technology; administrative science; and archives administration.

The provision of access to the information recorded in documents is represented by terms related to subject cataloging, classification, indexing and abstracting, and information-retrieval systems employing machine-readable databases and records management files in microform.

The names of persons and corporate bodies are excluded, as are the names of commercial products, systems, and services, with the exception of a few generically used trade names such as Monotype.

The definitions of terms in the GLOSSARY are generally compatible with definitions that have been standardized by such organizations and associations as the Association for Educational Communications and Technology, the National Micrographics Association, the Society of American Archivists, and the National Center for Education Statistics. Any differences are as a rule the result of placing the terms in a broader context or bringing the definitions into conformity with the vocabulary of the GLOSSARY. In the case of definitions that have not been standardized, the definition considered to be the most generally acceptable is presented in the GLOSSARY, and the term is used consistently with that meaning when it appears in the definitions of other terms.

In the case of terms used in different forms by different professional groups, the definition in the GLOSSARY appears under the form considered to be generally acceptable to the group with whom the term is most closely related. For example, the definition of a disc on which sounds are recorded is under *audiodisc,* the form used by media specialists, rather than under *sound disc.*

In those instances when a term has a different meaning in different fields, the first definition is the one used in the field with which the term is considered to be most closely associated. For example, the term *editor* is defined first as it is used in publishing and then as it is used in computer science.

As a rule, terms for which acronyms are only sometimes used are entered under the full term, with a reference from the acronym. However, when the full term is rarely, if ever, used and is generally unknown, entry is under the acronym, as in the case of COBOL and PRECIS.

Generally, definitions are given for specific terms in uninverted form; the user will, for example, find the definition of *star network* under that form, rather than under *network, star,* or under the general term *network,* along with the definitions of other types of networks. In some instances, however, the definitions of specific terms are contained within the definition of a broader term, as, for example, under *contrast.* In those instances, a "see" reference is made from the specific to the general term.

The GLOSSARY includes two types of references: "see" and "compare with." Synonymous terms are represented not only by "see" references; they also appear at the end of definitions. For example, the definition of *impact printing* includes the statement, "Synonymous with direct-impression, strike-on, and struck-image printing." The "compare with" references that are included in the definitions refer either to antonymous terms or to related terms, the definitions of which are intended, when compared, to reveal distinctions between the definitions and elucidate them. For example, the definition of *duplex transmission* contains the reference, "Compare with *half-duplex transmission, simplex transmission.*" Italicized terms found within references are terms under which definitions appear.

The user who does not understand terms used within a definition will frequently find those terms also defined in the GLOSSARY. For example, the definition of *bibliographic control* contains the following terms for which definitions appear in the GLOSSARY: bibliographic description, bibliographic record, bibliographic service center, document, library consortium, library network, and union list.

Alphabetization is letter-by-letter, except in the instance of a few inverted or qualified headings, when the term with modification is not separated by filing from the term unmodified.

As advances are made in technology, changes will occur in the form of documents, in the processes by which they are produced, and in the equipment that is needed for some of them to be read, viewed, or heard. Changes will occur also in the information delivery systems of libraries and similar information agencies. In using the GLOSSARY, one should bear in mind that many of the definitions reflect the state of technology at the beginning of the 1980s.

Sources

The editor and members of the revision committee gratefully acknowledge their debt to the many books and articles consulted in the search for definitions to include in the GLOS-SARY.

The definitions of categories of professional and supportive staff in libraries and media centers are based on the categories recommended by ALA in its policy statement, *Library Education and Personnel Utilization,* and the categories recommended by the American Association of School Librarians and the Association for Educational Communications and Technology in *Media Programs, District and School* (Chicago: American Library Association, 1975). The definitions of cartographic terms used as specific material designations in the *Anglo-American Cataloguing Rules,* second edition, are those of the Anglo-American Cataloguing Committee for Cartographic Materials.

Major sources consulted are listed below. Short titles or abbreviations for these sources are used in the GLOSSARY to indicate the source of a quoted definition.

American Library Association. Committee on Library Terminology. *A.L.A. Glossary of Library Terms.* Chicago: The Association, 1943. (ALA Glossary)

American National Standards Institute. *A Compilation of Terms and Definitions Appearing in Z39 Standards.* New York: The Institute, 1977. (Z39)

American Paper Institute. *The Dictionary of Paper.* 4th ed. New York: The Institute, 1980.

Anglo-American Cataloguing Rules. 2nd ed. Chicago: American Library Association, 1978. (AACR2)

Association for Educational Communications and Technology. *Educational Technology: A Glossary of Terms.* Washington, D.C.: The Association, 1979. (AECT)

The Bookman's Glossary. 5th ed. New York: Bowker, 1975. (Bookman's Glossary)

Buchanan, Brian. *A Glossary of Indexing Terms.* Hamden, Conn.: Linnet Books, 1976.

Cartographic Materials: A Manual of Interpretation for AACR2. Chicago: American Library Association, 1982.

Dataflow Systems. *A Glossary for Library Networking.* Network Planning Paper, no. 2. Washington, D.C.: Library of Congress, 1978.

Glaister, Geoffrey Ashall. *Glaister's Glossary of the Book.* 2nd ed. Berkeley: University of California Press, 1979.

Harrod, Leonard Montague. *The Librarians' Glossary.* 4th rev. ed. London: A. Deutsch, 1977.

Lee, Marshall. *Bookmaking.* 2nd ed. New York: Bowker, 1979.

Library Binding Manual. Edited by Maurice F. Tauber. Boston: Library Binding Institute, 1972.

Library Data Collection Handbook. Edited by Mary Jo Lynch. Chicago: Distributed by the Office for Research, American Library Association, 1981. (LDCH)

Sources

Mintz, Patricia Barnes. *Dictionary of Graphic Arts Terms*. New York: Van Nostrand Reinhold, 1981.

National Micrographics Association. *Glossary of Micrographics*. 6th ed. Silver Spring, Md.: The Association, 1980. (NMA)

Neumann, A. J. "A Guide to Networking Terminology." *Information Reports and Bibliographies* 7 (1978): 15–24.

Pettipas, Lisa Anne and Judith Paris. "Glossary of Terms." *Videodisc/Videotex* 1 (1981): 180.

Primer of Business Terms and Phrases Related to Libraries. Edited by Sherman Hayes. Chicago: Library Administration Division, American Library Association, 1978.

Rebsamen, Werner. "A Study of Simple Binding Methods." *Library Scene* 8, nos. 2–4 (June–Dec. 1979), 9, no. 1 (March 1980). (Rebsamen)

Rosenberg, Kenyon C. and John S. Doskey. *Media Equipment: A Guide and Dictionary*. Littleton, Colo.: Libraries Unlimited, 1976.

Saffady, William. *Micrographics*. Littleton, Colo.: Libraries Unlimited, 1978.

Sippl, Charles J. *Microcomputer Dictionary*. 2nd ed. Indianapolis: H.W. Sams, 1981.

Society of American Archivists. Committee on Terminology. "A Basic Glossary for Archivists, Manuscript Curators, and Records Managers." *American Archivist* 37 (1974): 415–33. (SAA)

U.S. National Center for Education Statistics. *Educational Technology: A Handbook of Standard Terminology and a Guide for Recording and Reporting Information about Educational Technology*. State Educational Records and Reports Series: Handbook X. Washington, D.C.: Government Printing Office, 1975. (NCES)

Glossary

abbreviated cataloging see *brief cataloging*

aberration A general term covering a variety of optical defects in a lens which result in the improper formation of an optical image, such as astigmatism and spherical aberration.

abrasion A fine surface defect on processed photographic film which does not penetrate to the film base. Abrasion generally results from moving contact with another surface and does not fully remove the image. Compare with *scratch.*

abridged edition see *abridgment*

abridgment A shortened version of a written work, produced by condensation and omission but with retention of the general meaning and manner of presentation of the original, often prepared by someone other than the author of the original. Sometimes used synonymously with *abstract, compendium* (2), *digest* (1), *epitome* (2), and *synopsis,* all of which denote the abridgment of a larger work, though with different connotations. Synonymous with abridged edition and condensation.

abscissa see *X-axis*

absence circulation system A circulation system in which a loan record is created for items at the time they are borrowed. Compare with *inventory circulation system.*

absolute address 1. In computer science, an address assigned permanently by a machine designer to identify a data storage location. 2. In computer science, a pattern of characters that identifies a unique storage location without further modification. Synonymous with machine address.

absolute language see *machine language*

absolute location see *fixed location*

abstract An abbreviated, accurate representation of a work, usually without added interpretation or criticism, accompanied by a bibliographic reference to the original work when appearing separately from it. Compare with *synopsis.*

abstract bulletin A bulletin issued by a special library which contains abstracts of works of interest to its target group, primarily as a selective dissemination of information service.

abstracting and indexing service A serial issued on paper, in microform, or as a machine-readable database which provides subject access to works in a specific subject field or a group of subject fields by means of abstracts and indexes and is available by subscription or fee.

abstract journal A journal which consists wholly or substantially of abstracts of works in a specific subject field or a group of subject fields.

a/c see *alternating current*

academic library A library forming an integral part of a college, university, or other academic institution for postsecondary education, organized and administered to meet the information needs of students, faculty, and affiliated staff of the institution.

academic status An official recognition by an institution of postsecondary education that librarians are part of the instructional and research staff, but normally without entitlement to ranks and titles identical to those of faculty, and frequently without commensurate benefits, privileges, rights, and responsibilities. Compare with *faculty status.*

academy publication A publication issued by an academy. Sometimes, in an inclusive sense, a publication issued by any learned society.

access 1. In computer-based information retrieval, the method by which a computer refers to records in a file, dependent upon their arrangement. 2. In archives, the general ability to make use of the records of a government, government agency, or other corporate body.

accession 1. In technical processing, to enter documents added to a library collection in an accession record. 2. A document that has been accessioned and added to a library collection. 3. In archives, the act and procedures involved in a transfer of legal title and the taking of records or papers into the physical custody of an archival agency, records center, or manuscript repository. (SAA) 4. The records or papers taken into physical custody by an archival agency, records center, or manuscript repository. (SAA)

accession book see *accession record*

accession catalog see *accession record*

accession file see *accession record*

accession number A consecutive number assigned to each document as it is added to a library collection.

accession order The arrangement of stored documents in the order of their addition to a library collection.

accession record A record of documents added to a library collection, arranged in the order of their addition. For each document the record includes its bibliographic identification, source, cost, and accession number. Synonymous with accession book, accession catalog, and accession file.

access point 1. A name, term, code, etc., under which a bibliographic record may be searched and identified. Compare with *heading* (1). (AACR2) 2. In computer-based information storage and retrieval, a field designated as a means of access to a record or file.

access time In computer-based information retrieval, the interval between the time when data are requested from a storage device and the time delivery begins.

accident In classification theory, an attribute which is incidental to a class, may or may not belong to it, and therefore is not essential to its definition.

accompanying material A complementary part of a work, physically separate from the document containing the predominant part of the work and frequently in a different medium, such as maps in a pocket inside a book cover, an answer book accompanying a textbook, and a pamphlet accompanying an audiodisc.

accountability In the organization of work, the liability on the part of a responsible person or institution to be called on to answer for the performance of assigned duties. Compare with *responsibility*.

accredited library school A library school whose program is accredited by the American Library Association. Compare with *approved library school*.

accrual accounting A method of accounting whereby in financial reports revenues are reported when earned (accrued), and materials and services are reported as expenditures when received. Compare with *cash-flow accounting*.

acetate film A safety film with a film base of cellulose acetate or cellulose triacetate. Most film in use today has an acetate base. Compare with *nitrate film*.

acetate tape A tape of cellulose acetate used as a magnetic tape base.

achromatic colors see *color*

acid-free paper see *permanent-durable paper*

acid resist The light-sensitive coating on a photomechanical printing plate. The degree of light passing through the film negative or positive onto the plate as it is processed determines the hardness of this coating, its resistance to the action of the acid used to etch the printing or nonprinting area on the plate, and thus the depth of the etch.

acoustic coupler A modem connecting a remote terminal with the central processing unit of a computer system by means of the handset of a conventional telephone receiver and dialing over a public or private telephone line. Compare with *modem*.

acoustic feedback In a sound system, the loud noise caused by sound reentering the device which transmitted the original sound. Most often this occurs when sound from the loudspeaker reenters the microphone, causing a shrill howl.

acquisition number The unique number used by a library to identify a bibliographic item on a purchase order. Sometimes standard codes such as the International Standard Book Number and the International Standard Serial Number are used as acquisition numbers.

acquisitions department The administrative unit of a library which performs acquisition services. Synonymous with order department.

acquisition services Activities related to obtaining library materials by purchase, exchange, or gift, including preorder bibliographic searching, ordering and receiving materials, processing invoices, and the maintenance of the necessary records related to acquisitions.

acquisitions files A general term referring to the order records kept by an acquisitions department. May include such files as the on-order/in-process file, outstanding-order file, in-process file, order-number file, date-of-order file, and dealer file. Synonymous with order files.

acquisitions librarian A librarian in charge of or assisting in the work of an acquisitions department. Synonymous with order librarian.

acquisitions searching see *preorder bibliographic search*

across the grain see *against the grain*

acting edition An edition of a play which gives the text as used in stage production (sometimes in a particular production), with entrances and exits, and other stage business. Compare with *script* (1).

actinic light Light rays of short wavelength, occurring in the violet and ultraviolet parts of the spectrum, which are capable of producing photochemical changes in a photosensitive material, such as photographic film.

action group see *task force*

active file A file that is currently in use. Compare with *inactive file, dead file.*

active records (archives) see *current records*

activity In information storage and retrieval, the frequency of referral to records in a file.

activity ratio In information storage and retrieval, the ratio of records referred to or updated to the total number of records in a file.

acutance An objective measure of the sharpness or resolution of a photographic image.

adaptation The modification of a work for a purpose, use, or medium other than that for which the original was intended, such as a dramatization, the free transcription of a musical work, or an engraving from an original painting.

added copy An additional copy of an item already in a library collection which is to be, or has been, added to the collection. Compare with *duplicate* (1). In the plural, sometimes called multiple copies.

added edition An edition of a bibliographic item added to a library collection that differs from editions already in the collection.

added entry 1. An access point other than a main entry. Compare with *main entry* (1). 2. In a unit entry catalog, a bibliographic record, additional to the main entry, by which a bibliographic item is represented. There may be added entries for joint author, editor, translator, illustrator, title, series, subject, etc. Compare with *main entry* (2).

added title page In cataloging, a title page preceding or following the title page chosen as the basis for the description of the bibliographic item. It may be more general, such as a series title page, or equally general, such as a title page in another language. (AACR2)

addendum Brief additional matter, less extensive than a supplement, which is essential to the completeness of the text of a bibliographic item and is usually added at the end of it. Compare with *appendix.*

address A name or number identifying a specific computer-storage device or location of data in storage.

adhesive binding Various methods of leaf affixing which rely on the application of adhesives to hold together the leaves of a volume. The back edges of the volume are trimmed to produce a block of separate leaves, and the edges may be roughened or notched before the adhesive is applied and the case is attached. Among the most common methods of adhesive binding are *fan* *adhesive,* double-fan adhesive, *perfect,* and *thread sealing.*

adhesives A large group of sticky substances used to hold two surfaces together, either by mechanical or chemical binding, or both. In library binding and preservation work, three main groups are used: starch pastes, animal glues, and synthetics. Of the latter group, polyvinyl-acetate emulsions have become widely used in recent years.

ad hoc committee A committee established for a limited time to address a given issue or accomplish a particular task or purpose. Compare with *task force.*

ad interim copyright Under the U.S. copyright law from 1909 to July 1982, a temporary copyright, lasting for a maximum of five years, for books and periodicals in the English language published abroad, and which might be extended to a full copyright if certain conditions were met, including the manufacture of a U.S. edition within the temporary period. The U.S. copyright law of 1976 so liberalized the manufacturing requirement, effective July 1982, that ad interim copyright was excluded from the law as no longer needed.

Adjustable Classification A classification system devised by James Duff Brown in 1897. Designed for smaller libraries, the system used an integral notation, with numbers left vacant to allow for the insertion of new subjects.

adjustable shelving Shelving in which the individual shelves may be adjusted to accommodate library materials of different heights. Compare with *fixed shelving.*

administration 1. A term used variously as a broader term than "management" or synonymously with "management." "Administration" may be defined as the process of coordinating the total resources of an organization toward the accomplishment of the desired goals of that organization through the execution of a group of interrelated functions such as planning, organizing, staffing, directing, and controlling. So defined, "administration" is usually used synonymously with "management" in current literature. "Administration" may be considered to be a broader term, emphasizing the planning function, involving goal setting and major policy formulation, with management variously limited to the process of coordinating certain functions and activities of an organization toward

the accomplishment of its goals. 2. Those persons in an organization with primary responsibility for executing the process of administration.

administrative and support services Those activities related to the provision of general administrative services for the operation of an organization. Specific services included are personnel management, public relations, fiscal management, planning, program management, publications, advertising, and plant and logistical services.

administrative assistant An assistant to the head of an organization or an organizational unit, usually with staff authority, who performs specified duties in support of the activities of the head.

administrative centralization see *centralization, administrative*

administrative code A set of administrative rules and regulations defining acceptable conduct for an organization.

administrative control see *control*

administrative decentralization see *decentralization, administrative*

administrative discretion Authority delegated to an administrative officer or supervisor within an organization to make decisions within a defined area of responsibility.

administrative manual A compilation of policies, rules, and procedures issued by the top administration of an organization which documents officially accepted practices for employees. Compare with *staff handbook, organization manual.*

administrative policy A policy which is officially sanctioned by the appropriate administrative officers of an organization.

administrative procedure A procedure which is officially sanctioned by the appropriate administrative officers of an organization.

administrative staff The group of individuals, usually the top management of an organization, with primary responsibility for administering and providing direction for the organization.

administrator A term frequently used to designate any individual in an organization whose position consists entirely or primarily of administrative duties.

admission record A permit, pass, attendance slip, or other form, used to check a student's attendance in a school library media center with the student's classroom and study hall schedules. Synonymous with library pass and library permit.

ADP see *automatic data processing*

ADSTARS see *automatic document storage and retrieval system*

adult education The education of adults beyond school age through regularly organized programs which have as their purpose the development of skills, knowledge, habits, or attitudes.

adult services The provision of library materials, services, and programs to meet the specific interests and needs of adults by a public library.

advance copies Copies of a book sent out before publication date for review or promotional purposes, sometimes unbound or in a binding different from the publisher's binding. Copies sent out unbound are generally in folded signatures and are termed advance sheets or early sheets. Compare with *review copies.*

advance sheets see *advance copies*

advertisement file A file of advertisements for products and services, found most frequently in the special libraries of business firms and corporations.

advertising types see *display types*

advisory services Special counsel rendered to a library or other agency by an expert or group of experts, usually external, commissioned to study the overall operation or specific areas of concern. Synonymous with consulting services and consultative services.

aerial chart see *aeronautical chart*

aerial remote-sensing image see *remote-sensing image*

aerial view see *bird's-eye view*

aeronautical chart In cartography, a specialized representation of mapped features of the earth, or some part of it, produced to show selected terrain, cultural and hydrographic features, and supplemental information required for air navigation, pilotage, or for planning air operations. Synonymous with aerial chart.

affiliated library A library which, as a member of a library system, is associated with other members of the system under common ownership or control, but which has its own board and maintains a high degree of administrative autonomy, such as a law library or medical library in a university library system.

affirmative action Systematic practices on the part of an employer to ensure that applicants are recruited and employed and that employees are treated without discrimination on the basis of race, color, religion, sex, national origin, age, marital status, sexual orientation, physical and mental handicaps, political affiliation, or other categorical criteria rather than established objective criteria.

AG (average gradient) see *contrast* (1)

against the grain Said of paper which has been folded or cut at right angles to the grain. Synonymous with across the grain.

agent An individual or company from whom, or through whom, library materials are purchased. Used most often to refer to the subscription agent, the intermediary who places periodical subscriptions and secures back issues of periodicals. Compare with *wholesaler.*

agitation The movement of photographic film, paper, or developing solution during processing to ensure maximum contact between the photographic material and chemicals.

aide A person who assists a superior staff member in the fulfillment of his or her duties by performing assigned tasks; frequently used to identify volunteer assistants in a library.

air bells Undeveloped spots that form on negatives or prints as a result of poor agitation during film processing. The defect is generally due to air bubbles that form in washing, preventing effective contact between the developer and photographic material. The term is sometimes used to describe tiny bubbles that form in optical glass.

à la grecque A style of binding with boards cut flush with the cut edges of the book and with headbands protruding above and below the boards; common on Greek printed books of the 16th century.

albertype see *collotype* (1)

alcove A recessed portion of a room enclosed on three sides by walls, partitions, or bookcases placed at right angles, and equipped to accommodate a small number of persons.

ALGOL A common international procedure-oriented programming language (algorithm-oriented language) designed for programming numerical computer applications.

algorithm A defined set of rules or instructions for solving a problem in a finite number of steps. Compare with *heuristic*.

alienation In archives, the act of transferring or losing custody or ownership of records to an agency or person not officially related to the institution or organization whose records are involved. (SAA)

alkaline-buffered paper see *permanent-durable paper*

alkaline reserve paper see *permanent-durable paper*

all along In binding, a style of hand-sewing in which the thread is passed through the fold and around every cord or tape all along the length of each section from the head to the tail kettle stitch. Synonymous with one sheet on and one on. Compare with *two along*.

allocation 1. The process of distributing the available financial, personnel, or material resources at the disposal of an organization for specified purposes and functions. The distribution may be based upon quantitative formulas or administrative judgment. 2. The plan resulting from the allocation process.

allotment The amount of resources assigned to units in an organization to perform specified functions or to be used for specified purposes.

all-over style In binding, a style of decoration in which a small, repeated pattern covers the whole of the side of the cover of a book (as distinct, for example, from a center-and-corner motif).

all published A note used in the description of a multipart item, the publication of which was started but was then discontinued or suspended.

all rights reserved A statement in a printed document indicating that reproduction in any medium of any work contained therein in whole or in part requires the consent of the copyright owner.

almanac 1. A compendium, usually an annual, of statistics and facts, both current and retrospective. May be broad in geographical and subject coverage, or limited to a particular country or state or to a special subject. Compare with *yearbook*. 2. An annual containing miscellaneous matter, such as a calendar, a list of astronomical events, planting tables, astrological predictions, and anecdotes.

alphabetic code A code which uses alphabetic letters to represent other data. Synonymous with alpha code. Compare with *alphanumeric code, numeric code*.

alphabetico-classed catalog A catalog in which the headings of bibliographic records are arranged alphabetically, but in which subject headings display the generic relationships of subjects, in the manner of a classification system. For example, the subject heading for a work on comets would appear as "Science—Astronomy —Comets." Compare with *alphabetico-direct catalog, classed catalog*.

alphabetico-direct catalog A catalog in which the headings of bibliographic records are arranged alphabetically and each subject heading expresses directly and specifically the subject of the work it represents. Synonymous with alphabetico-specific catalog. Compare with *alphabetico-classed catalog*.

alphabetico-specific catalog see *alphabetico-direct catalog*

alphabetize To arrange in alphabetical order. This may be done according to the letter-by-letter method, in which word divisions and punctuation are ignored (e.g., paper covers, papermaking, paper permanence), or according to the word-by-word method, in which entries having the same first word are arranged in the alphabetical order of the next word (e.g., paper covers, paper permanence, papermaking).

alphabet length The length in points of a complete lower case alphabet in any type face and size. The length in points, divided into 341, gives the number of "characters per pica."

alpha-cellulose That portion of a pulp or other cellulosic material which resists solution by aqueous caustic alkalies of mercerizing strength at room temperatures.

alpha code see *alphabetic code*

alphameric see *alphanumeric*

alphanumeric A contraction of "alphabetic-numeric," pertaining to a character set containing alphabetic letters, numbers, and usually special characters. Synonymous with alphameric.

alphanumeric code A code which uses alphabetic letters, numbers, and usually special characters to represent other data. Compare with *alphabetic code, numeric code.*

alternating current (a/c) An electric current that reverses its direction in regular cycles. In the United States, current reverses 60 times a second and is said to have 60-hertz frequency. Compare with *direct current.*

alternative entry Any one of a set of equal access points under which a bibliographic record of a bibliographic item may be searched and identified, such as an access point in a machine-readable bibliographic database. Compare with *main entry* (1), *added entry* (1).

alternative hypothesis A statistical hypothesis accepted after the rejection of the null hypothesis; e.g., that a relationship of specified or unspecified magnitude exists between population parameters.

alternative publications Publications which express views or treat subjects not normally presented in the daily or establishment press. May be politically or culturally right or left of center, but the left usually is emphasized. Sometimes called *underground publications.*

alternative title The second part of a title proper that consists of two parts, each of which is a title; the parts are joined by the word "or" or its equivalent in another language, e.g., *The tempest; or, The enchanted island.* (AACR2)

AM see *amplitude modulation*

ambient light In photography, the general level of illumination surrounding an object or available in a location.

Americana Documents containing works about the Americas or published in the Americas, as distinguished (properly) from documents containing works by American authors. The term usually refers to both North and South America, but it is sometimes loosely used to refer specifically to the United States.

American Standard Code for Information Interchange (ASCII) A standard code designed to facilitate information interchange between unstandardized data-processing and communications equipment. The code, consisting of eight bits including a parity bit, can represent a character set of 128 alphabetic, numeric, and special symbols.

ammonia print see *diazotype process*

ammonia process A dry process in which developing is achieved by using ammonia fumes to neutralize the acidic stabilizers in a two-component diazo material.

amplifier An electronic device for increasing the amplitude of the signal fed into it, while at the same time minimizing any distortion of the signal. The term is usually modified to indicate the kind of signals amplified, such as "audio amplifier" and "video amplifier."

amplitude The intensity of an audio or other signal.

amplitude distortion see *harmonic distortion*

amplitude modulation (AM) A system of radio broadcasting which adjusts the amplitude of the radio carrier wave in accordance with the amplitude of the signal, or sound wave, it carries. Compare with *frequency modulation.*

-ana A suffix denoting anecdotes, literary gossip, and other forms of literary works about a subject, generally a person or a place, as in Columbiana or Johnsoniana; the i is often added for the purpose of euphony.

analog channel A channel used to transmit analog data. Compare with *digital channel.*

analog computer A computer which translates continuous, physical conditions such as voltage or current, pressure, or rotation of a shaft, into related electrical or mechanical quantities, and then performs physical operations on the data. Compare with *digital computer* and *hybrid computer.*

analog data   Data represented in a continuous and physical variable form, such as voltage or current, pressure, rotation of a shaft. Compare with *digital data.*

analog data transmission   The movement of analog data from one point to another along a channel. Compare with *digital data transmission.*

analysis of covariance   A statistical analysis consisting of a combined application of linear regression and analysis of variance techniques to identify and control the effects of one or more independent variables on the dependent variable.

analysis of variance (ANOVA)   A statistical procedure for testing the equality of the means of two or more populations, using the F-distribution.

analytic   see *analytical entry*

analytical bibliography   The study of books as physical objects: the details of their production and the effects of the method of manufacture on their text. Analytical bibliography may deal with the history of printers and booksellers, with the description of paper or bindings, or with textual matters arising during the progression from writer's manuscript to published book. Analytical bibliography (sometimes also called critical bibliography) may be divided into three types: *historical bibliography* (the history of books and of the persons, institutions, and machines producing them); *textual bibliography* (the relationship between the published text and the text as conceived by its author), sometimes also called textual criticism; and *descriptive bibliography* (the close physical description of books). Compare with *enumerative bibliography.*

analytical entry   1. An access point to part of a bibliographic item for which a comprehensive bibliographic record has been made, e.g., to the author and title of a poem in an anthology, to the subject of a chapter of a monograph, or to the title of a separately titled volume of a multivolume set of books. 2. A bibliographic record of part of a bibliographic item for which a comprehensive record may be made. Synonymous with analytic.

analytical index   1. An alphabetical subject index under specific topics to a work that is arranged under relatively broad topics, such as an encyclopedia. 2. A classified index to a work arranged alphabetically by specific topics.

analytical note   The statement in an analytical entry relating to the work or part of a work analyzed to the bibliographic item that contains it, or the document analyzed to the bibliographic item of which it is a part.

analytico-synthetic classification   A classification system which represents a subject by analyzing it into its fundamental constituent elements and synthesizing a class number from the notations for those elements, linked by appropriate connecting symbols. Compare with *enumerative classification.*

anamorphic map   A map which is characterized by an areal distortion in proportion to a factor other than a linear one.

ancillary map   1. A small supplementary or secondary map outside the neat line of the principal or main map. 2. A generic term for small supplementary or secondary maps located either inside or outside the neat line of the principal or main map. Compare with *inset map.*

animation   In motion picture and videotape production, the process of photographing a series of drawings, with each showing slightly changed movement, so that the final film sequence gives the illusion of motion.

annals   1. A periodical which records the transactions of an organization or events and developments in a special field. 2. A record of events arranged in chronological order. 3. In a general sense, any historical narrative.

anniversary issue   see *special number*

annotation   A note accompanying an entry in a bibliography, reading list, or catalog intended to describe, explain, or evaluate the publication referred to.

annual   1. A serial issued once a year. 2. A *giftbook.*

annual report   An official document describing and reviewing the activities, programs, and operations of an organization or one of its divisions for the previous, and usually fiscal, year. It is frequently used for administrative reporting or public relations and usually submitted to the next higher level of administrative authority.

annual review A bibliographic survey of the major publications in a subject field. Used in a general way to refer to serials which may or may not be annual and may be called "Advances in . . . ," "Progress in . . . ," "Year's Work in . . . ," etc. Such surveys provide a state-of-the-art summary when they emphasize the significance and implications, rather than the specific content, of the publications.

anonym 1. A person whose name is not known. 2. A *pseudonym.*

anonymous Said of a work published without any acknowledgment of authorship.

anonymous classic A work of unknown or doubtful authorship, commonly designated by title, which may have appeared in the course of time in many editions, versions, and/or translations.

ANOVA see *analysis of variance*

antenna An aerial of metal rods, wires, or set of wires used to radiate electromagnetic waves in radio transmission, or a similar device used to receive the electromagnetic waves which reach it from the transmitting antenna.

anthology A collection of extracts from the works of various authors, sometimes limited to poetry or to a particular subject.

antihalation The reduction of halation by the use of a light-absorbing dye to tint or coat film and thereby absorb the image light and prevent it from reflecting back into the emulsion. One method is to introduce a layer of light-absorbing dye between the emulsion and the film base; this is referred to as antihalation undercoat. Film with a dye backing on the base side (opposite the emulsion side) is called dye-back film. Film with a dye-tinted base is called tinted stock, an example of which is blue-base film.

antihalation undercoat see *antihalation*

antiqua 1. A German name for roman type. 2. Early types derived from scripts used for 11th- and 12th-century manuscripts in northern Italy.

antiquarian bookseller A dealer in old, rare, and secondhand books.

antique-finish paper An uncoated book paper with a finish that is perceptively rough by sight and touch. Generally considered to be rougher than eggshell-finish paper.

aperture see *lens aperture*

aperture card A card with one or more rectangular holes or apertures designed to hold frames of microfilm. The card is usually a combination of a standard computer punched card and a chip of 35mm microfilm. Synonymous with image card.

aperture slot A narrow rectangular opening in the optical system of rotary cameras for copying moving source documents.

aperture stop see *diaphragm (2)*

APL (A Programming Language) A problem-oriented machine language with special capabilities for handling arrays and for performing mathematical functions.

apocryphal work A work of unknown authorship or doubtful authenticity.

appendix A complementary part of a written work which is not essential to the completeness of the text, such as a list of references, statistical tables, and explanatory matter. Compare with *addendum, supplement.*

application card A printed form which a person fills out to apply for library borrowing privileges, on which are recorded such data as name, address, telephone number, occupation, and signature. Synonymous with registration card.

application program A computer program written by or for a user to process data or perform calculations.

applied research Research which represents investigation directed toward the solution of practical problems, usually with commercial objectives rather than for the advancement of knowledge and discovery of new facts, theories, and laws. Compare with *basic research.*

appraisal 1. The monetary evaluation of books, manuscripts, and other documents for insurance, tax, or other purposes. 2. The process of determining the value (and thus the disposition) of records according to their current administrative, fiscal, or legal use; their informational or research value; their arrangement; and their relationship to other records.

apprentices' library see *mechanics' library*

approach term In information retrieval, the term that an inquirer chooses as the most likely first word to begin a subject search. Compare with *search term*.

appropriation An amount of money made available by the governing body of a library or other agency for expenditure by the agency according to established budgetary and accounting procedures.

approval plan An arrangement by which a publisher or wholesaler assumes the responsibility for selecting and supplying, subject to return privileges, all publications, as issued, fitting a library's collection profile specified in terms of subjects, levels, formats, prices, languages, etc. Some approval plans provide for the library to receive advance notification slips rather than the publications themselves. Compare with *blanket order, on approval.*

approved library school A library school whose program is recognized by a state certification board or education agency as meeting its standards, irrespective of accreditation by the American Library Association. Compare with *accredited library school.*

A Programming Language see *APL*

aquatint 1. A method of etching that produces tones as a network of white dots, through the application of powdered resin to the plate before it is eaten by acid. 2. A print so produced, similar in appearance to a wash or watercolor drawing.

arabesque A style of decoration (especially of bindings) marked by interlacing straight and curved lines in more or less geometrical patterns; derived from Arabian decorative designs.

arbitrary symbol In classification, a notational symbol, such as a punctuation mark or mathematical sign, which has no self-evident place in the filing order.

arbitration The process by which an employer and a union or employee group submit their differences to an impartial party appointed by mutual agreement or statutory provision for resolution after a formal hearing.

architectural barriers Structural or design features of buildings, grounds, or equipment which limit the access of handicapped persons to library services, collections, or facilities.

architectural drawings The various renderings, sketches, and drawings which are developed by an architect or architectural firm in phases over a period of time for a given building project and which are included in the architect's professional services. They include schematic plans, which show floor layouts; preliminary plans, which show structural building elements and the location and space requirements for everything to be included in the building; and working drawings, which show architectural, structural, and mechanical details, and which, together with accompanying specifications, are used for bidding purposes and for the construction of the building.

architectural rendering A pictorial representation of a building intended to show, before it has been built, how the building will look when completed. (AACR2)

archival arrangement The process and results of organizing and arranging records and other documents in accordance with accepted archival principles, particularly provenance, at as many of the following levels as necessary: repository, record group (or comparable control unit), record subgroup, record series, file unit, and document. The process is intended to achieve basic identification of holdings and their physical and administrative control.

archival document A document expected to be kept permanently, as closely as possible in its original form, for the bibliographical or other evidence which it potentially offers.

archival film Photographic film with an interminable shelf life, if properly processed and stored under archival conditions. Synonymous with permanent record film. Compare with *long-term film, medium-term film, short-term film.*

archival integrity The standard requiring that archival holdings be identified and arranged by provenance, as originally compiled, assembled, and administered, and preserved without alteration, mutilation, or unauthorized destruction of any portion.

archival permanence The degree to which documents retain their original characteristics and resist deterioration for a lengthy, specified period of time. Documents that do not undergo significant physical change for such a period of time are said to be of archival quality. For some documents the time period can be considered to range from 100 years to forever. In most cases, controlled storage and use are necessary to achieve archival permanence.

archival value The decision after appraisal that records or other documents are worthy of indefinite or permanent preservation.

archives 1. The organized body of noncurrent records made or received in connection with the transaction of its affairs by a government or a government agency, an institution, organization, or other corporate body, and the personal papers of a family or individual, which are preserved because of their continuing value. 2. The agency responsible for selecting, preserving, and making available such materials. 3. The repository itself. In American usage, the term "archives" is a collective noun, though the form "archive" is increasingly seen.

archivist A person responsible for or engaged in one or more of the following activities in an archival repository: appraisal and disposition, accessioning, preservation, arrangement, description, information service, exhibition, and publication. (SAA)

area In cataloging, a major section of the bibliographic description, comprising data of a particular category or set of categories, such as the title and statement of responsibility area and the edition area. (AACR2, mod.)

area bibliographer see *area specialist*

area diagram see *pie chart*

area of service see *service area*

area specialist A library staff member with responsibilities for the selection and evaluation of documents related to a geographical area of the world, such as Africa or Latin America, and sometimes with the added responsibilities of information service dealing with the area and with the bibliographic organization of the documents. Sometimes called area bibliographer.

arithmetical notation see *integral notation*

arithmetic-logic unit The part of the central processing unit of a computer containing circuits to perform arithmetic and logic operations.

arithmetic mean see *mean*

arithmetic unit see *arithmetic-logic unit*

arm The horizontal stroke(s) of a letter, such as L, Z, and E. Compare with *bar*.

armed services editions Editions of works in oblong, double-column paperback, issued by the Council on Books in Wartime from New York in 1943–47 for free distribution to members of the U.S. Armed Forces.

armorial binding A binding decorated with the coat of arms or other device of its original or a subsequent owner.

armorial bookplate A bookplate based on or incorporating the owner's coat of arms.

ARMS see *automatically retrieved microfilm system*

arrangement (music) 1. A musical work, or a portion thereof, rewritten for a medium of performance different from that for which the work was originally intended. Synonymous with transcription. (AACR2) 2. A simplified version of a musical work for the same medium of performance. (AACR2)

array 1. In classification, the group of coordinate classes formed by dividing a higher class by one characteristic. 2. In information storage and retrieval, an orderly and meaningful arrangement of words, letters, or numbers into a list or matrix.

arrowgraph A graph displaying groups of related terms with relationships shown by the use of arrows. Synonymous with association map.

art see *artwork*

artefact see *artifact*

art file see *picture file*

article A work of prose, identified by its own title or heading and frequently by its author, in a document that contains many such works, e.g., an article in a periodical or encyclopedia.

artifact Any object made or modified by human workmanship. In classification theory, a distinction is sometimes made between artifacts (physical objects) and mentifacts (mental conceptions). Also spelled "artefact."

artificial characteristic In classification, a quality common to the things classified, but not essential to their being. Compare with *natural characteristic.*

artificial classification A classification in which some accidental property of the things classified, such as size or color, is used as the characteristic of arrangement. Compare with *natural classification.*

artificial language A language based on a set of rules established before its construction or use, such as a programming language. Synonymous with synthetic language. Compare with *natural language.*

artist's proof A proof of an engraving, usually with the signature of the artist in pencil, and sometimes with a small sketch, known as a remarque, in the margin. Synonymous with remarque proof.

art original The original two- or three-dimensional work of art (other than an art print or a photograph) created by the artist, e.g., a painting, a drawing, or sculpture, as contrasted with a reproduction of it. (AACR2)

artotype see *collotype* (1)

art paper A high-grade printing paper, coated or calendered to give it a smooth, highly finished surface good for reproducing halftones.

art print An engraving, etching, lithograph, woodcut, etc., printed from the plate prepared by the artist. Compare with *art reproduction.* (AACR2)

art reproduction A mechanically reproduced copy of a work of art, generally as one of a commercial edition. Compare with *art print.* (AACR2)

artwork In publishing, the illustrative matter to be prepared for printing, as distinguished from the textual matter. Synonymous with art.

ASA film speed see *sensitivity*

ascender 1. That part of a lowercase letter that projects above the x-height. 2. A lowercase letter with such an extender, such as b, h. Compare with *descender.*

ASCII see *American Standard Code for Information Interchange*

ASF (assignable square feet) see *assignable space*

as issued In the antiquarian trade, a term indicating that a book offered for sale is in its original format.

as new In the antiquarian trade, a term indicating that the physical condition of a book offered for sale approaches the condition of newness.

assemble To translate a computer program written in symbolic language into a machine-language program.

assembler A computer program which directs the translation of other programs written in symbolic language into a machine-language program. Synonymous with assembly program. Compare with *compiler* (2).

assembler language A low-level computer language used to write programs with symbolic instructions, rather than the binary instructions (i.e., machine language) that can be understood by a computer system. The computer uses a program called an assembler to translate the instructions into its own machine language. Synonymous with assembly language. Compare with *compiler* (2).

assembly language see *assembler language*

assembly program see *assembler*

assertive library service see *proactive library service*

assignable space The total area of floor space in a library, expressed as assignable square feet (ASF), that is available for direct library purposes. It includes space for users, including meeting rooms and conference areas; space for staff and for services to users, including public service desks and the public catalog area; stack and related storage areas for the collection; space for copying, audiovisual, and other equipment; and aisles between stack ranges, furniture, equipment, and functional areas. It excludes nonassignable space, such as vestibules, lobbies, or other traffic areas; janitorial or custodial storage and service areas; rest rooms; elevator and stairway space; building corridors; mechanical areas; and other space not used specifically for library functions. Compare with *gross space.*

assignable square feet (ASF) see *assignable space*

assigned indexing An indexing method by which the indexer uses descriptors from a controlled list to represent the subject matter of a work. Synonymous with assignment indexing. Compare with *derived indexing.*

assignment indexing see *assigned indexing*

assistant/associate director A title assigned to one or several staff members ranking next to the chief executive officer in a library system who have broad administrative authority over particular parts of the library's activities and operations, such as assistant director for public services or technical services. Depending upon the title of the chief executive officer (e.g., director, dean, chief librarian, librarian), the title for such staff members will vary accordingly (e.g., assistant director, assistant librarian). Although the designations of assistant and associate are not applied uniformly, associate as a modifier frequently denotes broad administrative authority with the rank of second in command or the status of deputy.

assistant department head A title assigned to those staff members having delegated administrative duties in a major administrative unit in a library system and overall administrative responsibility for the unit in the absence of the department head.

assistant librarian 1. A title assigned to one or several staff members ranking next to the head librarian. 2. A title sometimes used in a classification for librarians, particularly in an academic library, which parallels the faculty rank of assistant professor.

associate director see *assistant/associate director*

associate librarian 1. A title assigned to a professional staff member ranking next to the head librarian. 2. A title sometimes used in a classification for librarians, particularly in an academic library, which parallels the faculty rank of associate professor.

associate specialist see *library associate/associate specialist*

association see *society*

association copy A book which has had some special connection with the author (or someone associated with the author), a distinguished individual, or a celebrated library or collection, as evidenced by bookplate, special binding, autograph, presentation inscription, correspondence, acquisition list, etc. Compare with *inscribed copy.*

association library A library owned or controlled by the members of an association which elects the governing board. Membership is usually obtained by subscriptions to annual or life memberships, and service may be limited to members or persons designated by them, or it may be provided free to the community. Title to the property is held by the members acting as a single person, in the manner of a common-law corporation, not by members individually.

association map see *arrowgraph*

association publication see *society publication*

associative retrieval system A computer-based information retrieval system in which an association value is established for terms in an index vocabulary on the basis of frequency with which they occur together in the same work by means of a statistical algorithm. In the search process, the starting list of terms may be expanded by the identification of other terms that are statistically associated, with a resultant higher recall ratio.

astigmatism An optical fault in a lens whereby light rays from an object do not meet at a focal point, resulting in blurred images.

ASTM CODEN see *CODEN*

asynchronous data transmission A mode of data transmission which requires start and stop signals at the beginning and end of each character. Usually, the end signal initiates the transmission of the next character. Synonymous with start-stop data transmission. Compare with *synchronous data transmission.*

asyndetic catalog A catalog without references. Compare with *syndetic catalog.*

athenaeum A name given to certain proprietary libraries, reading rooms, or buildings used as libraries, particularly in New England in the early part of the 19th century.

atlas A volume of maps, plates, engravings, tables, etc., with or without descriptive letterpress. It may be an independent publication or it may have been issued to accompany one or more volumes of text. (AACR2)

atlas folio see *book sizes*

attribute 1. A quality or characteristic of a thing. In classification, one line of theoretical development has proceeded on the assumption that whole subject areas can be divided into two categories: entities (concrete things and mental constructs) and attributes (properties of things, time, space, activities, etc.) 2. In computer-based information storage and retrieval, a characteristic of data, such as name, length, format, or use.

attributed author see *supposed author*

audible frequency range A range from the lowest frequency (about 15 hertz) to the highest frequency (20,000 hertz) which can be heard by the normal human ear.

audiocard A thin card with a strip of ¼-inch audiotape across the bottom of its width (usually less than 12 inches). Sounds recorded on the tape are usually 30 seconds or less in length. Space is provided above the audiotape for pictures or words. It is played on a special device or adapter which plays only audiocards. (AECT)

audiocard recorder A special form of audiotape recorder which records and plays only audiocards. (AECT)

audiocartridge An audiotape permanently enclosed in a plastic container with a single reel. The audiotape ends are joined together to form an endless loop that plays continuously. Synonymous with audiotape cartridge, cartridge audiotape, and sound cartridge.

audiocassette An audiotape permanently enclosed in a plastic container with two audiotape reels and with each of the ends of the tape attached to a separate reel. Synonymous with audiotape cassette, cassette audiotape, and sound cassette.

audiodisc An audiorecording on a thin, flat disc, usually of vinyl, on which is impressed a continuous fine spiral groove carrying recorded sounds. As the audiodisc revolves, it causes a stylus on the playback device to vibrate and produce electric impulses which are converted to sound. While the most common speed of audiodiscs is currently 33⅓ rpm, other speeds are 78, 45, and 66⅔ rpm. Synonymous with phonodisc, phonograph record, phonorecord, and simply disc.

audiodisc player A device, with built-in amplifier and speaker(s), which reproduces sound from audiodiscs. Synonymous with phonograph and record player. (NCES)

audio induction loop The loop of wire used to broadcast in an audio induction system. (AECT)

audio induction system A low-power audio broadcast system using a large loop of wire as a transmitting antenna. The wire is usually installed around the perimeter of a room (or area) in a large loop often attached to the walls. Only those within the loop wearing special headphones to receive the transmission can hear the broadcast. Devices in the system include amplifiers, special headphones for the listeners, and program sources such as an audiotape player or audiodisc player. (AECT)

audiopage A specially prepared page or sheet backed with a magnetic oxide (similar to that on audiotape) on which may be or are recorded electrical impulses which can be converted to sound. An audiopage requires a special playback device and is not the same as an audiocard. Synonymous with sound page and sound sheet. (NCES)

audiopage recorder A special form of audiotape recorder which records and plays only audiopages. (AECT)

audioplayer A generic term for any device which plays but does not record audiorecordings. Compare with *audiorecorder*. (AECT)

audiorecorder A generic term for any device which records sounds electronically and can also play back sounds from audiorecordings. Compare with *audioplayer*. (AECT)

audiorecording A generic term for material on which are stored (recorded) sounds only, which can be reproduced (played back) mechanically and/or electronically. Includes audiocards, audiodiscs, audiopages, audioslides, and audiotapes. Synonymous with sound recording.

audioreel An open reel holding recorded audiotape which is to be played reel to reel. Synonymous with audiotape reel and sound tape reel.

audio response unit see *voice response unit*

audioslide A 2-x-2-inch slide with a brief audiorecording on a magnetic coating on the slide mount or a special holder for the slide. An audioslide requires a special projector. Synonymous with sound-on-slide, sound slide. (NCES)

audioslide projector A slide projector which projects audioslides and plays back the sound recorded on the slide or slide mount. Most audioslide projectors have provision for recording sound on the audioslide. (AECT)

audiotape A strip of magnetic tape on which may be or are recorded electrical signals which can be converted to sound. While audiotape ranges in size from 150 mils to 1 inch, the most common sizes in instructional applications are 150 mils (in cassettes) and ¼ inch (reels). Audiotape is stored on reels, in cassettes, and in cartridges. A tape on which sounds are recorded is also called a tape recording. Synonymous with phonotape.

audiotape cartridge see *audiocartridge*

audiotape cassette see *audiocassette*

audiotape deck A device equipped with a tape transport and electronic components for recording and/or playing back sounds on audiotape, but not with amplifiers and loudspeakers.

audiotape monitor see *monitor* (1)

audiotape player A device which can play back but cannot record audiotapes. It has a tape transport, amplifiers, speaker(s) and playback head, but not a record head. Compare with *audiotape recorder.* (AECT)

audiotape recorder A device which can record and generally play back sound on audiotape. It contains heads for erasing, recording, and playback; amplifiers; and tape transport mechanisms. The recorder may be monaural, stereophonic, or quadraphonic. Compare with *audiotape player.* (NCES)

audiotape reel see *audioreel*

audio-tutorial method A self-pacing multimedia method of instruction that utilizes audiotape, in combination with materials in other formats, for individual learning.

audiovisual area An area within a library or serving as adjunct to the library, designed and provided with special equipment for storing, projecting, playing back, and producing audiovisual materials. Synonymous with listening and viewing area.

audiovisual communications The transmission of information by audio and/or visual methods rather than through the printed page.

audiovisual equipment The special equipment designed for projecting, playing back, or producing audiovisual materials.

audiovisual materials Materials in audio and visual formats which convey information primarily by sound and image rather than by text, e.g., charts, graphs, maps, pictures, slides, filmstrips, audiorecordings, videotapes, motion pictures, and models. Many of these materials require the use of special equipment in order to be seen or heard. Sometimes called nonbook and nonprint materials in the sense that they are not intended to be read. Synonymous with visual aids.

audit 1. A systematic examination of the financial records of an organization, frequently conducted by an external party, to verify their accuracy and determine their conformance with established financial criteria. 2. To examine the financial records of an organization.

audit trail A means of tracing the steps involved in processing data to verify the accuracy of the results from input through output.

augmented keyword index see *enriched keyword index*

authentication In archives, the determination that a record or other document (or a reproduction thereof) is what it purports to be. Compare with *certification.*

author see *personal author.*

author affiliation In an abstract or in the catalog of a special library, a statement of the organization with which the personal author of the work abstracted or the bibliographic item cataloged is affiliated, to assist in the identification and evaluation of the author.

author authority file see *name authority file*

author bibliography A list of works by, or by and about an author. It can range in scope from a simple enumeration of titles to descriptive bibliography.

author catalog A catalog consisting of bibliographic records with the names of personal authors and corporate bodies as access points.

author entry 1. The name of a personal author used as an access point to a bibliographic record. 2. A bibliographic record with the name of a personal author as the heading. Compare with *corporate entry, personal name entry.*

author index An index in which the headings of index entries are the names of persons and/or corporate bodies responsible for the intellectual content of the work(s) indexed. Compare with *name index.*

authority The right of a manager, legitimatized by virtue of the position held in an organization, to direct the activities and exact the compliance of others.

authority control The methods by which the authoritative forms of names, subjects, uniform titles, etc., used as headings in a file of bibliographic records are consistently applied and maintained. Includes the file of authority records containing the authoritative forms with appropriate references and, for a file of machine-readable records (a database), the mechanism whereby all records can be updated automatically to maintain consistency with the authority file.

authority file A set of authority records establishing the authoritative forms of headings to be used in a set of bibliographic records and the references to be made to and from the headings. Categories of authority files include name authority file, series authority file, and subject authority file. Synonymous with authority list.

authority list see *authority file*

authority record A record which shows a heading in the form established for use in a set of bibliographic records, cites the sources consulted in establishing the heading, indicates the references to be made to and from the heading, and notes information found in the sources as justification of the chosen form of heading and the specified references.

authorized edition An edition issued with the consent of the author or other holder of rights in the work, the subject of a biography, or the subject's family.

author mark A symbol following the class number in the call number of a bibliographic item to represent the name of the person or corporate body that is the main entry heading; used as a device to facilitate alphabetical arrangement

by the name of the person or corporate body responsible for the content of bibliographic items with the same class number. Synonymous with author number. Compare with *work mark.*

author number see *author mark*

author's edition 1. An edition of the complete, or nearly complete, works of an author, including previously published and unpublished works. Issued in one volume or in several uniform volumes, usually with a collective title. Synonymous with uniform edition, complete works. Compare with *collected edition, inclusive edition.* 2. An edition authorized by the author.

author's proof A proof sent to the author for correction after the correction of compositor's errors on the galley proof.

author's rights see *rights*

author statement see *statement of responsibility*

author table see *Cutter Table, Cutter-Sanborn Table*

author-title entry see *name-title entry*

author-title index An index in which the headings of index entries are the names of the persons and/or corporate bodies responsible for the intellectual content of the work(s) indexed and of the titles of the works, arranged in one or separate alphabetical sequence.

author-title reference see *name-title reference*

autoabstract see *automatic abstract*

autoanswer In data communications, the capability of a network station to respond automatically to a call received over a switched line.

autocall In data communications, the capability of a network station to initiate automatically a call over a switched line.

autocratic management An approach to management in which administrators or supervisors make decisions with minimal input from employees. Compare with *consultative management* and *participative management.*

autograph 1. A manuscript in the author's own handwriting. 2. A person's own signature. Compare with *holograph.*

autographed edition An edition of a bibliographic item, copies of which are signed by the author.

autoinstructional material and device A system and machine for individual instruction including individual reading pacers, individual viewing and listening equipment, language laboratories, programmed printed materials, and a teaching machine which presents verbal and pictorial programs in various ways, electronic and mechanical, so that the individual responds and is informed of errors and progress.

autoinstructional materials Materials for individual instruction, both self-displaying and for use with autoinstructional devices. (AECT)

automated circulation system see *computer-based circulation system.*

automatic abstract An abstract prepared from keywords selected from the text of a work by a computer. Synonymous with autoabstract.

automatically retrieved microfilm system (ARMS) A microfilm system which automatically retrieves microimages according to machine search instructions by means of a code appearing on the film, such as a code line or binary code, as distinct from a system in which an external index is searched to determine the location of relevant images.

automatic assigned indexing A form of automatic indexing in which a computer is used to assign descriptors to a work from an index vocabulary. Compare with *automatic derived indexing.*

automatic data processing (ADP) Operations performed automatically on data by a machine such as a digital computer without human intervention, but according to a predetermined set of instructions or computer program.

automatic data-switching Data-switching performed by a machine such as a computer, without human intervention in the process. Synonymous with automatic message-switching.

automatic data-switching center A data-switching center that receives and analyzes data or messages, then routes them to other destinations without human intervention. Synonymous with electronic data-switching center.

automatic derived indexing A form of automatic indexing in which a computer is used to assign descriptors to a work by selecting keywords from the text, using predefined rules. Synonymous with automatic extraction indexing. Compare with *automatic assigned indexing.*

automatic dictionary A dictionary of machine-readable words or codes used in a machine coding or translation system. A machine such as a computer substitutes words or codes in the dictionary for those in another language or code. Synonymous with electronic dictionary and mechanical dictionary.

automatic document storage and retrieval system (ADSTARS) A broad range of microform systems which use automatic or semiautomatic techniques for the storage and retrieval of specific microimages within a microform database.

automatic extraction indexing see *automatic derived indexing*

automatic format recognition The automatic sensing and recognition of the individual data elements or data fields of a record by a machine such as a computer.

automatic generic posting In a computer-based indexing system, the automatic assignment by a computer of additional descriptors, hierarchically higher than those assigned to a work by an indexer from an index vocabulary. Synonymous with posting-up and up-posting.

automatic indexing A method of indexing in which a computer is used to select, from the text or title of works or from an index vocabulary, terms to be used as the headings of index entries.

automatic message-switching see *automatic data-switching*

automatic reverse A means of changing the direction of travel of a magnetic tape during recording or playback, usually by applying a foil-sensing tape at the point at which reverse play is desired.

automatic rewind A device which automatically reverses the winding of an audiotape, videotape, or motion picture from the take-up reel to the supply reel once the tape or film has been played or shown to its conclusion.

automatic routing see *routing*

automatic shutoff A device which shuts off the motor of a player, recorder, or projector after an audiotape, videotape, audiodisc, set of slides, etc., has been played or shown to its conclusion.

automatic term classification In information retrieval, the analysis of the text of works by computer to form classes of terms, or a thesaurus, based on some form of correlation coefficient, usually the frequency with which words occur together in the same work.

automation The performance of an operation, a series of operations, or a process by self-activating, self-controlling, or automatic means. Automation implies the use of automatic data-processing equipment such as a computer or other laborsaving devices.

autothreading A feature on specific motion picture projectors which automatically performs threading operations from supply reel to take-up reel, except for the insertion of the film in the film slot and the final operation of inserting the film in the take-up reel.

auxiliary enterprise An enterprise that is operated by a library for services to a particular user group and is intended to be self-supporting.

auxiliary equipment see *peripheral equipment*

auxiliary schedule see *auxiliary table*

auxiliary storage In computer science, data storage that supplements other storage, particularly main storage; e.g., magnetic tape, magnetic disk, magnetic drum. Synonymous with backing storage, backup storage, secondary storage. Compare with *main storage, mass storage.*

auxiliary table A table of common subdivisions appended to the schedules of a classification system. Synonymous with auxiliary schedule.

availability rate A measure used to evaluate a library collection; refers to the percentage of items requested by users or the percentage of items in a standard list or subject bibliography that the library holds. Sometimes the term is used to refer to the percentage of items actually found in their proper place when requested.

average gradient (AG) see *contrast* (1)

axis A fixed, vertical or horizontal line used as a reference on a graph or chart.

azo dye A moderately transparent light-sensitive dye used in diazotype film.

azure tooling The process of tooling a decoration consisting of parallel lines or bars on a book cover; derived from the use of thin horizontal lines in heraldry to indicate blue.

back The back edges of the leaves of a book after leaf affixing. Compare with *backstrip, spine.*

backbone see *spine*

backcoat see *backing* (1)

back cover see *cover* (2)

backed 1. In binding, said of a book which has passed through the rounding and backing step. 2. Said of a leaf which has been repaired or strengthened by being mounted upon or backed by a new leaf.

back edge The left edge of a recto, corresponding to the right edge of a verso. It is the binding edge in the ordinary bound book.

back file The file of back issues of a periodical.

background The part of a source document, photographic negative, or print not occupied by an image.

background density A measure of the opacity of the background (the area not occupied by an image) of a source document, photographic negative, or print. Compare with *line density.*

background processing The execution of computer programs with low priorities when high-priority programs are not being run. Compare with *foreground processing.*

background program A low-priority computer program which is executed at a time when no other programs with a higher priority are being run. Compare with *foreground program.*

backing 1. In photography, a dark layer affixed to a film base in order to reduce halation or to improve daylight loading characteristics of the film. Synonymous with backcoat. 2. In binding, see *rounding and backing.*

backing storage see *auxiliary storage*

back issue An issue of a periodical preceding the current issue. Synonymous with back number.

back lighting A light coming from behind an object. Generally the light is used to illuminate a transparent or translucent object, such as a film slide on a light box. Synonymous with rear illumination.

back lining 1. In binding, the fabric (crash, canton flannel) and/or paper strip glued to the back of a volume in order to strengthen it. Gluing a paper strip over the fabric produces a stronger, neater result. 2. Loosely, the paper strip or *inlay* used to stiffen the spine of a case.

backlist Publications that are no longer new, but which the publisher keeps in stock because of a continuous demand.

back margin In the ordinary book, the margin at the binding edge of the page: at the left of the printed recto and the right of the printed verso. The back margins of facing pages together form the gutter. Synonymous with inside margin.

back matter The leaves following the body of a book that contain notes, bibliography, appendixes, etc. Synonymous with end matter, reference matter, and subsidiaries.

back number see *back issue*

back order An order which was not completed when originally placed, but is being held for future delivery.

back projection see *rear projection*

backstrip In binding, that portion of the covering material which extends from joint to joint. Compare with *spine* and *back,* which are sometimes used synonymously, and with *inlay.*

back title see *spine title*

backup In computer science, files, equipment, or procedures maintained in case those ordinarily used fail or are destroyed.

backup storage see *auxiliary storage*

Baconian classification A classification of knowledge based on the three faculties (memory, imagination, and reason) proposed by Francis Bacon in his *Advancement of Learning* (1605). This scheme has had great influence on library classification systems.

balance In playing back sounds from an audiorecording or videorecording through the loudspeakers of stereophonic or quadraphonic audio systems, the approximation of the original sounds by equalizing the amplitude of each loudspeaker.

balance sheet A written statement describing the financial position of an organization in terms of assets and liabilities at a specified date, usually at the end of a fiscal period.

balopticon see *opaque projector*

band 1. In computer science, a group of recording channels or tracks on such storage media as magnetic disk, magnetic tape, and magnetic drum. Data are recorded along the tracks. 2. The group of radio or television broadcasting frequencies within two limits assigned to a channel by the Federal Communications Commission for public broadcast as well as shortwave transmission. Synonymous with frequency band.

band printer see *printer* (2)

bands The cords on which the sections of a book have been sewed.

bandwidth 1. The range within a band of radio or television frequencies, expressed in hertz. 2. The frequency range applied to amplifiers and receivers for output within a distortion or harmonic distortion tolerance.

bank letter A bulletin issued at regular intervals by a bank, usually on general financial and business conditions.

banned see *suppressed* (1)

banned book A book that has been suppressed.

bar The crossing stroke of a letter, such as H, t, e. Compare with *arm.*

bar chart A chart presenting statistical data in graphic form; it uses rectangular bars whose widths are equal but whose heights (or lengths) are proportional to the frequencies or values of the data being represented.

bar-coded label A label containing machine-readable data in the form of vertical bars of varying widths and distances apart representing binary digits.

bar coding see *code lines*

bar gamma see *contrast* (1)

Barrow process A process of paper document repair and restoration named after William J. Barrow (1904–67) which involves deacidification and lamination. The process is not easily reversible, and it has lost ground in recent years in paper conservation to encapsulation.

base of notation In classification, the number of symbols available for use in the notation of a given classification system.

base stock The supporting material for a photographic emulsion, such as film or paper.

BASIC (Beginner's All-Purpose Symbolic Instruction Code) A popular programming language which is simple and easy to use, designed for timesharing.

basic research Research which represents original investigation directed toward the advancement of knowledge and discovery of new facts, theories, and laws, rather than toward the attainment of commercial or solely pragmatic objectives. Synonymous with pure research. Compare with *applied research.*

basis weight The weight in pounds, measured under standard conditions, of a ream of paper (usually 500 sheets, but may be 1,000 for U.S. federal agencies) of a determined "basic" size which differs according to the kind and quality of paper. Compare with *substance number.*

bass The low end of the audible frequency range (15 to 256 hertz, or middle C on the piano).

bastarda A group of informal gothic types used for vernacular works in the 15th and 16th centuries, including the type William Caxton introduced to England. The French form was lettre bâtarde; the German, Schwabacher, which was succeeded by Fraktur.

bastard title see *half title* (1)

batch processing 1. In computer science, a technique of collecting or accumulating data in groups or batches before they are processed. Compare with *online processing.* 2. A technique of executing computer programs in which one program is completed before another is begun.

bathymetric map A relief map of the ocean floor, or of a lake bed, etc.

battledore see *hornbook*

baud In data transmission, a unit of signaling speed equal to the number of discrete conditions or signal events per second. For example, one baud can equal one bit per second in a stream of binary signals.

baudot code A code of five binary digits representing one character of data, used for transmission of teletype messages. Synonymous with teletype code.

bay see *module* (1)

BCD see *binary coded decimal*

beading The twist of the silk in headbands; so called from its resemblance to a series of beads.

Beginner's All-Purpose Symbolic Instruction Code see *BASIC*

bell-shaped curve A frequency distribution that has the shape of a vertical cross-section of a bell. Normal (i.e., Gaussian) distributions are among those having this shape.

belt drive The rotational drive system found in some audiotape decks, audiodisc players, and motion picture projectors which employs a band or belt to provide motion from the motor to another part of the drive system.

belt press A printing press on which flexible plates are mounted on two continuous belts that revolve against a roll of paper.

bench-sewing In binding, joining sections together by hand-sewing them through the fold onto cords or tapes. So called from the use of a sewing frame set on a bench. There are various styles of hand-sewing, e.g., all along, two along, raised bands, and sunk bands.

Benday process A process for adding a flat tone in the reproduction of line drawings by applying a screen pattern from an inked transparent film onto the drawing, a plate before etching, or a film negative of the drawing before the photomechanical plate is made. So named for its originator, Benjamin Day.

Berne Convention The common name of a copyright agreement signed in 1886 and its revisions establishing the International Union for the Protection of Literary and Artistic Works. To receive protection under this convention, first publication of a work must occur in a signatory country. The United States is not a member, but a work published in the United States is protected under the convention if it is simultaneously published in a signatory country.

best seller 1. A current popular book in most active demand in bookstores. 2. In a broader sense, a standard book having a steady sale over a period of years.

beveled boards In binding, slant-edged boards, now seldom used except for very large books or in imitation of antique work.

biannual A serial publication issued twice a year.

bias The amount of departure by the average of a set of values from a reference value.

biased sample A sample into which an error has been introduced by selecting elements from a wrong population or wrong elements from the correct population.

bias phase In classification, the phase relationship occurring in a work in which one subject is presented from the point of view of those whose primary interest is in another field.

Bible paper A very thin, strong, opaque paper made from cotton or linen rags, flax fiber, or chemical wood pulp, used for printing Bibles, prayer books, and other books requiring many pages in compact form. The paper was first developed in England under the name India Bible or India Oxford Bible paper.

Bible style A term commonly used to designate any flexible, round-cornered leather binding.

Biblia pauperum Literally, Bible of the Poor. A type of medieval picture book, in either manuscript or printed (either from movable type or from blocks) form, containing illustrations of scriptural subjects, with descriptive texts.

bibliographer 1. One who writes about books, especially in regard to their authorship, date, typography, editions, etc.; one skilled in bibliography. 2. One familiar with systematic methods of describing the physical characteristics of books, who prepares bibliographies, catalogs, or lists. 3. A title sometimes accorded an *area specialist* and *subject specialist.*

bibliographical ghost A work or an edition of a work, recorded in bibliographies or otherwise mentioned, of whose existence there is no reasonable proof. Also called ghost.

bibliographical note 1. A note, often a footnote, set apart from the text of a document, which contains a reference to one or more works used as sources. 2. A note in a catalog or bibliography, relating to the bibliographical history or description of a book.

Bibliographic Classification A classification system devised by Henry Evelyn Bliss, first published in outline form in 1910, characterized by the organization of knowledge in consistency with the scientific and educational consensus.

bibliographic control A term which covers a range of bibliographic activities: complete bibliographic records of all bibliographic items as published; standardization of bibliographic description; provision of physical access through consortia, networks, or other cooperative endeavors; and provision of bibliographic access through the compilation and distribution of union lists and subject bibliographies and through bibliographic service centers.

bibliographic coupling The theory that if any two scientific papers contain a citation in common, they are bibliographically related, as are papers in a group, if each of the group contains at least one citation in common with a given paper used as a criterion. The strength of the relationship is measured by the number of citations in common between each paper and the criterion paper.

bibliographic database A database consisting of computer records that represent works, documents, or bibliographic items.

bibliographic description In cataloging, the description of a bibliographic item, divided into the following areas: title and statement of responsibility; edition; material (or type of publication) specific details; publication, distribution, etc.; physical description; series; notes of useful information which cannot be fitted into other areas; and standard number and terms of availability. Each area is divided into a number of bibliographic elements. Compare with *level of description.*

bibliographic information interchange format see *communication format*

bibliographic instruction An information service to a group, which is designed to teach library users how to locate information efficiently. The essential goals of this process are an understanding of the library's system of organization and the ability to use selected reference materials. In addition, instruction may cover the structure of the literature and the general and specific research methodology appropriate for a discipline. Compare with *library use presentation.*

bibliographic item A document or set of documents in any physical form, published, issued, or treated as an entity, and as such forming the basis for a single bibliographic description. (AACR2, mod.)

bibliographic network A network established and maintained for the sharing of bibliographic data through the use of a standard communication format and authority control. Compare with *information network.*

bibliographic record A record of a bibliographic item which comprises all data contained in or accommodated by a bibliographic format such as MARC.

bibliographic reference A set of bibliographic elements essential to the identification of a work, document, or bibliographic item to which a reference is made.

bibliographic search The process of identifying a work, document, or bibliographic item and obtaining bibliographic data about it through a systematic search of bibliographic tools and other sources.

bibliographic service center An organization that serves as a distributor of computer-based bibliographic processing services (i.e., activities that assist libraries in establishing bibliographic control over their collections and in gaining access to mechanisms for their identification and retrieval). The center may also provide other services, such as interlibrary loan facilitation and maintenance of union catalogs. It gains access to external resources through the facilities of a bibliographic utility.

bibliographic utility An organization which maintains online bibliographic databases, enabling it to offer computer-based support to any interested user. It provides a standard interface by which bibliographic records are available to libraries either directly or through bibliographic service centers.

bibliographic volume see *volume*

bibliography 1. The study of books as physical objects, as a means of determining the history and transmission of texts. 2. The art of correctly describing books with respect to authorship of the work(s) they contain, editions, physical form, etc. 3. A list of works, documents, and/or bibliographic items, usually with some relationship between them, e.g., by a given author, on a given subject, or published in a given place, and differing from a catalog in that its contents are not restricted to the holdings of a single collection, library, or group of libraries.

bibliology The study of books, embracing knowledge of the physical book in all its aspects, such as paper, printing, typography, illustration, and binding; bibliography in its widest sense. The term has never gained wide currency.

bibliomania A mania for collecting and possessing books.

bibliometrics The use of statistical methods in the analysis of a body of literature to reveal the historical development of subject fields and patterns of authorship, publication, and use. Formerly called *statistical bibliography.*

bibliophile A lover of books, especially as regards their physical format.

bibliothecal classification A classification system devised for arranging library materials. Compare with *knowledge classification.*

bibliotherapy   The use of books and other reading materials in a program of directed reading which is planned and conducted as an auxiliary in the treatment of mental and emotional disorders and social maladjustment.

bidding   The process of soliciting prices for defined services, equipment, or supplies from various potential providers in order to obtain the desired services, equipment, or supplies at the most desirable cost.

biennial   A serial publication issued every two years.

bifurcate classification   A method of classification in which classes are created by dividing the genus by a single significant difference into two species, e.g., the division of the genus Alphabet into Roman and Non-Roman on the basis of its derivation.

bill   1. A draft of a proposed law introduced in a legislative body. 2. A term designating money owed for goods or services. 3. A written statement of money owed for goods or services.

bill drafting   The writing of a legislative bill in which the library serving legislative bodies might cooperate with the drafting agent by gathering and preparing background information.

bimodal distribution   A frequency distribution having two modes.

bimonthly   A serial publication issued every two months.

binary   1. Pertaining to a characteristic or property involving a selection, choice, or condition in which there are two possibilities. 2. Pertaining to the binary number system which has a base of two; that is, only two numbers are possible, 0 and 1.

binary code   A code with only two possibilities, usually 0 or 1.

binary coded decimal (BCD)   A code in which a decimal number is represented by a group of four binary digits or bits.

binary coded microfilm   On roll microfilm, the numerical encoding of descriptors by binary digits represented by an optical pattern of small clear and opaque rectangles placed between frames and adjacent to the image of the document to which the descriptors apply.

binary digit   Either of the two characters, 0 and 1, of the binary number system. By contraction, commonly called "bit."

binary number system   A number system with a radix or base of two, using the numbers 1 and 0.

binary search   A search whereby a set of records or data is divided into two parts, one with a specified characteristic or property, the other without. The part without is rejected, and the process repeated on the remaining part until a desired record or data item is located. Synonymous with dichotomizing search.

binder's board   A high-quality, single-ply pulpboard used for book covers, made to full thickness in one operation. The board is hard, flat, and nonwarping. Synonymous with millboard.

binder's leaves   see *flyleaves*

binder's slip   see *binding slip*

binder's title   The title lettered on the cover of a volume by a binder, as distinguished from the title on the publisher's original cover (the *cover title*). (AACR2, mod.)

bindery   An establishment performing one or another of the various kinds of binding.

bindery preparation department   see *binding department*

bindery record   see *binding record*

bindery slip   see *binding slip*

bind in   To fasten supplementary material securely into a bound volume.

binding   1. Various methods by which leaves, sheets, sections, signatures, etc., are held together or affixed so that they will be usable and resistant to wear for a prolonged period. Major subcategories of binding are machine binding, mechanical binding, and hand binding. Binding operations often are grouped into three large series of operations: sewing or leaf affixing, forwarding, and finishing. Synonymous with bookbinding. 2. The cover of a volume.

binding cloth   see *book cloth*

binding department   The administrative unit of a library that prepares materials for binding or rebinding outside the library and may do mending and minor repairs. Synonymous with bindery preparation department.

binding edge In binding, the edge at which the leaves are affixed to one another.

binding proof A few rough fore-edges left on a volume to show that it has been slightly trimmed in binding.

binding record A record of library materials sent to a bindery; usually includes information on title, style of binding, etc. Synonymous with bindery record.

binding slip The form that accompanies an item to a bindery and supplies instructions to the binder on how the item is to be handled. Synonymous with binder's slip, bindery slip, specification slip.

binding specifications Specifications of materials and methods of manufacture of library binding. Those commonly used are: 1. *Library Binding Institute Standard for Library Binding* (1981), or Class A binding. Includes specifications for binding unbound materials, rebinding worn volumes, and binding new books (prior to sale). Incorporates the American Library Association *Minimum Specifications for Class "A" Library Binding* (1933) and American Library Association *Standards for Reinforced (Pre-Library-Bound) New Books* (1939). 2. American Library Association *Minimum Specifications for Lesser Used Materials for Libraries* (1959), usually referred to as LUMSPECS. 3. *Official Minimum Manufacturing Standards and Specifications for Textbooks* (1965). Specifications for binding new textbooks approved by the National Association of State Textbook Directors, the American Textbook Publishers Institute, Inc., and Book Manufacturers' Institute.

biobibliography A list of works by various authors (or occasionally, one author) which includes brief biographical data.

biography file A card file, or vertical file of clippings, etc., giving information and additional sources of information about individuals of potential interest to users. Synonymous with who's who file.

bird's-eye view A perspective representation of the landscape, as it might be visible from a high viewpoint above the surface of the earth or other celestial body, in which detail is shown as if projected onto an oblique plane. Synonymous with aerial view, map view.

bit A contraction of binary digit.

bit density The number of binary digits or bits which can be stored in a specified space such as a length of magnetic tape.

bit pattern An arrangement or grouping of binary digits or bits.

bit rate The speed by which binary digits can be sensed or recorded by a machine or transmitted over a channel, expressed usually as bits per second or bps.

bits per inch (bpi) The number of binary digits or bits which can be recorded per inch of a medium such as magnetic tape. Common numbers of bits per inch are 800 and 1600.

bits per second (bps) The number of binary digits or bits which can be sensed or recorded by a machine or transmitted over a channel.

biweekly see *semimonthly*

blackening field The surfaces of a microfilm emulsion which can be exposed.

black-faced type see *boldface type*

blackface type see *boldface type*

black letter see *gothic* (1)

black light A common term referring to light radiation of wavelengths normally invisible to the human eye, in particular ultraviolet rays. Black light can be produced by electrode or mercury arc lamps for purposes such as diazotype process copying.

black-line method see *woodcut* (1)

blank character In data processing, a special character representing a space or a blank. Synonymous with space character.

blanket A rubber-covered cylinder which transfers the ink from plate to paper in offset lithography.

blanket order A plan by which a publisher or wholesaler agrees to supply to a library one copy of all publications, as issued, within the specified limits of the plan, generally without return privileges. Synonymous with gathering plan. Compare with *approval plan.*

blank stamping see *blind stamping*

bleed   1. In printing, to run an illustration off the edge of the page. 2. In binding, to trim a volume so that the text or illustration is cut into. 3. In photocopying, an undesirable thickening of lines, generally due to overexposure or overdevelopment. Synonymous with bleed line and line spread.

bleed line see *bleed* (3)

bleed through   In photocopying, a defect that occurs as a result of images showing through from the opposite side of the source document being copied. Synonymous with show through.

blemish   A film defect, caused by aging and other factors, that appears as microscopic spots, usually reddish or yellowish in color. Redox (oxidation-reduction) blemishes were common, even in archival film, until it was discovered that they were due to the deterioration of film containers.

blind blocking see *blind stamping*

blind reference   A reference in a catalog or index to a heading which does not appear in the catalog or index.

blind stamping   The stamping of a design on a book cover without the use of ink or other coloring material, especially gold leaf, though sometimes preliminary to their use. Also called blank stamping and, in British usage, blind blocking.

blind tooling   The tooling of a design on a book cover without putting on gold leaf, sometimes preliminary to gold tooling of the design.

blip see *document mark*

Bliss Classification see *Bibliographic Classification*

blister   A bubble-shaped defect in photographic materials resulting from the separation of the emulsion from the base.

block   1. A type-high piece of wood, engraved for printing. 2. A piece of wood or metal on which an engraving or cut is mounted to make it type-high. 3. In data processing, a group or string of contiguous digits, characters, words, or records treated or transmitted as a unit. Synonymous with transmission block and transmission frame. 4. To mount an engraving or cut on a wood or metal base for printing. 5. To paint over a part of a film negative to prevent or modify its printing. Synonymous with block out.

block accession   To accession documents in groups, assigning a block of consecutive numbers to each group without giving individual numbers to individual documents.

block book   A book printed from wooden blocks cut in relief, with illustrations and text for each page on one block; a type of book common at about the time of the introduction of printing with movable type. Synonymous with xylographic book.

block diagram   1. A graphic representation of the hardware components of a computer system which shows both basic functions and functional relationships between the parts. A less detailed and less symbolic representation than a flowchart. 2. A representation of the landscape in either perspective or isometric projection, usually with some vertical exaggeration. Block diagrams may also be used to illustrate subterranean structures.

blocked up   Said of photographic negatives with loss of detail due to overexposure or overdevelopment.

block indexing   A system of separating related microimages, as they appear on roll microfilm, into groups or blocks by the use of targets, which identify the block of microimages that contains the particular image to be retrieved.

blocking   1. In reprography, a problem that occurs when film, coated sheets of sensitized paper, or aperture cards stick together. 2. In binding, see *stamping.*

block letter see *sans-serif*

block out see *block* (5)

block print   A print made from a wood, linoleum, or metal block cut in relief.

block sort   In computer science, a sort of items or records on the first or first few characters of a file key, with the purpose of segmenting a file into more manageable parts.

blowback see *enlargement*

blowup see *enlargement*

blue see *diazotype process, proofs*

blue-base film A film whose base contains a blue dye for the purpose of reducing halation.

blue book 1. A popular name for a government publication issued in a blue cover. 2. A popular name for state manuals listing officials and giving other data about the government organization. 3. In Great Britain, lengthy official reports in the *Parliamentary Papers,* some of which are issued in the traditional blue color, but many of which are issued in various other colors.

blueline see *diazotype process, proofs*

blueprint A print with a white image on a blue background, produced by the blueprint process.

blueprint process A wet process for producing a same-size reproduction of a single-sided, translucent original. The original is exposed on copy paper treated with a preparation of ferroprussiate to produce a latent image. The paper is developed in running water to produce an image in white on a blue background. Used primarily to reproduce architectural and mechanical drawings. Synonymous with ferroprussiate process.

blue-sensitive Said of photographic paper and film sensitive primarily to the blue and ultraviolet range of the light spectrum.

blurb A description and recommendation of a book prepared by the publisher and generally appearing on the book jacket. Synonymous with puff.

board An official body consisting of several individuals which has comprehensive authority for governing an organization or agency. Its members, commonly called trustees or directors, may be elected, appointed, or selected by some other legally established procedure. A governing body common to most public libraries, it in most cases retains authority in broad policymaking areas but delegates considerable authority to the chief administrative officer. Known variously as board of directors, board of trustees, and, as the governing body of a library, library board and library trustees.

board of directors see *board*

board of trustees see *board*

board papers see *endpapers*

boards A general term for various types of paperboard used in book covers, including binder's board, chip board, pasted board, and strawboard.

bock A kind of sheepskin leather, sometimes used as a substitute for morocco.

body In printing, the block of metal upon which the face of a type character is cast. Synonymous with shank.

body of a book The main part of a book that follows the front matter and precedes the back matter.

body of the description That part of the bibliographic description which begins with the title proper and ends with the imprint.

body size The height and width of type. The standard height of metal type from the surface on which it stands to the printing surface, called type high, is .918 of an inch in the United States. The horizontal dimension of metal type and phototype, measured in vertical segments of an em, is called the set; the vertical dimension, which allows for ascenders and descenders and extends above or below the face of most characters, is measured in points and determines the size of the font.

body type see *text type*

bold-faced type see *boldface type*

boldface type Type thicker and darker than the normal font, usually used for emphasis. Also called bold-faced type. Synonymous with blackface or black-faced type.

bolt A fold of paper at the top edge, fore-edge, or occasionally the foot of an uncut or unopened book.

BOM proof see *book club proof*

bonded leather A material consisting of leather particles bonded together with rosin, which can be used just as cloth or paper on book covers.

bond paper Originally a grade of writing or printing paper with the great strength, durability, and permanence required for government bonds and legal documents. The term has come to designate papers within a wide range of quality for uses where those characteristics are a consideration. May be made from bleached chemical wood pulps or with rag content.

bone folder A flat piece of bone six or eight inches long and about one inch wide, used for folding paper and in book repairing.

book 1. A collection of leaves of paper, parchment, or other material, in some way affixed to one another, whether printed, written, or blank, and considered apart from any container or case. 2. According to Unesco, a nonperiodical literary publication containing 49 or more pages. 3. According to the U.S. Postal Service, a publication qualifying for fourth-class postal rate, which consists of 24 or more pages, at least 22 of which are printed, and which contains primarily reading matter, with advertising limited to incidental announcements of books. 4. A literary work or one of its major divisions.

bookbin 1. A box on wheels for moving books. Sometimes equipped with self-depressing cushion and used as a book drop under a return slot at the circulation desk. 2. A space in a circulation desk in which books are placed while waiting for later discharging routine.

bookbinding see *binding* (1)

book box see *cumdach*

book capacity see *shelving capacity, stack capacity*

book card see *charge card*

book carriage In reprography, a device consisting of a carriage with two balanced or spring-loaded platforms and clamps which facilitates the photographing of two opposite pages in a large bound book by holding the volume open at a level or near-level plane. Synonymous with book cradle and book holder.

book carrier see *conveyor*

bookcase A framed set of two or more shelves, single- or double-faced, for storing library materials.

book catalog A catalog in the form of a loose-leaf or bound book. It may be conventionally printed, produced from a computer printout, or put together by hand, e.g., a guard book or sheaf catalog.

book charging machine see *charging machine*

book chute see *chute*

book cloth A cotton material used for book covers which comes in various qualities and grades, measured mainly according to the weight of the thread and the number of threads per square inch. A variety of colors and textures can be obtained by adding fillers, which may be primarily starch or plastics such as pyroxylin or vinyl, before or after dyeing and preparing the surface. Three major surfaces are natural finish, vellum finish, and linen finish. Book cloths coated rather than impregnated with plastic may resemble leather. Synonymous with binding cloth.

book club 1. A business organization that sells books through the mail to subscribing members, who usually agree to purchase a minimum number yearly. Books offered by the clubs may be specially reprinted for club distribution, purchased by the club from a publisher's stock, or produced as original editions for subscribers only. General interest clubs offer selections of fiction and nonfiction on a variety of subjects; special interest clubs limit selections to one subject. 2. A noncommercial club of book collectors or readers.

book club proof A proof specially printed and bound for submission to book clubs. Sometimes called BOM proof, because such proofs were first used for the Book-of-the-Month Club.

book collecting The assembling of books according to a logical principle, e.g., according to their contents, their place or origin, their provenance, their bibliographical interest, or their rarity.

book collection see *book stock*

book collector One who acquires books according to some sort of logical principle.

book conveyor see *conveyor*

book cover see *cover*

book cradle 1. A rack or stand, often of plexiglass or a similar material, used to support an open book in an exhibition. 2. A *book carriage.*

book display case see *display case*

book distributor see *conveyor*

book drive A systematic campaign to obtain gifts of books for a library.

book drop see *drop*

book elevator see *lift*

bookend Any of a variety of devices, usually made of plastic or metal, placed at the end of a row of library materials on a shelf to keep them upright. Synonymous with book support, end support.

book fair An exhibit of books sponsored by groups of booksellers and publishers, a library, or other group, often conducted as a market. In the tradition of the Frankfurt and Leipzig fairs, which flourished in the 16th and 17th centuries, may include the negotiation of publishing agreements, as well as the display of books available for sale or resale.

book hand The handwriting used by scribes in preparing manuscript books before the introduction of printing, as distinguished from the cursive hand used for letters and other, less formal records.

book holder see *book carriage*

book jacket A detachable, protective paper jacket placed around a book by the publisher. The jacket fits flush with the head and tail of the cover and is attached to the book by flaps folded over the fore-edges of the cover. Commonly contains a blurb, a biographical sketch of the author, quotes from reviews, and a list of other books by the author or issued by the same publisher. Synonymous with dust cover, dust jacket, dust wrapper, jacket, jacket cover.

booklet A small book, usually with paper covers; a pamphlet.

book lift see *lift*

book list A selected list of books, sometimes with descriptive notes and usually in a systematic order (subject, author, etc.)

book mark see *book number*

bookmark A piece of paper, plastic, or other material to be slipped between the leaves of a book to mark a place. It may also take the form of a piece of thin ribbon fastened to the top of the spine of a book, and long enough to extend the length of the leaves.

bookmarker see *bookmark*

bookmobile A large enclosed truck or van especially equipped to carry books and other library materials and which serves as a traveling branch library in small communities, city neighborhoods, or rural areas not otherwise served by a library.

book number The combination of symbols in a call number which distinguishes an item in a library collection from all other items in the same class number; ordinarily includes an author mark and a work mark. Synonymous with book mark. Compare with *class number* (2).

Book of Hours A liturgical book containing prayers and other private devotions, designed for a general user, in widespread use throughout the Catholic church from the 14th to the 16th century. Both before and after the invention of printing with movable type, such books were often beautifully illuminated.

book paper A generic term for all paper used in the manufacture of books, including paper made from rag pulp, chemical wood pulp, groundwood pulp, and esparto pulp. It may be coated or uncoated.

book piracy see *pirated edition*

bookplate A label affixed to a book to indicate ownership and, sometimes, its location in a library.

book pocket see *card pocket*

book preparation see *physical processing*

book press A device for pressing books to effect adhesion of pasted or glued surfaces, or for some other purpose, during the repair or binding process.

book processing see *physical processing*

book processing center see *processing center*

book rack see *rack*

book repair department see *repair department*

bookrest A device for holding a book at a convenient angle for reading.

book return see *drop*

book review see *review* (1)

books-by-mail service The provision of library materials by mail to authorized borrowers who request them through a mail-order catalog or by telephone.

book scout A person who travels, visiting obscure shops, in search of books which may be desired by librarians, private book collectors, or antiquarian booksellers.

book selection see *selection*

bookseller A person whose business is selling books; especially the owner of a bookstore. Compare with *dealer*.

books for the blind Books and periodicals with text printed in embossed braille characters and talking books, with the spoken text recorded on audiotape or audiodisc.

book shrine see *cumdach*

book sizes There is much confusion about the definition of book sizes and little consistency in usage. The common book trade designation of sizes was based originally on the relation to a sheet of paper measuring approximately 19 x 25 inches. When folded once to make two leaves (4 pages), it was a folio; when folded twice to make four leaves (8 pages), it was a quarto; when folded to eight leaves (16 pages), an octavo; when folded to 12 leaves (24 pages), a duodecimo or twelvemo; when folded to 16 leaves (32 pages), a sixteenmo, etc. This is the historical background of book sizes and is the basis of terms still used in the rare book trade. In exact bibliographical descriptions, as in describing rare books, the historical definition applies.

However, present trade practice almost invariably refers to a measurement of the height of the binding, not the size of the leaf. Usual library practice calls for the use of centimeters, the measurement again referring to the height of the binding.

With the present variety of paper sizes, all dimensions are approximate:

Folio, F, over 30 cm. (approx. 15 in.) high.
Quarto, 4to, 30 cm. (approx. 12 in.) high.
Octavo, 8vo, 25 cm. (approx. 9¾ in.) high.
Duodecimo or twelvemo, 12mo, 20 cm. (approx. 7¾ in.) high.

Sixteenmo, 16mo, 17½ cm. (approx. 6¾ in.) high.
Twentyfourmo, 24mo, 15 cm. (approx. 5¾ in.) high.
Thirtytwomo, 32mo, approx. 5 in. high.
Fortyeightmo, 48mo, approx. 4 in. high.
Sixtyfourmo, 64mo, approx. 3 in. high.
Other sizes include:
Double elephant folio, approx. 50 in. high.
Atlas folio, approx. 25 in. high.
Elephant folio, approx. 23 in. high.

Any book wider than it is high is designated as oblong and such descriptive note is abbreviated "obl." or "ob." and precedes such terms as quarto, octavo, etc. If the width of the book is less than three-fifths of its height, it is designated narrow and such descriptive note is abbreviated "nar." If the width of a book exceeds three-fourths of its height, but is no greater than its height, it is designated square. (Bookman's Glossary)

book stack see *stack*

book stamp see *ownership stamp*

book stock A library's collection of books. Synonymous with book collection.

book support see *bookend*

book trade Usually refers to the complex of arrangements for the distribution and sale of books to the general public. It includes a nation's retail bookstores, booksellers' organizations, and publishers and their organizations.

book trade journal A periodical issued by publishers or booksellers, individually or collectively, calling attention to books published or for sale, and sometimes including information about book production and distribution and a current record of new books.

book trough A V-shaped shelf or rack for the display of books, sometimes a part of a counter, circulation desk, case, or book truck.

book truck A small cart on wheels provided with two or three shelves, used for transporting books within a library.

Book Week see *Children's Book Week*

bookworm 1. The larvae of various insects that injure books by boring small holes in the binding and leaves. 2. A person devoted to books who reads voraciously.

boolean   Referring to logical or algebraic operations, formulated by George Boole, involving variables with two values, such as Value 1 *and* Value 2; Value 1 *or* Value 2; and Value 1 but *not* Value 2.

boom microphone   A microphone which has been mounted on a long, movable arm to permit the placement of the microphone in an optimal recording position. These are found in television studios, sound recording studios, etc.

bootstrap   A method of loading a computer program by entering the first few instructions into the system to initiate entry of the remaining instructions.

bootstrap loader   An automatic routine built into the hardware to load a computer program by entering the first few instructions into the system to initiate entry of the remaining instructions.

border   1. An ornamental design along one or more sides of an illuminated manuscript or of any body of printed matter, or surrounding an illuminated miniature. 2. In printing, a continuous decorative design arranged around text or illustration, consisting of cast strips of plain or patterned rule, or repeated units of flowers. Compare with *compartment*. 3. A binding ornamentation that runs close to the edges of the sides and/or the spine of a volume. Compare with *frame* (1).

borrower   A person who charges out library materials.

borrowers' file see *registration file*

borrower's identification card   A card issued by a library to a person, bearing usually his or her name, address, and identification number. The card is used to identify the person as an authorized borrower and to provide information for the loan record in the charging process. Also called library card or simply identification card.

borrower's identification number   The unique number assigned to an authorized library borrower for identification purposes.

boss   A metal knob, often ornamented, fixed upon the covers of books, usually at the corners and center, for protection and decoration.

bounce   A sudden, unanticipated brightness in a television picture.

bound book   Originally, a hand-bound book with boards attached to the handsewn sections before gluing or pasting the covering material to the boards. The term as now generally used includes cased books.

bound term   In coordinate indexing, a term that cannot be used alone but must be used with another term.

bound volume see *volume* (2)

bound with   One of two or more bibliographically independent books or pamphlets which have been published separately and subsequently bound together. Synonymous with independent.

bow   The tendency of photographic film or paper to bend into a curve across the width. Compare with *curl.*

bowdlerize   To expurgate the text of a literary work by omitting or changing objectionable words or passages; from the name of Thomas Bowdler, who in 1818 issued an expurgated edition of Shakespeare.

bowdlerized edition see *expurgated edition*

boxed   Said of a set of documents enclosed in a boxlike protective container for display purposes, or to keep several physical units together.

box file   A container made to stand on a shelf, and intended primarily to contain flimsy material such as loose papers and correspondence.

bpi see *bits per inch*

bps see *bits per second*

bracket shelving   A type of adjustable metal shelving in which the shelves are supported by brackets with lugs on the back that fit into precut slots in stack uprights. In one type, shelves are suspended from brackets which not only support the shelf but also serve as bookends. A type in which brackets support the shelves from underneath is also called cantilever shelving. Compare with *standard shelving*.

Bradford's law of scattering   A law of diminishing returns in the use made of scientific journals, based on C. S. Bradford's analysis of journal references related to specific topics in selected subject fields. Bradford found that a small number of journals in a field yielded a high proportion of all the relevant articles and identified zones of less productive journals, each zone producing a reduced yield of relevant articles.

braille A system of embossed print for the blind which uses all the combinations of six dots arranged in groups or cells, three dots high and two dots wide; named for its inventor, Louis Braille.

braille book see *hand-copied braille book, press braille*

braille music notation An internationally recognized system of embossed music symbols based on the character used in braille print.

braille slate A device for writing braille consisting of two metal blades, one pitted with rows of braille cells, the other with openings to locate the pitted cells. Paper is inserted between the blades and the dots are made with a stylus, moving from right to left. Also called braille tablet.

braille tablet see *braille slate*

braillewriter A machine for writing braille, having six keys corresponding to the six dots of the braille cell.

branch To transfer or depart from one sequence of computer instructions to another sequence in a computer program.

branch department The administrative unit of a library that supervises the work of branch libraries.

branch librarian The administrative head of a branch library or a professional librarian working in a branch library.

branch library An auxiliary library service outlet with quarters separate from the central library of a system, with no less than a basic collection of materials, a regular staffing level, and an established service schedule.

branch registration see *separate registration*

Bray library see *parish library* (2)

brief cataloging The limitation of the bibliographic description to those data elements considered by a library or other cataloging agency to be essential to the identification of bibliographic items and of the number of access points to the bibliographic records of the items, applied to all items cataloged or to certain categories of items. Synonymous with abbreviated cataloging, limited cataloging, simplified cataloging. Compare with *full cataloging, selective cataloging.*

brieflisting see *temporary cataloging*

brittleness A defect in paper, film base, or other substance, which causes it to crack as a result of age, temperature, or other factors.

broad band see *wide band*

broad classification 1. A classification system which provides broad general classes with very little subdivision. 2. A method of classifying which uses only the broader classes of a classification system, omitting detailed subdivision.

broadsheet see *broadside*

broadside Originally a sheet of paper printed only on one side to be read unfolded. Now also used for variously folded sheets printed on one or both sides. Synonymous with broadsheet.

brochure see *pamphlet* (2)

broken Said of a book which tends to fall open at a place where the binding has been strained.

broken file see *incomplete file*

broken order The arrangement of the library collection in discontinuous order, as when materials in a particular range of class numbers are removed from regular sequence and located elsewhere to provide better user access or service.

broken over Said of plates folded or turned over a short distance from the back edge before being placed in a book preparatory to binding, so that the plates may lie flat and be easily turned. Synonymous with hinged.

broker's circular A circular published by a brokerage house, sometimes at regular intervals, containing descriptions of securities, usually of new issues.

bromide film Sensitized photographic film with an emulsion of silver bromide suspended in gelatin.

bromide paper Sensitized photographic paper with an emulsion of silver bromide suspended in gelatin.

brownline see *diazotype process, proofs*

Brown's Adjustable Classification see *Adjustable Classification*

Brown's Subject Classification see *Subject Classification*

browse 1. To look through a library collection or to scan the records in a file in a general, rather than a specific, search for items of interest. 2. In micrographics, to rapidly scan a multi-image microform using a manual or automatic reader.

browsing period see *free reading period*

browsing room A room in an academic or public library with a collection of books for cultural and recreational reading, selected for their broad contemporary interest.

Brussels Classification see *Universal Decimal Classification*

bucket In computer science, a general term for a specific part of storage designed for accumulating data or totals.

buckles In binding, the severe wrinkles near the head and back of the folded signatures where the paper is folded at right angles. Synonymous with gussets.

buckram A filled book cloth with a heavy-weave cotton base. Originally applied only to a starch-filled fabric of this type; now, loosely, any filled fabric with a heavy base.

budget A comprehensive financial plan for a given time period which estimates, by established categories, the expenditures required to accomplish the goals or programs of an organization based upon estimated income.

budgetary control The process of periodically reviewing the activities of an organization by monitoring the actual expenditures against the estimated expenditures established in the budget. This review process ensures fiscal control and integrity and identifies the need for prescrip-

tive adjustments in the budget. Compare with *fiscal control.*

budget binding see *economy binding*

budget hearing A formal session, in which the head of an organization or organizational unit has the opportunity to present testimony and evidence in justification of a proposed budget.

buffer A temporary storage area or device for data being transferred or transmitted between other storage devices, used to equalize the differing speeds of input/output devices. Synonymous with data buffer and storage buffer.

bug An error or malfunction in a computer program, a piece of equipment or hardware, or a procedure.

building code A set of legal regulations and standards governing new construction and building alterations within a particular government jurisdiction, such as a municipality. The code may establish requirements and restrictions in such areas as safety, size, building use, and acceptable electrical and mechanical standards.

building department see *maintenance department*

building-in In binding, the process of drying the paste used to attach the case to a bound volume so that the boards will not warp.

bulk The thickness of a specified number of sheets of paper when under a specified pressure.

bulk borrowing The borrowing, usually for an extended period of time, of a large quantity of library materials from another library. The borrowed materials remain under the control of the lending library which owns them, but they are housed in the borrowing library.

bulk lending The lending of a large quantity of materials from a library's collection to another library, usually for an extended period of time.

bulk storage see *mass storage*

bulletin 1. A periodical issued by a government department, a society, or an institution. 2. In a special library, a selective dissemination of information service in fields of interest to the host organization, produced and issued by the library, usually weekly or monthly, and with some form of subject arrangement.

burn-in 1. To give additional exposure to selected areas of a photographic print, typically an enlargement, so as to alter the density locally. Compare with *dodge*. 2. In reprography, to give greater than normal exposure to all or a portion of a photosensitive material so as to produce a desired density.

burnished edges Colored or gilt edges of a book that have been polished smooth and bright, usually with an agate or other polishing tool.

burn out To overexpose a reversal film or reversal paper, causing a complete loss of image when developed.

burst 1. To separate fanfold or continuous computer forms into individual sheets. 2. In data transmission, a sequence of signals transmitted as a single group and at one time.

bus A circuit or channel for transmitting or transferring data or electrical power.

business branch A branch of a metropolitan public library system conveniently located in the commercial or financial district which specializes in collections and services required by that community.

business firm borrower's card A borrower's identification card issued to a business firm or corporation to which library materials are charged for the use of the organization. Synonymous with corporate borrower's card, corporation borrower's card, and firm borrower's card.

butt splice see *splice*

buying around The term used to describe the purchase from a foreign dealer of an edition that is cheaper than the domestic edition which is, according to the publishers' contracts, the only edition legally offered for sale in the domestic market.

by authority Published by permission of a legally constituted official or body.

byte A group of adjacent binary digits, usually eight bits, treated as a unit.

cable Electrical conductors insulated from each other and arranged in a variety of patterns to perform signal transmission, control, audio, and power supply functions in an electrical system. (AECT)

cable television see *closed circuit television (CCTV), community antenna television (CATV)*

cadastral map A map showing the boundaries of subdivisions of land, usually with the bearings and lengths thereof and the areas of individual tracts, for purposes of describing and recording ownership. Synonymous with property map.

cadenza In music, a technically brilliant solo passage toward the close of the first or last movement of a concerto, in which the main themes are given further development.

CAI see *computer-assisted instruction*

calendar 1. In archives, a chronological list of documents, either selective or comprehensive, usually with a description giving one or more of the following: writer, recipient, date, place, summary of content, type of manuscript, and page or leaf count. (SAA) 2. A schedule of events or discussions in the order in which they are to take place, as of cases in court or of bills in a legislative body. 3. A page or series of pages within a periodical on which is printed a chronological schedule of events such as meetings or other activities relevant to the subject matter.

calender Part of a papermaking machine that passes newly made, dried paper under pressure through a series of metal rollers to smooth the surface.

calendered paper Paper with a very smooth machine finish imparted by passing the newly made, dried paper between the metal rolls of the calender.

calf A binding leather made from calfskin, usually from an animal not more than six weeks old, popular because of its smooth, slightly porous surface, unblemished appearance, relatively large size (8–10 square feet), and ease of tooling. Calf can be stained or painted in various ways for decorative purposes (e.g., marbled, mottled, speckled, sprinkled, and tree).

call 1. To request a computer program from a program library. 2. To transfer control in a computer program to another set of instructions or program.

calligraphy The art of beautiful writing; fine penmanship.

call mark see *call number*

call number The set of symbols identifying a particular item in a library collection and indicating its location. Usually includes a class number and a book number. Synonymous with call mark and shelf mark.

call slip A form filled out by a borrower to request the delivery of an item from the closed stack of a library; used also as a charge card.

cameo binding A style of binding having the center of the boards stamped in relief, in imitation of antique gems or medals. Synonymous with plaquette binding.

camera 1. A device with a light-proof enclosure for forming an image on photographic film when light is admitted to the enclosure through a lens or lens system. 2. In television, a device equipped with a lens and a pickup tube containing a photosensitive plate on which the image is projected for conversion into an electric video signal.

camera card An aperture card containing unexposed and unprocessed microfilm and used for filming source documents. The card is designed to be exposed and processed in a processor-camera. Compare with *copy card.*

camera copy see *camera-ready copy* (1)

camera head The portion of a camera which contains the film, film-advance mechanism, and the lens.

camera lens An optical device which forms the image on photographic film.

camera microfilm The film image of a source document, produced directly by the camera. The film, generally of high quality and subject to rigid standards, is usually kept by the producer to make distribution copies or for archival purposes. Synonymous with first-generation microfilm, master film, master negative film, and original film.

camera processor see *processor camera*

camera-ready copy 1. Type or artwork assembled in place and ready to be photographed for the production of a plate photomechanically. Synonymous with camera copy. 2. A source document suitable for microfilming. The term generally refers to the physical characteristics of the document, e.g., typography, color of paper, margins, line density.

cancel Any leaf or leaves intended to be substituted for the corresponding part of the book as originally printed; also called a cancellans. The term "cancel" applies only to the new part, and not to the original, offending part (called a cancellandum) which it is intended to replace.

cancellandum see *cancel*

cancellans see *cancel*

candela A unit of luminous intensity equal to $\frac{1}{60}$ of the luminous intensity per square centimeter of a blackbody radiator operating at the temperature of freezing platinum. Formerly called candle.

candle see *candela*

canonical class In classification, a subdivision of a main class derived from tradition or convention rather than from the natural characteristics of the class.

canonical order In classification, an arrangement of classes derived from tradition or convention rather than from natural characteristics of the things classed.

canopy top The flat top or rooflike cover over a section of shelving which contributes to the stability and aesthetics of the shelving unit.

cantilever shelving see *bracket shelving*

canton flannel Cotton cloth that is fleeced on only one side. When used as back lining, it provides the additional strength required for library binding.

Cape morocco   A durable goatskin leather used in binding, made from Cape (South African) goatskin, and resembling Levant.

capital equipment   Items of equipment involving a significant expenditure of funds and representing a long-term investment.

capital improvement   Acquisition of or additions to fixed assets, such as building sites, new buildings and additions, new equipment, initial book stock, furnishings for new or expanded buildings, and new vehicles. Excludes replacement and repair of existing furnishings and equipment, regular purchase of library materials, and investments for capital appreciation.

capital letter   1. A large letter, the only form of the written Roman alphabet until approximately the 4th century. Latin manuscripts of the period were written entirely in square or rustic capitals. 2. Any letter written or printed in a form larger than, and often different from, that of the corresponding small letter. 3. An upper-case letter.

capsa   A cylindrical box used in Roman libraries to hold one or more rolls standing upright.

capstan   The spindle in an audiotape recorder that rotates the tape against the pinch roller at a relatively constant speed during recording or playback. The capstan disengages for fast forward or rewind.

caption   1. The brief title or description above an illustration. By extension, the legend below an illustration. Synonymous with cut line. 2. A headline at the beginning of the text of a chapter, section, etc., of a book or periodical. 3. The brief title/subtitle which describes, identifies, or explains the frame(s) of a film or filmstrip. 4. On a microform, the brief identification of the photographed material that is readable without magnification.

caption title   The title of a work given at the beginning of the first page of the text or, in the case of a musical score, immediately above the opening bars of the music. Synonymous with head title. (AACR2)

CAR   see *computer-assisted retrieval*

cardboard   A general term applied to boards .006 of an inch or more in thickness, popularly used to denote any stiff board of moderate thickness. In the paper industry the term has been supplanted by the term "board" in combination with words indicating its character or use.

card catalog   A catalog in which bibliographic records, references, etc., are on separate cards of uniform size arranged in any desired order in card trays. 2. The aggregate of furniture containing the cards and the area in which the furniture is located. Synonymous with manual catalog.

card catalog case   A filing cabinet of drawers or trays for holding a card catalog.

card code   A code in which characters of data are represented as patterns of holes punched in a card.

card column   A vertical column of punching positions in a punched card, used to code one character of data. Compare with *card row*.

card field   A set of columns in a punched card format dedicated to the storage of a specific kind of data.

card image   In computer science, data stored in main or auxiliary storage exactly as it would be stored on a punched card (usually as it was input from punched cards or will be output to them).

card jacket   A clear plastic cover, often preprinted with a brief message (e.g., Closed Reserve, On Order), slipped over a catalog card or temporary slip to convey information or to protect the card or slip.

card pocket   A flat pouch or envelope usually made of stiff paper and affixed inside the front or back book cover or the cover or container of other documents to hold the charge card. Frequently called book pocket from its common use in books.

card punch   A device which records data in cards by punching holes representing letters, numbers, and other special symbols or characters. Compare with *keypunch*.

card reader   A device which senses or reads the holes in punched cards and converts the coded patterns of holes into electrical or electronic pulses or signals for entry into a computer for processing.

card read-punch   A device containing both a card reader and a card punch.

card reproducer see *reproducer*

card row A horizontal row of punching positions across the width of a punched card. Compare with *card column.*

card service A serial publication which is revised, cumulated, or indexed, or any one of these, by means of new or replacement cards. It is used where latest revisions of information are important, as with scientific materials.

card-to-card printer A contact copy printer for producing duplicate card-mounted microfilm.

card-to-roll printer A step printing device which creates duplicate microimages from microfiche onto roll film.

career information center see *education and job information center*

Carnegie library A library building built fully or in part with funds contributed by Andrew Carnegie and characterized by a common architectural style.

Carolingian Relating to a variety of book hands developed in France from the 8th to 11th centuries, and employing capitals and minuscules.

carrel 1. A small room with a door which usually can be locked or an alcove in a library stack for individual study. It may be assigned to one user for a designated time period, during which the user can store in it the materials being used. 2. A freestanding, unenclosed desk or table for individual study, often with a shelf or low partition on the back and partitions on the sides. Called a wet carrel when equipped with one or more electrical outlets for using audiovisual equipment and a dry carrel when it lacks such outlets. Synonymous with study carrel.

carrier In xerography, that portion of the developer which carries the toner, but does not actually form a part of the image.

cartobibliography 1. The study of the bibliography of maps. 2. A bibliographic item resulting from such study.

cartographic material Any material representing, in whole or in part, the earth or any celestial body at any scale. (AACR2)

cartouche A scroll-shaped or other ornamental frame with a space containing an inscription, as on a map; also seen on bindings, frequently surrounding an armorial device.

cartridge 1. A container with a single reel permanently encasing an audiotape, videotape, or motion picture film which has its ends joined together in a continuous loop. Compare with *cassette.* 2. A container with a single reel permanently encasing processed roll microfilm. The microfilm is threaded onto a take-up reel in the microfilm reader and must be rewound before the removal of the cartridge from the reader.

cartridge audiotape see *audiocartridge*

cartridge film A motion-picture film of short duration, with or without a sound track, which has been spliced into a continuous loop and sealed into a cartridge. For viewing, the cartridge is inserted into a projector and the film plays continuously.

cartridge tape see *audiocartridge, videocartridge*

cartridge videotape see *videocartridge*

cartulary (chartulary) 1. A collection of charters, deeds, and other records, as of a monastery. 2. A register in which these are recorded. 3. A keeper of such archives.

case 1. In printing, a compartmentalized drawer for holding type. 2. The hard cover of a book, made separately from the book and later attached to it.

case binding A method of binding in which a hard cover is made wholly separate from the book and later is attached to it. A case binding usually consists of two boards and an inlay covered with cloth, paper, leather, or some other material. (AACR 2, mod.)

casebook A book that records for study and reference real cases in law, sociology, psychology, or other fields.

cased book A book with a hard cover, or case, that has been prefabricated and attached to the book by machine.

case file In archives, a folder or other file unit containing documents relating to a specific action, event, person, place, project, or other subject. Sometimes called a project file or dossier.

case shelving A type of stack shelving, each section of which consists of a bookcase, usually providing storage on six shelves and the base.

case study The careful and thorough examination and analysis of the behavior of one individual or event in a population.

cash-flow accounting A method of accounting whereby in financial reports revenues are reported when cash is received and materials and services are reported as expenditures when cash is disbursed. Compare with *accrual accounting.*

casing-in The process of attaching a case binding to the book, usually by pasting the endpapers to the boards.

cassette A container with two reels permanently encasing an audiotape, videotape, or motion picture film, the ends of which are each attached to a separate reel. Compare with *cartridge* (1).

cassette audiotape see *audiocassette*

cassette tape see *audiocassette, videocassette*

casual mnemonics In classification, the mnemonic device of using letters in the notation to indicate a topic, the letter usually being the first letter of the name of the topic. Used only when order permits, casually, and not consistently throughout the classification schedule. Similar to *literal mnemonics.* Compare with *systematic mnemonics, variable mnemonics.*

catalog 1. A file of bibliographic records, created according to specific and uniform principles of construction and under the control of an authority file, which describes the materials contained in a collection, library, or group of libraries. (AACR2, mod.) 2. In a wider sense, a list of materials prepared for a particular purpose, e.g., an exhibition catalog, a sales catalog. (AACR2)

catalog card 1. One of the cards composing a card catalog. 2. A plain or a ruled card, generally of standard size, 7.5 cm. high and 12.5 cm. wide, to be used for entries in a catalog or some other file. (ALA Glossary)

catalog case see *card catalog case*

catalog code A set of rules for the preparation of bibliographic records; designed to ensure consistency in the construction of a catalog.

catalog department The administrative unit of a library which catalogs and classifies new materials and prepares and maintains the library's catalogs. In some libraries, this department also performs accessioning, physical processing, and the preparation of library materials for binding or rebinding outside the library.

catalog editing The regular inspection of a catalog to check or test its conformity to established standards, and to make appropriate alterations or additions, such as the correction of obsolete and conflicting headings, the provision of needed explanatory references, etc.

cataloged materials Any library materials which have been described in the catalog of a collection, library, or group of libraries, as distinct from library materials which are merely physically arranged for use and are not described in a catalog.

cataloger A librarian who performs descriptive and/or subject cataloging and may also perform such related tasks as classifying, shelflisting, etc.

cataloging Those activities performed in the preparation of bibliographic records for a catalog.

cataloging in publication (CIP) A prepublication cataloging program through which participating publishers provide galley proofs or front matter of their books to the national library or other centralized cataloging agency, where a bibliographic record is prepared and returned to the publisher. The record, except for the elements of description between the title proper and the series statement, is printed in the book, usually on the verso of the title leaf. Originating in the Library of Congress in 1971, the program is now internationally operational.

catalog librarian A librarian in charge of or assisting in the work of a catalog department.

catalog maintenance The total of all the work of maintaining an existing file of bibliographic records, including addition, correction, and deletion of records, as well as the production of a syndetic structure to connect individual records. Maintenance of a card catalog includes the physical maintenance of the cards, their disposition in the catalog, and maintenance of the catalog trays and cases.

catalogue raisonné see *classed catalog*

catch letters see *catchword* (1)

catch stitch see *kettle stitch*

catch title see *catchword title*

catchword 1. A word or part of a word placed prominently at the top of a page or a column, repeating the first and/or the last heading of the page or the column, as in a dictionary. Synonymous with catch letters, direction word, guide word. 2. In early books, the word or part of a word given below the end of the last line of a page (in the direction line) or of the last verso of a signature, anticipating the first word of the following page or leaf. 3. In indexing, a *keyword*.

catchword title A partial title consisting of some striking word or phrase likely to be remembered and sought as a heading by catalog users. May coincide with the subtitle or alternative title. Synonymous with catch title.

categorical funding The process of assigning monies to a clearly defined activity or use.

category In classification, any of the various basic concepts of high generality and wide application into which all possible objects of human thought can be classified.

cathedral style Said of cloth and leather bindings with Gothic architectural motifs, often including a rose window, done between 1815 and 1840 in England and France.

cathode-ray tube (CRT) A vacuum tube with a televisionlike screen upon which data or information can be displayed. Synonymous with display tube.

cathode-ray-tube (CRT) recorder see *computer-output-microfilm recorder*

cathode-ray-tube terminal A computer terminal equipped with a cathode-ray tube for visual display of output. Synonymous with video display terminal. Compare with *visual display unit, printer terminal, touch terminal.*

CATV see *community antenna television*

causal relationship A relationship between two variables in which a change of one brings about a change in the other.

CCTV see *closed circuit television*

celestial globe see *globe*

celestial map A map representing the heavens. Synonymous with star map.

cellulose The basic fiber in paper; cellulose forms a significant proportion of many plants, including trees, in fibers of various lengths.

cellulose acetate A transparent plastic produced by the action of acetic acid on cellulose, used as a film base for safety film and as a magnetic tape base. As a film base, compare with *cellulose nitrate.*

cellulose nitrate A transparent plastic produced by the action of nitric acid on cellulose, once used extensively as a film base. Because it is extremely flammable, it has been largely replaced by *cellulose acetate* and *cellulose triacetate.*

cellulose triacetate A transparent plastic more dimensionally stable than cellulose acetate, used as a film base for safety film and as a magnetic tape base. As a film base, compare with *cellulose nitrate.*

censor To prohibit or object to the production, distribution, circulation, or display of a work on the grounds that it contains offensive material.

central catalog The catalog located in the central library of a library system and usually containing bibliographic records of materials held by all service outlets in the system. Synonymous with general catalog and main catalog.

centralization, administrative The practice of limiting authority and decision-making to a selected number of administrative officers and supervisors as a means of closely controlling the activities and operations of an organization. It is sometimes associated with a tall organizational structure. Compare with *decentralization, administrative.*

centralization, organizational An organizational arrangement within a library system which is characterized by consolidated collections and service points in one central facility with few, if any, separate libraries outside that facility. Compare with *decentralization, organizational.*

centralized cataloging   1. The original cataloging of bibliographic items by some central organization (such as the Library of Congress or the British National Bibliography) which makes the bibliographic records accessible to other libraries. 2. The cataloging of all library materials for members of a library consortium, network, or other cooperative endeavor by a processing center. Compare with *cooperative cataloging, shared cataloging.*

centralized network   A network in which management and control functions and services are performed in a central location or node. Compare with *decentralized network.*

centralized processing   The processing of library materials for a group of libraries by a processing center.

central library   A single-unit library or the library which is the administrative center of a library system, where usually processing is centralized and the principal collections are housed. Synonymous with main library.

central limit theorem   The theorem that as the number of cases in each sample increases, and as the number of samples increases, the distribution of sample means approaches the normal distribution.

central processing unit (CPU)   The unit of a computer system containing the circuits used to interpret and execute instructions in a computer program and perform essential arithmetic and logic operations on data. Synonymous with central processor and mainframe.

central processing unit time   The amount of time a user requires use of the central processing unit of a computer system. Compare with *connect time.*

central processor   see *central processing unit*

central registration   A method of recording all authorized borrowers in a union registration file at the central library of a library system, although borrowers' identification cards may be issued at the central library and at branch libraries. Compare with *separate registration.*

central serial record   see *serial record*

central shelflist   The shelflist located in the central library or headquarters unit of a library system, usually containing entries for materials held by all service outlets in the system. Synonymous with main shelflist. Sometimes called union shelflist.

central tendency   A term generally meaning the average or center of a distribution, such as the mean, median, mode.

certificate of issue   The statement in a limited edition which certifies the number of copies printed, sometimes bearing the autograph of the author and/or illustrator.

certification   In archives, the act of attesting the official character of a record or other document, or a reproduction thereof. Compare with *authentication.*

certification of librarians   The process of establishing professional qualifications and competencies for librarians and conferring upon acceptable candidates a certificate to practice. Such action may be taken by a legally authorized state body, as in the case of school media specialists, or on a voluntary basis by a professional association, as in the case of medical librarians.

certified bindery   A library bindery which adheres to the binding specifications of the Library Binding Institute.

certified librarian   A professional member of a library staff who has been endorsed officially as having met the requirements for employment established by a governmental agency or a professional association.

chafed   Said of a surface worn by rubbing, as the covers of a book.

chain   In classification, a hierarchy of terms in a classification system, each term including all those that follow it.

chained book   A book attached to a shelf or a reading desk by a chain to prevent theft; common in libraries in the 15th–17th centuries.

chain index   An index produced by chain procedure.

chaining   In computer science, a method of storing data items, operations, computer programs, or records in groups or lists, with linking fields to trace each in the chain.

chain lines   see *laid paper* (1)

chain of command The formal lines or channels of vertical communication, reporting, and control between administrative officers, supervisors, and subordinates within an organization.

chain printer see *printer* (2)

chain procedure The standardized procedure for constructing an alphabetical index which provides for an entry under each of the terms of a complex subject notation. Terms are listed in reverse order (specific to general), and index entries are made by progressively deleting the first term in the previous entry.

chain stitch see *kettle stitch*

chalkboard A smooth surface of slate, glass, or other material used for presentation by writing or drawing with chalk, crayon, pen, or other easily erased materials. (NCES)

chalk engraving see *crayon engraving*

chance The possibility or probability that an event will occur.

changed title The title proper of a bibliographic item that differs from the one under which the item was earlier published.

channel 1. A path for the electrical transmission of data between two or more points. 2. The connection between the point of entry of data into a network and the point of usage of the data (a data sink). 3. A track or row on a storage medium such as a magnetic disk or magnetic tape along which signals can be recorded. 4. The band of frequencies assigned by the Federal Communications Commission to a particular transmitting station, as in radio and television. Synonymous with communications channel.

channel capacity In data communication, the maximum rate, usually measured in bits per second or characters per second, at which data can be transmitted over a channel.

channel multiplexer see *multiplexer*

channel noise see *noise* (1)

chapbook 1. A small, cheap paperback book, usually containing a tale, legend, poem, or ballad of a popular, sensational, juvenile, moral, or educational character. Chapbooks were sold by hawkers or "chapmen" in the 16th–18th centu-

ries. 2. A modern pamphlet suggestive of this type of publication.

chapter heading A heading consisting of the number and title of a chapter.

character 1. Any conventional mark, sign, or symbol used in writing and printing. 2. In data processing, a coded group of binary digits or electrical pulses representing a letter of the alphabet, a number, or other special mark or symbol.

character generator The electronic portion of a computer output microfilm recorder which converts electrical signals to visible characters. One method uses a dot matrix consisting of light-emitting diodes to form the characters. Other methods include the projection of light through the holes of a dot matrix to form characters on a cathode-ray-tube screen, and an electron-beam-stroke generator which writes characters directly on dry silver or vesicular film.

characteristic curve see *contrast* (1)

characteristic of a classification The distinguishing property or quality which is used to define a class and which forms the basis of division at each level of a classification.

character printer A computer printer which prints a single character at a time. Compare with *line printer*.

character recognition The sensing, identification, and conversion to patterns of electronic pulses or signals of characters of a language by a machine.

character set In data processing, the particular set of characters to be used for a specific purpose or by a particular device or machine.

characters per inch (CPI) The number of characters which can be recorded per inch on a medium such as magnetic tape.

characters per pica In any type font, the average number of characters that will fit into one pica of width of average copy.

characters per second (CPS) The number of characters per second which can be sensed or recorded by a machine or transmitted over a channel.

character string see *string*

character transfer rate The maximum speed at which characters can be transferred from one point or location to another, such as from magnetic disk to main storage, measured usually in characters per second.

charge 1. A library's record of the loan of an item from the library collection, including identification of the item, identification of the borrower, and the date due. 2. To lend an item from the library collection to a borrower and enter a record of the loan in the charging file. Compare with *discharge.*

charge card A card identifying an item loaned from the library collection (e.g., by call number, main entry heading, title) which is used as a loan record in the charging file. The card may be prepared by the library and found inside the cover or other container of the document, in which case it is synonymous with book card, or it may be filled out by the borrower.

charging desk see *circulation desk*

charging file A complete record of all items charged from the library collection in any format, e.g., card, punched card, computer printout, magnetic tape, magnetic disk, or microfilm. Synonymous with circulation file, circulation record, and loan record.

charging machine Any of various mechanical and electronic devices used for recording circulation transactions.

charging system The method used to charge out and maintain records of the materials lent by a library. Synonymous with loan system.

chart 1. An opaque sheet that exhibits data in the form of graphs or tables, or by the use of contours, shapes, or figures. 2. A special-purpose map, generally designed for navigation or other particular purposes, in which essential map information is combined with various other data critical to the intended use, e.g., *aeronautical chart, hydrographic chart.*

chartulary see *cartulary*

chase A rectangular frame of steel or iron into which a letterpress form is locked for printing or platemaking.

chased edges see *gauffered edges*

check bit A binary check digit added to a character to verify that hardware does not lose or add a bit during the handling or processing of data. Compare with *check digit, parity bit.*

check digit A redundant digit added to a pattern of binary digits, used to perform a check for inaccurate storage, retrieval, or transfer of data. Compare with *check bit, parity bit.*

check-in record The file in which a library records receipt of the numbers or parts of serials and continuations.

checklist 1. A *finding list.* 2. A finding aid, usually for a particular accession, created by an archival agency and consisting of a preliminary listing of records with or without summary description of their informational content. With the development of the record group concept, this finding aid evolved into the inventory. (SAA)

Checklist Classification see *Documents Office Classification*

checkout routine see *test routine*

chemical wood pulp A pulp used in practically all grades of paper, prepared by chemically treating wood chips to remove the lignin.

chiaroscuro 1. A method of printing engravings by the successive use of several blocks or plates to represent light and dark shades. The word means clear-obscure, that is, balanced light and shade. Synonymous with claro obscuro. 2. A print so produced.

chief librarian The title used to designate the chief administrative officer of some libraries and library systems.

chief source of information The source of bibliographic data to be given first preference as the source from which a bibliographic description (or a portion thereof) is prepared. (AACR2)

chiffon silk A strong and durable silk material used for repairing and reinforcing paper, so sheer that the finest print is clearly legible through it.

children's books Books that match the reading ability level and interests of children of a particular age group or educational level between preschool and sixth grade.

Children's Book Week A week in November set aside for special celebration and exhibits by booksellers, librarians, and other groups, to stimulate interest in books and reading for children and young people, under the sponsorship of the Children's Book Council. Sometimes referred to as simply Book Week.

children's department 1. The part of a library devoted to collections and services for children. 2. The administrative unit of a public library system that has charge of work with children in the central children's room and all other service outlets offering services to children. Synonymous with junior department and juvenile department.

children's librarian A librarian responsible for developing and providing services and collections for children.

children's room A room in the central library or in a branch of a public library set aside for services and collections for children.

china paper A soft and very thin yellowish paper, handmade in China from bamboo fiber and used for proofs of wood engravings.

Chinese style see *traditional format (Oriental books)*

chip 1. An integrated circuit of diodes, transistors, and resistors mounted on a small wafer of semiconductor silicon. 2. A unit of microfilm, usually 35mm in width and three inches or less in length, which contains coded indexing information and one or more microimages. Chips are intended for use in automatic retrieval systems.

chip board A thin, cheap paperboard used in book covers, made from recycled paper and other fibrous materials.

chi-square distribution A sampling distribution derived from the sums of the squares of the deviations from the mean obtained from a large number of random samples of the same size drawn from a normally distributed population. Like the t- and F-distributions, the shape of the chi-square distribution is dependent upon the number of degrees of freedom.

chi-square test A test of significance that compares frequencies, derived from sample data, with expected frequencies that have been predicted by some hypothesis. The extent of the discrepancies between the observed and expected frequencies is interpreted through the use of the chi-square distribution.

chloride film Sensitized photographic film and paper with an emulsion of silver chloride, used mainly for contact copying.

chloride paper Sensitized photographic paper with an emulsion of silver chloride, used mainly for contact copying.

chorus score In music, a score of a vocal work showing only the chorus parts, with accompaniment, if any, arranged for keyboard instrument. (AACR2)

chrestomathy A collection of extracts from literary works with notes and explanations, used in studying a language or as literary specimens.

chromatic aberration An optical defect in a lens which results in a distorted image forming on the film plane. The problem is due to light of different colors focusing in different planes. It can be recognized by a rainbow effect which forms at the edges of the image. Synonymous with chromaticity.

chromaticity see *chromatic aberration*

chromolithography Lithographic printing in colors by means of separate stones or plates for the various colors, with some colors printed over others. Synonymous with color lithography.

chronogram A motto, sentence, or inscription in which occur roman numerals, often written as upper-case letters, which, added together and read in sequence, express a date. Thus the following tag from Horace, feriaM siDera VertIce, contains the capital letters MDVI, giving the date 1506.

chronological file see *reading file*

chronological order The order of time, or the point or period when something occurs; sometimes employed as a characteristic of classification and as the basis of arranging groups of documents and/or their records in a file in the order of date of publication, date of copyright, or period covered.

chronological subdivision see *period subdivision*

chrysography The art of writing in gold letters, as practiced by medieval writers of manuscripts.

chunk A string of consecutive words treated as a unit in preparing an automatic index.

chute A sloping channel through which books or other library materials may slide to a lower level.

CIM see *computer input microfilm*

cinching The undesirable practice of pulling the end of a roll of film to tighten the film when wound on a reel. This may result in straight longitudinal scratches called cinch marks.

cinch marks see *cinching*

cinefilm see *motion picture*

cinéma vérité A filmmaking technique which attempts to portray reality. Usually produced with a hand-held camera, actual events, interviews, and natural activities are recorded rather than the filming of actors performing roles.

cine orientation Said of images on roll microfilm which are positioned perpendicular to the edge of the film, in the manner of images on motion picture film. Technically referred to as 1A orientation (a type of image placement recognized by the American National Standards Institute in *USA Standard Specifications for 16mm and 35mm Silver-Gelatin Microfilms for Reel Applications*). Synonymous with motion picture orientation. Compare with *comic orientation*.

CIP see *cataloging in publication*

circuit Any series of electrical connections which give a continuous path through the various parts for the conduction of electrical energy for the transmission of signals between two or more remote points. Communications circuits may provide one-way transmission (simplex); two-way transmission, in one direction at a time (half-duplex); or two-way transmission, in both directions simultaneously (duplex).

circuit edges see *divinity circuit edges*

circuit switching A method of handling communications in a network whereby a connection is made first between the sending and receiving points before a message is transmitted. Compare with *data switching*.

circulation department 1. The part of a library from which items from the library collection are lent to members of the user group, generally for outside use. 2. The administrative unit in charge of all the activities connected with lending items to members of the user group, generally for outside use. Synonymous with loan department.

circulation desk A counter or desk where items from the library collection are charged and discharged. Synonymous with charging desk, discharging desk, and loan desk.

circulation file see *charging file*

circulation record see *charging file, circulation statistics*

circulation services Those activities connected with charging and discharging items borrowed from the library collection, generally for outside use. Included are the loan of items from special and reserve collections; maintaining loan records; monitoring and collecting overdues; renewing loans; reshelving items; stack maintenance; equipment rental and loan for use in reading, viewing, or listening to materials; copying services provided to users; and the distribution of audiovisual materials by dial access, closed-circuit television, or other technique whereby the items remain in the library/media center while the image and/or sound is disseminated by electronic or mechanical means.

circulation statistics The cumulative record of materials lent by a library which may include analyses by time periods and categories or classifications of materials and borrowers, and related statistics, such as the number of overdues, renewals, and recalls.

circulation system The sum of all policies, procedures, and methods used in the execution of circulation services.

circulation transaction The act of charging an item from the library collection to a member of the library's user group for use outside or within the library and discharging the item upon its return. Compare with *renewal transaction*.

citation 1. A note referring to a work from which a passage is quoted or to some source as authority for a statement or proposition. 2. Especially in law books, a quotation from, or a reference to, statutes, decided cases, or other authorities.

citation index An index consisting essentially of a list of works which have been cited in other, later works and a list of the works from which the citations have been collected. Used to identify subsequently published works that are related by subject to the cited work.

citation order In a faceted classification system, the order of precedence in which the elements of a composite class are arranged to produce a class number or heading. Synonymous with facet formula and combination order.

civil service 1. All branches of government service except the judiciary, legislative, and military; especially one in which appointment is dependent upon competitive examination. 2. Collectively, the employees of all branches of government service, except the judiciary, legislative, and military.

claim A notice sent to a dealer that an order has not been received within a reasonable period of time.

clandestine publications see *underground publications* (1)

Clapp-Jordan formula A quantitative formula developed by Verner Clapp and Robert Jordan in 1965 to establish a benchmark for measuring the adequacy of collection size for academic libraries. Statistics such as student enrollment, faculty size, and number of academic programs at a given institution are multiplied by preestablished volume numbers to obtain total level of adequacy for gross collection size. The Clapp-Jordan formula served as a prototype for the development of many similar formulas in subsequent years.

claro obscuro see *chiaroscuro*

clasp A metal, ivory, or plastic fastening hinged to one board of a book or album and made to clip or lock into a loop or bar on the other board.

class 1. In classification, a group of concepts or things formed on the basis of a common characteristic. 2. In personnel management, a group of positions in the organization with comparable duties, responsibilities, and required qualifications; a common class title (e.g., librarian, library assistant); and the same pay scale.

class A library binding The most rigorous library binding category as specified in the *Library Binding Institute Standard for Library Binding*.

class catalog see *classed catalog*

classed catalog A subject catalog with primary arrangement of bibliographic records by the class numbers of a classification schedule; also includes an alphabetical index to the class numbers used. Synonymous with catalogue raisonné, class catalog, classified catalog, classified subject catalog, and systematic catalog. Compare with *alphabetico-classed catalog.*

class entry The representation of a work or bibliographic item in a catalog or index under a subject heading or descriptor that is broader than its subject content, with a resultant increase in recall ratio and decrease in precision ratio. Synonymous with generic entry. Compare with *specific entry.*

classification 1. A series or system of classes arranged in some order according to some principle or conception, purpose, or interest, or some combination of such. The term is applied to the arrangement either of the class names, or of the things, real or conceptual, that are so classified. The term "classification" is also by derivation and use the name for the classifying or arranging of classes, or things, as a process or method. 2. In archives, the predesigned filing system for a record series, or the act of identifying records or other documents, in accordance with a predesigned filing system. (SAA)

classification and pay plan In personnel management, a systematic scheme which groups all positions in an organization into classes based upon the nature of the work performed, and the required qualifications for each, establishes a schedule of compensation for the classes, and incorporates rules for salary adjustments and promotions.

classification chart An outline of a classification schedule.

classification code The rules and principles to be followed in applying a particular classification system.

Classification Décimale Universelle see *Universal Decimal Classification*

classificationist A person who develops a classification system. Compare with *classifier.*

classification number see *class number* (1)

classification schedule A list of class terms which represents a classification system, and which may be accompanied by notation, or system of symbols which represent the terms. For a hierarchical classification system the schedule displays the hierarchical levels of the main classes, divisions, subdivisions, sections, and subsections into which classes are divided.

classification scheme see *classification system*

classification system A particular series or system of classes arranged in some order according to some principle or conception, purpose, or interest, or some combination of such. Synonymous with classification scheme.

classified catalog see *classed catalog*

classified filing system The arrangement of a file in some logical sequence, usually indicated by numbers or symbols, as distinct from alphabetical sequence.

classified index An index characterized by hierarchical structure, in which topics are grouped under broad subjects of which they form a part.

classified information see *classified material*

classified material Records and other documents emanating from government agencies and other corporate bodies which are of a secret or confidential nature and which receive protection against unauthorized disclosure. The U.S. government uses the following degrees of protection: Top Secret, Secret, Confidential, Restricted Data, Formerly Restricted Data, and (before 1953) Restricted. Synonymous with classified information.

classified report A technical report whose distribution is limited by security classification regulations of the U.S. Department of Defense, or other issuing agency.

classified subject catalog see *classed catalog*

classifier A person who arranges books or other documents in the order of a classification system by assigning each a class number from the classification schedule. Compare with *classificationist.*

classify 1. To make or conceive a class, or classes, from a plurality of things. Also, to arrange classes in some order or to relate them in some system according to some principle or conception, purpose, or interest. 2. To arrange actual things, such as books or other documents, in the order of a classification system by assigning each a class number from the classification schedule.

class interval The size or range of each group or class of values within a frequency distribution, usually measured as the difference between the upper and lower values in a group.

class letter The letter used to designate a particular class of a classification system whose notation begins with a letter of the alphabet.

class limit The upper or largest and lower or smallest value in a group or class of data.

class mark see *class number* (2)

class name see *class term*

class number 1. The combination of notational symbols, taken from the classification schedule, and used to denote a particular class of a classification system. Synonymous with classification number. 2. Such a combination of notational symbols placed on a bibliographic item and its record in a catalog to place the item in the classification system and to show its physical location. Synonymous with class mark. Compare with *book number.*

classroom collection A semipermanent collection of library materials sent to the classroom by the school library media center or the public or academic library for use by teachers and students. This collection is selected for general use rather than for use with a specific topic.

classroom library A permanent collection of library materials in a classroom for use by the teacher and students in that classroom.

classroom loan A temporary collection of library materials on a special topic or supplementing a special curriculum unit and sent to the classroom for a limited period.

class specification In personnel management, a written description of the group of positions in one class, including the class title; a general summary of the nature of the class, including types of duties and responsibilities; minimum qualifications required for positions in the class; and the pay and promotion scale.

class term The word or phrase that designates a class in a classification system or in a classed catalog. Synonymous with class name.

class title In personnel management, the official designation for a group of positions in a class.

clay tablet An ancient Mesopotamian form of record inscribed in cuneiform writing on a piece of clay; perhaps the earliest form of books.

clean The absence of audio-distorting elements such as drop-out, flutter, rumble, and wow in the reproduction of sound.

clear see *erase* (1)

clearance An administrative determination of the U.S. government or other agency that an individual may have access to classified materials of a specified nature.

clear-base film A colorless film coated with a photographic emulsion.

clearinghouse see *information clearinghouse*

cleat binding A method of leaf affixing in which sections are joined to one another by a single thread pasted in a figure-eight pattern through slits cut into the back of the book in a dovetail pattern. Compare with *saw-kerf binding.*

cleat lacing see *cleat binding*

cleat sewing see *cleat binding*

clerical positions Those positions in a library which entail duties of a library clerk.

clerk see *library clerk*

clientele see *user group*

clinical medical librarian A librarian member of a health care team who participates in clinical settings, assisting patients in participating more knowledgeably in their own health care and assisting health professionals in applying information from biomedical literature to patient care.

clipped article see *tear sheet*

clipping bureau A commercial organization which clips articles on specific subjects from current newspapers and periodicals and forwards them to clients on a fee basis.

clipping file A file of clippings from current newspapers, periodicals, and other sources arranged in some definite order in a vertical file. Its scope is usually determined by anticipated needs of potential users.

clipping service A daily activity in many special libraries which consists of clipping items of concern to the work of the host organization from current newspapers and periodicals and sending them to the appropriate staff member of the host organization.

clippings file see *clipping file*

close classification 1. A classification system which provides minute subdivision of classes. 2. A method of classifying in which the class number assigned to a document is coextensive with its subject. Synonymous with specific classification.

closed access see *closed stack*

closed catalog A catalog in which the filing of new bibliographic records is discontinued or limited to certain categories. Existing records may be removed or deleted from the catalog as they are corrected, revised, converted to machine-readable form, etc. Compare with *frozen catalog, integrated catalog, open catalog.*

closed-circuit television (CCTV) A television transmission system for the distribution by cable of instructional and educational information programs, live or on tape, for relatively short transmission distances (e.g., a building, school district, campus, or intracity). Reception is restricted to television receivers within the prescribed area. Compare with *community antenna television (CATV).*

closed entry A bibliographic record which contains complete bibliographical information for all parts or volumes (a complete set) of a continuation or serial.

closed file In archives, a file containing documents on which action has been completed and to which additions are unlikely, or one to which access is limited or denied.

closed indexing system see *controlled vocabulary indexing system*

closed joint The type of joint obtained when cover boards are laced on tight against the spine. Synonymous with tight joint. Compare with *French joint.*

closed reserve A reserve collection in a closed stack area, from which requested items are delivered by a library staff member.

closed shelves see *closed stack*

closed stack Any library stack area not open to the general public or open only on a selective basis. Synonymous with closed access and closed shelves. Compare with *open stack.*

close score A score of vocal music in which the separate parts are written on two staves, as with hymns. (AACR2)

close-up A photograph made with the subject at very close range.

cloth A term applied to any binding, with or without boards, that is fully covered in cloth. Compare with *clothbound.*

cloth board see *feltboard*

clothbound Bound in full cloth over stiff boards. Compare with *cloth.*

cloth joint A fold of endpapers which has been reinforced with a strip of cloth. It may be a concealed joint or an exposed joint.

cloth sides A book cover which has cloth sides, but a spine of other material.

clump In an associative retrieval system, a grouping of terms based on the frequency with which they occur together in the same works.

cluster In sampling, a group of elements of a population; used in cluster sampling, in which the first stage of selection of a sample consists of choosing some of the clusters, all of which together contain all the individual elements of the population.

cluster sampling A sampling method, in which the elements of a population are selected from groups or clusters in the population rather than directly from the elements of the population as a whole.

CMOD see *customer-must-order-direct*

coated paper A paper finish that is very smooth. It is prepared by treating the surface of the paper with clay or other pigments and an adhesive mixture to improve appearance, surface uniformity, and printing quality. It is in high demand for halftone and color printing. Synonymous with enamelled paper.

coating A general term for any substance covering or spread over the surface of paper, film base, or magnetic tape base.

coauthor see *joint author*

coaxial cable An insulated transmission cable with an outer metal tube shielding the central conducting core.

COBOL (Common Business Oriented Language) A problem-oriented programming language used with a wide range of business data-processing applications.

cockle A wrinkle or pucker in paper or boards resulting from nonuniform shrinkage and drying, usually under little or no tension.

code 1. A set of letters, numbers, or other symbols arbitrarily used to represent other letters, numbers or symbols. Synonymous with coding scheme. 2. To put into the form of a code. 3. A set of rules, such as a catalog code.

code area The nonimage portion of a film frame reserved for indexing the location of particular documents on roll microfilm by the use of a code such as document marks.

codebook 1. A list of words or terms with their corresponding equivalents in a coded form. 2. A manual that describes the organization and content of one or more machine-readable data files. (AACR2)

coded tape A length of plastic, paper, or other material which contains data coded as magnetic spots or punches, to be used as input into a computer or other device.

code lines On roll microfilm, a set of parallel lines located between film frames which serves as a visual index to the contents. The position of the lines indicates numeric information, such as a frame number, or a numerically encoded subject descriptor. Synonymous with bar coding.

CODEN A concise, unique, alphanumeric code assigned to serial and monographic publications and used as an unambiguous, permanent identifier. Developed in 1963 by the American Society for Testing and Materials for scientific and technical publications, but since expanded in scope. In 1975 Chemical Abstracts Service assumed responsibility for the assignment and dissemination of CODEN designations.

code of ethics A statement of ideal professional standards adopted by a professional group or organization to guide its members in carrying out their professional responsibilities.

coder see *programmer*

codex 1. Sheets of writing material fastened at one side and enclosed in a binding: the physical form of the modern book. The name was originally given to two or more tablets of wood or ivory, hinged together and written upon with a stylus. Later, the term was given to books of this type consisting of a smaller or greater number of sheets of papyrus, vellum, or parchment and, more recently, of paper. Compare with *tablet book*. 2. A collection of Roman laws, e.g., Codex Theodosianus.

coding The process of translating characters or words of data into a code.

coding scheme see *code* (1)

coefficient A number that serves as a measure of a relationship between variables or parameters.

coefficient of alienation A measure of the lack of linear association or relationship between two variables, resulting from computing the square root of the coefficient of nondetermination.

coefficient of association A measure of independence or association between two or more variables.

coefficient of contingency A measure of the strength of the relationship between two variables on the basis of a contingency table.

coefficient of determination The square of the Pearson product-moment correlation coefficient of a pair of variables. It expresses the proportion of the variability of one of the variables that is attributable to the variability of the other.

coefficient of multiple correlation A measure of the closeness of fit or association between a dependent variable and two or more independent variables.

coefficient of nondetermination A measure indicating the proportion of the total variability of one variable that is not attributable to a second variable. It is computed by subtracting from 1 the coefficient of determination.

coefficient of partial correlation A measure of the magnitude of the relationship (i.e., correlation) of two variables from among three or more variables. It expresses the best assessment of the correlation between the chosen pair of variables that can be made using information about all the variables.

coefficient of reflection see *reflectance*

coefficient of variation A measure that compares the standard deviation of a variable to its arithmetic mean. It is usually expressed as a percentage and is obtained through multiplying by 100 the ratio of the standard deviation to the mean.

coextensive subject indexing The assignment of a subject heading, descriptor, or class number to a document which is neither broader nor narrower than the subject of the work(s) contained in the document.

coil binding see *spiral binding*

cold light A light source emitting luminous energy but without incandescence, such as phosphorescent light.

cold stamping see *stamping*

cold type Composition by direct impression, as by typewriter, and, by extension, photosetting, as distinguished from so-called *hot metal composition,* which uses type cast from molten metal.

collaborator One who works with one or more associates to produce a work; all may make the same kind of contribution, as in the case of shared responsibility, or they may make different kinds of contributions, as in the case of collaboration between an artist and a writer. (AACR2)

collage An artistic composition of bits of flat objects of any material, pasted together on a surface for a variety of uses, such as use as a learning tool or as a display on a bulletin board.

collate 1. To ascertain, usually by examination of signatures, leaves, and illustrations, whether or not a copy of a book is complete and perfect; also to compare it with descriptions of perfect or apparently perfect copies found in descriptive (or other) bibliographies. 2. To compare minutely, page for page, and line for line, in order to determine whether or not two books are identical copies, or variants. 3. The checking by the binder of the sections of a book, after gathering. 4. In data processing, to compare and merge two or more sets of data into one set arranged in a specified order that is not necessarily the same as any of the original sets. Compare with *merge*.

collateral reference A reference between two subject headings at the same level of hierarchy, both headings being subsumed under a common generic term. Synonymous with horizontal reference.

collation 1. In cataloging, the *physical description area*. 2. A list of the signatures of a book with indications of the number of leaves in each. Various formulae have been devised for the efficient presentation of such information, the best known being those devised by McKerrow, Greg, and Bowers.

collator 1. A device for collecting in proper order one copy of each of the printed sheets required to make a set. 2. A punched-card machine that matches, selects, and files identical cards of two sets fed into the machine. Synonymous with interpolator.

collected documents Annual or biennial reports of the various offices of a state collected in a bound volume under a collective title, e.g., *Connecticut Public Documents, Legislative Documents of New York State.*

collected edition An edition of an author's works previously published separately (sometimes by different publishers) issued in one volume or in several volumes in uniform style. May not be the complete works. Synonymous with uniform edition. Compare with *author's edition, inclusive edition.*

collected set A monographic series treated as a bibliographic entity and held together physically with the same class and book number.

collection 1. A number of separate works or parts of works, not forming a treatise or monograph on a single subject, combined and issued together as a whole. 2. Three or more independent works or parts of works by the same author, published together; or two or more independent works or parts of works by more than one author, published together, and not written for the same occasion or for the publication in hand. (AACR2, mod.) 3. An accumulated group of library materials having a common characteristic, such as Pamphlet Collection, Chemistry Collection. For a library's total holdings, see *library collection.* 4. Any body of material indexed. In this sense, a collection may consist of a single or composite text (e.g., treatise, anthology, encyclopedia, periodical); a group of such texts; or a set of representations (e.g., maps, drawings, reproductions of works or art or of other objects). (Z39.4)

collection (archives) 1. An artificial accumulation of manuscripts or other documents devoted to a single theme, person, event, or type of record. 2. A body of manuscripts or papers having a common source. If formed by or around an individual or family, such materials are usually termed personal papers. If the collection concerns an institution, it is usually termed records. 3. For the total holdings of a repository, see *repository collection.*

collection assessment see *collection evaluation*

collection development A term which encompasses a number of activities related to the development of the library collection, including the determination and coordination of selection policy, assessment of needs of users and potential users, collection use studies, collection evaluation, identification of collection needs, selection of materials, planning for resource sharing, collection maintenance, and weeding.

collection evaluation The process of assessing the quality of a library collection, usually in terms of specific objectives or the needs of the target group of that particular collection; one aspect of collection development. Synonymous with collection assessment.

collection maintenance A term covering all of the activities carried out by a library to preserve the materials in its collections; includes binding, mending, repairing, materials conversion, etc. One aspect of *collection development.*

collection management A term used to refer specifically to the application of quantitative techniques (statistical analyses, cost-benefit studies, etc.) in collection development.

collective bargaining Negotiation between employees represented by a union or other officially recognized group and the employing organization for reaching an agreement on wages, hours, or other terms or conditions of employment.

collective biography A work consisting of separate accounts of the lives of a number of persons, such as a biographical dictionary.

collective cataloging The cataloging of materials of secondary importance by grouping a number of the documents, such as pamphlets, on a particular subject, and treating the group as a bibliographic item, assigning a collective title.

collective microreproduction see *microreproduction*

collective record group In archives, a modification of the record group concept which for convenience or other purposes brings together the records of a number of relatively small or short-lived agencies which have an administrative or functional relationship, the records of each agency constituting a separate subgroup.

collective title A title proper that is an inclusive title for a bibliographic item containing several works. (AACR2)

college library 1. A library established, supported, and administered by a college to meet the information needs of its students, faculty, and staff and to support its instructional and research programs. 2. In a university library system, a library with a collection related to the work of a particular college, administered separately by the college or as a unit of the university library.

collocation 1. In classification, the arrangement of coordinate classes to stand together in the classification schedule to show their relationships. 2. In cataloging, the assemblage in a catalog, by means of access points, of bibliographic records of bibliographic items by the same author, of different editions of the same item, of the same series, on the same subject, etc.

collotype 1. A planographic, photomechanical printing process using an unscreened gelatin-coated plate to print continuous tone copy. It is capable of excellent reproduction of illustrations but is suitable for only short runs. Used for special purposes, it has been known by many process names, such as albertype, artotype, and heliotype. Synonymous with gelatin process, photogelatin process. 2. A print made by this process.

Colon Classification A faceted classification scheme devised by S. R. Ranganathan, so called because of its use of a colon to separate certain parts of class numbers.

colophon 1. In early printed books, the statement given at the end of the text proper which provides some or all of the following particulars: author, title, subject, printer, publisher, place, and date. 2. In modern books, a statement given at the end of the text proper or on the verso of the title leaf which provides some or all of the following particulars: printer, typeface, type of paper, the materials used in binding, the printing equipment employed, the names of the personnel engaged in the production of the item. Not to be confused with *printer's mark*.

color In photography, the visual sensation resulting from light of different wavelengths striking the eye, or the sensitivity of film emulsions to light waves of a particular length. Achromatic colors are those perceived as having no hue.

color-blind film A photographic film that is not sensitive to all colors.

color coding The use of colored signals as a code in a file or on documents to represent subject, language, format, frequency of publication, etc., as the basis for primary or secondary arrangement, or as an additional access point not provided by the file or storage arrangement.

colored illustration An illustration in two or more colors of ink, with black considered to be a color.

color filter see *filter*

color lithography see *chromolithography*

color printing In addition to black-and-white or single-color printing, printing may be done in several colors. Among the ways of achieving this are: by applying the colors to different areas of a single block or plate; by printing each distinct color area from a separate block or plate; by inking separate blocks or plates with different colors and printing them over one another for a wide range of color. The principal processes are multicolor printing, in which the colors of the inks used are chosen to match the important colors to be reproduced, and full-color printing, in which the overprinting of three basic colors is regulated to reproduce the range of colors in the original.

color sensitivity   An attribute of certain light-sensitive materials to absorb light waves of particular length, resulting in images of different colors. A complete absorption of all light rays results in a black appearance, and white is the result of a complete reflection of all light rays.

color separation see *full-color printing*

color slide see *slide*

column   1. One of two or more vertical sections of printed matter separated from each other by a rule or a blank space, as in newspapers and some books. 2. The part of a planetary camera which projects vertically from the base and supports the camera head above the object being photographed. 3. A vertical series of microimages on a microfiche or microopaque.

COM see *computer output microfilm*

COMARC (Cooperative MARC)   A project, initiated in 1974 and terminated in 1978, under which the Library of Congress accepted bibliographic records based on Library of Congress card copy but converted to MARC format by other libraries.

combination coding   The joint notching of two or more positions in an edge-notched card to code a specific subject.

combination order see *citation order*

COM catalog see *computer-output-microfilm (COM) catalog*

comic orientation   Said of images on roll microfilm which are positioned parallel to the edge of the film, in the manner of the panels of a newspaper comic strip. Technically referred to as 1B orientation (a type of image placement recognized by the American National Standards Institute in *USA Standard Specifications for 16mm and 35mm Silver-Gelatin Microfilms for Reel Applications*). Compare with *cine orientation.*

command   A signal or message telling a computer or other device to execute a specific program or operation.

command language   A programming language which consists primarily of procedural instructions, each of which is capable of specifying a function to be executed by a computer.

command paper   A paper presented to the British Parliament by a minister without a formal request from either of the Houses of Parliament, theoretically by command of the sovereign. Such papers are limited to matters likely to be the subject of early legislation or which may be regarded as otherwise essential to members of Parliament as a whole to enable them to discharge their responsibilities.

commentary   Explanatory or critical notes on a work, either accompanying the text in an edition of the work or issued independently, with the notes predominant.

commercial processing service   A commercial firm which offers the services of a processing center.

commercial television   Television programming and broadcasting which is designed to attract the widest possible viewing audience with little concern for content beyond an analysis of what will attract viewers. Compare with *public television.*

Common Business Oriented Language see *COBOL*

common carrier see *communications common carrier*

common facet   A facet, such as one designating time or place, which is commonly used to subdivide classes in a classification system.

common subdivision   A subdivision, such as one designating time, place, or form of presentation, which is commonly used to subdivide classes in a classification system.

communication format   A format for the exchange, rather than the local processing, of bibliographic records. Synonymous with bibliographic information interchange format, exchange format, information interchange format, and interchange format.

communications The process and means of interchanging or transmitting and receiving messages or information over communications channels.

communication satellite A manmade vehicle placed in orbit around the earth for relaying electromagnetic signals, including carriers of sound, image, and digital and analog data, from earth station to earth station(s).

communications channel see *channel* (4)

communications common carrier A government-regulated public utility company that provides communications services to the public; e.g., a telephone company. Synonymous with data carrier, data communications common carrier.

communications computer 1. A computer which controls the flow of data in a network. 2. A computer used between another computer or terminal device and a network.

communications link The physical means of connecting one location or node to another for the purpose of transmitting and receiving data.

communications protocol see *protocol*

community antenna television (CATV) The transmission of television programs received from regular broadcasting stations by a common antenna, and of locally initiated programs on magnetic tape and films or live to cable subscribers in a designated area. Reception by cable is usually high quality, and cable stations may transmit many programs at the same time. Libraries may use a free channel allocated to education. Compare with *closed-circuit television (CCTV).*

community college library/media center A library or media center established, supported, and administered by a community college to meet the information needs of its students, faculty, and staff and to support its instructional and community service program.

community services Special services provided by a library for the community as a whole or for some segment of the community, e.g., lectures, concerts, book or art exhibits, discussion programs, and story hours.

compact shelving Any type of shelving which is designed to increase the storage capacity of library materials to be shelved in a given space, such as drawout shelves, movable ranges, and swinging-case shelving.

compact storage 1. A shelving area, usually for little-used library materials, in which some type of compact shelving is utilized to maximize capacity. 2. A shelving area, usually for little-used library materials, in which the sections or bookcases are designed or arranged to maximize capacity, e.g., by narrow aisles and higher than normal shelving.

company file see *corporation file*

comparison In classification, the type of phase relationship in which two subjects are compared.

compartment A decorative frame enclosing the letterpress of a title page, etc. In descriptive bibliography, distinguished from borders by being cut as one piece or designed for use as one piece. Compare with *border* (2).

compass map see *portolan chart*

compatibility 1. The capability of one computer, system, or device to accept and process data or software intended for another, without modification. 2. The capability of any audiovisual equipment or system to integrate and operate with elements of a similar system, e.g., the capability of playing any audiorecording on any audiorecorder.

compatible headings As applied to the adoption of *Anglo-American Cataloguing Rules,* those headings derived from an earlier catalog code which are so close to the form prescribed by the new code that they are left unchanged.

compendium 1. A written work containing the substance of a subject in brief and sometimes outline form. Sometimes used synonymously with *epitome* (1). 2. A brief statement of the substance of a larger written work, especially of a treatise, often prepared by someone other than the author of the original. Sometimes used synonymously with *digest* (1), *epitome* (2), and *synopsis.*

compensation guard see *guard*

compensatory time off Authorized time off, instead of overtime pay, to compensate for a comparable period of overtime work.

competitor file In special libraries, a file containing material about companies and other organizations carrying on activities similar to those of the library's host organization.

compilation A bibliographic item formed by collecting and putting together works of various authors without editorial alteration of the text, such as an anthology.

compile In computer science, to translate a computer program written in a symbolic language into machine language.

compiler 1. One who produces a collection by selecting and putting together matter from the works of various persons or bodies. Also, one who selects and puts together in one publication matter from the works of one person or body. Compare with *editor* (1). (AACR2) 2. In computer science, a special computer program which directs the translation of other programs written in symbolic language into machine language. Unlike an *assembler,* the compiler generates more than one computer instruction for each statement written in symbolic form.

compiler program see *compiler* (2)

complete works see *author's edition* (1)

complex class In classification, a composite class whose elements are in a phase relationship.

composing (printing) see *composition*

composite class In classification, a class composed of two or more elements which are related through their interaction, such as micrographics education for librarians. Composite classes may be complex or compound.

composite terminal A terminal which has both optical scanner and keyboard built into one cabinet or unit.

composite volume A bound volume made up of two or more separately published works, such as pamphlets.

composite work An original work consisting of separate and distinct parts, by different authors, which constitute together an integral whole.

composition Originally the assembling of type, spacing, cuts, etc., by hand for printing; now includes the preparation of copy for printing by either hand or machine typesetting, direct-im-

pression composition, or various methods of nonimpact composition, some of which use electronic aids such as computers.

compositor A person who assembles type for printing.

compound class In classification, a composite class whose elements have their extension decreased by the relationship, such as photography of plants.

compound name see *compound surname*

compound subject heading A subject heading which includes two or more words, sometimes separated by punctuation.

compound surname A surname consisting of two or more proper names, often connected by a hyphen, conjunction, or preposition. (AACR2)

comprehensive records plan In archives, a U.S. government term for a document describing all or part of the records of an agency or institution, specifying records to be preserved as having archival value, and authorizing, on a continuing basis, the disposition of specified recurring series of records. Compare with *records retention plan.* (SAA)

compulsory arbitration The process by which the employing agency and the union are required by law to submit their dispute or differences to a designated government agency or panel for resolution and to accept its decision.

compulsory retirement Retirement at a fixed age established by an organization's personnel policy and in accordance with the law.

computer A machine which accepts and automatically performs prescribed sequences of operations on data to achieve a desired end result.

computer application A specific job or series of related routines to be performed by a computer, e.g., online cataloging.

computer application program A computer program written or prepared for a specific application of a user.

computer-assisted instruction (CAI) A system of individualized instruction in which a computer provides programmed instructional material.

The computer provides the learner with self-paced steps resulting in gradual increments in learning and immediate feedback of the learner's mistakes, allowing learning with minimal intervention from a teacher.

computer-assisted retrieval (CAR) The retrieval of information stored on microforms using a computer-stored index to identify and locate relevant microimages and drive a microform reader or reader-printer to automatically display them.

computer-based circulation system A circulation system in which some or all activities related to the loan of items from the library collection are performed by computerized procedures. Such systems range from a totally online system to a partially computerized batch-processing system and from a record-keeping system to one that yields management statistics resulting from the recording of circulation transactions and their characteristics, e.g., type of user, type and age of items borrowed, and subject categories.

computer center see *data-processing center*

computer configuration The specific pieces of models of hardware forming a particular computer system or installation. Compare with *computer system.*

computer-dependent language see *machine-oriented language*

computer graphics Pictorial representations such as drawings and graphs produced by a computer on a cathode-ray tube or paper.

computer-input microfilm (CIM) Any microform on which data are recorded in such a way that they can be used as input to a computer using optical character recognition for the conversion of human-readable information to digital data.

computer instruction An instruction or command that a machine such as a computer can recognize and execute.

computer instruction code The code which represents a set of computer instructions. Synonymous with machine code.

computer language see *machine language*

computer network Two or more interconnected computers.

computer-oriented language see *machine-oriented language*

computer-output microfilm (COM) Any microform on which human-readable data are recorded directly from digital data by a computer without a printout as the intermediary. The data may be transferred directly from the central processing unit or from some intermediary such as magnetic tape. The conversion is handled by a computer-output-microfilm recorder.

computer-output-microfilm (COM) catalog A catalog produced by computer-output-microfilm recorder on microfilm or microfiche. Compare with *microfiche catalog, microfilm catalog.*

computer-output-microfilm recorder The computer device which converts machine-readable digital data into human-readable data and records it on microfilm. The unit may operate online or receive data offline from magnetic tape. Four basic types of recorders are used: (1) cathode-ray-tube (CRT) recorder, (2) electron-beam recorder (EBR), (3) light-emitting diode (LED) recorder, and (4) laser-beam recorder (LBR). They differ primarily in the way images are created by a character generator, type of film, and the extent to which they can generate graphics.

computer printer see *printer* (2)

computer program A set of computer instructions which the machine follows in processing data or solving a problem.

computer program maintenance see *program maintenance*

computer programmer see *programmer*

computer programming language see *programming language*

computer-readable see *machine-readable*

computer run The execution of a single computer program without manual interruption or intervention. Synonymous with machine run.

computer storage see *storage*

computer system A central processing unit and its associated main storage unit, input devices, and output devices. Compare with *computer configuration*.

computer word A group of consecutive binary digits or bits, treated as a unit, which can be stored in one location in a computer or storage device.

computer word length The size of a computer word, measured usually in terms of a number of characters or binary digits.

concatenate To join together two or more data fields into a single field.

concealed joint A cloth joint in which the cloth strip reinforcing the fold of the endpapers is glued next to the cover board and back of the book and is concealed by the paste-down endpaper. Compare with *exposed joint*.

concentrator In data communications, a device which collects several low-speed signals and transmits them over a single high-speed channel.

concept The recognition of a pattern of qualities, or a structure, which enables the mind to externalize the object of thought by name with recurrent consistency.

concordance An index of all words or the principal words in any work or in the works of a single author, showing location in the text, generally giving context, and sometimes defining the words.

concurrent processing The simultaneous performance of two or more processing operations or tasks by a data processing system such as a computer system. Synonymous with simultaneous processing. Compare with *multiprocessing, multiprogramming*.

condensation see *abridgment*

condensed score The score of an orchestral or band work reduced to two, three, or four staves as required. (AACR2)

condenser In optics, a lens or a combination of lenses used to collect and focus the light from a light source in order to project a clear image. Condensers are commonly used in enlargers and projectors.

conditional exclusion In computer-based information retrieval, a search strategy stated in terms of A but not B, unless C.

conditioning 1. The act of placing a material in a special environment in order to put it in a proper state for work or use. 2. A process of restoring film for active use after a period of storage or excessive use, generally involving cleaning and rehumidifying. 3. The addition of equipment to a private line to maintain signals at a specified minimum quality for error- and distortion-free data transmission.

conductor part In music, the score which contains parts for all instruments in the ensemble.

conference 1. A meeting of individuals or representatives of various bodies for the purpose of discussing and acting on topics of common interest. (AACR2) 2. A meeting of representatives of a corporate body that constitutes its legislative or governing body. (AACR2)

conference proceedings see *proceedings*

confidence interval A range of values which, one believes with a predetermined degree of confidence, will contain the value of a quantitative characteristic of a population or parameter.

confidence limits The upper and lower limits of a confidence interval.

confidential file In a special library, a file of material which is segregated for security and restricted for use according to certain preestablished conditions.

conflict detection An aspect of automated authority control whereby incompatible headings and references, such as the coincidence of a "see" reference from a heading used on a bibliographic record, are discovered. Discrepancies may be repeated or suppressed, input may be inhibited, etc., depending upon the particular computer program.

Congressional Edition see *United States Serial Set*

Congressional Set see *United States Serial Set*

conjugate leaves Two leaves which, when traced through the fold, are found to form a single piece of paper.

conjunctive search In computer-based information retrieval, a search to locate every item in a file matching all of a specified set of search keys.

connective catalog see *syndetic catalog*

connective index entry In a chain index, an entry which is justified not on the basis of its place in an hierarchical chain, but because it will show a relationship that might be important to searchers.

connect time The amount of time a user is connected to, or online, to a computer system. Compare with *central processing unit time*.

connotation In classification, the set of attributes constituting the definition of a term and determining the range of things to which the term may be applied. Compare with *denotation*.

CONSER (Cooperative Conversion of Serials) A U.S.-Canadian project, designed as a component of a national bibliographic system to develop a comprehensive machine-readable bibliographic database of serials held by libraries in the two countries. The Library of Congress and the National Library of Canada are responsible for the verification of records contributed to the database by participating libraries. The project, which became operative in 1975, was first managed by the Council on Library Resources and is now managed by the Online Computer Library Center.

conservation The use of chemical and physical procedures in treatment or storage to ensure the preservation of books, manuscripts, records, and other documents. Compare with *preservation*.

conservation binding Binding and rebinding procedures in which materials are used which contribute to the long-range preservation of the book, and which strive insofar as possible to maintain the original integrity of the artifact; as distinct from binding procedures in which materials or structures are employed that may provide an immediately useful or strong book, but which impair long-term preservation.

conservator A specialist with advanced training in the arts and sciences related to the theoretical and practical aspects of conservation, who is able to prescribe and undertake various physical and chemical procedures and techniques in order to ensure the preservation of books, manuscripts, records, and other docu-

ments, and who adheres to ethical standards established by the profession. Book conservators have traditionally come from bookbinding backgrounds; but formal training in both book conservation and the more general paper conservation is now available.

consideration file A list of publications under consideration for purchase by a library.

console 1. In audio and television production, a desk-type structure equipped with electronic devices for use in processing audiorecordings of live performances and audio signals during recording, playback, or radio broadcast; and in monitoring pictures and sound in the production of television programs and videorecordings, for creating special effects, and for making technical adjustments to maintain signal quality. 2. In computer science, a terminal device used for communication between an operator or maintenance person and a part of a computer.

consolidated index A combined index to several volumes or a long run of a serial publication, or to several independent works or serial publications.

consolidated system A public library system established by vote of several municipal governing bodies or by action of voters, and governed by the board of trustees of the system, with individual units operating as branches of the system.

consolidated trade catalog A trade catalog of products of several manufacturers in a single industry or group of allied industries; published for sale or rent by commercial publishers, or, more often, as an advertising venture, when it is usually free to certain libraries. Sometimes published by trade journals, either free to subscribers as a special number or at an additional fee. Synonymous with union trade catalog.

consolidation The merging of two or more libraries or organizational units into a single administrative unit, usually for the purpose of improving services or establishing greater economic viability.

consortium see *library consortium*

constant A quantity whose value remains unchanged.

construct An idea or perception resulting from the mental synthesis of facts, impressions, etc.

consultant An expert in a specialized field brought in by a library or other agency for professional or technical advice.

consultative management An approach to management in which administrators or supervisors actively solicit the views of employees before making decisions. Compare with *autocratic management, participative management.*

consultative services see *advisory services*

consulting services see *advisory services*

contact copy A copy made by direct contact of a photosensitive material and a film positive or negative or an original. Contact copies are produced by a number of lensless copying methods involving either reflex copying or transmission copying. The choice of method is generally determined by the characteristics of the original. Two specific processes are the thermal process and the diazotype process. These two direct-contact copying processes are nonreversing, i.e., a positive original produces a positive copy. Synonymous with direct-contact copy.

contact paper A photographic paper, generally low in sensitivity, used for making contact prints.

contact print A print made by direct contact of a film negative or positive and photographic paper or film.

contact printer An exposing device containing a light source, a transparent or translucent support, and a platen to press together the surfaces of the film negative and the photographic paper to which the graphic image is to be transferred, used to make 1:1-scale contact prints. Compare with *projection printer.*

content analysis Analysis of the manifest and latent content of a body of communicated material (as a book or film) through a classification, tabulation, and evaluation of its key symbols and themes in order to ascertain its meaning and probable effect.

content designators Characters which identify the data elements of a machine-readable bibliographic record or provide additional information about a data element, such as tags, indicators, subfield codes, and delimiters.

contention In data communications, a situation whereby two or more communications devices attempt at the same time to transmit data over the same channel.

contents see *table of contents*

contents note A note in a bibliographic record that lists all or part of the individual works contained in the bibliographic item.

contingency fund A special fund established in a budget to cover unexpected expenditures and to provide for possible emergencies.

contingency table A table in which a set of items, on each of which the values of two different variables can be observed, has been classified according to the jointly occurring values of the variables. Also called a cross tabulation.

continuation 1. A part issued in continuance of a monograph, a serial, or a series. (AACR2) 2. A *supplement* (1).

continuation card A card that continues a bibliographic record from a preceding catalog card. Synonymous with *extension card.*

continuation order An order to a dealer to supply the various parts of a continuation until otherwise notified. Compare with *standing order, 'til forbid.*

continuing education The activities by which library and other information agency personnel purposefully seek to improve, diversify, or change their professional- or job-related knowledge, attitudes, or skills. Continuing education activities include short courses, full-term courses, institutes, workshops, conferences, home study courses, learning packages, and other educational activities undertaken by staff members individually by their own initiative.

continuity file see *reading file*

continuous-flow camera see *rotary camera*

continuous pagination The numeration, in one continuous series, of the pages of two or more parts or volumes of a bibliographic item, or the issues of a periodical that constitute a volume.

continuous printing A rapid method of making film prints, in which unexposed film and the negative or positive film being copied are in direct contact as they move synchronously past a lens aperture during exposure. This method is employed in rotary cameras.

continuous processing Processing photographs or films in equipment which automatically transports the material through the processing stages.

continuous revision The practice of updating reference works, especially encyclopedias, by altering the text and illustrations of part of the contents with each printing to reflect changes in knowledge and in educational curricula rather than completely revising the contents periodically and publishing a new edition.

continuous tone Said of printed or photographic images with gradation in tone from light to dark so gradual as to appear continuous.

continuous variable A variable that may have any value within a specific range.

contour line A line on a map or chart connecting points of equal elevation.

contour map A topographic map which portrays relief by the use of contour lines.

contract services 1. Services provided *to* a library by another library or other agency through a contractual agreement specifying terms and cost, e.g., physical processing and maintenance services. 2. Services provided *by* a library to another library or other agency or organization through a contractual agreement specifying terms and cost.

contrast 1. The range of tones in a photographic negative or print. It is measured in terms of the difference between extreme densities ranging from low contrast to high contrast. Maximum contrast is black and white. Gamma, a measure of contrast, is based on the rate of change in density versus the logarithm of exposure as shown on a sensitometric curve. This curve is also referred to as the characteristic curve, H and D (Hurter and Driffield) curve, or D log E curve. Gamma is useful in general photography, but is not sufficient for high-contrast microfilming. A measure known as the average gradient (AG), also measured on the sensitometric curve, is considered to be better for expressing contrast values. A related value termed bar gamma is often used for measuring the contrast in duplicating film and paper. 2. The range of tones or brightness in a television picture.

contributed materials Supplies or materials provided by an organization for which there is no direct compensation; used as a budget or ac-

counting concept to indicate the contribution of an organization to a special project or program for which a grant or other external funding has been received.

contributed services 1. Services rendered to a library or other organization for which little or no compensation is paid, the full monetary value of which can be determined on the basis of payments to other staff members having equal qualifications, training, experience, and responsibilities. Synonymous with volunteer services. 2. Services provided by an organization for which there is no direct compensation; used as a budget or accounting concept to indicate the contribution of an organization to a special project or program for which a grant or other external funding has been received. Synonymous with contributed time.

contributed time see *contributed services* (2)

contributory retirement system A retirement system in which the funds are built up by regular and prescribed contributions by both the employing agency and the employee.

control The process of assuring the accomplishment of desired organizational goals by establishing standards, measuring and evaluating performance, and making necessary adjustments.

control field In computer science, a field within a record containing data whose purpose is to initiate, change, or end a specified operation, task, or function.

control group In experimental research, the collection of subjects which receive no experimental treatment, to be used as a check for the experimental group.

controlled access The limitation of entry into or use of a library or collection to members of the library's target group and, sometimes, to certain other classes of persons, some of whom are granted access upon payment of a fee. For example, a private university library may limit access to its collections to members of the university community.

controlled circulation journal A serial financed largely by advertising and available (usually without charge) only to those specified by the authors or publisher. According to the U.S. Postal Service, a journal which is issued at regular intervals of four or more times a year, each issue of which consists of at least 24 pages containing no more than 75 percent advertising, and which is not conducted as an auxiliary to and essentially for the advancement of the main business or calling of the business organization or individual who owns or controls it.

controlled-vocabulary indexing system An indexing system in which the indexer, in assigning descriptors to works, is limited to a specified list of terms called the index vocabulary. Synonymous with closed indexing system. Compare with *natural-language indexing system.*

control panel A panel on a computer console or punched-card machine used to direct and control the operation of a computer or other device. Synonymous with patch panel and plugboard.

control program A part of an operating system designed for overall management of a computer and its facilities and work.

control station see *network control station*

control unit The part of the central processing unit of a computer which controls the interpretation and execution of instructions for processing data.

convenience copy In reprography, a copy of an original intended for short-term use. The copies are made quickly and economically, thus are generally not of archival quality.

convenience file In archives, copies of records, personal papers, or other documents maintained for ease of access and reference.

convenience outlet A jack on a piece of audiovisual equipment into which the line cord of another piece of equipment may be plugged.

conventional name A name, other than the real or official name, by which a corporate body, place, or thing has come to be known. (AACR2)

conventional processing The processing of photographic film or paper using accepted practice. For silver halide film this involves a processing sequence of developing, stopping, fixing, washing, and drying. For diazotype film, an alkaline environment is needed. For vesicular and dry silver film, processing involves the application of heat.

conventional title see *uniform title*

conversational mode see *interactive mode*

conversion see *data conversion, materials conversion, file conversion*

Conversion of Serials see *CONSER*

conveyor A mechanical or electrically powered device for carrying things from place to place, especially one which operates horizontally or vertically on the endless-chain principle. Occasionally used in libraries for materials return, shelving, and physical processing.

cooperating library A library that joins with another library or group of libraries in some common plan, such as coordinated development of collections and services or contribution of entries to a union catalog.

cooperative acquisition A system whereby two or more libraries coordinate their selection and purchase of new materials so as to avoid unneeded duplication.

cooperative book buying see *cooperative purchasing*

cooperative book selection see *cooperative acquisition*

cooperative cataloging The original cataloging of bibliographic items through the joint action of a group of independent libraries which make the bibliographic records accessible to group members and sometimes to nonparticipating libraries as well. Sometimes called *shared cataloging* because cataloging responsibility and cataloging product are shared. Compare with *centralized cataloging, shared cataloging.*

cooperative collection resource facility A facility supported cooperatively by a group of libraries to acquire, maintain, and provide access to materials not generally available in any or all of the cooperating libraries. Materials may be acquired by cooperative purchase or through the transfer of little-used materials from the collections of participating libraries. To be distinguished from a *storage center,* in which materials stored cooperatively remain the property of the library that deposited them rather than becoming the property of the facility.

Cooperative Conversion of Serials see *CONSER*

Cooperative MARC see *COMARC*

cooperative purchasing An arrangement between two or more libraries through which one of them, or a separate processing center, purchases new materials for all libraries in the group in order to obtain larger discounts and other advantages unavailable to a single customer.

cooperative services The common services planned and coordinated by a cooperative system.

cooperative system A group of independent and autonomous libraries banded together by informal or formal agreements or contracts which stipulate the common services to be planned and coordinated by the policymaking body of the cooperative system.

coordinate classes In a hierarchical classification system, classes of equal rank in the hierarchy; that is, removed by the same number of steps of division from a main class.

coordinate indexing system see *precoordinate indexing system, postcoordinate indexing system*

coordination In information retrieval, the expression of a logical product.

coordination of terms In classification, the joining of two or more terms in order to define distinct concepts by the intersection of the classes represented by these terms.

coordinator A title designating an individual in an organization who administers several programs or coordinates the activities of several programs, such as a coordinator of children's services in a public library system who has overall administrative authority for all such activity within the system.

copper engraving An engraving made from a copperplate.

copy 1. Graphic matter to be reproduced by printing, photography, or other means. 2. A single specimen of a document. 3. In reprography, a duplicate of an original document, including enlargements and microimages. 4. In reprography, to make a duplicate of an original document using any one of a variety of copying processes, usually on a sensitized material. 5. In data processing, to reproduce data from one location or medium to another, without altering the original.

copyboard In reprography, a flat, level platform on which copy is placed for reproduction by photography.

copy card An aperture card containing unexposed and unprocessed microfilm, used to make a copy of a camera card image. Compare with *camera card.*

copy cataloging see *derived cataloging*

copyholder In reprography, any device used to prevent the movement of copy being photographed.

copy number 1. The symbol added to a call number to distinguish multiple copies of the same item. 2. The identifying number assigned to each copy of a book issued in a limited edition.

copyright The legal provision of exclusive rights to reproduce and distribute a work. Under U.S. Public Law 94–553 (Sec. 106) these rights are granted to the author, composer, artist, etc., and with certain limitations are those of (1) reproduction; (2) preparation of derivative works; (3) distribution to the public by sale, rental, lease or lending; (4) public performance; and (5) public display. These rights may be transferred to others.

copyright clearance center An independently organized and financed organization providing publishers and, as appropriate, authors with a centralized mechanism through which they can collect self-designated fees for authorized copying of copyrighted works other than that permitted under the fair use standards of the 1976 U.S. Copyright Act (Public Law 94–553, Sec. 107).

copyright date The year as it appears in the copyright notice. The 1976 U.S. Copyright Act (Public Law 94–553, Sec. 401) specifies that this will be the year of first publication.

copyright deposit see *legal deposit*

copyright depository library A library designated to receive a specified number of free copies of published works under the terms of a national copyright law. Synonymous with copyright library.

copyright library see *copyright depository library*

copyright notice A notice appearing on all copies of works protected by law and published by authority of the copyright holder. In U.S. law

(Public Law 94–553, Sec. 401) it should consist of three elements: (1) the symbol ©, the abbreviation "Copr." or the word "Copyright"; (2) the year of first publication of the work; and (3) the name of the copyright owner. The notice is to be affixed in such a manner and location as to make it conspicuous.

coranto An early 17th-century newssheet devoted to foreign news, appearing first in Holland and Germany and in 1620–21 in England, issued irregularly and printed as a half-sheet in folio. After 1622 in England, a quarto newsbook, usually appearing weekly. The coranto is the earliest form of newspaper.

cords 1. Heavy hemp, cotton, or linen strings to which sections are sewed in the process of binding a book by hand. Compare with *tapes* and *bands*. 2. Heavy string reinforcements of the top and bottom edges of the spine.

core 1. The center portion of a reel, spool, cartridge, magazine, or cassette. 2. An unflanged spool for holding film or paper.

core collection 1. A separate collection that is representative of the major information interests of the library's target group, with selection for inclusion in the collection based on anticipated high demand and retention in the collection based on frequency of use. 2. The initial collection of a library, developed from a comprehensive standard list or other bibliographic guide.

core list A list of works considered essential for the study of a particular discipline or subdiscipline; often used to designate a basic list of periodical titles in a subject field.

core-set The tendency for film or other materials to remain curled after unwinding from a reel or other cylindrical holder.

core storage see *magnetic core storage*

corner 1. Where the turn-in of one edge of the book cover meets another. Various types include Dutch or library corner, mitered corner, round corner, square corner. 2. The leather or other contrasting material over the corners of a cover in half binding and three-quarter binding.

corner cut A diagonal cut at the corner of an aperture card, punched card, microfiche, or similar rectangular cards or sheets which aids in positioning them for a specific use, such as image orientation, storage, or identification of the photosensitive side of film.

cornerpiece A metallic or other guard used to protect the corners of books in shipping.

corporate body An organization or group of persons that is identified by a particular name and that acts, or may act, as an entity. Typical examples of corporate bodies are associations, institutions, business firms, nonprofit enterprises, governments, government agencies, religious bodies, local churches, and conferences. (AACR2)

corporate borrower's card see *business firm borrower's card*

corporate entry 1. The name of a corporate body used as an access point to a bibliographic record. 2. A bibliographic record with the name of a corporate body as the heading. Compare with *author entry, personal name entry*.

corporate name The official title by which a corporate body is known.

corporation borrower's card see *business firm borrower's card*

corporation file In a special library, a file of materials about the activities, securities, etc., of individual companies, such as annual reports and other publications issued by the corporations, stock exchange listings, prospectuses, and clippings. In a financial library the term "corporation file" is generally used; in other kinds of special libraries the term "company file" is sometimes used because it covers any type of business enterprise.

corporation library 1. A library owned or controlled by a governing board legally constituted as a corporate body and including or not including municipal representatives. The library may or may not provide free public library service to its community. 2. A special library that serves a particular incorporated organization.

corrective maintenance Maintenance performed on hardware or software to correct an identified problem or malfunction. Synonymous with remedial maintenance and unscheduled maintenance. Compare with *preventive maintenance, scheduled maintenance*.

correlation The interdependence between two or more variables. If the values of the variables tend to vary together, the variables are said to exhibit "positive correlation"; if the values tend to vary opposingly (inversely), the variables are said to exhibit "negative correlation."

correlation coefficient A measure of the magnitude of the interdependence (i.e., correlation) of two variables and the direction of the interdependence as positive or negative.

correlative indexing system see *precoordinate indexing system, postcoordinate indexing system.*

correspondence management Application of records management techniques to correspondence to increase efficiency, improve quality, and reduce costs. In Canadian usage, treatment of correspondence. (SAA)

corrigenda see *errata*

cost accounting The process of maintaining records of all expenditures incurred by an organization for purposes of planning, analyzing, or controlling operations or activities. In a broad sense, includes procedures for cost studies, methods of determining costs, comparison costing, and a formal cost-basis accounting system whereby the various types of costs are charged or assigned to accounts for activities, products, or services, in order to derive a unit cost.

cost-benefit analysis A management technique for comparing the cost of providing a program, service, or activity with its value or effect, stated in financial and social terms. The purpose is to select the alternative which yields the greatest benefits from existing resources or to determine whether the program or service is worth the cost of providing it.

cost-effectiveness analysis A management technique used for comparing the efficiency, or level of performance, of a program, service, or activity, and the cost of achieving that level. The purpose is to select from among several choices the least costly method of achieving a particular level of performance.

cottage binding see *cottage style*

cottage style A binding style in which the top and bottom of the center panel are given a gable-like, broken-pediment design, and the spaces are filled with a variety of small patterns. It is characteristic of English bindings of the late 17th century.

cotton linters The short fibers adhering to cottonseed after the ginning operation. Linters are used increasingly in the manufacture of cotton-content paper, but the relative shortness of the fibers makes a paper less strong than that made from rag fiber.

countermark A secondary watermark on handmade paper, usually positioned in the center of the half-sheet opposite the principal watermark and often recording initials of maker, place, or date. Date watermarks of the early 19th century are frequently placed near one edge. Compare with *watermark.*

countersunk In binding, a book cover with a depression pressed or stamped to receive a label, an inlay, or a decoration.

county library 1. A free public library maintained by county taxation for the use of the whole or a part of a county, established as an independent agency, or combined with a municipal or other library. 2. A municipal or other library which provides library service to a county by contract.

coupler 1. In a diazo-coated material, the chemical compound or coupling agent which reacts with unexposed diazo compound to produce an azo dye. It is the azo dye which forms a visible image. 2. In data transmission, see *acoustic coupler.*

coupling agent see *coupler* (1)

course-integrated bibliographic instruction Any bibliographic instruction which is designed as a part of course objectives. The instruction is viewed as essential to knowledge of the subject and therefore to successful completion of the course. Compare with *course-related bibliographic instruction.*

course-related bibliographic instruction Any bibliographic instruction designed to provide students in a given course with the skills in the use of the library that are necessary to meet the course objectives. In contradistinction to *course-integrated bibliographic instruction,* it supports course objectives but is not an integral part of those objectives.

courtesy card see *visitor's card*

courtesy storage see *deposit*

court hand A medieval cursive hand used in court records, charters, and other official documents.

cover 1. The outer covering of a document, of whatever material. 2. Popularly, either of the two parts of the cover on either side of the spine of a book; the front cover and the back or lower cover.

coverage 1. The scope or degree of completeness of a library collection; of a particular group of library materials within the collection, such as the Chemistry Collection; or of a bibliographic item. 2. The geographical extent of a cartographic item.

cover date The publication date which appears on the cover of a publication, as opposed to the date which may appear on the title page or elsewhere in the publication.

covering materials Cloth, leather, paper, or other materials affixed to the boards and inlay, and forming the outer surface of the book cover.

cover paper Heavy, durable paper used for making covers of booklets, pamphlets, etc.

cover pocket A special adaptation of the inside of a book cover (usually the back cover) in which a pocketlike arrangement is provided as a receptacle for loose maps, and the like, accompanying the book.

covers bound in The original covers included, or to be included, in a later binding of a volume.

cover title A title printed on the cover of a publication as issued by the publisher. Compare with *binder's title, side title.*

CPI see *characters per inch*

CPM see *Critical Path Method (CPM)*

CPS see *characters per second*

CPU see *central processing unit*

Crabtree-Ross method see *Ross-Crabtree method*

cradle books see *incunables*

crash Coarse, open-weave starched cotton goods used in edition binding for reinforcing backs of books. Also called gauze, mull, and

super. When reinforced at intervals with heavier cross threads, it is known as law super.

crayon engraving 1. A method of etching by which the broken or dotted lines of chalk drawings are imitated through the use of various toothed wheels or disks called roulettes and other tools. Synonymous with chalk engraving. 2. A print made by this method.

credit line A statement giving the name of a photographer, artist, author, agency, or publication responsible for the picture, photograph, article, or quotation being reproduced. Usually printed flush right below an illustration, or as the last line of the caption. Credit lines are sometimes printed in one paragraph on one page in a periodical or included in the back matter of a book.

criblé Minute punctures made in a surface of wood or metal.

critical abstract An abstract which provides not only an abbreviated representation of a work but also an evaluation of it by the abstracter.

critical apparatus The introduction, footnotes and other marginalia, glossary, list of references, commentary, and related material which appear in a scholarly edition of an author's works; can include information concerning variant readings or doubtful or obscure passages.

critical bibliography see *analytical bibliography*

critical edition An edition of a bibliographic item which reflects the results of scholarly research and examination of earlier editions and manuscripts by the editor.

Critical Path Method (CPM) A mathematically ordered system of planning and scheduling for program management, similar to the *Program Evaluation and Review Technique (PERT),* concerned with establishing the sequence of dependent and interrelated activities that make possible a balanced, optimum, time-cost schedule to assure timeliness and minimum use of resources.

crop To cut part of the top, bottom, or sides of a photograph or piece of artwork before reproducing or mounting.

cropped Said of a book so severely trimmed that the text has been cut into. Compare with *shaved.*

cross aisle A passageway which runs at right angles to the ranges and range aisles in a shelving area. It separates two banks of ranges or a bank of ranges from public areas or other functional spaces. Compare with *range aisle.*

cross classification In classification, the act of placing two or more works with the same composite subject in more than one place in the classification system. This can occur when, in the process of forming a classification system, more than one characteristic is used in a single step of division.

cross reference see *reference* (2)

cross tabulation see *contingency table*

CRT see *cathode-ray tube*

CRT recorder see *computer-output-microfilm recorder*

CRT terminal see *cathode-ray-tube terminal*

crushed morocco Goatskin leather intended for binding, in which the grain has been flattened and highly polished and then crushed by plating.

cubook The volume of space required to shelve the average-size book, taking into account books of varying height and thickness, and allowing for vacant space 10 percent of each shelf length. Devised for measuring stack capacity, a cubook equals a hundredth part of a standard single-faced shelving section 3 feet wide and 7½ feet tall.

cultural, recreational, or educational presentation An information service to a group which enriches the intellectual life of the participants, provides wholesome entertainment, or provides formal instruction in some subject other than the use of the library. Examples are book reviews and discussions, media presentations, musical events, lectures, and story hours.

cumdach An Irish term for a bronze, brass, or wooden box, often elaborately decorated in silver or gold, for holding a precious bound or unbound medieval manuscript. Synonymous with book box and book shrine.

cum licentia A notice in a book indicating that permission for the printing had been obtained from a religious or secular authority. Compare with *cum privilegio.*

cum privilegio A notice in early printed books indicating that permission and usually exclusive rights to print had been obtained from a religious or secular authority, the permission and rights being applicable to a single book or to a class of books. Compare with *cum licentia.*

cumulative frequency distribution A frequency distribution which indicates either the number of cases in and below the limits of each class interval, or the number of cases in and above the limits of each class interval.

cumulative index An index in which several previously published indexes are combined into one sequence.

cumulative volume A volume in which several previously published issues of an index or bibliography have been combined in one sequence.

cuneiform writing The wedge-shaped writing of Assyrian and Babylonian inscriptions.

curator 1. One who has the care and superintendence of something; especially, one in charge of a museum, art gallery, or other place of exhibit. 2. A title sometimes used to designate a person in charge of a special collection, especially one trained to aid in the interpretation of the materials.

curiosa Said of books containing curious or unusual subject matter; sometimes used euphemistically for *erotica.*

curl The tendency of photographic film or paper to roll up into the shape of a cylinder. The lengthwise distortion is often a result of core-set. The problem is often solved by reverse winding. Compare with *bow.*

current-awareness journal A periodical containing reproductions of the tables of contents of journals in a particular subject field.

current-awareness service see *selective dissemination of information (SDI)*

current records In archives, records necessary for conducting the current business of a corporate body and which must therefore be kept readily accessible. In Canada, called active records.

curriculum guide A written plan including one or more aspects of curriculum and instruction, such as goals and objectives, resources, a variety of learning activities, and evaluation techniques. This plan may cover a single unit of instruction or may be used to describe the entire curriculum of a school district or an entire state.

curriculum laboratory see *curriculum materials center*

curriculum materials center A central collection for a school district or for a school of education in a college or university in which are kept the professional books, professional periodicals, sample textbooks, teaching aids, curriculum units and guides, and other instructional materials for teachers or for students in teacher education programs. Compare with *laboratory collection* (2).

cursive 1. Said of writing in which the letters within words are joined together. Applies specifically to writing used in Renaissance papal documents and humanistic manuscripts. 2. In printing, a class of typeface that has the appearance of handwriting.

cursor A special rectangle of light on the screen of a cathode-ray tube used to indicate the position where the next character will be displayed or is to be entered by an operator.

curvature of field In optics, the aberration of a lens which causes an object being photographed to be focused into a curved surface rather than into a flat plane.

curve A line that can be accurately defined by an equation; also often loosely used for a line connecting two specific points on a graph.

curve fitting Representing or approximating an observed frequency distribution by means of a probability function or density.

custody In archives, the guardianship of books, manuscripts, records, and other documents. May include either or both physical possession (protective responsibility) and legal title (legal responsibility).

custom binding A book which has been bound according to the order of a dealer or owner; a book bound to specific instructions rather than in accordance with general instructions.

customer-must-order-direct (CMOD) A restriction stipulated by some publishers, particularly of law-related materials, who do not want to deal with wholesalers or retailers.

cut 1. A general term referring to metal blocks for the letterpress printing of illustrations. 2. A print made from such a printing block.

cut-corner pamphlet file A box file which has the upper-back corners of the sides cut away diagonally to half the height of the box and with the upper half of the back and the top unenclosed. The file is designed to hold pamphlets, unbound issues of periodicals, and other materials unbound or in paper covers.

cut edges In binding, the three edges of a book which have been smoothly trimmed with a guillotine. Not to be confused with *opened*. Compare with *trimmed edges*.

cut flush Said of a bound volume which has had its cover trimmed after binding, so that the edges of the cover are even with the edges of the leaves. Synonymous with trimmed flush and flush boards.

cut-in boards see *in boards* (1)

cut-in heading A subheading set in the text of a page in a rectangular space that is surrounded by the text on three sides. Synonymous with cut-in note, cut-in side note, let-in note, and incut note.

cut-in index see *thumb index*

cut-in note see *cut-in heading*

cut-in side note see *cut-in heading*

cut line see *caption* (1)

cut mark A mark added to roll microfilm during microfilming which triggers an automatic device for cutting of microfiche.

Cutter Classification see *Expansive Classification*

Cutter number An alphanumeric code for a main entry heading, the first word other than an article of the bibliographic description, the name of a biographee, etc., taken from or based on a Cutter Table or the Cutter-Sanborn Table and forming part of the book number assigned to a bibliographic item.

Cutter-Sanborn Table A modification of the two-figure Cutter Table by Kate E. Sanborn; uses single letters and three numbers to provide symbols to be used as author marks.

Cutter Table   Either one of two tables constructed by Charles A. Cutter to provide an alphanumeric code for author names which, when included in call numbers as author marks, provides under each class number an alphabetical subarrangement by author. One of the tables uses two numerals in the author mark, the other, three.

cybernetics   The theory of mechanical, electronic, and electrical control systems designed to replace human functions.

cycle   1. In computer science, the time required to complete a sequence of specific operations or events. 2. The time required for the reversal of an alternating electric current from positive to negative and back again.

cyclopedia   see *encyclopedia*

cylinder   1. On a printing press, a roller carrying the printing plate or the paper. 2. In computer science, all tracks of data on a magnetic disk pack which can be accessed without repositioning the read-write heads.

cylinder press   A printing press on which type or plates are on a flat bed and the paper is carried on a cylinder.

daisy wheel printer   see *printer* (2)

dandy roll   A cylinder used in the manufacture of machine-made paper to smooth the surface and impress designs such as the watermark, countermark, the cross lines of laid paper, and the mesh pattern of wove paper.

dark line image   see *positive-appearing image*

darkroom   A room with no light or with a safelight in which unprocessed photosensitive materials are handled during camera loading and unloading, or developing. Some films and paper have daylight-loading characteristics which do not require a darkroom.

data   The symbols or characters of a language which have been selected and combined to convey information.

data acquisition   In data processing, pertaining to the identification and collection of data, usually at decentralized locations, for later processing in a usable form at a central site.

database   An organized collection of computer records, standardized in format and content, that is stored in any of a variety of computer-readable modes. It is the basic set of data from which computer-readable files are created. In the database, all records are interrelated by some common denominator. (LDCH)

database management system (DBMS)   The software designed to organize, store, maintain, and retrieve data in a database.

data buffer   see *buffer*

data carrier   see *communications common carrier*

data channel   see *channel* (1)

data collection   The process of accumulating data at one location from a number of remote locations or remote terminals by telecommunication before data processing.

data communication   An interchange of data or messages between people or machines over communications channels. Compare with *data transmission.*

data communications common carrier   see *communications common carrier*

data compression   In data processing, the reduction of the amount of space required to store data or increasing the amount of data which can be stored in an amount of space. Synonymous with redundancy reduction.

data conversion   The process of converting data from one form to another, usually from a human-readable form to a machine-readable form, or from one recording medium to another. Compare with *file conversion.*

data element 1. A defined unit of information which constitutes all or part of a field in a computer record. 2. In a bibliographic record, a word, phrase, or group of characters representing a unit of bibliographic information and forming all or part of an area of the bibliographic description. (AACR2, mod.)

data field see *field* (1)

data file see *file* (1)

data hierarchy In data processing, a means of organizing or structuring subsets of specific data within larger sets of more general or broader data.

data item In data processing, a single unit of data within a set of data.

data link The assemblage of communications equipment and interconnecting channels that allows data to be exchanged between two or more network stations.

data management see *information management*

datamation A term implying the combination of data processing and automation.

data processing The systematic performance of an operation or sequence of operations upon data by one or more computer-processing units to achieve a desired end result. Synonymous with information processing.

data-processing center A location where one or more computer systems, peripheral equipment, and staff to manage and operate the equipment and provide data-processing services are housed. Synonymous with computer center, EDP center, and service bureau.

data reduction In data processing, the transformation of a mass of unprocessed or raw data into organized and useful information.

data retrieval see *information retrieval*

data set see *file* (1)

data set name In certain computer systems, the name that the software recognizes as the identifier of a given machine-readable data file. (AACR2)

data sink 1. The point of usage of data in a network. 2. A computer or terminal that re-

ceives and processes data from a connected channel.

data storage see *storage*

data switching A technique of handling data or messages over a network. A message is transmitted to an intermediate point, analyzed, then transmitted to the next point. Synonymous with message switching, store-and-forward switching. Compare with *circuit switching.*

data-switching center A point in a network where data or messages are received, then routed to the next point, depending upon their content and according to prearranged instructions. Synonymous with message-switching center.

data terminal see *terminal* (2)

data transfer The movement of data from one point or location to another, usually via data transmission facilities.

data transfer rate The rate at which data are moved or transmitted from one point or location to another over a channel, usually measured in bits per second or characters per second. Synonymous with data transmission rate and transmission rate.

data transmission The movement of data from one point to another along a channel. The data usually will be in the form of coded, electrical pulses or signals. Synonymous with information transmission. Compare with *data communication.*

data transmission line see *transmission line*

data transmission rate see *data transfer rate*

data validity The measurement of the extent or degree to which tests have been made and the tests performed accurately and correctly to ensure the reliability of data.

date due The last day of the loan period (the period of time allowed for the use of an item charged from a library collection). Synonymous with due date.

date due card/slip A card or small strip or piece of paper inserted in an item charged from the library collection, or a printed, ruled form, usually attached to an inside cover or free endpaper of a volume, on which is indicated the date the borrowed item is due to be returned.

date file A file of the records of items charged from the library collection, with primary arrangement by date due.

date-of-order file An acquisitions file of documents on order, with primary arrangement by date of order to facilitate the claim of orders past due.

date of publication see *publication date* (1), (3)

day file see *reading file*

db see *decibel*

DBMS see *database management system*

d/c see *direct current*

deacidification The process by which the acidity of paper (a major factor in its deterioration) is neutralized, with, in some cases, the addition of an alkaline buffer to neutralize future acidity. The most common method of deacidification involves aqueous solutions of mildly alkaline compounds; nonaqueous methods are at present being developed for mass application and for items that are sensitive to water.

deacquisition see *discard* (1)

dead file 1. A file that is not currently in use and never expected to be used again, but retained for some specific reason. Compare with *active file, inactive file.* 2. An acquisitions file containing information on documents ordered, received, and processed, or on documents requested but never received for various reasons.

dead time A time delay between successive computer runs or sequences of operations of a computer or other machine.

dealer An individual or company who buys and sells books or other materials acquired by libraries. Compare with *bookseller, wholesaler.*

dealer file An acquisitions file of documents on order, with primary arrangement by the dealers with whom the orders are placed. Synonymous with vendor file.

dealering A term used to refer to the process of selecting the dealers from whom a library will order certain materials.

dean 1. The title used to designate the chief executive of some academic library systems, in which the professional staff members usually have full or modified faculty status and the chief executive of the library is head of the library faculty. The term is usually modified by a phrase such as "dean of library services" or "dean of media services." 2. The title used to designate the chief academic and administrative officer of most library schools in the United States.

deblinding An aspect of automated authority control whereby blind references (i.e., references that do not lead to a heading on a bibliographic record) are detected. Blind references may be reported or suppressed, input may be inhibited, etc., depending upon the particular computer program.

debug To locate and correct or remove the defects in a computer program, a piece of equipment, or a procedure. Synonymous with troubleshoot.

decatalog To withdraw from the public catalog the bibliographic record(s) of a bibliographic item which is to be removed from public access but retained in the library.

decentralization, administrative The practice of delegating authority and decision-making power to a relatively large number of administrative officers and supervisors as a means of encouraging initiative and staff development. The practice necessitates the development of mechanisms for coordination and lateral communication. It is sometimes associated with a flat organizational structure. Compare with *centralization, administrative.*

decentralization, organizational An organizational arrangement within a library system which is characterized by numerous geographically dispersed collections and service points. Compare with *centralization, organizational.*

decentralized network A network in which all or some management and control functions and services are distributed among several locations or nodes. Compare with *centralized network.*

decibel (db) A standard unit used to express the relative intensity (amplitude) of a sound wave or an electric signal. This measurement is used in specifications for audio equipment. To the average human ear one decibel is the softest audible sound and 120 decibels can be painful. A sound above 130 decibels may cause permanent loss of hearing.

decile One of the nine points that divide a frequency distribution into ten equal parts.

decimal classification In general, any classification system which uses a notation based on decimal numbers. Specifically (and capitalized), the classification system by Melvil Dewey, first published in 1876, which divides knowledge into ten main classes, with further subdivisions, accompanied by decimal notation.

decimal notation In classification, a notation which uses decimal numbers to indicate subjects so that classes may be subdivided indefinitely without disruption of the logical order of the notation scheme.

decimal number system A number system with a radix or base of ten.

decision table An array or table of possible courses of action or choices to be considered in describing or solving a problem, with the actions which can be taken. Synonymous with decision tree.

decision tree see *decision table*

deck 1. The space occupied by one level of a stack, including ranges, aisles, elevators, and necessary working facilities. Synonymous with stack level. 2. A set, group, or collection of punched cards. Synonymous with pack. 3. In magnetic recording, see *audiotape deck* and *videotape deck.*

deckle edge The uneven or feather edge of handmade paper where the stock has flowed against the deckle or frame. Also can be produced in machine-made paper by a jet of water or air. Synonymous with *feather edge.*

declassification The determination that classified material no longer requires protection against unauthorized disclosure. A removal or cancellation of the security classification designation is normally involved.

decode To use a code to reverse a previous encoding.

decoder 1. A device, located in the control unit of a computer, which interprets signals and initiates execution of computer instructions. 2. A matrix of switching elements which can select one or several output channels depending upon the nature of the input signals.

decollate To separate the parts of a multipart form and, possibly, remove any interleaving carbon paper.

decollator A device or machine which decollates multipart forms.

decorated covers In library binding, front covers which bear an illustration, design, or special lettering. Synonymous with illustrated covers.

decorated papers Sheets of colored paper, usually with a pattern, suitable for endpapers and covers.

decreasing concreteness, principle of In classification, a rule used to establish citation order. The most concrete, or important, aspect of the subject is cited first, then less concrete aspects follow in order.

dedicated computer A computer which is used solely for one particular function or application or a series of related functions or applications. Compare with *general-purpose computer, special-purpose computer.*

dedicated storage Storage which has been reserved or allocated to a specific application, user, or other purpose.

dedication copy A copy of a book inscribed by the author to the person to whom the work is dedicated.

deduping The act of reconciling records within the same catalog, authority file, etc., which are discovered to be the same in substance but different in form, e.g., differing bibliographic records of the same bibliographic item and differing authority records of the same series.

deed of gift A signed document containing a voluntary transfer of title to real or personal property without a monetary consideration. A deed of gift frequently takes the form of a contract establishing conditions governing the transfer of title and specifying any restrictions on access or use. Synonymous with instrument of gift.

deferred cataloging see *temporary cataloging*

definition see *resolution*

definitive edition The complete works of an author presented in a form considered final and authoritative.

degrees of freedom Used to characterize a statistic; it is the number of free (unrestricted and independent) values or observations of a variable (or variables) from which the statistic is calculated. For example, if the mean of three scores is 4.00, the sum of the three must equal 12. Any two of the scores are free to take on any value, but the third must have a value such that the sum of the three is 12.

degressive bibliography Varying the details of a bibliographical description according to the difference in the period treated or the importance of the publication to be described; thus more space might be devoted to the description of the first edition than to later reprintings of the same work.

delete To remove a portion of data from a record, file, or storage. Compare with *erase* (1).

delimiter In data processing, a character or special symbol which separates or marks the boundaries of items of data. Synonymous with separator. Compare with *field terminator.*

delinquent borrower A borrower who fails to return items charged from the library collection, to pay fines, or to pay for lost items.

delphi technique A method of predicting trends or events based upon the assessments, judgments, and opinions of a group of experts or advisers. Usually the group is given a series of questionnaires, after each of which the results are tabulated, analyzed, and reported back to the group; the process continues until a level of agreement is reached among the group.

deluxe binding A fine leather binding, lettered and tooled by hand. So-called deluxe bindings are often machine products, and the term is now seldom used for individually ordered fine-leather bindings.

deluxe edition An edition characterized by superior materials and fine workmanship, usually a limited edition.

demodulation The process of converting a signal to its original form after modulation, such as the process of converting digital data to a signal suitable for analog data transmission over a telephone channel and then reconverting it to digital data for its acceptance by a receiving terminal.

demonstration library A library designated or organized for an experimental purpose, in which

a certain type of service is carried on for a specified period of time to test its value and potential for broader application.

demonstration program A program of an experimental or innovative nature which is actualized for a specified period of time to test its value and potential for broader application.

denotation In classification, the range of things represented by a term or symbol. Compare with *connotation.*

densitometer A photoelectric instrument used for measuring the density of a photographic image. A transmission densitometer is used for processed film and a reflection densitometer for paper prints. A microdensitometer is a densitometer designed to measure the density of very small areas of an image.

density 1. A measure of the degree of opacity of film and of blackness of paper prints. Density is the result of exposure of photographic materials to light. It is a function of the intensity of incident light reflected or transmitted. Density values for processed film range between the lowest density obtainable, D-MIN, and the highest, D-MAX. Density values are plotted against the logarithm of exposure (D log E) and can be obtained using a densitometer. A frequently used measure of film density is diffuse transmission density or, more formally, background visual diffuse transmission density. The measure is used primarily for silver halide and diazo film. Density of paper prints is measured as diffuse reflection density. Synonymous with optical density. 2. In data processing, the amount of data which can be contained in a specific amount of area or space, usually measured in bits per inch or characters per inch. 3. In typography, the number of type characters fitted into a given space.

dentelle A style of toothlike or lacelike ornamentation on the borders of a binding. It is particularly (but not only) associated with 18th-century leather bindings.

department 1. A major administrative unit of a library system set up to perform a definite function or set of related functions and having its own staff and definite responsibilities, with an administrative head directly reporting to the head administrative officer or an assistant head administrative officer of the library system. 2. A subject section in a library in which library materials, whether for reference or circulation, are separated by subject into several divisions (as in some large public libraries). Sometimes used synonymously with division.

Departmental Edition   The publications of the executive departments and independent establishments of the U.S. government, issued with no uniformity in contents, format, or binding, as distinguished from their appearance as Senate and House Documents in the *United States Serial Set*. Synonymous with Plain Title Edition and Departmental Set.

departmental library   In an academic library system, a separate library supporting the information needs of a specific academic department. May be a branch library, external to the central library, or housed within the central library. Compare with *division library*.

Departmental Set see *Departmental Edition*

department head   A title assigned to those staff members in charge of a major administrative unit in a library system.

dependent variable   In an experiment, the variable that is (or is hypothesized to be) affected by an independent variable.

dependent work   In cataloging, a work which depends in some way on an earlier work by another author, such as a revised edition, abridgment, and dramatization. Synonymous with related work.

deposit   Records or other documents which have been placed in a repository, sometimes for security reasons and sometimes to make them more readily available for consultation, the depositor retaining ownership. Synonymous with courtesy storage.

deposit copy   A free copy of a new publication sent to the copyright office or designated libraries under the terms of the national copyright law.

deposit fee   Money deposited by a person who is not a member of the library's target group in order to qualify for borrowing privileges. The deposit is refundable upon the return of all borrowed materials.

deposit library see *storage center*

depository see *repository*

depository catalog see *Library of Congress depository catalog*

depository invoice   A list of the publications sent by the U.S. Superintendent of Documents to a depository library on a specified date.

depository library   1. A library legally designated to receive without charge all or a selected portion of the U.S. government publications supplied by the Government Printing Office and other federal agencies for distribution by the Superintendent of Documents. 2. A library legally designated to receive without charge state government publications supplied by the state agencies of a particular state for distribution by the state library. Synonymous with documents depository and government documents depository.

deposit station   A public library service outlet in a store, school, factory, club, or other organization or institution, with a small and frequently changed collection of books, and open only at limited and designated times.

depth indexing   The indexing of each specific subject contained in the text of a document, as contrasted with using relatively fewer generic descriptors.

depth of field   The distance between the points nearest and farthest from the camera that are acceptably sharp, at a given lens setting. At a given distance from camera to subject, the smaller the lens aperture and focal length, the greater the depth of field.

depth of focus   The allowable tolerance in lens-to-film distance within which an acceptably sharp image of the subject focused upon can be obtained.

deputy   An individual in an organization who is second in command, with authority to represent another or act in another's place.

derived cataloging   The cataloging of a bibliographic item by using an existent bibliographic record and altering it as needed to fit the item in hand and to conform to local cataloging practice. Synonymous with copy cataloging.

derived indexing   An indexing method by which the indexer uses as descriptors words occurring in the text or title of a work. Synonymous with extraction indexing, indexing by extraction, and word indexing. Compare with *assigned indexing.*

descender 1. That part of a lowercase letter that extends below x-height. 2. A lowercase letter with such an extender, as j, p. Compare with *ascender.*

descriptive bibliography 1. The close physical study and description of books, including details about the author, exact title, date, place, and circumstances of publication, the format, pagination, illustrations, binding, and other particulars. 2. A book which is the result of such study, providing full physical descriptions of the books and other works it includes, and usually dealing with the output of a particular author, illustrator, printer, publisher, period, or place.

descriptive cataloging The aspects of cataloging concerned with the bibliographic description of a bibliographic item and the determination of headings, other than subject and form headings, under which it will be represented in the catalog; the identification and description of the item.

descriptive statistics Statistical methods used to describe with precision a collection of quantitative data in a form that facilitates interpretation and communication. Compare with *inferential statistics.*

descriptor 1. In indexing, a term, notation, or other string of symbols used to designate the subject of a work. 2. As used by Calvin Mooers, a limited list of subjects.

desiderata see *want list*

desk duty A work assignment at the circulation, reference, or other public service desk to assist library users.

desk schedule An outline indicating hours when staff members in public service departments are assigned to desk duties in order to assure continuity of services.

desktop reader see *microform reader*

destruction see *disposition*

destruction schedule see *disposition schedule*

destructive read The reading by a computer device of data in a process which erases or destroys it at the same time.

desuperimposition As applied to the adoption of *Anglo-American Cataloguing Rules,* the full adoption of the rules following their partial adoption, or superimposition, with resultant revision of those headings left unrevised while superimposition was in effect. Compare with *superimposition.*

detail file In data processing, a file of current data or data collected during a period of time which later is to be processed against or used to update a master file. Synonymous with transaction file.

developer see *developing*

developing The process by which latent images on exposed photosensitive materials are rendered visible, as the first step in photographic processing. A developer, consisting of such substances as chemical reagents, dry powders, water, or gas, is used to convert the latent images to visible ones. Liquid developers, such as PQ developer, contain chemical agents for reducing the density of images on materials sensitized with silver halide.

deviation The value of a variable measured from some standard point of location, usually the mean.

device 1. An electrical, electronic, or mechanical contrivance having a specific purpose or function. 2. In publishing, a *printer's mark.*

Dewey Decimal Classification see *decimal classification*

diagnostic Pertaining to the discovery or detection of errors or malfunctions in a computer program or equipment.

dial-up The use of a rotary or push-button telephone to establish a data transmission circuit between a terminal and another communications device or computer system over a switched line.

diaper A small repeating pattern of binding ornament in geometrical form, usually a diamond or a lozenge.

diaphragm 1. A thin disc in a microphone which is activated by receiving or producing sound waves. 2. In an optical system, a device which limits the amount of light entering through the lens aperture, or the field covered by the lens, or both, depending upon its location. Synonymous with *stop*.

diazo A light-sensitive compound consisting primarily of diazonium salts used on diazo-coated materials. The term is often used as an abbreviation for the *diazotype process.*

diazo-coated material A slow, direct image (nonreversing) duplicating film, paper, or cloth, sensitized by means of diazonium salts. In the case of film, the diazo emulsion is impregnated in the film base. An image is formed on the material using a diazotype process.

diazo film see *diazo-coated material*

diazo print see *diazotype process*

diazotype process A direct image (nonreversing) contact copying process during which a diazo-coated material is exposed to ultraviolet light passing through a photographic positive or negative master. Diazonium salts on the portion of the material exposed to light are bleached, resulting in a latent image. The unbleached salts are then developed with a liquid developer of ammonia fumes to produce a copy in any one of a variety of colors, depending on the type of diazo coating used. A print made by this process is called diazo print, ammonia print, whiteprint, and, from the color used to make the print, a blue or blueline and brownline or vandyke. Synonymous with dyeline process and whiteprint process.

diced Said of the cover of a binding which has been ruled or stamped into a pattern of small diamond squares.

diced russia A diced cowhide tanned by a special process; frequently used in late 18th-century books.

dichotomizing search see *binary search*

dictionary catalog A catalog in which all the entries (author, title, subject, series, etc.) and their related references are arranged together in one alphabet. The subarrangement frequently varies from the strictly alphabetical.

die 1. A piece of engraved metal used for stamping. 2. In American usage, an engraved plate, usually of brass or copper alloy, used for stamping book covers.

difference In classification, the attribute by which one species is distinguished from all the other species of the same genus.

diffused light Light rays that have become scattered and no longer travel in a linear, parallel fashion. The scattering is generally due to a material which either transmits or reflects the light rays striking it. A frosted lamp acts as a diffusing screen to create a soft light. Diffusing screens are used in microfilm readers to provide a better viewing surface by reducing glare.

diffuse reflection density see *density* (1)

diffuse transmission density see *density* (1)

diffusing screen see *diffused light*

diffusion transfer process Any transfer process in which image-forming materials, such as silver salt or dye, move from one surface to another through a thin liquid layer. A transfer process in which the negative and positive images are formed at approximately the same time is termed a diffusion transfer reversal process.

diffusion transfer reversal process see *diffusion transfer process*

digest 1. A systematic, comprehensive condensation of a written work, often prepared by someone other than the author of the original, generally larger in scope than a synopsis, and sometimes with headings and subheadings for quick reference. Sometimes used synonymously with *compendium* (2) and *epitome* (2). 2. A periodical containing condensations of works gathered from many sources, frequently arranged in classified order. 3. In law, a compact summary of laws, reported cases, decisions, etc., systematically arranged.

digit In classification, any single symbol that occurs in a class number.

digital channel A channel used to transfer digital data without need for its conversion to analog form. Compare with *analog channel.*

digital computer A type of computer which performs arithmetic and logic operations on data represented as discrete binary digits. Compare with *analog computer, hybrid computer.*

digital counter A device found in audiotape recorders which counts the rotations of one of the reels or the amount of tape passing a fixed point. This device permits finding a specific point on the tape for editing or indexing purposes.

digital data   Data represented in the form of discontinuous or discrete binary digits. Compare with *analog data.*

digital data transmission   The movement of digital data from one point to another along a channel. Compare with *analog data transmission.*

dime novel   A story, usually of a romantic and sensational nature, published in paper covers and generally priced at ten cents a copy; popular during the second half of the 19th century.

dimensional stability   The ability of any material to resist dimensional change during production, processing, subsequent handling, and storage. The term is generally applied to photographic materials, but may include books and other objects.

diode   A small semiconductor crystal with two terminals used in nearly all types of electronic equipment, characterized primarily by its ability to convert alternating current into direct current.

diorama   A three-dimensional representation of a real-life scene created by placing life-size or miniature objects in front of a painted background. Children create these in shoe boxes, while museums provide life-size dioramas.

diplomatics   The study of official (as opposed to literary) documents, including handwriting and chancery practices, abbreviations, etc.; usually refers to the study of ancient and medieval materials.

diptych   An ancient hinged writing tablet consisting of a pair of panels of wood, metal or ivory, covered with wax on the inside surfaces, on which writing was done with a stylus.

direct access   In computer-based information storage and retrieval, a method of referring to records arranged in nonsequential order in a file. Access time to records is not related to their location in the file, because all those preceding a desired one are ignored. Synonymous with random access. Compare with *serial access.*

direct-access processing   A technique of processing data by computer as it is received or as transactions occur, in random order and without preliminary sorting. Synonymous with random processing. Compare with *sequential processing.*

direct-access storage   In computer-based information storage and retrieval, the storage of data in a device in which the time required to record or retrieve the data is independent of its location. Synonymous with random-access memory (RAM) and random-access storage. Compare with *sequential storage.*

direct-broadcast satellite   A process of distributing one-way television signals directly by satellite to any television receiver which is connected to a special antenna (often called a dish) without intervention of a cable television distributor or a local broadcast television station.

direct-contact copy see *contact copy*

direct copying see *lensless copying*

direct current (d/c)   An electric current that flows in one direction. Its magnitude does not vary or varies only slightly. It is often produced by batteries or by special components within electronic equipment. Compare with *alternating current.*

direct electrostatic process see *electrostatic process*

direct image film   A duplicating film which, with conventional processing, retains the same polarity as the original or the previous film generation; that is, a negative from a negative or a positive from a positive. Synonymous with nonreversing film. Compare with *image reversing film.*

direct-impression printing see *impact printing*

directional transaction   An information contact which facilitates the use of the library in which the contact occurs, or its environs, and which may involve the use of sources describing that library, such as schedules, floor plans, handbooks, and policy statements. Compare with *reference transaction.*

direction line   The line below the last line of text on a page. It carries the signature mark, signature title, and catchword when present.

direction word see *catchword* (1)

directive An official, downward communication within an organization prescribing a particular action or practice on the part of subordinate personnel.

director 1. The title used to designate the chief executive officer of some libraries or library systems and most frequently denoting authority over more than one library. The title is usually modified with a word or phrase such as "library director," "director of libraries," or "director of library services." 2. The title used to designate the chief executive officer of some library schools in the United States. 3. Sometimes a librarian in charge of a particular type of work in a library system, such as children's work. 4. In a few libraries, the administrative head of one of the larger divisions, as in the Library of Congress. 5. A member of the governing board of a library; a trustee. 6. In medieval manuscripts and early printed books, a small letter placed in a space left blank for an initial, as a guide for the illuminator or rubricator. Synonymous with guide letter.

direct order The purchase of materials directly from the publisher.

directory 1. A list of persons or organizations, systematically arranged, usually in alphabetic or classed order, giving address, affiliations, etc., for individuals, and address, officers, functions, and similar data for organizations. 2. In computer science, a list or table of identifiers with references to corresponding data fields, items, or entries within a record, file, or computer program.

direct positive A positive copy made from a positive original, using a reversal process. Synonymous with self-positive.

direct-reversal film see *reversal film*

direct subdivision The subdivision of subject headings by name of province, county, city, or other locality without intermediate subdivision by name of country or state. Compare with *indirect subdivision*.

disc see *audiodisc, videodisc*

discard 1. To officially remove an item from a library collection for subsequent disposal and to remove all entries for the item from library records of holdings. Synonymous with deacquisition. 2. An item which has been discarded.

discharge 1. The cancellation of the loan record of an item borrowed from the library collection upon its return. 2. To cancel the loan record of an item borrowed from the library collection upon its return. Compare with *charge*.

discharging desk see *circulation desk*

discography A list of audiodiscs giving all or some of the following details: composer, title, performer, date and circumstances of recording, maker, maker's catalog number, date of release.

discount A percentage deducted from the list or retail price of an item. Bookselling has a complicated discounting system, including among the most common: library discounts, offered to library purchasers; trade discounts, given by publishers to wholesalers and retailers; and short discounts, generally offered on professional or textbooks likely to be sold directly to individuals.

discretion, administrative see *administrative discretion*

discretionary funds 1. Funds to be used at the discretion of those with the authority to purchase. 2. Funds available after all essential, required expenditures have been made, which are subject to fewer guidelines or restrictions than normal funds.

discrimination The act of differential treatment or bias in any aspect of personnel management toward an individual on the basis of race, color, religion, sex, national origin, age, or any other categorical rather than individual basis.

disk A round metal disk coated with a magnetizable material on which data can be recorded and stored along concentric tracks as small magnetic spots forming patterns of binary digits or bits.

diskette A flexible plastic disk available in a standard 8-inch square size and in a 5¼-inch miniature size called minidiskette. Synonymous with floppy disk.

disk operating system (DOS) The programs responsible for the housekeeping and communications between the disk storage device and the computer, and for communications between the computer and other peripheral devices.

disk pack   A group of disks which can be mounted interchangeably on a machine or device for access to the stored data.

disk storage see *disk*

dispersion   1. In optics, the separation of a ray of light into light of the various elementary colors when it passes through the surface of a transparent medium and is refracted. 2. In statistics, the scatter or variability of the observed values of a variable, usually with respect to some measure of central tendency.

display case   A free-standing bookcase with open shelves for showing books and other library materials from which library users may select.

display rack see *rack*

display terminal see *cathode-ray-tube terminal*

display tube see *cathode-ray tube*

display types   Large (usually 18-point and larger) or decorative typefaces intended to attract attention, used primarily for headings and advertisements.

disposal see *disposition*

disposal list   In archives, a document providing authorization for the destruction or preservation of specified existing records.

disposition   In archives, the actions taken after the appraisal of noncurrent records and other documents, including transfer to another repository for temporary or permanent storage, reproduction in microform, or destruction. The term includes (but is not synonymous with) disposal, which in U.S. government usage means destruction.

disposition schedule   In archives, a document governing, on a continuing basis, the retention and disposition of the recurring records of an organization or agency. Also known as a records schedule and records control schedule. (SAA)

dissolve control   A device which controls the illumination from two or more slide projectors so that images on the screen seem to dissolve from one into another. The unit is usually electronic in nature and dims one projection lamp while simultaneously raising the intensity of the other. (NCES)

distortion   1. Any change from the original audio or video program caused by mechanical or electrical faults in recording or reproducing equipment. 2. In data communication, any undesired change in the signal being transmitted over a channel. Compare with *noise* (1).

distributed network   A network whose members or nodes are interconnected either directly with other nodes or indirectly through intermediate nodes. Compare with *fully connected network, ring network, star network.*

distributed processing   A data-processing system in which some computing functions are shared among the nodes of a computer network.

distribution   In statistics, a set of values of a variable together with the frequencies of occurrence of each value.

distribution copy   A microform copy, normally produced from camera microfilm, which is used to produce additional copies or is distributed for end use. Synonymous with service copy.

distribution rights   The arrangements publishers make which give the exclusive right to distribute a publication in a specified geographic area.

distributor   An agent or agency that has exclusive or shared marketing rights for a publication. (AACR2, mod.)

district media program see *school district media program*

ditto see *spirit duplication*

divided catalog   A card catalog which has been divided into two or more sequences, such as (1) bibliographic records with headings other than subject and form and (2) records with subject and form headings.

divinity calf   1. A dark calf binding with blind stamping and no gilding. 2. A binding leather used chiefly for the inside cover lining of well-bound limp-leather prayer books and small Bibles, especially in the 19th century.

divinity circuit edges   The edges of a limp-leather book cover which overlap the edges of the book. Synonymous with Yapp edges, divinity edges, and circuit edges.

divinity edges see *divinity circuit edges*

division 1. In library organization, see *department* (2). 2. In classification, see *hierarchical classification system.*

divisional plan In a large general library, the subdivision of the collection and services into administrative units according to broad subject divisions (e.g., humanities, social sciences). In its purist application, the plan includes the division of all functional activities, including technical services, but in actual application the division usually encompasses only user services and collection development.

divisional title 1. A leaf preceding the first page of the text of a major subdivision of a book, with the title and/or number of the subdivision appearing on the recto. 2. The title of a major subdivision of a book as it appears on a divisional title leaf or elsewhere. Synonymous with part title and section title.

division library A library attached to a division or a group of related departments of a university or a college, administered either by the central library or by the division, with some form of cooperative arrangement with the central library. Compare with *departmental library.*

D log E curve see *contrast* (1)

D-MAX see *density* (1)

D-MIN see *density* (1)

document 1. A physical entity of any substance on which is recorded all or part of a work or multiple works. Documents include books and booklike materials, printed sheets, graphics, manuscripts, audiorecordings, videorecordings, motion pictures, and machine-readable data files. 2. In reprography, a single piece of paper containing text or other graphic matter on one or both sides. 3. Short for government document, a synonym for *government publication.*

document address A number, symbol, or label which designates the location of an item in a document store.

documentalist see *information scientist*

documentary film A film based on fact that has been dramatically structured to enhance the real-life situations and the people. Made up of shots of actual places, people and events, a docu-

mentary film probes relationships between people and their environment.

documentary information Information about or in documents.

documentary reproduction see *reprography*

documentation 1. Broadly, the systematic collection, organization, storage, retrieval, and dissemination of specialized information, especially of a scientific or technical nature. 2. More specifically, the acquisition, organization, storage, retrieval, and dissemination of documents. 3. A collection of documents on a given subject. 4. Descriptive information required to initiate, develop, operate, and maintain machine-readable files and systems. Data file documentation describes the condition of the data, the creation of the file, and the location and size of the data elements contained in the records. System documentation usually is quite technical and defines the relationship among the various hardware components or software elements. Program documentation explains the purpose and procedures of a given set of software instructions. 5. The description of any procedure or set of procedures or policies.

documentation center An organization that acquires, organizes, and stores documents for delivery in response to requests for specific documents. Its purpose is distributive, not archival.

document card In a unit-card system, a card which contains complete bibliographic and indexing information for a document.

document case A letter- or legal-sized container, usually 3 to 5 inches deep, made of acid-free cardboard, used for the flat storage of archives or manuscripts.

document copying see *reprography*

document delivery service 1. In information retrieval systems, the provision of documents, published or unpublished, in hard copy or microform, at an established cost upon request. 2. The delivery of requested documents from the library collection to the office or residence of library users.

document mark An optical mark placed below each image on roll microfilm, used to count automatically the number of frames (images) and to serve as an image-mark retrieval code through the use of an external index indicating the location of documents on the roll by their frame number. Synonymous with blip and image mark.

document number An identifying number assigned to a government publication. Particularly, in the *United States Serial Set,* the number assigned to documents within each series.

document overlap see *double document*

document plane The position and space occupied by a document during exposure; for example, the document is flat and parallel to the ground during filming with a planetary camera.

document retrieval The activity or process of locating or retrieving and providing documents on demand from a document store on a specific topic or subject.

document retrieval system A system in which complete copies of documents, rather than information about them, are located or retrieved and provided on demand from a document store.

documents depository see *depository library*

Documents Office Classification The classification system used by the U.S. Superintendent of Documents for the arrangement of federal government publications. Arrangement is basically by issuing agency. Synonymous with Checklist Classification and Superintendent of Documents Classification.

document stop see *double document*

document store In a document retrieval system, the location where the documents themselves are housed.

dodge To vary the density of selected areas on a photographic print by temporarily shielding them during exposure. Synonymous with hold back. Compare with *burn-in* (1).

door checker see *guard* (5)

dormitory library A library in a residence hall of a college or university, which provides students with recreational reading and, sometimes, with reference books and materials for required reading. Synonymous with residence library.

DOS see *disk operating system*

dos-à-dos A form of binding in which two books are bound together so as to open in opposite directions, one of the three boards used being common to both volumes, and with the two spines and, respectively, the fore-edges, opposed. Compare with *tête-bêche.*

dossier In archives, an accumulation of documents in a folder or other file unit, concerned with the same purpose and gathered together to give information about a person or corporate body. The term is sometimes applied to a case file or a particular transaction or proceeding.

dot printer see *matrix printer*

dotted print 1. An early relief method of engraving in which the parts cut in relief print black, and tone is obtained by punching small holes in the plate or block, which appear in the print as white dots on a black background. Synonymous with Schrotblatt and manière criblée. 2. A print so produced.

double document A defect in a microfilm which occurs when a double image of a document appears on a frame, or when one document covers or partially overlaps with another document during filming. The defect occurs most frequently with planetary and rotary cameras. A device termed a document stop is built into some cameras to prevent more than one document from entering the filming area. Synonymous with document overlap.

doubledot halftone A halftone process in which the copy is photographed twice with different exposures and the two halftone negatives are placed one over the other and photographed to make a single negative or positive to achieve a greater range in tone. Compare with *duotone.*

double elephant folio see *book sizes*

double endpapers Endpapers constructed so that in both front and back two are pasted down and two remain free.

double entry (cataloging) see *duplicate entry*

double-entry charging system A charging system in which two records of each circulation transaction are generated. One is maintained in a file arranged by date due and the other in a file arranged by call number, author, or title. Synonymous with two-card charging system. Compare with *single-entry charging system.*

double exposure   In photography or microfilming, the exposure of all or part of the image area twice in succession. This may give the appearance of a double document or create a double image if the images are not exactly superimposed. Double exposure is often done intentionally in order to produce a desired effect.

double-faced shelving   A bookcase, section, or range with accessible shelving on two opposite sides. Shelves are frequently supported by common uprights or shelf supports.

double-fan adhesive binding   see *fan adhesive binding*

double fold   see *double leaf*

double fore-edge painting   see *fore-edge painting*

double image   Two photographic images of one object not exactly superimposed.

double leaf   A leaf of double size with a fold at the fore-edge or at the top edge of the book. The inner pages are not printed. Synonymous with double fold. (AACR2, mod.)

double letter   see *ligature*

double numeration   The numbering of illustrations, often used in textbooks, whereby the first number is the chapter number and the second the number of the illustration within the chapter, such as Figure 6.1.

double-perforation film   see *motion-picture film*

double plate   A single illustration extending across an opening, often printed on a leaf of double size folded in the center and attached at the fold. Compare with *folded plate.*

double slipcase   A slipcase in two parts, one of which fits into the other. Synonymous with telescope box.

double-spread   Two facing pages on which printed matter, either textual or illustrative, is spread across as on a single wide page.

double-spread title page   A term used for two facing pages on which the usual contents of a single title page are spread across.

double-tailed test   A test of a hypothesis for which the rejection region comprises areas at both extremes of the sampling distribution of the test statistic.

double title page   A term used for two title pages that face each other, such as title pages in two languages and, in the case of a volume of an author's complete works, one title page for the complete works and one for the individual work contained in the volume.

doublure   The ornamental lining (frequently decorated) of leather, silk, vellum, or other material mounted on the inner face of the cover of a book, especially one that is leatherbound.

doubtful authorship   Authorship not proved, but ascribed to one or more authors without convincing evidence.

downgrading   1. The assigning of classified material to a less restricted security classification. A change of the classification designation to reflect an appropriate lower degree of protection is involved. 2. The process of lowering the grade level of particular positions within a position classification to reflect a lowered level of complexity, responsibility, etc. Compare with *upgrading.*

down time   The time that a computer or other machine is not operable, due to a malfunction or other problem. Compare with *up time.*

downward reference   A reference from a term used as a subject heading or descriptor to a term that is more specific. Compare with *upward reference.*

drawing   An original representation by lines. A sketch or design made by pencil, pen, ink, crayon, or typewriter drawn on transparent or translucent material.

drawn-on covers   In binding, covers which have been glued to the backs of flat-backed periodicals and paperbacks. Called drawn-on solid when endpapers are also pasted down.

draw-out shelves   A type of compact shelving in which the shelves are wide enough to accommodate two rows of books with facing fore-edges. The shelves are fitted into sections like the drawers of a card catalog case and are pulled out into the aisle to permit access to either row of books.

drier   In reprography, any of a number of ink additives which speed drying.

drop A receptacle with a slot or below a chute, to which borrowers may return library materials, particularly when the library is closed. Synonymous with book return.

drop folio A page or folio number at the foot of the page.

drop initial see *initial letter*

drop-out 1. In data communication, the loss of a signal due to transmission noise or equipment malfunction or the failure to read or write a character on such media as magnetic tape or magnetic disk. 2. In magnetic recording, a brief loss of signal which occurs when the magnetic tape loses contact with the tape head.

dropout halftone A halftone in which the screen is dropped out of areas where pure white is desired. Synonymous with highlight halftone.

dropping fraction The part of a file of records in an edge-notched card system which falls out during the needle sorting process.

drum see *magnetic drum*

drum printer see *printer* (2)

dry ammonia process see *ammonia process*

dry carrel see *carrel*

drying The last step in conventional processing of silver halide film. This step involves the removal of moisture from the photographic material by using a dryer.

dry mounting see *mounting*

dry-mount press An electrically heated press which applies heat and pressure for mounting and/or laminating flat graphic and photographic materials.

dry offset A form of offset printing which, because the plate used to create the image on the offset blanket is in low relief rather than being lithographic, does not use water. Synonymous with letterset.

drypoint 1. An engraving method in which a metal surface is scratched with a pointed tool. The roughened metal burrs hold the ink for transfer to the paper. 2. A print produced by this method.

dry process Any method of producing a copy from a film positive or negative or from an original which does not involve wet chemicals. The ammonia process for diazo film and a photothermographic process using heat for dry silver film are examples. Most electrostatic processes are also dry. Compare with *wet process*.

dry silver film A nongelatin silver film which is developed by the application of heat. The film is used in some types of computer-output-microfilm recorders. Synonymous with thermally processed silver (TPS).

dual programming see *multiprogramming*

dual-spectrum In reprography, a two-stage dry-process copying method which uses ultraviolet light to produce the master and infrared light to produce subsequent generations.

dub 1. To transfer sound from one audiorecording or videorecording to another. 2. To record sound after the filming has been completed.

due date see *date due*

dull-coated paper A coated paper smooth enough to take fine halftones but having a minimum of surface gloss.

dumb terminal A terminal device with no capabilities of processing data before its transmission to a computer. Compare with *intelligent terminal.*

dummy 1. An unprinted, partially printed, or sketched sample of a projected publication to suggest the appearance of the completed work. Elements of the dummy may be used in a prospectus. 2. A piece of wood or some other material used to replace an item out of its regular shelf position, on which is placed a label identifying and indicating the location of the item. 3. A computer record used as a receptacle for certain types of data, or upon which certain types of actions can be performed without affecting other records.

dump In computer science, to copy the contents of a storage device onto another recording medium.

duo A roll microfilm format consisting of two rows of images running parallel to the sides of the film. Typically, the film is put through a rotary camera so that one-half of one side is exposed. The film is then reloaded in order to expose the other half. Documents of various size can be filmed in either cine or comic image orientation.

duodecimo see *book sizes*

duotone A halftone two-color process in which the copy is photographed twice with different exposures and a plate is made from each negative, one of which prints in black and the other in a color or in gray. The result is a monochromatic print with a full range of tones. Synonymous with two-color process. Compare with *doubledot halftone.*

duplex method In microphotography, a technique for filming both sides of a document simultaneously and positioning them as side-by-side images across the width of microfilm by means of mirrors inside the camera. The term is also used to describe the resulting double-row format or cameras capable of duplex photography.

duplex paper see *photographic paper*

duplex stock In reprography, material that has a different color or finish on each side.

duplex transmission Data transmission over a channel simultaneously and independently in both directions. Synonymous with full-duplex transmission and two-way simultaneous transmission. Compare with *half-duplex transmission, simplex transmission.*

duplicate 1. An additional copy of an item already in a library collection which is surplus to the library's needs. Compare with *added copy.* 2. In reprography, an exact copy of an original which can be used in the same way or in place of the original. The copy may be positive or negative and be made from either a film or print master, such as a contact copy. 3. In data processing, see *copy* (5). 4. To make single or multiple copies of an original.

duplicate card An aperture card in which a microfilm copy is mounted. Generally 35mm microfilm containing a single frame is used.

duplicate detection The determination, usually through a computerized routine, of the exis-

tence in the same catalog, authority file, etc., of records which are the same in substance but different in form, e.g., differing bibliographic records of the same bibliographic item and differing authority records of the same series.

duplicate entry The assignment of two subject headings to represent the same subject matter in order to bring out different aspects of it, e.g., "United States—Foreign relations—Great Britain," and "Great Britain—Foreign relations—United States." Synonymous with double entry.

duplicate exchange see *exchange* (1)

duplicate negative A negative image obtained from a negative original or from a positive original using a reversal process.

duplicate paging The duplicate numbering of pages, as is sometimes the case with books having parallel texts.

duplicating film A film used to make exact copies from a master. The film may be referred to as either image reversing or direct image (nonreversing). Image-reversing film changes polarity with every generation. Direct-image film maintains the master's polarity for each successive generation.

durable paper see *permanent-durable paper*

dust cover see *book jacket*

dust development see *xerography*

dust jacket see *book jacket*

dust wrapper see *book jacket*

Dutch corner see *library corner*

dye-back film see *antihalation*

dyeline process see *diazotype process*

dye transfer process see *gelatin transfer process*

dynamic range The ratio of dynamic extremes, given in decibels, between the lowest (quietest) part and the highest (loudest) part of a specific audio program.

E&G see *educational and general expenditures, exchange department*

early impression see *state* (2)

early sheets see *advance copies*

easy books Easy-to-read books, picture books, and picture storybooks within the interests and reading ability of children from preschool to third grade, frequently shelved in a separate section in the children's room of a library.

eau-forte see *etching* (1)

EBCDIC see *Extended Binary Coded Decimal Interchange Code*

EBR (electron-beam recorder) see *computer-output-microfilm recorder*

EBR film A special type of microfilm, sensitive to direct electron-beam energy, used in electron-beam recorders.

echo check A means of checking the accuracy of transmission over a channel by returning the received data for comparison with the original.

economy binding Any of a variety of inexpensive methods for binding library materials. Synonymous with budget binding.

edge fog The darkening of film or paper edges after developing due to excessive light, aging, improper storage, or any of several other adverse conditions.

edge-notched card A card with one or more of its edges notched or cut to represent coded data. Cards with the same coded data may be sorted by passing a rod or needle through the appropriate holes; those cards with notched holes will drop from the pack. Synonymous with margin-punched card.

edge-notched charging system A manual circulation system which utilizes edge-notched cards as the basis for maintaining the record of items charged. Typically the charge file is arranged by call number, with the date due notched in the card margin, permitting the sorting of overdues.

edge printing Letters, numbers, or other symbols on film outside the normal image area, generally obtained by exposure of a small portion of the film edge. They may identify the manufacturer, film quality, or other parameters. The edge may also be used as a code area for indexing the location of documents on roll microfilm. Editing symbols that aid in cutting and loading microfilm may also be placed on the edge, although these are normally large enough to be read with the unaided eye and appear at the beginning of the roll.

edges The three outer edges of the leaves of a book: the head, fore-edge or front edge, and foot or tail.

editing 1. In publishing, the practice of revising and preparing material for publication. Five editorial functions which may overlap or be combined are those of: acquisition editor, recommending works to the firm; manuscript editor, helping the author shape the work; copy editor, perfecting grammar and style; managing editor, coordinating resources and scheduling; and production editor, connecting editorial and production activities. 2. In data processing, modification of the format of data by its rearrangement or the addition or deletion of other data. 3. In audiotape production, the activity of selecting and rearranging recorded sounds into a new continuity. It may be done by rerecording from and mixing several sources or by cutting and splicing audiotape. (NCES) 4. In videotape production, the activity of selecting television sequences from videorecordings and arranging them in a continuous, orderly fashion. With videotape, editing is usually done electronically, by rerecording the selected portions onto another videotape. (NCES)

editing symbols see *edge printing*

edition 1. In the case of books and booklike materials, all those copies of a bibliographic item produced from substantially the same type image, whether by direct contact or by photographic methods. (AACR2) 2. In the case of nonbook materials, all the copies of a bibliographic item produced from one master copy and issued by a particular publishing agency or a group of such agencies. Provided the foregoing conditions are fulfilled, a change of the identity of the distributing body or bodies does not constitute a change of edition. (AACR2) 3. One of the various printings of a newspaper for the same day, an issue published less often, such as a weekly edition, or a special number devoted to a particular subject, such as an anniversary number. 4. In edition binding, all of the copies of a book or booklike materials produced and issued in uniform style.

edition area The part of a bibliographic description which pertains to the edition of the bibliographic item being cataloged.

edition bindery A bindery in which books are bound in quantity for publishers.

edition binding The binding in uniform style of a large number of copies of a bibliographic item. Speed and economy are primary concerns. Includes publisher's binding. Compare with *library binding*.

editions file A list of editions which a library plans to acquire.

editio princeps see *first edition*

editor 1. One who prepares for publication a bibliographic item containing a work or works not his or her own. The editorial labor may be limited to the preparation of the item for the manufacturer, or it may include supervision of the manufacturing, revision (restitution) or elucidation of the text, and the addition of an introduction, notes, and other critical matter. For certain items it may involve the technical direction of a staff of persons engaged in writing or compiling the text. Compare with *compiler* (1). (AACR2, mod.) 2. The administrator of an editorial department. 3. In computer science, a software routine which edits data or computer programs as they are input, during processing, or before output. Synonymous with edit routine.

editorial copies see *review copies*

edit routine see *editor* (3)

EDP see *electronic data processing*

EDP center see *data-processing center*

educational and general expenditures (E&G) That part of the total annual budget of a college or university expended on instruction, research, libraries, extension and public service, operation and maintenance of the physical plant, student services, general administration, and development, but excluding sponsored research and auxiliary enterprises such as student housing.

educational games see *games, educational*

educational media Audiovisual materials which have been designed and produced for instructional purposes.

educational technology A complex, integrated process involving people, procedures, ideas, devices and organization, for analyzing problems, and devising, implementing, evaluating and managing solutions to those problems, involved in all aspects of human learning. Compare with *instructional technology*. (AECT)

educational television (ETV) Any television programming, broadcast or closed circuit, designed to cover a broad range of educational and cultural subjects for information enrichment. Such programming may be used for instruction but is not always specifically designed to be instructional. A general term used in reference to noncommercial television operations. Public television, school television, and instructional television are classified as educational television. (NCES)

educational toy see *toy, educational*

education and job information center A public service unit in a public library system which provides job and career information and information and resources in support of adult continuing education. Synonymous with learners' advisory service, job information center, and career information center.

Edwards of Halifax binding A binding made of specially prepared transparent vellum with a painting or drawing on the underside (and thus protected from wear); the process was patented by the Halifax (and London) bookbinder, James Edwards, in 1785; Edwards of Halifax bindings frequently have fore-edge paintings.

eggshell-finish paper An uncoated book paper with a slightly smoother finish than antique-finish paper, so called because its surface resembles that of an eggshell.

eight-track An audiotape, usually an audiotape cartridge, with eight tracks recorded on it.

eight-up format A single frame of 35mm microfilm which contains images of eight standard-sized documents, normally 8½ x 11 inches.

electrofax see *electrostatic process*

electrographic process see *electrostatic process*

electron-beam recorder (EBR) see *computer-output-microfilm recorder*

electronic computer see *computer*

electronic data processing (EDP) Data processing using electronic equipment such as a digital computer.

electronic data-switching center see *automatic data-switching center*

electronic dictionary see *automatic dictionary*

electronic mail The sending and receiving of point-to-point or multipoint personalized messages, typically using a microcomputer and a cathode-ray-tube terminal with keyboard and printer. The output may be hard or soft copy.

electronic photoengraving machine A machine which produces metal or plastic halftone printing plates automatically by means of a cutting or burning stylus controlled by a scanning device with a photoelectric cell which traces the image to be reproduced.

electronic security system An electronic system installed at the exit of a library building or facility to detect items from the library collection being removed without loan authorization. The various commercial systems available entail an electrically charged device attached to or inserted in items which, when carried through a detection gate, trigger an alarm unless they have been desensitized in the charging process.

electrophotographic film A film base coated with a light-sensitive photoconductor, which retains its sensitivity through repeated exposures and which, through electrostatic processing, permits the updating of microfilm and microfiche by the addition of new microimages and the overprinting of superseded images.

electrophotographic process see *electrostatic process*

electrostatic copying see *electrostatic process*

electrostatic printer see *printer* (2)

electrostatic process In reprography, a process of document reproduction using static electricity and heat to form and fuse images on paper. The process involves the exposure of a source document on an electrically charged surface; the image area that remains charged attracts oppositely charged pigment particles, or toner, which are fused by heat to copy paper in the development of the latent image. The direct electrostatic process called electrofax forms images from a source document directly onto zinc oxide-coated copy paper. The transfer electrostatic process forms the images on a selenium-coated intermediary, from which the images are transferred to the copy paper. This process is often referred to as *xerography.* Synonymous with electrographic process and electrophotographic process.

electrotype plate A duplicate letterpress plate made by using electrolysis to deposit copper on the face of one or more pages of a metal relief-printing surface.

element see *data element*

elephant folio see *book sizes*

em A unit of linear measurement in printing, being equal, or nearly equal, to the point size of any font (or roughly the size of the uppercase letter M, which in early type fonts was cast on a square body).

emblem book A type of book in which designs or pictures called emblems, expressing some thought or moral idea, are printed with accompanying proverbs, mottoes, or explanatory writing, or in which verses are arranged in symbolic shapes such as crosses; especially common in the 17th century.

embossing The process of producing a relief design on a surface by the use of a sunken die and a raised counterpart, as on leather.

embroidered binding A binding in which embroidered cloth (often velvet) is used as the covering material. Synonymous with needlework binding.

empirical Pertaining to data or information obtained through experiment, experience, or observation, and which can be verified.

employee evaluation see *performance appraisal*

employee handbook see *staff handbook*

employee magazine see *house organ*

empty digit In classification, a digit of notation which has no subject meaning, but is used to separate other digits with subject meaning and show their interrelation.

em quad see *quad*

emulsion A suspension of light-sensitive chemicals, such as silver halide suspended in gelatin, used as coating on photographic film, paper, plates, or other base. Upon exposure, a latent image is formed in the emulsion.

en In printing, a unit of type measurement the same height, but half the width, of a corresponding em.

enamelled paper see *coated paper*

encapsulation The process whereby a flat document of paper or other fibrous writing material (such as papyrus) is held between two sheets of transparent plastic film by sealing around the edges, providing physical support against handling and storage hazards. The process is widely used for protecting large paper objects such as posters and maps, and it is increasingly used to protect smaller items; it is a quick, simple, and completely reversible process which has found wide acceptance among paper and other conservators.

encode To translate data into a code so that it can be recognized, accepted, and processed by a machine such as a computer.

encumbrance A sum of money charged against a fund in the budget to cover a purchase commitment. The encumbrance is removed when payment is made and payment becomes an expenditure.

encyclopedia A book or set of books containing informational articles on subjects in every field of knowledge, usually arranged in alphabetical order, or a similar work limited to a special field or subject. Synonymous with cyclopedia.

endleaves see *endpapers*

end matter see *back matter*

endnote see *note* (1)

endowment fund A fund or sum of money, received as a gift or bequest, which is invested by the recipient. The earnings or part of the earnings are expended, usually for a purpose designated by the donor, while the principal remains intact for future earnings.

endowment income Monies earned from the investment of an endowment fund.

end panel A panel covering a range end facing the aisle of a stack area. Constructed of wood, steel, or other appropriate material and frequently covered with vinyl or paint, it contributes to the aesthetics of the stack area. Compare with *range end*.

endpapers The leaves a binder adds to the front and end of a book to join the text block to the cover; also called endleaves and endsheets. Usually endpapers consist of a sheet folded to provide two or more leaves which are affixed to the text block. The leaf which is pasted to the inside of the cover or board is known variously as the paste-down endpaper, board paper, and lining paper. The leaf (or leaves) which remains free is the free endpaper, sometimes incorrectly called a flyleaf. Endpapers may be blank, decorated, or printed.

endsheets see *endpapers*

end support see *bookend*

engineering drawing see *technical drawing*

English Braille, American Edition see *Standard English Braille*

English-finish paper 1. In general, all smooth-finished, uncoated book papers. 2. More specifically, an uncoated book paper with a finish between machine-finish and supercalendered, and low in gloss.

engraved title page A decorated title page, printed from an engraved plate, facing the title page in letterpress type; popular in the 17th century.

engraver's proof A proof taken from an engraved plate or block, or a lithographic stone, used for checking the quality of the work and for making up in pages. Synonymous with trial proof.

engraving 1. An intaglio process in which the image to be printed is cut into a metal plate, block of wood, or other surface. Compare with *photoengraving* (1). 2. A print so produced. According to the material engraved, a copper, steel, or wood engraving.

enlargement The print or copy produced as a result of enlarging a film negative or positive or an original (a source document or intermediate copy). Although an image produced on a microform reader is also an enlargement, the term usually refers to a hard copy. Synonymous with blowup and blowback.

enlargement ratio A measure of the scale of enlargement of photographs or microimages, expressed as 18X, 23X, etc. It is the ratio of the enlarged image to the original image, expressed in diameters. Compare with *reduction ratio*.

enlarger see *projection printer*

enlarger-printer An optical device containing a lens system which enlarges a film positive or negative or an original and can also produce an enlarged copy of it. Normally the original is a microimage.

enlarger-reducer see *image modifier*

enlarging The process of producing an enlargement.

enlarging-reducing machine see *image modifier*

en quad see *quad*

enriched keyword index An automatic index, prepared by computer selection of keywords, which has been checked and augmented by a human indexer. Synonymous with augmented keyword index and machine-aided index.

entity see *attribute*

entrance-level position A position at the first grade of a position classification, designated for an individual without previous experience. Promotion to a higher grade or classification is usually dependent upon vacancies, rather than on the evolvement of the entrance-level position into a higher level one.

entry 1. An access point to a bibliographic record, under which the record may be searched and identified. 2. A record of an item in a catalog. (AACR2)

entry-a-line index An index in which each entry is brief enough to be printed on one line.

entry point In the execution of a computer program, a location or point in a routine to which control can be transferred by another routine.

entry word The word by which an entry is primarily arranged in a catalog or searched in a bibliographic database, usually the first word (other than an article) of the heading. Synonymous with filing word. (AACR2, mod.)

enumerative bibliography The listing of books, etc., according to some system or reference plan, e.g., by author, subject, or date. The implication is that the listings will be short; enumerative bibliography (sometimes called systematic bibliography) attempts to record and list, rather than to describe minutely. A library's catalog is an example of enumerative bibliography, as is the list at the back of a book of works consulted. Compare with *analytical bibliography*.

enumerative classification A classification system with each subject developed to an indivisible species and with a notation for every term from the most general to the most minute. Compare with *analytico-synthetic classification*.

enumerative notation see *fenced notation*

ephemera 1. Materials of transitory interest and value, consisting generally of pamphlets or clippings, which are usually kept for a limited time in vertical files. 2. Similar materials of the past which have acquired literary or historical significance.

epigraph A motto or brief quotation prefixed to a book or a chapter, intended to indicate an idea to be developed in the text that follows.

epitome 1. A written work containing the essence of a subject, characterized by extreme brevity. Sometimes used synonymously with *digest* (1), *compendium* (2), and *synopsis*. 2. A statement of the main points of a written work, characterized by extreme brevity and accuracy, often prepared by someone other than the author of the original. Sometimes used synonymously with *compendium* (2).

equipment Items of a nonexpendable nature which retain their basic identity and utility over a period of time. For budgeting and accounting purposes equipment is sometimes further defined to designate items costing more than a certain amount. Compare with *supplies*.

erase 1. To remove data from a storage device, a recording medium such as magnetic disk or magnetic tape, or cathode-ray-tube screen, without leaving a form of data representation. Synonymous with *clear*. Compare with *delete*. 2. To remove the audio and/or video signal from magnetic tape by passing the tape next to an erase head or by recording over previously recorded signals.

erase head see *head* (5)

erotica Works with strong sexual overtones, and with some claim to artistic integrity. Compare with *pornography*.

errata A list of errors discovered after the printing of a book, number of a periodical, etc., and their corrections, printed separately and tipped in, or printed on a spare page or part of a page. Synonymous with corrigenda. Compare with *paste-in*.

error A discrepancy between results obtained from a computation, measurement, or observation and a true or correct value.

error of grouping In statistics, an error introduced when it is assumed that all values within a group are located at the midpoint of that group.

error of sampling see *sampling error*

escalator clause Provision within a contract which allows the payments to increase or decrease in correlation with agreed-upon factors, such as the adjustment of rent up or down in correlation with the Cost of Living Index.

escape character In data processing, a special character which must precede any character or group of characters which are to be interpreted differently from a code being used at the moment.

esparto paper Paper made from the pulp of esparto grass mixed with chemical wood pulp. Although the fibers are short, they provide a uniform finish, fine texture, and bulk considered suitable for better grades of book paper.

essay periodical Popular in the 18th century, a periodical consisting usually of a single essay; well-known examples are *The Spectator* and *The Rambler*.

estray The legal term applied to a record not in the custody of the original records creator or its legal successor.

etching 1. An intaglio process in which the design to be printed is chemically (rather than physically) incised by the action of acid on a metal plate. The areas to be etched are controlled by the removal of an acid-resistant surface on the plate. The artist may do this by hand with a needle. In photogravure, the printing and nonprinting areas are controlled photomechanically. Also known by its French name, eau-forte. 2. A print produced by this process.

ethnic number A symbol in the notation of a classification system to indicate a racial, ethnic, or national group.

ETV see *educational television*

evaluation of employees see *performance appraisal*

evolutionary order In classification, the arrangement of subjects in their presumed order of creation or development.

exchange 1. The arrangement by which a library sends to another library its own publications, or those of the institution with which it is connected, such as a university, and receives in return publications from the other library; or sends duplicates from its collection to another library and receives other materials in return. Also called, respectively, publication exchange and duplicate exchange. 2. A publication given or received through this arrangement. 3. A data-switching center or a defined geographical area served by a communications common carrier.

exchange department The administrative unit of a library that handles exchanges; may also have the responsibility for acquiring library materials through gift, in which case the unit may be designated exchange and gift (E&G) or gift and exchange (G&E) department.

exchange format see *communication format*

exchange of librarians A formal arrangement by which two libraries, or administrative units within a library system, lend to each other simultaneously one or more staff members for a specified period. Synonymous with interchange of librarians.

exciter lamp   The device which scans the optical sound track of films, activating the photoelectric cell of motion picture projectors.

execute   In computer science, to interpret and carry out a computer instruction.

executive   A person with total or shared responsibility for the overall direction and effectiveness of an organization. In a library agency, the term applies to the head librarian or director and a few upper-level personnel.

executive program (computer science) see *operating system*

exempt employee   Any employee in a bona fide executive, administrative, or professional position, whose conditions of employment and compensation are not subject to the provisions of the U.S. Fair Labor Standards Act of 1938 as amended. Exempt employees are not eligible for overtime payment.

exhibition case   A glass-enclosed cabinet, either built into or against a wall, or free standing, in which selected books, manuscripts, artifacts, or other items are placed for display. It is usually lighted and secured to protect the contents.

exit   In computer science, a way of leaving or the act of leaving a sequence of operations or a computer program.

exit interview   An interview with an employee at the time of separation from the organization by the personnel officer or other designated official to determine such information as reason for leaving, attitude toward the organization, and opinions on various aspects of the employment experience. Its aim is to monitor the perceptions of employees regarding the organization and to determine the need for future corrective actions on the part of the employing organization.

ex-library copy   The term used by a dealer to indicate that a book was once owned by a library and therefore shows signs of wear and damage.

ex libris   1. "From the books of," a Latin phrase preceding the owner's name on a bookplate; hence, a bookplate. 2. In the antiquarian trade, books from a subscription or other library, usually with marks of ownership and use, and implying less than desirable physical condition.

expansibility   The ability of the notation of a classification system to accommodate the insertion of any new class or part of a class without dislocating the sequence of the system.

Expansive Classification   A classification system devised by Charles Ammi Cutter in 1891. The system provided seven expansions, the first listing only broad classes and the seventh providing very detailed subdivision, suitable for close classification in a large library.

experimental group   In experimental research, the collection of subjects that receive an experimental treatment and will be compared to the control group.

experimental research   A type of research in which two groups of subjects are studied, a control group and an experimental group, to determine the changes or effects when members of the experimental group are manipulated in a controlled manner, i.e., undergo an experimental treatment.

explanatory guide card   A guide card placed at the beginning of a group of cards in a file to explain the arrangement of cards within the group.

explanatory reference   An elaborated "see" or "see also" reference that explains the circumstances under which the headings involved should be consulted, such as a reference defining the scope of a heading, referring from the name of a corporate body to earlier and/or later headings used for the body, or referring to the multiple headings used for one series of meetings. Compare with *general reference*. (AACR2, mod.)

explicit   A statement at the end of the text of a manuscript or early printed book, or at the end of one of its divisions, indicating its conclusion and sometimes giving the author's name and the title of the work. (AACR2)

exposed joint   The cloth joint made by joining the paste-down endpaper to the free endpaper with fabric glued to the surface of the endpapers. Synonymous with visible joint. Compare with *concealed joint*.

exposition phase   In classification, the phase relationship occurring in a work in which one subject is expounded through the techniques of another subject.

exposure 1. The process of submitting light-sensitive materials to a light source for a predetermined time period in order to produce a latent image. The latent image is subsequently made visible by developing. Exposure time, frequently measured in fractions of a second, is a function of film speed and intensity of light. Exposure tolerance is the time range during which the material can be exposed without significant loss of detail. An exposure meter (or light meter) is used to measure the intensity of light falling on or reflected from the subject with a light-sensitive photoelectric cell in order to arrive at a desirable camera setting before exposure. 2. A section of film which has been subjected to a light source.

exposure meter see *exposure* (1)

exposure time see *exposure* (1)

exposure tolerance see *exposure* (1)

expressive notation A notation which displays the basic structure of the classification system it accompanies. It reveals the hierarchy of the system in the sense that notations of similar length and structure indicate subjects that are equal in rank.

expurgated edition Said of an edition from which objectionable parts in the original text have been deleted, usually on moral grounds. Synonymous with bowdlerized edition.

Extended Binary Coded Decimal Interchange Code (EBCDIC) A coding scheme in which characters of data are represented as unique patterns of eight binary digits or bits, in a special version of the binary coded decimal code.

extension In classification, the whole range of things to which a term is applicable. Compare with *intension.*

extension card see *continuation card*

extension center library A library branch located in an extension center of an institution of postsecondary education which provides a collection and limited library services in support of the classes or other extension services offered at the center.

extension library service 1. The provision by a library of materials and services (including advisory services) to individuals and organizations outside its regular service area, especially to an area in which library service is not otherwise available. 2. The provision of library materials and services to individuals and agencies outside the campus by an academic library, frequently in support of the parent institution's off-campus instructional programs.

external storage Data storage which is not immediately accessible, but which can be made accessible when needed, by a computer.

extra binding In binding, a trade term for the best work; the binding of books with more than ordinary care and handling, and/or with a higher quality of material, usually with ornamentation, marbled, or other decorated endpapers, etc.

extraction indexing see *derived indexing*

extra-illustrated Said of a volume illustrated by the insertion of engravings, pictures, variant title pages, etc., which were not part of the volume as issued. This additional matter, though often from other books, may consist of original drawings, manuscripts, etc. Synonymous with privately illustrated and grangerized (a term derived from the vogue begun by the publication, in 1769, of James Granger's *Biographical History of England,* which had pages left blank for the insertion of engraved portraits).

extramural loan The loan of library materials to individuals or organizations outside the normal constituency of a library.

extrapolation In statistics, the process of estimating the value of a variable beyond its observed or known range.

face 1. The entire unbroken front of shelving on the one side of single-faced shelving, or on each of the sides of double-faced shelving. 2. In printing, see *typeface.*

facet 1. In classification, the set of subclasses produced when a subject is divided by a single characteristic. 2. Any of a number of aspects of a subject.

facet analysis In classification, the analysis of a subject to determine its fundamental characteristics. A basic step in constructing a faceted classification.

faceted classification A classification system based on the analysis of subjects according to a group of fundamental concepts or facets, such as those proposed by S. R. Ranganathan in his *Colon Classification*—personality, matter, energy, space, time.

faceted notation In classification, a notation which uses facet indicators.

facet formula see *citation order*

facetiae 1. Witty sayings or writings. 2. Literary works distinguished by coarse and obscene wit.

facet indicator In classification, a symbol which occurs as part of a notation and indicates which facet is to follow. Compare with *fence*.

facilities A library building or the part of a building in which the library is housed and its equipment. Compare with *plant*.

facsimile catalog A catalog which incorporates reproductions of slides, pictures, designs, etc., as part of the catalog entry for each.

facsimile edition In the case of books and booklike materials, an exact reproduction of a bibliographic item, usually by a photomechanical process. Compare with *type-facsimile*.

facsimile reprint see *type-facsimile*

facsimile reproduction In the case of books and booklike materials, a reproduction of a bibliographic item that has as its chief purpose to simulate the physical appearance of the original document(s) as well as to provide an exact replica of the text. The facsimile need not reproduce the size of the original. Includes *facsimile editions* and *type-facsimiles*.

facsimile transmission The electrical transmission over a channel of a facsimile of graphic matter, such as a printed work, from one point or location to another.

factor analysis In statistics, a technique for analyzing or studying the interconnection among many variables.

faculty status An official recognition by an institution of postsecondary education that librarians are part of the instructional and research staff by conferment of ranks and titles identical to those of faculty, and commensurate benefits, privileges, rights, and responsibilities. Compare with *academic status*.

fading In reprography, loss in density of images over a period of time on exposed and processed photographic materials.

fair employment practices The application of all personnel policies, such as employment, compensation, and promotion, on the basis of individual merit rather than on categorical bases such as race, sex, religion, and national origin.

fair use Conditions under which copying is not an infringement of U.S. copyright (PL 94–553, Sec. 107), which permits copying for purposes such as criticism, comment, news, reporting, teaching (including multiple copies for classroom use), scholarship, or research. Though not specifically defined, fair use must meet several criteria: the use should not impair the value of the copyright by reducing demand for the original; the copier should not have used the copyright owner's efforts as a substitute for his or her own intellectual labor; the use should be "fair" as a reasonable person would view it, not unjust or damaging to the original.

fairy tale 1. A traditional, fanciful story that commonly contains a supernatural element affecting human beings, animals, and inanimate objects. 2. A modern story of known authorship having similar characteristics.

fall-out ratio In information retrieval, the ratio of the number of irrelevant documents retrieved to the total number of irrelevant documents in a file.

false code see *illegal character*

false combination In information retrieval, an irrelevant reference produced when descriptors are combined in a postcoordinate indexing system. Synonymous with false sort and false drop.

false drop see *false combination*

false first edition   An edition called first edition by the publisher when there has been a previous edition issued by another firm.

false imprint   see *fictitious imprint*

false link   In classification, the meaningless entry which is produced in a chain index when the notational chain has been lengthened by a symbol (such as a zero introducing a standard subdivision) which does not have an appropriate verbal term.

false sort   see *false combination*

fan adhesive binding   A method of adhesive binding used in library binding. After the back edges of the book have been trimmed, they are fanned to allow the application of a thin strip of adhesive to the back margin. When the back edges are fanned first on one side and then the other for the application of adhesive, the method is called double-fan adhesive. Thus each leaf is joined to the ones on either side of it. Should be distinguished from *perfect binding* used in edition binding, in which adhesive is applied to the back edge rather than the back margin.

fanfare binding   A style originally of 16th-century Parisian binding with interlaced ribbons, defined by a double line on one side and a single one on the other, which divide the cover into symmetrical compartments (which may or may not be filled with gold tooling) of varying sizes.

Farmington Plan   A cooperative acquisition plan, undertaken by a group of major university and research libraries in the United States in an attempt to ensure that every book or pamphlet of research value from every country would be available in some library in the United States. Collection responsibilities were divided by subject and geographical area. The plan, drawn up at Farmington, Connecticut, was operative from 1948 until the end of 1972.

fascicle   One of the temporary divisions of a bibliographic item that, for convenience in printing or publication, is issued in small installments, usually incomplete in themselves; they do not necessarily coincide with any formal division of the item into parts, etc. Usually the fascicle is protected by temporary paper wrappers and may or may not be numbered. A fascicle is distinguished from a *part* (1) by being a temporary division of an item rather than a formal component unit. (AACR2, mod.)

fast   1. Having a high photographic sensitivity. 2. Said of paper or a film base which has been made resistant, by special treatment, to changes caused by light, acid, alkali, heat, etc.

fat-faced type   see *fatface type*

fatface type   A bold display type combining hairlines and exaggeratedly thick strokes. Synonymous with fat-faced type.

favored category   A class given prominence in a classification system because of local needs or interests. A class may be favored because it represents the strength or the subject specialization of the collection. Synonymous with favored focus.

favored focus   see *favored category*

fax   Colloquially, the product of facsimile transmission or the facsimile transmission system.

F-distribution   A sampling distribution derived from the ratios of the variances of samples drawn from two normally distributed populations with the same variance. It is used for comparing the homogeneity of the variances, or (in analysis of variance) for testing the quality of the means of two or more sets of observations. So called for its formulator, Sir Ronald Fisher. Like the t- and chi-square distributions, the shape of the F-distribution is dependent upon the number of degrees of freedom. Synonymous with variance-ratio distribution.

feasibility study   A systematic and objective examination of a possible course of action designed to determine its cost, practicality, and consequences.

feather edge   see *deckle edge*

featherweight paper   Very light, porous, bulky paper, usually made from esparto.

featuring   In a classified catalog, the verbal translation, immediately following each class number, of the digit of greatest intension in the number.

federated system   A library system formed by joining action of governing bodies, but in which existing libraries continue to be governed by local boards; the central administration of the system coordinates and advises on cooperative services.

fee card see *nonresident's card*

feedback Output from a system or machine returned to control or correct future input.

feeder Equipment designed for guiding documents of a similar size into the exposure area of a camera, such as bank checks in a rotary camera. The term is sometimes also used to describe the mechanical devices on a card punch which move the cards from one location to another.

feltboard A visual display board for letters or simple shapes. Pieces stick to this board when applied to the felt surface. Synonymous with cloth board, flannel board, and hook and loop board.

felt side see *wire side*

fence In faceted classification, the symbol in a notation which separates facets without indicating the type of facet which will follow. Compare with *facet indicator*.

fenced notation In faceted classification, a style of notation which uses a fence to separate one facet from another. Synonymous with enumerative notation.

fere-humanistica A group of typefaces based on the formal book hand used by the earlier Italian humanists for scholastic works. Of the gothic or black-letter types, it most closely resembles early roman forms. Synonymous with gotico-antiqua.

ferric oxide tape A magnetic tape whose coating is made of Fe_2O_3, a dark-red, crystalline, water-insoluble solid. Since ferric oxide occurs naturally as rust, audiotape and videotape recorders which use this common brand of tape should be cleaned regularly.

ferroprussiate process see *blueprint process*

ferrotype see *glossy print*

ferrotype plate A highly polished plate, frequently chromium plate on copper, used to produce glossy prints.

festschrift A complimentary or memorial publication in the form of a collection of essays, addresses, or biographical, bibliographical, scientific, or other contributions, often embodying the results of research, issued in honor of a person, an institution, or a society, usually on the occasion of an anniversary celebration.

fiche see *microfiche*

fictitious imprint An imaginary imprint used for the purpose of evading legal or other restrictions, to mask a pirated edition, to protect anonymity of the author, etc. Synonymous with false imprint and spurious imprint.

field 1. In computer science, a defined subdivision of a record used to record only a specific category of data or a data element. 2. A column or group of columns on a tabcard allocated for punching or otherwise entering a specific category of data. 3. In cataloging, an element or group of elements (an area) in a bibliographic record.

field length The physical length of a data field, expressed usually as a specified number of characters, card columns, or binary digits.

field lens A lens placed near the focal plane of an optical system to provide a larger view of the image or an image of more uniform brightness.

field terminator In computer science, a special character or delimiter designating the end of a variable-length field. Compare with *delimiter*.

field visit A direct, personal contact by a librarian or library consultant with a library agency, individual, group, organization, institution, or government body in the interest of stimulation, administration, or development of better library service. Synonymous with site visit.

figure In letterpress printing, an illustration printed from a cut locked into the chase along with the metal type, as an integral part of a page.

file 1. A collection of related records treated as a unit and organized or arranged in a specific sequence to facilitate their storage and retrieval. In computer science, synonymous with data set. 2. A group of library materials kept together for certain reasons or purposes, e.g., a group of extra large books in a file called oversize. 3. In archives, a homogeneous collection of records or other documents maintained according to a predetermined physical arrangement. Used primarily in describing current records, the term may refer either to a record series or to a file unit such as a folder or dossier.

file conversion The transfer of all or a part of records in a file from one medium to another, usually from a non-machine-readable to a machine-readable form. Compare with *data conversion*.

file integrity A term used in records management to mean that all relevant records are in their proper physical location. File integrity is lost when records are misfiled.

file key In computer science, a character or characters used to identify, locate, control, or retrieve a record in a file. Compare with *search key*.

file maintenance The process of adding, changing, or deleting data in a file.

files administration In archives, the application of records management techniques to filing practices, in order to maintain records properly and to retrieve them easily, and to ensure their completeness and the disposition of noncurrent records.

file search see *search*

file unit In archives, a body of related records within a record series, such as a dossier.

filing code The set of rules used to arrange bibliographic records in a catalog. Synonymous with filing rules.

filing element A word or character that affects or is used in filing. Compare with *nonfiling element*.

filing indicator A character added to a machine-readable bibliographic record to control the filing order of data in a field, such as a character indicating the suppression of the initial article of a title in filing.

filing order The order in which bibliographic items or their bibliographic records are arranged on a shelf or in a file.

filing medium The word, name, phrase, or other symbol which determines the filing order of a bibliographic item or bibliographic record.

filing position Any position in an access point that would affect filing order in a machine-readable bibliographic database.

filing rules see *filing code*

filing title see *uniform title* (2)

filing word see *entry word*

filler The blank leaves added at the end of a thin pamphlet to produce a sizable volume when bound. Synonymous with padding.

fillet 1. A line or band impressed on the sides of a book cover. 2. The wheel-shaped tool used when heated to impress these lines, either in blind or gilt. Compare with *roll* (2).

filling The addition of clay or other white pigments during the manufacture of paper in order to improve appearance and receptivity to ink. When the filler is calcium carbonate, an alkaline buffer is provided. Synonymous with loading.

film 1. A thin sheet or strip of transparent or translucent material coated with a light-sensitive emulsion. The base is usually a plastic material such as cellulose acetate. 2. A term synonymous with both educational and commercial motion pictures which are produced in 8, 16, 35, and 70mm widths.

film advance 1. The apparatus which positions film for exposure or projection. The portion of film moved after exposure or projection is referred to as pull-down. Some techniques of roll microfilm indexing rely on film pull-down to drive odometers on microfilm readers. 2. In printing, see *leading*.

film base The layer of photographic film which supports the emulsion. Film base normally consists of a plastic material, such as cellulose acetate.

film base density A measure of the degree of opacity of a film base. The measure does not include density produced by other layers such as the emulsion, subbing, or protective layers added to prevent scratching.

film bow see *bow*

film can A plastic or metal can designed to hold a reel of film.

film cartridge A cartridge containing a motion picture spliced in a continuous loop. Compare with *filmloop*.

film cassette see *cassette*

film chip see *chip* (2)

film core see *core*

film curl see *curl*

film drying see *drying*

film edition   An edition of a printed bibliographic item on film, published simultaneously with, after, or in place of an edition in printed form. Synonymous with film issue.

film facsimile   A photographic facsimile on film. The term is sometimes used with reference to facsimile transmission of graphic matter in microform.

film frame see *frame* (3)

film gate   The device in a projector, camera, printer, or reader that holds the film in position and momentarily still as light is transmitted to it or through it during projection or exposure.

film insert   Unitized microfilm, used primarily for insertion into a film jacket, or for stripping up a master microfiche.

film issue see *film edition*

film jacket   A transparent plastic sleeve into which individual frames or strips of microfilm may be inserted. Film that has been stored in this manner is referred to as jacketed film. The jacket may be notched in order to facilitate the insertion of the film. Ribs between the plastic sheets form multiple sleeves, allowing the storage of several strips. Jackets can be used on aperture cards or on sheets the size of microfiche.

film jacket rib see *film jacket*

film jacket set   Said of film jackets that assume a curved shape due to improper storage or aging.

film library   1. A collection of 8, 16, 35, or 70mm motion-picture films available for loan. Some film libraries charge rental fees for use of the collection, while others are free to a special group of users. 2. A collection or reproductions of printed or manuscript materials on microfilm.

filmloop   A motion picture spliced into a continuous loop for playing without rewinding. When the film is sealed in a cartridge, the film and the cartridge containing it are called a *film cartridge.*

film measure indexing   For roll microfilm, any method of indexing that is based on the linear distance of film travel to determine the approximate location of an image, such as an odometer reading.

film mottle   Spots, blotches, and uneven density on processed film. Film mottle can be a result of a defective emulsion, poor processing techniques, or improper storage.

film plane   The surface (plane) occupied by an image on photographic film. Synonymous with image plane.

film processing   The activity of subjecting exposed photographic film to a special process or treatment in order to develop and stabilize the images which have been recorded on it and prepare it for end use. Several conventional processing methods, including both wet and dry processes, are used.

film projector see *projector*

film reconditioning see *conditioning* (2)

film reel   A reel holding motion-picture film.

filmsetting see *photosetting*

film size   The width of a film, usually expressed in millimeters (e.g., 8, 16, 35, and 70mm). The larger sizes (35 and 70mm) are used for commercial motion pictures, while the smaller sizes are used by educational institutions and home moviemakers. For microfilm, 16 and 35mm are generally used.

filmslip   A short filmstrip not on a roll and usually in a rigid holder.

film speed see *sensitivity*

film splice see *splice*

film stability   A term which refers to the shelf life of film or relative resistance to physical deformation such as stretching or contraction. The term includes resistance to image fading in processed films.

film strip see *microstrip*

filmstrip   A length of film that represents a sequence of related still pictures for projection one at a time. Most filmstrips are on 35mm film, but some are 16mm or smaller. A filmstrip is single frame if the horizontal axis of the pictures is perpendicular to the sprocket holes; it is double frame if the pictures are twice the size of the single frame and their horizontal axis is parallel to the sprocket holes. It may or may not have provision for sound accompaniment.

A silent filmstrip is one without an accompanying audiorecording but is usually accompanied by a script or captions are printed on the frames.

A sound filmstrip is accompanied by a separate audiorecording which may also have a signal for the filmstrip to be advanced as well as a sound track related to the filmstrip. (NCES)

filmstrip projector A device designed to project filmstrips, normally a single frame. Sound filmstrip projectors are available for playing accompanying audiorecordings. Some models have automatic advance mechanisms keyed to the audiorecording.

filmstrip/slide projector A filmstrip projector (usually silent) equipped with an adapter or carrier for projecting 2-x-2-inch slides. (NCES)

filmstrip viewer A device equipped with a built-in viewing glass or rear projection screen for viewing filmstrips, usually single frame. Models are available with provision for playing audiorecordings. Some models have automatic advance mechanisms keyed to the audiorecording.

film viewer A small optical device for viewing or editing film. The term is sometimes used for a more specific device called a *hand viewer*.

film washing see *washing*

film weld see *splice*

filter In photography, a piece of optical glass or other colored transparent material designed to selectively transmit radiation through a lens to the film.

filtering technique The process of selecting the amount of input into an information retrieval system in order to avoid or minimize its overloading.

financial report A report on the financial position of an organization, giving income received and expenditures made, with balances of budget accounts and explanatory remarks, for the period covered.

finding aids In archives, documents which provide direction to information contained in other documents. Basic finding aids include guides (general or subject), inventories, local registers, card catalogs and files, shelf and box lists, indexes of various kinds, calendars, and (for machine-readable records) software documentation.

finding list A list of items in a library collection with very brief entries, usually indicating only author, title, and location.

fine A penalty assessed borrowers for keeping library materials after they are due, usually based upon a fixed charge per day.

fine-grain see *grain* (2)

finish (paper) see *paper finishes*

finishing In binding, the processes of making, attaching, lettering, and decorating the cover or case, unless the covers are attached before being decorated, in which instance it includes only lettering and decorating.

firm borrower's card see *business firm borrower's card*

firm order An order placed with a dealer specifying a time limit for delivery and a price which must not be exceeded without the customer's prior approval.

firmware The use of a combination of both hardware and software to control the operations of a computer. Compare with *microcode.*

first edition The edition of a bibliographic item that is printed first. The terms editio princeps, princeps edition, and princeps are generally used as synonyms, but are reserved by some bibliographers for the first printed editions of ancient authors.

first-generation image The picture or first reproduction of an object or document. A copy made from the first-generation image is termed a second-generation image, etc. Normally, the term refers to images reproduced on film.

first-generation microfilm see *camera microfilm*

first-line index An index to poetry, songs, or hymns, with entry under first line only.

first-line supervisor A supervisor at the bottom tier of an organizational hierarchy.

first published edition Said of a bibliographic item previously released for restricted distribution, but now offered for sale to the public.

first reproduction microfilm The first copy of a document made from camera microfilm, thus a second-generation copy. Synonymous with second generation microfilm.

fiscal control The process of regulating the activities of an organization in accordance with its actual income or the established budget. Compare with *budgetary control.*

fiscal period A specified accounting period, usually 12 months, at the end of which the financial condition of an organization is determined by comparing income against expenditures.

fiscal year A 12-month accounting period based upon the established budget of the organization. With many governmental and educational agencies, the fiscal year begins on the first day of a month other than January.

fist see *index* (2)

five predicables see *predicables, five*

fix see *fixing*

fixed charges A regularly recurring and unavoidable expense, such as rent, depreciation, and insurance.

fixed costs Indirect costs that stay constant regardless of the level of activity or production, such as rent, payments on construction bonds, and interest.

fixed field In data processing, a field of fixed length that has been reserved or allocated to a specific category of data to be entered in a record. Compare with *free field, variable field.*

fixed focus Said of photographic instruments and microform readers that have a preset focus arrangement, with no provision for varying the focus.

fixed-length record In data processing, a record whose length is limited to a defined number of characters. Compare with *variable-length record.*

fixed location A method of arranging library materials. Each item is assigned a definite storage location and is given a mark to indicate that location. Synonymous with absolute location. Compare with *relative location, sequential location.*

fixed shelving Shelving in which the position of shelves is permanently fixed by attachment to the stack upright or vertical standard of a bookcase. Compare with *adjustable shelving.*

fixed storage see *read-only storage*

fixer A solution used for fixing the image that has been developed on a film negative or print, usually containing a hypo, a hardener, and an acid or acid salt.

fixing 1. In photographic processing, the removal of undeveloped silver halide from the film or photographic paper. Through the use of a fixer, light-sensitive crystals are dissolved in water and washed away. This permanently fixes the image on the film negative or print and prevents further reaction with light. 2. In the electrostatic process, the bonding of toner to the copy paper by heating.

flag 1. In computer science, a special character used to indicate the occurrence of a specified condition. Compare with *tag.* 2. The title of a newspaper displayed on the front page.

flange see *ridge*

flannel board see *feltboard*

flap 1. Either of the two turned-over ends of a book jacket, on which the blurb or other flap copy is printed. 2. The projecting, bent-over edge of a limp cover of a book, such as *divinity circuit.*

flare Undesirable extraneous light which reaches photographic film during exposure. It is a non-image-forming light which generally lowers the contrast of the desired image by fogging the film. Flare can be caused by reflection of light from dirty or scratched lenses or defective equipment.

flash card A small card containing an image (words, numbers, pictures, etc.) designed to be displayed briefly for drill, recognition training, or in a teaching presentation.

flash index On roll microfilm, a target which facilitates the rapid location of subfields within a document or set of documents. Generally, a readily recognizable image, which does not require magnification to read, is filmed in predetermined locations and serves as a means of block indexing. The image can be quickly recognized as the film frames "flash" by in a viewing device or during manual inspection. Synonymous with flash target.

flash target see *flash index*

flat back In binding, a back which has not been rounded and which is, therefore, at right angles to the front and back covers.

flat-bed camera see *planetary camera*

flat-color printing see *multicolor printing*

flatness of field The property of an optical lens which permits it to focus an image over the entire focal plane, or the extent to which a focal plane is perpendicular to the axis of a lens.

flat organization A formal organizational structure in which supervisors at each level of the hierarchy have a relatively large number of subordinates reporting to them, or a wide span of control. Compare with *tall organization.*

flat paper conservator see *paper conservator*

flats Two pieces of matched optical glass for holding film flat during projection or viewing, as in a microfilm reader. Synonymous with optical flats.

flat sewing or **stitching** see *side stitching*

fleuron see *flower* (1)

flexbinding see *flexible binding*

flexible binding 1. In binding, any cover made with boards that are flexible, not stiff. 2. Any binding that permits the book to open perfectly flat. Synonymous with flexbinding.

flexible budget see *variable budget*

flexible notation In classification, a notation which has the expansibility to allow new subjects to be inserted and at the same time maintain the logical sequence of the notation and the classification schedule.

flexography A rotary letterpress printing process using flexible rubber or photopolymer plastic plates with a raised printing surface wrapped around a cylinder and quick-drying, liquid ink.

flip Exchanging one heading for another in a catalog, usually in response to a change in cataloging rules, by automated means, often through appropriately coded authority records or through a specially constructed computer program. Compare with *global change.*

flipchart A set of graphic representations hinged together so they can be flipped over during a presentation.

flip-flop A small electrical or electronic device or circuit which can assume either of two possible states at a given time.

floor case A free-standing, double-faced case of varying height.

floor duty A work assignment away from a public service desk to assist users in selecting materials or in finding particular items desired.

floor model reader see *microform reader*

floor space see *assignable space*

floppy disk see *diskette*

floret see *flower* (1)

flow camera see *rotary camera*

flowchart A diagram using predefined and standardized symbols to show step-by-step progression of the flow of work or data through a complicated operational procedure or system.

flower 1. In printing, a type ornament originally shaped like a leaf or flower, used for decoration, as in a page border. Now any small ornament without a border line or frame. Synonymous with floret, printer's flower, and fleuron. 2. A leaf-shaped flower ornament used on bindings.

flush Said of type aligned along a side margin, without indention.

flush boards see *cut flush*

flutter Distortion, usually mechanical, in the form of a rapid wavering of pitch.

flyleaves Blank leaves inserted by the binder which are in addition to the endpapers and which are not conjugate with any leaf of the text block. Synonymous with binder's leaves.

fly title A term sometimes used synonymously with *half title* (1) and *divisional title* (2).

FM see *frequency modulation*

f-number The ratio of the focal length of a camera lens to the aperture. Simple cameras have a fixed f-number, but more sophisticated cameras can vary the f-number to suit the characteristics of the film, the light source, and the exposure time. An exposure meter can provide a suitable range of f-numbers. Compare with *f-stop*.

focal length The distance between the optical center of a lens and the focal plane when the lens is focused at infinite distance. Focal length is usually specified in millimeters.

focal plane The surface (plane) occupied by film in a camera, on which a sharp image is formed by the lens. The plane is normally perpendicular to the axis of the lens.

focal-plane shutter A shutter usually found in the single-lens reflex camera which is situated directly in front of the film.

focal point A point on the focal plane at which converging rays of light form the sharpest image.

focus 1. In photography, to adjust a camera lens so as to produce the sharpest possible image on the focal plane. The lens-to-object distance is converted to the appropriate lens-to-image distance through the use of a calibrated focusing scale found on most adjustable lenses. 2. In synthetic classification, one of the subclasses produced when a facet is divided on the basis of a single characteristic.

focusing scale see *focus* (1)

fog Undesirable density in photographic emulsions caused by flare, improperly stored or dated film, defective chemicals in the emulsion, or other reasons.

foil 1. Diazo-sensitized plastic film. 2. In stamping, see *leaf* (2).

foil tape sensing The sensing by some open-reel recorders of a piece of metal-foil tape applied to a certain point of magnetic tape, causing the recorder to change to automatic rewind or automatic reverse, depending on the machine and the way it is programmed to react.

folded leaf A wide leaf bound in at one edge and folded one or more times to fit within the fore-edge.

folded book A form of book consisting of a strip of paper folded accordion-fashion and attached at one or both ends to stiff covers. Used commonly in the Orient, but in other parts of the world used mostly for books of an unusual nature, generally pictorial, such as views and panoramas. Synonymous with folding book. Compare with *traditional format (Oriental books)*.

folded plate An oversize plate bound in by one edge and folded to fit the book. Synonymous with folding plate. Compare with *double plate*.

folder 1. A publication consisting of one sheet of paper folded into two or more leaves, but not stitched or cut. The pages of a two-leaf folder are in the same sequence as those of a book, but a folder of three or more leaves has its printed matter imposed so that when the sheet is unfolded the pages on one side of the paper follow one another consecutively. 2. A large sheet of heavy paper folded once, or with additional folds at the bottom, usually with a projecting tab at top of the back flap; used as a holder for loose papers, etc.

folding In binding, the process of folding the flat printed sheets of a book into sections.

folding book see *folded book*

folding plate see *folded plate*

fold sewing see *sewing through the fold*

fold symbol A symbol indicating the number of leaves into which the sheets of paper of which a book is made are folded, and thereby the approximate book size. For a list of fold symbols, see *book sizes*.

foliation 1. The consecutive numbering of the leaves (folios) of a book or manuscript on the recto, as distinct from the numbering of the pages (pagination). 2. The total number of leaves, whether numbered or unnumbered, contained in a book or manuscript.

folio 1. The format of a book printed on full-size sheets folded in half to make two leaves or four pages. Also used to designate the book size resulting from folio format. 2. A leaf of a book or manuscript numbered on the recto only. 3. The number of a leaf (folio) appearing on the recto. When only the leaves are numbered, a book or manuscript is said to be foliated rather than paginated. 4. In modern printing, a page number.

folio line The line upon which the number of a page is printed.

folio recto see *recto*

folio shelving Specially designed shelving with greater than standard depth to accommodate oversize books, such as elephant folios, by laying them flat.

folio verso see *verso*

follow-up file see *tickler file*

fonds In archives, a French term widely used in Europe (and to some extent in North America) to indicate the chief archive unit and the basis of all rules for arrangement of the contents of archives. The term is comparable to the concept of the record group; that is, the archives resulting from the work of an agency or office which was an organic whole, complete in itself, and capable of undertaking business independently, without any added or independent authority.

font A complete assortment of type of one style and size, including uppercase letters, lowercase letters, small capitals, punctuation marks, and special characters. Related fonts may be designed in condensed, expanded, bold, and/or italic forms. Also spelled "fount."

foot The bottom of a book or page; the opposite of the head. Synonymous with tail.

footcandle A unit of luminous intensity equal to one lumen per square foot, or the illumination on a surface that is everywhere one foot from a uniform point source of one candle. Full sunlight with the sun in the zenith is of the order of 10,000 footcandles on a horizontal surface.

footline see *running foot*

footnote see *note* (1)

fore-edge The front, or outer edge of a book opposite the spine. Synonymous with front edge.

fore-edge painting A picture painted on the fore-edge of a book, and seen when the pages are splayed out. A double fore-edge painting has two paintings which can be seen singly by fanning the leaves first one way, then the other. Popular in the late 18th and early 19th centuries in England.

foreground processing The execution of computer programs which have priority over other programs. Compare with *background processing*.

foreground program A computer program which has a priority over any other program being executed. Compare with *background program*.

foreword Introductory remarks preceding the text of a book, written by someone other than the author of the work. Often used interchangeably with *preface*. Compare with *introduction*.

form In letterpress and offset printing, all the pages being printed on one side of the sheet at one time, or, in the case of letterpress, the type metal or plates arranged in proper order (imposed) for the printed sheet and locked in a metal frame called a chase. In England the word is spelled "forme."

format 1. The number of times the printed sheet has been folded to make the leaves of a book. For fold symbols, see *book sizes*. 2. The general appearance and physical makeup of a printed publication, including proportions, size, quality and style of paper and binding, typographical design, etc. 3. In information storage and retrieval, the arrangement of data in an input, output, or storage medium and the code or aggregate of instructions governing that arrangement. 4. In reprography, the dimensions of the material accepted by reprographic equipment, the size of copy material, the nature of the microform, or the arrangement of images on a material. Arrangement generally includes both image orientation and image formatting. 5. In its widest sense, any particular physical representation of a document.

format recognition   A computer program used in the production of MARC records, which can process unedited bibliographic records and supply all the necessary content designators required for the full MARC record.

form class   One of the classes formed when type of composition (literary, artistic, musical, etc.) or general format, as of a bibliographic item, is used as the characteristic of classification.

forme see *form*

form entry   1. An access point consisting of a form heading. 2. A bibliographic record with a form heading at the head of the record. Compare with *subject entry.*

form heading   An access point to a bibliographic record, consisting of a word or phrase which designates the type of composition (literary, artistic, musical, etc.) of the work(s) contained in the bibliographic item (e.g., Short stories, Portraits), or the general format of the item (e.g., Atlases, Encyclopedias and dictionaries). Compare with *subject heading.*

form number   In classification, the number or other symbol added to a notation to indicate form of composition (literary, artistic, musical, etc.) or the general format of a bibliographic item.

forms flash see *forms overlay*

forms overlay   A technique by which the image of a business form is merged with microimages of digital data by a computer-output-microfilm recorder. The superimposition is achieved by the use of a forms slide, a transparent piece of film or glass bearing the image of the form, and a mirror, with blank spaces on the form for variable information to be filled in by the recorder.

forms slide see *forms overlay*

form subdivision   1. In classification, the subdivision of a class based on type of composition (literary, artistic, musical, etc.) or on the shape, size, or general format, as of a bibliographic item. 2. In cataloging, the subdivision of a subject heading which designates the type of composition (literary, artistic, musical, etc.) of the work(s) contained in the bibliographic item or the general format of the item.

formula budget   A budget in which the allocations are based on preestablished standards, such as an established expenditure for materials per student in an academic library.

Formula Translator see *FORTRAN*

fortnightly see *semimonthly*

FORTRAN (Formula Translator)   A symbolic programming language designed to solve algebraic problems or problems expressed in mathematical formulas.

fortyeightmo see *book sizes*

forwarding   The binding processes that precede finishing but follow sewing or leaf affixing and trimming. Includes rounding and backing.

foundry proof   A proof used to check corrections of page proofs before electrotype plates are made from composed metal type.

fount see *font*

four-color process see *full-color printing*

four-track audiotape   An audiotape with four tracks recorded on it.

foxing   The discoloring of paper by dull, rusty patches, attributed to fungus, impurities in manufacture, dampness, or other causes.

fps see *frames per second*

fractional notation   In classification, a notation which can be divided so that new classes can be inserted in the proper logical order. Compare with *integral notation.*

fraktur   Narrow and pointed gothic type with breaks or "fractures" in the lines. Replaced Schwabacher as the standard text type in Germany.

frame   1. A binding ornamentation consisting of a simple hollow rectangle set in some distance from the edges of the cover of a book. To be distinguished from *border* (3). 2. In binding, an adjustable wooden rack which facilitates the attaching of gatherings to spine cords or tapes; a sewing frame. 3. One of the single images or pictures on a strip of motion-picture or other film. 4. The part of microfilm exposed to light in a camera during an exposure, consisting of the image area, frame margin, and frame line. A portion of the frame margin may be reserved for a code area. 5. A single unit of instruction in the series of programmed instruction modules. 6. One complete television picture, consisting of two fields of interlaced scanning lines.

frame line A line dividing two film frames.

frame margin The area within a film frame between the image area and the frame line. This part is sometimes used as a code area.

frame pitch The physical proximity of two specific points located in adjacent film frames.

frames per second (fps) The running speed of film in a projector or camera.

free endpapers see *endpapers*

free field In data processing, a field without predefined length or position in a record. Compare with *fixed field, variable field.*

free field coding The coding of data into a field without restrictions on its length or position in a record.

free floating subdivision A form or topical subdivision of a subject heading which catalogers at the Library of Congress may use under any existing appropriate subject heading for the first time without the usage being specifically authorized in the subject authority file. These subdivisions may have limited application and may be assigned only under limited categories of headings in specifically defined situations.

free indexing system see *natural-language indexing system*

free reading Reading done by students in school or college, voluntarily, apart from any course requirements.

free reading period A class period when voluntary reading is allowed in a classroom or in a school library media center. Synonymous with sustained silent reading and browsing period.

free-standing shelving see *free-standing stacks*

free-standing stacks Single-tier stacks which are self-supported by bases so broad that they do not require additional support, such as strut bracing or fastening to the floor, for stabilization. Synonymous with free-standing shelving.

free-term list An index vocabulary in which terms are not rigidly or precisely defined and to which additions may be freely made. Synonymous with open-ended term list.

free-text retrieval system see *natural-language retrieval system*

French Cape Levant see *Levant*

French fillet In binding, a fillet of three lines, unevenly spaced.

French fold A leaflet made from a sheet printed on one side only and folded into quarters but not cut.

French guard The back edge of an insert, turned over and folded around a signature.

French joint The free-swinging joint produced by forcing the cover material into the space between the edge of the board and the ridge of the back. Synonymous with open joint. Compare with *closed joint.*

frequency 1. The intervals at which a serial is published, e.g., weekly, monthly, annually. 2. The number of oscillations or cycles of an alternating electric current in a given period of time, expressed in hertz. 3. In statistics, the number of items, cases, or repetitions that occur or that fall into a category, classification, or unit of time.

frequency band see *band* (2)

frequency distribution A systematic arrangement of a collection of measures on a given variable, indicating the frequencies of occurrence of the different values of the variable.

frequency modulation (FM) A system of radio broadcasting which adjusts the frequency of the radio carrier wave in accordance with the frequency of the sound wave it carries, with resultant freedom from static and a more exact reproduction of sound than is achieved with *amplitude modulation.* Because FM waves travel in a straight line, a loss of broadcast quality occurs as the distance of the FM receiver from the transmitter increases.

frequency polygon A graph or diagram of a frequency distribution obtained by plotting, at the midpoint of each class interval, a point representing the frequency in that interval, and then connecting the points with straight lines.

frequency range A measure of the difference between the lower and upper limits of a frequency group other than a frequency band, such as audible frequency range, usually given in hertz.

Fresnel lens A plano-convex lens, with its convex side collapsed into a concentric series of simple lens sections to produce a lens that is very thin for its diameter and focal length. The lens is used in spotlights and in some cameras, microform readers, and other optical equipment to improve the uniformity of brightness. Named for its inventor, Augustin Fresnel.

friends of the library An organization of interested individuals formed to support a particular library through public relations and fund raising endeavors. Synonymous with library associates.

frilling The separation of a photographic emulsion from the film base.

fringe benefits Those benefits or rewards given to an employee in addition to wages or salary, such as various types of insurance coverage, retirement program, paid vacation, leave of absence, travel expenses, subsidized housing or meals, and educational expenses.

front cover see *cover* (2)

front edge see *fore-edge*

front-end computer A computer that handles communications functions such as data, error, and line control and message routing for a host computer.

front-end processor see *front-end computer*

frontispiece An illustration preceding, and usually facing, the title page.

front matter The pages that precede the body of a book. It includes some or all of the following, roughly in listed order: half title, frontispiece, title page, copyright page, dedication, acknowledgments, preface or foreword, table of contents, list of illustrations, and introduction. When printed as a separate signature or signatures, pagination is in lower case roman numerals. Synonymous with preliminaries and preliminary matter.

front projection The projection of images onto the front of an opaque screen or other viewing surface. Compare with *rear projection.*

front screen projection see *front projection*

frozen catalog A catalog in which incorporation of new bibliographic records is entirely discontinued, and from which existing records are not removed, even when revised, corrected, converted to machine-readable form, etc. Compare with *closed catalog, integrated catalog, open catalog.*

f-stop A camera lens aperture setting indicated by an f-number. Compare with *f-number.*

FTE see *full-time equivalent*

fugitive material Material printed in limited quantities and usually of immediate interest at the time of, or in the place of, publication, such as pamphlets, programs, and processed publications.

full binding A binding with covering material all of one kind. Strictly, the term should be applied only to leather bindings. Synonymous with whole binding.

full cataloging Cataloging that includes detailed bibliographic data in addition to the elements of bibliographic description that are essential to the identification of bibliographic items; the highest level of description according to the cataloging code being followed. Compare with *brief cataloging, selective cataloging.*

full-color printing A method of reproducing an infinite range of colors by regulating the overprinting of three colors of process ink (yellow, magenta, cyan), with black often added as a fourth. Extra colors may be added if needed; thus the terms "three-color process," "four-color process." The term "color separation" is given to the procedure by which a full-color original is photographed through color filters or scanned by a color-sensing machine that electronically separates the colors to produce color separation negatives that define the image to be printed with each color of ink. Also known as process color because the printing surfaces are produced by photomechanical means. Compare with *multicolor printing.*

full-duplex transmission see *duplex transmission*

full-name note A note, formerly added to Library of Congress bibliographic records below the tracings, giving the full name of the personal author when a shortened form of the name had been used as the main entry heading.

full score see *score* (1)

full-text database A database in which the data consist of the full text of one or more works.

full-text retrieval system see *natural-language retrieval system*

full-time equivalent (FTE) The numerical representation of part-time work activities (e.g., part-time employees, part-time students) as full-time equivalencies for such purposes as statistical analysis and accounting. Each part-time unit may be expressed as a full-time equivalent (e.g., an employee working 20 hours a week in a library with a 40-hour workweek is counted as .5 FTE) or the total of part-time units may be expressed as a full-time equivalent (e.g., nine half-time employees and four three-fourths-time employees are counted as 7.5 FTE).

full-time position A position requiring the employee to work the standard number of hours per week as established by the employing agency, usually 35 to 40 hours. Employees are entitled to the standard benefits as prescribed or defined by the employing agency.

fully connected network A network in which each node is linked or connected with all other nodes. Compare with *distributed network, ring network, star network.*

fumigation The process of exposing paper and other materials to a poisonous vapor in a vacuum or other airtight container to destroy insects or mildew.

functional authority The right conferred upon administrators or other individuals in an organization by virtue of their position to direct the activities of other administrators or other individuals in certain specified activities, tasks, or functions; e.g., a personnel officer with functional authority to develop, direct, and evaluate a staff training program for all employees in the organization. Compare with *line authority, staff authority.*

functional relationship In statistics, a relationship of several variables such that altering one will result in corresponding alterations of the others.

fund 1. A sum of money and/or other assets set aside for a specified purpose in the budget. 2. In governmental and institutional accounting, a sum of money and/or other assets constituting a separate accounting entity. A separate budget is prepared for each fund.

fundamental categories In classification, categories of facets which are thought to be applicable to any subject field. For example, S. R. Ranganathan proposed five fundamental categories of facets (personality, matter, energy, space, and time) as the basis of his Colon Classification.

fundamental class 1. In a classification system, the class which covers all aspects of a subject; the place to put general works. 2. The class to which a particular topic basically belongs, even though it sometimes appears in other contexts.

furnish The mixture of pulp, sizing, filler, dyes, and other additives from which paper is made.

galley proofs Proofs taken from matter set in type for publication in book form before make-up, or the arrangement of the type matter in page format. The name derives from the galley, or tray used for storing metal type after setting. Also known as slip proofs, proof in slips, and galleys.

game, educational A set of materials developed to be used according to prescribed rules for mental competitive play.

gamma see *contrast* (1)

gampi In paper conservation, a fine, silky-textured paper, frequently used as a removable slipsheet in protecting the face of a mounted, unframed print or document; from the Japanese.

G&E see *exchange department*

gangpunch To punch the same data into a deck of blank punched cards.

gap In data communication, an interval of space between data or records in a recording or storage medium, or an interval of time between signals being transmitted over a channel.

garbage In computer science, meaningless data resulting from incorrect input or an equipment malfunction. Synonymous with hash.

garbage in, garbage out (GIGO) A slang expression meaning that the result or output of data processing is only as good as the data fed in.

gas bells Bubbles forcing the emulsion to separate from the base during photographic processing. The bubbles can create pinholes in the negative.

gate see *film gate*

gatefold A folded illustration or other insert which is larger than the volume into which it is bound and must be unfolded for proper viewing. It opens horizontally to the left or right.

gathering 1. The process of collecting and arranging in proper order the folded sections of a book, preparatory to binding. 2. In bibliography, but not in the book trade, a synonym for *section* (2) and *signature.*

gathering plan see *blanket order*

gauffered edges Edges of a book decorated by impressing heated relief tools to indent small repeating patterns, usually (but not always) done after gilding; popular in the 16–17th centuries. Also spelled "goffered." Synonymous with chased edges.

Gaussian distribution see *normal distribution*

gauze see *crash*

gazette 1. A newspaper; now used mainly in newspaper titles. 2. Formerly, a journal containing current news. 3. A journal issued officially by a government; specifically, one of the official semiweekly journals issued in London, Edinburgh, and Dublin, giving lists of appointments and other public notices, called official gazettes.

gazetteer A geographical dictionary.

gear drive A disc, wheel, or shaft section with teeth which mesh with teeth of identical form, size, and spacing to move an audiodisc turntable platter.

gelatin process see *collotype* (1)

gelatin transfer process A transfer process using paper coated with a photosensitive gelatin emulsion containing a dye-forming agent as a master. The master is pressed into contact with plain paper, to which the dyed gelatin image, which is left unhardened in exposure and developing, is transferred. Synonymous with dye transfer process.

general catalog see *central catalog*

general classification A classification system which attempts to cover the universe of knowledge.

general collection That segment, usually the majority, of the collection in any library which constitutes the core of materials, as distinct from special or segregated subject collections or collections for a particular user group.

general cross reference see *general reference*

generalia class In a classification system, the main class which is reserved for bibliographic items which cover so many subjects (such as an encyclopedia or newspaper) that they cannot be put into any other class.

generalization The act or process of asserting or inferring something to be true about all or some of a class or population, based upon statistics or other facts obtained through study or observation.

general library 1. A library not limited to a particular field or special subject. 2. The central library of a university library system.

general material designation (GMD) In cataloging, a term indicating the broad class of material to which a bibliographic item belongs, such as "motion picture." Compare with *specific material designation.* (AACR2, mod.)

general-purpose computer A computer with interchangeable, stored programs designed to solve a broad class of problems or handle a wide range of different applications. Compare with *dedicated computer, special-purpose computer.*

general record groups Record groups with titles usually beginning: *General Records of*

..., established as a practical modification of the record group concept. General record groups include records of the head of the corporate body as well as other units concerned with matters that affect the corporate body as a whole, such as personnel.

general records schedule A records control schedule, also called a general schedule, governing the retention and disposition of specified recurring record series common to several or all agencies or offices.

general reference A blanket reference from one heading to a group of headings which is represented by an example, such as: Civilian defense. *See also subdivision under names of countries, cities, etc., e.g.,* Great Britain—Civilian defense. Compare with *explanatory reference.*

general schedule (archives) see *general records schedule*

general special concept In classification, a subdivision based on a characteristic which can be applied to the subdivision of a general class and also the subdivisions within that general class.

generation The relationship between an original document and copies made from it. On film, the first copy is called camera microfilm or first generation. Copies made from camera microfilm are called second generation, and copies made from the second generation are called third generation, etc.

generic entry see *class entry*

generic relationship In classification, the relation between genus and species, or between classes in a chain of subordinate classes.

generic search In information retrieval, a search in which all documents on a particular subject and all its subdivisions or aspects are to be retrieved.

genus In classification, a class or group of things which is capable of being divided into two or more subgroups called species.

geographic filing method The primary or secondary arrangement of the records in a file by place, either alphabetically or on the basis of a geographic classification system.

geographic subdivision 1. In classification, the subdivision of a class based on geographic order

(area, region, country, state, etc.) 2. The extension of a subject heading by a subheading which designates the place to which it is limited. Synonymous with local subdivision, place subdivision. Compare with *direct subdivision, indirect subdivision.*

ghost 1. A faint undesirable image which may appear in addition to the image of an object or document being photographed or reproduced. The unwanted image may be due to mechanical, chemical, or optical failure. 2. A double image in a television picture with one a shadowy image left or right of the desired image as a result of poor transmission. 3. In bibliography, see *bibliographical ghost.*

gift and exchange department see *exchange department*

giftbook An elaborately printed and bound book of prose and poetry, frequently an annual, popular in the earlier part of the 19th century. Synonymous with keepsake.

gigahertz One billion hertz.

GIGO see *garbage in, garbage out*

gilt Gold or something that resembles gold applied to a surface.

gilt edges In binding, the edges of a book which have been cut smooth, covered with gold leaf, and burnished. Edges are sometimes also tooled with a repeated pattern after binding.

global change In automatic data processing, the changing of every occurrence of a specified string of characters, or every occurrence of it in a specified context, in a database from an old or incorrect string to a new, correct form. Compare with *flip.*

globe The model of a celestial body, usually the earth or the celestial sphere, depicted on the surface of a sphere. (AACR2)

gloss A marginal or interlinear note explaining a word or expression in a manuscript text.

glossary An alphabetical list of unusual, obsolete, dialectical, or technical terms, all concerned with a particular subject or area of interest. 2. A collection of equivalent synonyms in two or more languages.

glossy print A photographic print with a hard, shiny surface that is created by drying on a ferrotype plate. Synonymous with ferrotype.

GMD see *general material designation*

goatskin Leather manufactured from the skins of goats and widely used in binding; also called *morocco,* especially in the antiquarian trade. It is usually produced with a natural grain but can be artificially grained to present a more even texture (e.g., pebble-grain, straight-grain). Different kinds of goatskin are generally named after the place of origin (or supposed origin), and include Levant, Cape, and Niger.

goffered edges see *gauffered edges*

gold leaf Gold which has been beaten very thin, either by hand or mechanically, and used by bookbinders in gold tooling and gilding the edges of books.

gold tooling The process of tooling an ornamental design or pattern in gold leaf on a book cover by means of individual heated tools, the surface of the cover (usually leather) having first been prepared by blind tooling. The practice became common for fine books in Europe in the early 16th century.

go list A list of significant words that are to be selected as keywords in automatic indexing. Compare with *stop list.*

goodness of fit In statistics, the degree of agreement between an observed and a hypothetical set of values, often measured by some criterion depending on the squares of differences between observed and theoretical values, for example, the chi-square test.

gothic 1. Typefaces based on the dark, angular writing of the Middle Ages. Can be considered in four general groups: textura, or lettre de forme; fere-humanistica, or gotico-antiqua; rotunda; and bastarda, which includes lettre bâtarde, Schwabacher, and Fraktur. Also known as black letter. 2. Sans-serif types (primarily an American usage, and properly avoided in favor of sans serif).

gotico-antiqua see *fere-humanistica*

gouge index see *thumb index*

government document see *government publication*

government documents depository see *depository library*

government library A library established in a government department or office.

government publication Any publication originating in, or issued with the imprint of, or at the expense and by the authority of, any office of a legally organized government or international organization. Often called government document, public document, and document.

goyu In paper conservation, a Japanese tissue paper frequently used for hinges in the mounting of paper objects.

grace period An established period of time subsequent to the date due during which a library borrower may return items without a fine or other penalty.

grade A term used in the classification of personnel designating levels of positions or jobs within a common position classification. Positions assigned a common grade share comparable levels of responsibility, duties of similar difficulty or complexity, similar qualification requirements, and a common salary range.

graduate library At a university with a separate undergraduate library or college library, the central library facility which houses the major research collections and emphasizes services to the graduate students and faculty.

graduate reading room A special room or area in a university library designated for the exclusive use of graduate students. It may contain relevant library materials and assigned study carrels.

grain 1. The direction in which most of the fibers lie in a sheet of machine-made paper, parallel to the forward movement of the paper in the machine. Paper curls, folds, and reacts most readily and flexibly along, or with, the grain. In books the grain of the paper should run parallel to the spine. On packages of paper, the grain direction is indicated on the label by underlining the dimension along which it runs or by the words "long" or "short." Handmade paper has little or no grain. 2. A silver halide crystal in a film emulsion. Film coated with an emulsion with relatively small silver halide crystals is termed fine-grain. 3. Microscopic silver grains, converted from silver crystals in the film emulsion in the developing process, which, in granular groupings of varying density, make up the film image.

graininess A defect in processed photographic film or print resulting from an uneven distribution of the grains that make up the image. The defect, most apparent in enlargements, may appear as a pattern of small dots or uneven color distribution. Graininess is a subjective property, as perceived by the viewer. An objective assessment of graininess is termed granularity.

grangerized see *extra-illustrated*

grant-in-aid Income from state or federal funds to subsidize the operational expenses of a library or for designated programs and activities of a library.

granularity see *graininess*

graphic A two-dimensional representation, whether opaque (e.g., art originals and reproductions, flash cards, photographs, technical drawings) or intended to be viewed, or projected without motion, by means of an optical device (e.g., filmstrips, stereographs, slides). (AACR2)

graphic display see *plotter*

gravure see *photogravure* (1), *rotogravure* (1)

gray scale A strip of material for measuring the tonal range in either reflex or transmission copying.

Greenaway Plan A type of blanket order plan, originated at the Philadelphia Free Library by Emerson Greenaway, whereby libraries arrange with publishers to receive at nominal price one advance copy of all trade titles in order that titles selected for acquisition can be ordered in advance of publication. The plan is based on the assumption that the library will purchase multiple copies of many of the titles.

green film Any film that has not dried sufficiently after washing.

green paper A printed document issued by any department or ministry of the British government to stimulate discussion of a proposed policy.

grid 1. On microfiche or microopaques, an array of horizontal and vertical lines defining the rows and columns of the microimages. 2. In binding, an ornament consisting of two horizontal lines with a few vertical bars between, the sides having a foliage character. 3. In cartography, an array of even squares, drawn in a specified projection, overprinted on a map to facilitate the location of particular points.

grievance An actual or perceived circumstance within a work situation which an employee or group of employees regards as unfair, unjust, discriminatory, or abusive and brings to the attention of a supervisor, grievance committee, or other appropriate party.

grievance committee A group of employees, usually selected by fellow employees, to serve for a prescribed time as a panel for the purpose of reviewing and assisting in the resolution of grievances.

grievance procedure An established process and mechanism within an organization which allows an employee or group of employees to air a grievance and seek resolution.

groove In binding, the depression running the length of the back margins of the covers which results from the formation of the ridge or flange during rounding and backing.

gross space The total area of floor space in a library, expressed as gross square feet (GSF) included within the outside faces of exterior walls, exclusive of architectural projections, for all stories or areas that have floor surfaces. Compare with *assignable space.*

gross square feet (GSF) see *gross space*

groundwood pulp A mechanically produced wood pulp which may be bleached or unbleached and is made in several grades or qualities. Because the process produces short cellulose fibers and does not eliminate noncellulose ingredients such as lignin, paper produced from groundwood pulp or admixtures of it is not durable or permanent. Synonymous with mechanical wood pulp.

group (archives) see *record group*

group notation A notation using two or more digits, decimally, to represent coordinate classes and thereby increase its expressiveness. Compare with *sector notation.*

GSF (gross square feet) see *gross space*

guard 1. A flexible strip of cloth or strong paper upon which to mount an insert too stiff to be broken over. Sometimes used synonymously with *hinge*. 2. One of several strips of paper or fabric put together to balance the space to be taken up by a bulky insert, such as a folded map or plate. Synonymous with compensation guard. 3. A strip of paper or other material reinforcing a signature. 4. A *guard leaf.* 5. A person assigned to control a library exit and assure that library materials taken from the building are properly charged. Synonymous with door checker.

guard book catalog A catalog made by pasting slips containing individual bibliographic records to the pages of a bound or loose-leaf book. Originally, only a few records are put on each page so that there will be room for insertion of later records into the proper order. The British Museum (now the British Library) has used this form of catalog. Synonymous with ledger catalog, page catalog.

guarded sections Sections, usually at the front and the end of a volume, that have had the back fold reinforced with fabric.

guard leaf In binding, a free endpaper faced with silk or other material to protect and complement the doublure which it accompanies.

guard sheet A sheet of paper (usually thinner than that on which the remainder of the book is printed) bearing descriptive text or an outline drawing, inserted to protect and elucidate the plate or other illustration over which it is placed. It is not normally included in the pagination.

May be termed a *leaf* if the descriptive text is printed on the same kind of paper as the rest of the book.

guide In archives, a finding aid which at the repository level briefly describes and indicates the relationships between holdings, with record groups, papers, collections, or comparable bodies of material as the units of entry. Guides may also be limited to the description of the holdings of one or more repositories relating to particular subjects, periods, or geographical areas. (SAA)

guidebook A handbook for travelers that gives information about a city, region, or country, or a similar handbook about a building, museum, etc.

guide card A card inserted into a card catalog to indicate arrangement; has a tab or a raised edge which projects higher than the other cards in the file.

guide letter see *director* (6)

guide word see *catchword* (1)

gulp A set of bytes of data treated or processed as a unit.

gussets see *buckles*

gutter The area formed by the inside or back margins of facing pages in an open book.

gypsographic print see *seal print*

hachures In cartography, a method of portraying relief by short, wedge-shaped marks radiating from high elevations and following the direction of slope to the lowland.

halation An undesirable reflection of light from the film base to the emulsion, causing a ghost image or fog. The defect is usually avoided through the use of an antihalation undercoat in dye-back film.

half-binding A style of book cover in which the spine and the corners are traditionally of one material and the sides of another. Hence, half cloth, half leather, etc.

half cloth A style of book cover in which the spine is of cloth and the sides usually of paper. Synonymous with *half linen.*

half-duplex transmission Data transmission over a channel which both transmits and receives, but in only one direction at a time. Synonymous with two-way alternate transmission. Compare with *duplex transmission, simplex transmission.*

half leather   A half binding in which the spine and corners are of leather, and the sides of some different material.

half linen   see *half cloth*

half title   1. The title of a book, in full or in brief, appearing on the recto of a leaf preceding the title page. When so defined, synonymous with bastard title. 2. The title of a book, in full or in brief, appearing on the recto of a leaf placed between the front matter and the first page of the text.

halftone   1. A technique for reproducing the different shadings of continuous tone illustrations by offset or letterpress. The original to be reproduced is photographed through a screen with fine cross markings that break up the tones into tiny dots. The human eye does not see the individual dots, but perceives the overall tonal effect created by the dots. 2. A print so produced.

halftone block   An engraved or etched metal plate, usually of zinc or copper, containing the image of a continuous tone illustration.

halftone cut   1. A photoengraved plate containing the image of a continuous tone illustration. 2. A print produced from such a plate.

halftone paper   A supercalendered or coated paper used for printing halftones.

half track   An open reel audiotape on which each of two recorded tracks occupies slightly less than one half of the width of the tape.

half-uncial   A style of handwriting used in Latin manuscripts in the 5th–9th centuries in which the uncial style took on cursive characteristics and the use of ligatures began; an intermediate step on the way to minuscules.

halide   A binary compound of a halogen and a more electropositive chemical element. Light-sensitive metallic halides, such as silver chloride, silver bromide, and silver iodide, are used in film and photographic paper emulsions.

hand   see *index* (2)

handbill   A small sheet containing an advertisement, to be distributed by hand.

hand-binding   The processes of binding books by hand, including sewing, forwarding, and finishing.

handbook   A compendium, covering one or more subjects and of basic or advanced level, arranged for the quick location of facts and capable of being conveniently carried.

hand-copied braille book   A book for the blind in which the braille transcription has been done by hand on a braille tablet or a braillewriter. Only one copy can be made at a time.

H and D curve (Hurter and Driffield curve)   see *contrast* (1)

handling charge   A flat rate charged to the library by a wholesaler in addition to the price the wholesaler paid the publisher for an item, in lieu of a charge based on list price less discount.

handmade paper   Paper made by hand-dipping a mold, or screen stretched over a wooden frame, and deckle, or removable wooden frame which fits over the mold, into paper pulp and lifting it with a particular motion necessary to tangle the cellulose fibers and form the sheet. It has little or no grain.

handshaking   In data communications, an exchange of predefined control signals between two terminals or other equipment once a connection has been established and before a message is transmitted.

hand tooling   see *tooling*

hand viewer   1. A small portable magnifying device for viewing filmstrips or slides. 2. A type of *microform reader*.

hanging indention   A form of indention in which the first line of a paragraph is set flush with the left margin and succeeding lines are indented.

Hansard   The popular name for the official, verbatim published reports of the British *Parliamentary Debates*. Named for their 19th-century publisher, Thomas Curson Hansard.

hardback   see *hardcover book*

hard copy   1. Data printed in human-readable form on paper or card stock by a machine such as a computer. 2. In reprography, the original paper document or an enlarged copy of a microimage, usually on paper. Compare with *soft copy*.

hardcover book A book bound or cased in boards. Synonymous with *hardback*. Compare with *paperback*.

hardener A solution of chemicals used in film processing to harden the gelatin of emulsions and to raise its melting point. The hardener makes the photographic material more resistant to scratches and prevents the emulsion from softening in the warm processing baths. Commonly used chemicals include aluminum potassium sulfate, chromium aluminum sulfate, and formaldehyde solution.

hard paper Photographic paper used to print negatives with very high contrast. The gradations in the tonal range are more limited than in normal and soft paper, producing a marked distinction between light and dark areas.

hardware The electronic, electrical, mechanical, or other physical equipment used for the projection and playback of audiovisual materials, or associated with a computer system. Compare with *software*.

harmonic distortion Distortion that occurs as a component of sound recording or reproducing equipment is saturated when a large signal is applied and new frequencies, which are some exact multiple of the frequency of the input signal, appear in the sound reproduction. Synonymous with amplitude distortion.

hash see *garbage*

head 1. A modifier used to designate the individual in charge of a library, or a particular type of library work (e.g., head librarian, head cataloger). 2. A title used to designate the individual in an organization in charge of a department or other organizational unit. 3. The top of a book or page; the opposite of *foot*. 4. A word or phrase used as a headline in a book or periodical. 5. In a magnetic tape recorder, an electromagnet across which the tape is drawn and which, depending on its function, can erase (erase head), record (record head), or play back (playback head). The heads may be separate or combined in various ways, such as a record/playback head.

headband A small ornamental (and sometimes protective) band, generally of mercerized cotton or silk, sewn or glued at the head and foot of a book between the cover and backs of the sections; originally a cord or leather thong similar to ordinary bands, around which threads were twisted, and laced in to the boards. Headbands are now generally made separately and have no structural function.

header A punched card or label containing data identifying or pertaining to cards or records that follow in a deck, file, or recording medium such as magnetic tape or magnetic disk.

heading 1. An access point to a bibliographic record in the form prescribed by a catalog code, under which the record may be searched and identified. In a unit entry catalog, such as a card catalog, the access point is at the head of the record. Compare with *access point* (1). 2. In data communications, machine-readable characters that indicate routing and destination at the beginning of a message. 3. In composition, type set apart from the text as a title or a summary of the text that follows.

head librarian The title used to designate the chief executive officer of some libraries and library systems.

headline see *running head*

headphone Two small loudspeakers placed on a headband so that a loudspeaker fits over each ear and an individual can listen to audio sources. In some headphones all sound is cut off except that coming from the headphones; in others the listener may hear external sounds as well. Synonymous with headset.

headpiece An ornament decorating the top of a page or the beginning of a chapter.

headset see *headphone*

head title see *caption title*

health sciences library see *medical library*

hearing In personnel management, a formal session, frequently involving a grievance, in which an employee has an opportunity to present testimony or evidence to a panel of individuals authorized to rule on the matter.

hearings United States government publications in which are printed transcripts of testimony given before the various committees of Congress. Many hearings are not published.

heat copying see *thermal process*

heat-developing film Any film which is developed by the action of heat, such as dry silver and vesicular film. The film is used in dry process copying, such as dual-spectrum.

heat filter A filter, usually of glass, placed between the light source and the film plane in a projector, film viewer, or other optical device to absorb infrared (thermal) radiation and reduce the heat that falls on the film without absorbing light from the visible range.

heat splice see *splice*

heliotype see *collotype* (1)

hertz (Hz) A unit of frequency equal to one cycle per second. Named for physicist Heinrich R. Hertz.

heterogeneous network A network whose members or nodes are dissimilar. Compare with *homogeneous network.*

heuristic Pertaining to a method of solving a problem in which a continuous evaluation of progress toward the solution is made and the results of the evaluations used as feedback. Compare with *algorithm.*

heuristic search A search of a file, database, or index in which the strategy is constantly modified as results of the search appear.

hexadecimal number system A number system with a radix or base of sixteen.

hidden link In chain indexing, a class which is properly part of the hierarchical chain but may be missed because the notation of the classification system is not hierarchical.

hierarchical classification system A classification system in which classes divide from the general to the specific by gradations of likeness and difference. It begins with the assembly of groups of the principal divisions of knowledge into main classes, which form the basis for the development of the classification system. A characteristic of classification is used to divide main classes into divisions, which form a second hierarchical level of classes. The process is continued to divide divisions into subdivisions, subdivisions into sections, and sections into subsections, until further subdivision is impossible or impractical.

hierarchical network A network in which control and processing are vested or performed at various levels.

hierarchical notation A notation which shows genus-species relationships. Compare with *ordinal notation.*

hierarchy The pyramidal arrangement of personnel in a formal organization according to rank or degree of authority. It reflects the chain of command.

hieroglyphics Ancient Egyptian picture writing; picture writing of any people, as that of the Aztecs.

high fidelity Sound reproduction using a wide range of audible frequencies. Since very little distortion occurs, the reproduced sounds appear to be very close to the original sounds.

high-level language In computer science, a programming language oriented toward a problem to be solved or procedural steps. Compare with *low-level language.*

highlight In reprography, the lightest part of an original document or of a copy, and the darkest part of a continuous tone or halftone negative.

highlight halftone see *dropout halftone*

high-order digit The most significant or highly weighted digit of a number in a positional notation system. For example, 8 is the high-order digit in the number 8957. Synonymous with most significant digit. Compare with *low-order digit.*

high reduction see *reduction ratio*

high-speed printer Any computer printer which operates at a speed close to or approximating that of the computer itself. Compare with *low-speed printer.*

high-speed storage Storage with a short access time.

hinge 1. A paper or muslin stub, or guard, which is affixed to the binding edge and permits the free flexing of an insert, leaf, section, or map. 2. Sometimes used synonymously with *joint* (1).

hinged see *broken over*

Hinman collator A collating machine, invented by Charlton Hinman, used to compare copies of the same edition of a printed work and identify variances by superimposing the text of two copies, page by page, by means of a series of mirrors.

historical bibliography The history of books broadly speaking, and of the persons, institutions, and machines producing them. Historical bibliography may range from technological history to the history of art in its concern with the evidence books provide about culture and society. Synonymous with material bibliography.

history reference An explanatory reference which includes brief information on the history and name changes of a corporate body.

hit Pertaining to a successful match of a search key with desired data or records during a file search.

hit rate The percentage of successful hits to the number of attempts during a file search.

hold (circulation) see *reserved item*

hold back see *dodge*

holdings 1. The issues of a serial in the possession of a library. 2. Sometimes used synonymously with *library collection.*

holdings card The catalog card which lists the parts received of a serial or multipart item.

holdings rate The percentage of documents requested by library users that are in the library collection.

Hollerith card see *punched card*

Hollerith code A code, developed in 1890 by Herman Hollerith, for representing alphabetic, numeric, and special characters in standard, 80-column punched cards.

hollow The open space between the spine and the back of a hollow or loose-back book.

hollow-back see *loose-back*

hologram see *holography*

holograph A document wholly in the handwriting of the person under whose name it appears. Compare with *autograph.*

holography A process of lensless photography utilizing laser beams. By splitting and deflecting the laser beam, three-dimensional images can be recorded on a photographic film. The recorded image, called a hologram, can be reconstructed in three dimensions by passing laser illumination through the film. A hologram of moving objects which may be viewed without laser illumination is an integram.

homogeneous network A network whose members or nodes are the same or similar. Compare with *heterogeneous network.*

hook and **loop board** see *feltboard*

horizontal reference see *collateral reference*

hornbook An early form of primer, consisting of a sheet of parchment or paper protected by transparent cattle horn, mounted on a thin oblong of wood with a handle at the bottom. Its paddlelike shape suggested its use in games, as a racket or battledore, and a simpler and later form of the hornbook was indeed called a battledore. It consisted of a tablet made from a piece of folded and varnished cardboard, but without the handle, and was common in the late 18th century.

hospitality of notation The quality attributed to a flexible notation, which allows new subjects to be inserted without disrupting the logical sequence of the notation or the classification schedule.

hospital library A library maintained by a hospital to serve the information needs of its medical, paramedical, nursing, research, administrative, and teaching staff, or its staff and patients.

host computer The principal or primary computer in a system or network of more than one computer.

host organization The organization of which a special library is an administrative unit.

host organization file see *organization file* (2)

hot-melt adhesives A group of synthetic adhesives having a thermoplastic base formulated from either homopolymers or copolymers. "Hot melts" are applied at temperatures between 300° and 400° F.

hot melts see *hot-melt adhesives*

hot metal composition A method of composition, such as Linotype and Monotype, which uses type cast from molten metal. Compare with *cold type.*

hot spot A bright spot in the center of an image projected on a screen or other viewing surface. The uneven illumination causes eyestrain when viewed over a period of time.

hot stamping see *stamping*

housekeeping operations Operations required to maintain and operate a computer or execute computer programs, but which do not contribute directly to the desired results or output of the machine. Synonymous with red-tape operations.

housekeeping records In archives, records of an agency or office which relate to budget, personnel, and similar administrative operations common to all organizational units, as distinguished from records which relate to an organization's primary functions. Compare with *program records.*

house organ 1. A type of periodical issued by a business, industrial, or other organization for internal distribution to employees; often concerned with personal and personnel matters. Synonymous with employee magazine and plant publication. 2. A periodical issued for external distribution to dealers, customers, and potential customers; generally including articles on the company's products and on subjects related to the business or industry.

howl see *acoustic feedback*

hum A low-frequency, continuous droning tone caused by improperly grounded electrical and electronic audio equipment.

humanistic hand A neo-Carolingian book hand, less angular than gothic, the precursor of fere-humanistica and roman type faces. Synonymous with lettera antiqua.

Hurter and Driffield curve see *contrast* (1)

hybrid computer A computer which can process data either in discrete, digital form or in the form of numerical quantities expressing continuously changing physical variables. Compare with *analog computer, digital computer.*

hydrographic chart A chart designed to assist navigation at sea or on other waterways. Synonymous with nautical chart.

hygrometer An instrument for measuring humidity of the atmosphere. It is used in determining storage conditions for documents, film, and other materials susceptible to damage from moisture.

hypo In photography, a solution used to fix photographic materials during processing, with sodium or ammonium thiosulfate as the main fixing agent. The solution may also contain a hardener and other chemicals. A hypo eliminator solution is used to remove the hypo after fixing.

hypo eliminator see *hypo*

hypo test see *residual hypo test*

hypothesis A statement about the existence of a relationship between two or more variables or events under study or examination. A tentative theory.

hypothetical construct An abstract concept constructed through a mental synthesis process, to be used in an experiment or in developing a theory.

hypsographic map see *relief map*

hypsometric map see *relief map*

Hz see *hertz*

I&R see *information and referral service*

iconography 1. The study of the pictorial representation of persons or objects in portraits, statues, coins, etc. 2. The book or other result of such study.

iconoscope A television camera pickup tube in which a beam of high velocity electrons scans a mosaic (photosensitive plate) on which an electron image of the optical image to be transmitted is formed to produce an electrical video signal.

The iconoscope has been largely replaced by the *image orthicon.*

ideal copy   A bibliographer's description of the most perfect copy of the first impression of an edition, constructed after the examination of as many copies as possible, against which all other copies of the first impression and copies of subsequent impressions are compared in the determination of issues and states.

identification card see *borrower's identification card*

identification strip   A short strip of film at the beginning of a roll or microfilm, on which has been photographed a description of the film, in letters large enough to be read without magnification.

identifier   In computer science, a symbol which identifies or labels a body of data such as a record, file, or database.

ideogram see *ideograph*

ideograph   A symbol or picture used in writing to represent an object or an idea, as in Chinese writing, or in hieroglyphics. Synonymous with ideogram.

idler wheel drive   A disc with a rubber rim which touches both the shaft of the motor and the inside rim of the turntable platter of an audiodisc player and transmits the motion of one to the other.

ILL see *interlibrary loan*

illegal character   A character that is invalid or unacceptable in a specific computer program or system. Synonymous with false code.

illuminated   Adorned by hand with richly colored ornamental initial letters, decorative designs, or illustrations. Illumination flourished with books intended for upmarket customers, especially during the late medieval period, but the practice never completely died out, and there was a revival of interest in the practice in the 19th century by (among others) the circle surrounding William Morris.

illumination see *illuminated*

illustrated covers see *decorated covers*

illustration   A photograph, drawing, map, table, or other representation or systematic arrangement of data designed to elucidate or decorate the contents of a publication. Narrowly defined, an illustration appears within the text, or on a leaf with text on the reverse side.

image   A representation of an object, person, or scene produced by radiant energy.

image area   The area within the film frame actually occupied by an image.

image card see *aperture card*

image density see *line density*

image mark see *document mark*

image-mark retrieval code see *document mark*

image modifier   A cameralike device used for enlarging or reducing images on two-dimensional artwork or a copy and projecting them onto a translucent plate in the device. The image can then be traced or (in some models) copied by using light-sensitive materials. Not the same as a photographic enlarger. Synonymous with enlarging-reducing machine, enlarger-reducer, Lacey-Luci.

image orientation   The arrangement of document images on microfilm, usually with respect to the film edge. The orientation or mode is described as cine or comic. Common image formats include simplex, duo, and duplex. The microfilm format, document size, reduction ratio, and type of reprographic equipment can influence the arrangement. For example, eight-up format is associated with single frames of 35mm microfilm.

image orthicon   A photoemissive television pickup tube, more sensitive than the iconoscope, in which light from the scene being televised falls upon a photocathode (a sensitive photoelectric surface) and forms an electron image of the scene. The photoelectrons emitted from this surface are forced toward a target surface, where there is a secondary emission of electrons. A beam of low-velocity electrons periodically scans the target surface; reflected electrons return to an electron multiplier, which produces an electric video signal.

image plane see *film plane*

image processing A general term, at one time associated with reprography, but having a broader scope, due in part to the merger of reprography with other technologies, such as electronic data processing. The term is no longer limited to the technology of reproduction, but may include the processing of both graphic and textual materials, using a wide variety of media and different means of representing information.

image reversing film A duplicating film which, with conventional processing, reverses the polarity of the original or the previous film generation; that is, a negative from a positive or a positive from a negative. Compare with *direct image film*.

image spacing A general term referring to the distance between film frames. The distance will vary depending on the nature of the objects being filmed, reduction ratios, and user requirements.

imaginary map A map of an imaginary place, such as Erewhon, Middle Earth.

imitation embossing see *thermography* (1)

immediate supervisor The staff member to whom a subordinate reports directly and who is responsible for the performance of that subordinate.

impact printing A printing method in which copy is composed by striking the image directly onto the paper, as with a typewriter. Synonymous with direct-impression, strike-on, and struck-image printing. Compare with *nonimpact printing*.

import A publication issued in one country and imported into another.

import license A license obtained from the U.S. Treasury Department in order to trade with certain countries where trade by U.S. citizens is prohibited by federal law.

imposition The arrangement of type or image pages so that they will be in proper sequence when the sheet is printed and folded.

impression 1. All copies of a bibliographic item printed at one time from one setting of type. There may be several impressions, presumably unaltered, of one edition, each new printing from standing type or original plates constituting a new impression of the item. 2. The pressure of the metal type, plate, or blanket against paper or other material, or by die, stamp, or type into the cover of a book. 3. Each occurrence of imprinting by pressing metal type, plate, or blanket against paper or other material.

imprimatur Literally, let it be printed. In early books (principally in the 16th and 17th centuries), a printed statement indicating that permission to print had been granted by a religious or secular authority. Still used in Roman Catholic doctrinal works to indicate official approval by a bishop of the church. Compare with *nihil obstat*.

imprint (binding) 1. The name of the owner of a volume as stamped on the binding, usually at the bottom of the spine. Synonymous with library stamp. 2. The name of the publisher stamped on an edition binding, usually at the bottom of the spine. 3. The name of the binder stamped on the cover (not used by U.S. library binders).

imprint (publishing) 1. In a book, the publisher's imprint, giving the publisher's name and place and date of publication, usually on the recto of the title leaf, and the printer's imprint, giving the printer's name and place of printing, usually on the verso of the title leaf. 2. By extension, the name of the publisher, distributor, manufacturer, etc., and the place and date of publication, distribution, manufacture, etc., of a bibliographic item. 3. In a bibliographic description, the data elements that give such information. 4. By extension, a book itself, such as early American imprint.

imprint date 1. The year of publication, distribution, manufacture, etc., as it appears in a bibliographic item. 2. In descriptive cataloging, the year of publication, distribution, manufacture, etc., as it appears in a bibliographic item or as determined from other sources.

imprint group In a bibliographic record, the group of data elements making up the imprint.

IMS see *information management system*

inactive file A file that is not currently in use but expected to become active again in the future. Compare with *active file, dead file.*

inactive records (archives) see *noncurrent records*

"in" analytic An analytical entry which includes a description of the work or document analyzed and an analytical note consisting of the word "In," followed by a short citation of the bibliographic item which contains the work or document.

in boards 1. An obsolete style of binding in which the book was trimmed after the board sides had been laced on; short for cut in boards. 2. A cheap style of binding common in the 18th and early 19th centuries, consisting of pasteboards covered with (usually) blue paper on a lighter-colored spine; it was superseded by edition cloth binding.

incident light The sum total of the light which falls on an object. All or some part of the light may then be absorbed, transmitted, or reflected, depending on the characteristics of the object.

incipit From the Latin, here begins: the opening words of a medieval manuscript or an early printed book, or of one of its divisions, and often introducing the name of the author and the title of the work.

inclusive edition An edition of all of an author's works, or all of a particular type, written or published up to the time of its publication. Compare with *author's edition, collected edition.*

income A generic term for all money or money equivalents received by an organization in an accounting period.

incomplete file A periodical or newspaper file or a series from which volumes or numbers are lacking. Synonymous with broken file, incomplete run.

incomplete run see *incomplete file*

incunables Books printed from movable type during the 15th century, from the Latin incunabula, meaning swaddling clothes, i.e., cradle. Also known as cradle books and incunabula (the latter term formerly the most common in North America, but in recent years losing ground to the Anglicization).

incunabula see *incunables*

incut note see *cut-in heading*

indention The blank space from the margin to the beginning of a line of text, as in the first line of a paragraph.

independent see *bound with*

independent variable In statistics, a variable that influences (or is hypothesized to influence) another variable (a dependent variable) during an investigation.

index 1. A systematic guide to the contents of a file, document, or group of documents, consisting of an ordered arrangement of terms or other symbols representing the contents and references, code numbers, page numbers, etc., for accessing the contents. 2. The character ☞ , an old style reference mark, used to point to printed material. Also known as a hand, a fist, or an index finger. 3. When capitalized, a common short form of *Index Librorum Prohibitorum.*

indexed sequential file In information retrieval, a file of sequentially organized records in which one or more keys determines the location of records. The location of each record is computed through the use of an index. The keys are contained in a separate index which can be rapidly searched to determine if records are in the file and, if so, their location.

index finger see *index* (2)

indexing by exclusion A form of automatic indexing in which a computer is used to select, from the text of works, keywords to be used as the headings of index entries, by excluding insignificant words specified in a stop list. Compare with *indexing by inclusion.*

indexing by extraction see *derived indexing*

indexing by inclusion A form of automatic indexing in which a computer is used to select, from the text of works, keywords to be used as the headings of index entries, by including significant words specified in a go list. Compare with *indexing by exclusion.*

index language see *index vocabulary*

Index Librorum Prohibitorum The list of books which Roman Catholics were forbidden by the highest ecclesiastical authority to read or retain without authorization. Ceased publication in 1966 and no longer has the effect of law in the church. Commonly referred to as the Index and the Roman Index.

index map A map showing the total geographic coverage encompassed by a set or series of maps, or by a segmented single map, which indicates the way in which the area is divided among the several maps and often also indicates the location of the map in hand. Compare with *map index.*

index number In statistics, a number used to indicate changes in a variable observed over a period of time, e.g., the Consumer Price Index.

index of refraction see *refraction*

index vocabulary The set of descriptors to be used in indexing the contents of documents in an information storage and retrieval system. Synonymous with index language.

India Bible paper see *Bible paper*

India Oxford Bible paper see *Bible paper*

India proof paper An extremely soft, absorbent paper of straw color which soaks up a large quantity of ink from the surface of an engraved plate and is used in the making of proofs of engravings.

indicative abstract An abstract which indicates the contents of a document, but contains little of the quantitative and qualitative information contained in the original and therefore usually cannot be used in place of it. Compare with *informative abstract.*

indicator A character added to a machine-readable bibliographic record to provide additional information about a field, to facilitate a specific method of data manipulation, or to show the relationship between one field and another.

indirect subdivision The subdivision of subject headings by name of country or state, with further subdivision by name of province, city, county, or other locality. Compare with *direct subdivision.*

inferential statistics Statistical methods for drawing inferences about large groups, or populations, on the basis of descriptive statistics derived from small groups, or samples, chosen from the populations. Compare with *descriptive statistics.*

influence phase In classification, the phase relationship between two subjects in which one subject is influenced by the other.

informal organization In organizational theory, the intricate, but inevitable, network of personal, social, and political interactions and relationships among employees. While distinct from the formal organizational structure, it can affect the formal lines of communication and authority in various subtle or overt ways.

informatics The study of the structure and properties of information, as well as the application of technology to the organization, storage, retrieval, and dissemination of information.

information All ideas, facts, and imaginative works of the mind which have been communicated, recorded, published and/or distributed formally or informally in any format.

information agency An organization whose primary function is the provision of information to a body of clients.

information analysis center see *information evaluation center*

information and referral service (I&R) A service, primarily by telephone, of providing specific information, frequently of a utilitarian or practical nature, to inquirers, or referring the inquirers to an organization, agency, or individual capable of providing the information required. Such service may be provided by a library or other public service agency.

information broker An individual or organization who, on demand and for a fee, provides information directly to individual and organizational consumers, using all sources available.

information center An independent organization or an administrative unit of an organization which normally collects, organizes, stores, retrieves, and disseminates documents and performs such services as literature searches, compilation of bibliographies, issuance of selective dissemination of information bulletins, and abstracting, but does not produce evaluative reports requiring the analysis and synthesis of the contents of documents.

information clearinghouse An independent organization or an administrative unit of an organization which serves as a central agency for the collection, organization, storage, and dissemination of documents and performs referral services, such as maintaining records of research in the planning stage, in progress, and in completion and referring questions regarding research to the source.

information contact An encounter in person, by telephone, mail, or other means, between a member of the reference staff and a library user, in which information is sought or provided. An information contact may be a *directional transaction* or a *reference transaction;* a *bibliographic instruction* or *library use presentation;* or a *cultural, recreational, or educational presentation.*

information desk A desk in a library staffed by personnel responsible for directional transactions and sometimes ready reference.

information evaluation center An independent organization or an administrative unit of an organization which performs the functions of an information center and also provides evaluative reports requiring the analysis and synthesis of the contents of documents or other information sources. Synonymous with information analysis center.

information interchange format see *communication format*

information management The management or administration of the acquisition, organization, storage, retrieval, and dissemination of information. Synonymous with data management.

information management system (IMS) A system designed to organize, store, retrieve, and disseminate information.

information manager A person who administers or manages information or an information system.

information network A network of organizations established and maintained to share information, as distinct from a network for the sharing of bibliographic data identifying information sources. Compare with *bibliographic network.*

information processing see *data processing*

information retrieval The process of searching, locating, and retrieving data from a file. Synonymous with data retrieval.

information science The study of the creation, use, and management of information in all its forms.

information scientist One who is highly competent or knowledgeable in the creation, use, and management of information, usually with an emphasis on the processes of acquiring, organizing, storing, and retrieving information rather than on its content. Sometimes called documentalist.

information service Personal assistance provided by members of the reference staff to library users in pursuit of information. Synonymous with reference service.

information specialist One who is highly competent or knowledgeable in the content of documents in a particular field.

information staff see *reference staff*

information storage The process of entering data into a file for temporary or permanent retention and later retrieval.

information storage and retrieval (ISR) A general term often used to encompass both information storage and information retrieval.

information system A complete system designed for the generation, collection, organization, storage, retrieval, and dissemination of information within an institution, organization, or other defined area of society.

information technology The application of computers and other technology to the acquisition, organization, storage, retrieval, and dissemination of information.

information theory A branch of learning concerned with the measurement and transmission of information.

information transmission see *data transmission*

informative abstract An abstract which concentrates on the quantitative and qualitative information contained in a document and therefore can frequently be used in place of it. Compare with *indicative abstract.*

infrared light   The part of the red end of the spectrum that is invisible to the naked eye.

initial letter   A large capital letter, often ornamental in design, at the beginning of the first word of a chapter or paragraph. Synonymous with ornamental initial. When it is aligned with the top of the letters which follow and displaces one or more lines of text below, it is called a drop initial.

ink jet printer   see *printer* (2)

ink jet printing   A nonimpact printing process in which a coded tape controls laser-activated jets that spray the ink onto paper in patterns that create type and other graphic images. Currently used primarily in computer printers.

inlaid   1. Said of a leaf, plate, or other piece of graphic material which has been set into a border or frame, or into a larger piece of paper by cutting out a portion of the larger piece and pasting the piece to be inset over the gap. Compare with *onlaid*. 2. Said of a leather-bound book in which the cover has had another color or kind of leather set in.

inlay   1. In binding, the paper strip used to stiffen the spine. Often confused with *back lining* and *backstrip*. 2. A piece of material that has been inlaid. Compare with *onlay*.

in-line   see *online*

in press   In process of being printed.

in print   Available from the publisher.

in-process file   A file of bibliographic items which have been received but for which cataloging and physical processing have not been completed. Synonymous with process file, process information file.

in progress   Said of a publication that is not complete, but with volumes or parts issued as they are ready.

input   1. The data to be entered or transferred into a data processing or computer system for processing, in contradistinction to the results of processing *(output)*. 2. The signal fed into an audio or video device, in contradistinction to the signal emanating from it *(output)*.

input device   An electronic or mechanical machine or unit, such as a card reader or cathode-ray-tube terminal, designed to enter or transfer data into a computer for processing. Compare with *output device.*

input/output (I/O)   A general term pertaining to all aspects of entering data as input into a computer and receiving the results of processing or output.

input/output control system (IOCS)   A group or set of computer routines for managing and handling the details of input and output operations for a computer.

in quires   Said of a book in unbound printed sheets that have been folded and gathered. Synonymous with in signatures. Compare with *in sheets.*

inquiry   A request for data or information from a system, network, or storage.

inquiry station   A device such as a cathode-ray-tube terminal from which an inquiry can be made.

inscribed copy   1. A copy of a book in which has been written a presentation inscription, usually consisting of the names of the donor and recipient and appropriate remarks. 2. A copy of a book in which the presentation inscription is by the author of that book. Compare with *association copy, presentation copy.*

insert   1. One or more folded sheets of four pages, or a multiple of four, placed inside a folded signature, in the middle or elsewhere. The supplemented signature forms a binding unit, or section, of a book. Synonymous with inset. Compare with *outsert*. 2. Any matter slipped loose into a book, newspaper, or periodical that is not an integral part of the publication, such as an advertisement. Synonymous with loose insert and throw-in.

in-service training   A continuing program of systematic instruction and practice developed and provided by an organization to aid in staff development.

inset   see *insert* (1)

inset map   Any map positioned within the neat line of a larger map. Compare with *ancillary map.*

in sheets   Said of a book in unbound printed sheets laid flat. Compare with *in quires.*

inside margin see *back margin*

inside strip see *joint* (1)

in signatures see *in quires.*

instantaneous audiorecording An audiorecording that can be played back at once, without processing, such as an audiotape recording.

institution An established corporate body with social, educational, religious, or other purpose, whose functions require a plant with buildings and equipment, such as a college or hospital.

institution library A library maintained by a public or private institution to serve its staff and persons in its care because of physical, health, mental, or behavioral problems, such as the library of a correctional institution or an institution for the care of the mentally ill.

instructional materials Materials used for the purpose of instruction in a learning situation that is purposive and controlled.

instructional materials center see *media center*

instructional materials, programmed see *programmed instruction materials*

instructional technology A complex, integrated process involving people, procedures, ideas, devices, and organization, for analyzing problems and devising, implementing, evaluating, and managing solutions to those problems, in situations in which learning is purposive and controlled. Compare with *educational technology.* (AECT)

instructional television (ITV) Television programs which have been designed commercially or locally for the student in the classroom or at home. While the contents pertain to subjects taught in school, the viewer may utilize the programs in a nontraditional setting.

instructional television fixed service (ITFS) A method of broadcasting using a special microwave frequency which can only be received by television installations equipped with a converter to change signals back to those used by a television set. Within a range of 30-50 miles, it is ideal for school systems. (Pettipas)

instruction code see *operation code*

instrument of gift see *deed of gift*

intaglio printing Printing from a design cut by hand (engraving) or etched by chemicals (etching) into the printing surface, usually a metal plate. The incised lines hold the ink for transfer to the paper or other surface.

integer notation see *integral notation*

integral notation In classification, a notation which uses whole numbers rather than decimal fractions. Integral notation does not allow new subjects to be incorporated logically into a classification system unless blocks of numbers have been left unassigned for expansion purposes. Sometimes called arithmetical notation, it is less hospitable than decimal notation. Synonymous with integer notation. Compare with *fractional notation.*

integral positional locating A microfiche indexing and retrieval technique which relies solely on the automatic location of specific images indexed by position rather than by specific search codes also present in the desired frame.

integram see *holography*

integrated catalog A catalog in which the incorporation of new bibliographic records is unrestricted, and in which some attempt is made to reconcile headings derived from an old cataloging code or policy and those derived from a new one. Compare with *closed catalog, frozen catalog, open catalog.*

integrated circuit An electronic circuit with all components fabricated on a small piece or chip of semiconductor material.

integrated shelving The shelving together of all materials in classified order, regardless of format, in a library or media center. All materials on a particular subject are intershelved, whether book, filmstrip, audiorecording, etc.

integrative levels In classification, the theory which proposes that there is a recognizable developmental order in nature which involves a progression from simple organization to a high level of complexity, thereby allowing subjects to be categorized according to their complexity and arranged in ascending order.

integrity of numbers The principle that a class number, once used to denote a term in a classification system, not be reused with a different meaning, and that subjects be relocated sparingly in subsequent editions of the classification schedule.

intelligent terminal A computer terminal having some built-in capabilities for processing data before it is transmitted to a computer. Synonymous with smart terminal. Compare with *dumb terminal.*

intension In classification, all the attributes that the things denoted by a term have in common, whether these attributes are known or unknown, essential or accidental. Compare with *extension.*

interactive mode Pertaining to an interchange of messages and data between an operator of a terminal device and a computer. Each exchange elicits a response from the other, similar to a conversation between two individuals. Synonymous with conversational mode.

interactive television A two-way cable system which allows interaction between the television viewer and whatever is on the screen. This capability, for example, allows the user to conduct a step-by-step search of databases, using a communication system such as videotex.

interborrowing and interlending The practice of borrowing or lending materials between two administratively independent special libraries of the same organization. Also called internal borrowing and lending.

intercalation The insertion of a new class term in a classification schedule.

interchange format see *communication format*

interchange of librarians see *exchange of librarians*

interest profile A list of subject terms related to a person's activities and interests, to be used in selecting documents in a selective dissemination of information system. Synonymous with user profile.

interface The point or process which joins two system components, such as a device that facilitates the interoperation of data communication equipment and data-processing equipment.

interference In a signal transmission system, the reception of unwanted signals that interfere with the desired signal, such as the interference of television reception by airplane or automobile engines.

interference rings An optical defect somewhat similar in form to chromatic aberration. The defect appears as rainbow-colored rings that occur because of trapped air space between film negatives and photomechanical plates during the platemaking process.

interfiling 1. The practice of filing two or more variations of a single heading as if they were the same. The degree of variation allowed varies with individual institutional policy. Interfiling is a common response to heading changes which result from changes in rules or from subject heading revision. Compare with *split files.* 2. The practice of incorporating bibliographic records with records derived from one catalog code into a catalog containing headings derived from another code.

intergovernmental body A corporate body created by the action of two or more governments.

interim copyright see *ad interim copyright*

interleave To insert parts of one computer program into another. When there are delays in executing one program, parts of the other can be processed.

interleaved Said of a book with blank leaves for note taking between printed pages, or with guard sheets or plain thin sheets over plates.

interleaved plate A plate over which a guard sheet or plain thin sheet is inserted.

interlending see *interborrowing and interlending*

interlibrary loan (ILL) A transaction in which, upon request, one library lends an item from its collection, or furnishes a copy of the item, to another library not under the same administration or on the same campus.

interlibrary loan code A code that prescribes policies and procedures to be followed in interlibrary loan transactions.

interlibrary reference service A cooperative agreement among autonomous libraries to provide reciprocal reference services to the members of one another's target groups.

interlinear Written or printed between the lines of a text, such as explanatory notes or translation set in small type.

intermediate copy In reprography, a photographic copy of a document used to make distribution copies, or a copy produced during an intermediate stage in a reproduction process, such as a negative from which a positive copy is made.

internal borrowing see *interborrowing and interlending*

internal lending see *interborrowing and interlending*

internal report A report giving details and results of a specific investigation by an organization for its own research program. Internal reports filed in special libraries are generally confidential within the organization and restricted for the use of its own personnel.

internal storage see *main storage*

International Classification A general classification system by Fremont Rider, published by the author in 1961 and not updated. Resembling the Library of Congress Classification in its main outline, it is characterized by its brief notation of no more than three digits.

international copyright The copyright protection afforded foreign works, governed by national law and international agreements. The most widely effective international copyright agreements are the *Berne Convention* and the *Universal Copyright Convention.*

International Standard Bibliographic Description (ISBD) A group of standards for preparing the descriptive part of bibliographic records, first adopted officially by the International Federation of Library Associations in 1971. As of 1982, standards have been published for the following types of materials: monographs, ISBD(M); cartographic materials, ISBD(CM); nonbook materials, ISBD(NBM); printed music, ISBD(PM); pre-1820 books, ISBD(A); serials, ISBD(S). There is a general standard, ISBD(G), which provides the framework for describing all types of materials.

International Standard Book Number (ISBN) A four-part, ten-character code given a book (a nonserial literary publication) before publication as a means of identifying it concisely, uniquely, and unambiguously. The four parts of the ISBN are: group identifier (e.g., national, geographic, language, or other convenient group), publisher identifier, title identifier, and check digit. Started by British publishers in 1967, the standard book number was adopted the next year in the United States and the following year as an international standard. The numbering system is administered among cooperating publishers in participating countries by a standard book numbering agency.

International Standard Serial Number (ISSN) The international numerical code that identifies concisely, uniquely, and unambiguously a serial publication, based on American National Standard Identification Number for Serial Publications, Z39.9–1971, and approved by the International Organization for Standarization as ISO 3297, International Standard Serial Numbering. The ISSN program became operative in the United States in 1971.

internship A specified period of planned and supervised professional training in a library or other information agency which allows the application of theory to practice in a variety of professional activities following the completion of course work for the master's degree in library and information science. Compare with *practicum.*

interpolate To estimate a value between two other known values.

interpolator see *collator* (2)

interpret To print data above the columns in which characters are punched in a punched card.

interpreter 1. A machine which prints data above the columns in which characters are punched in a punched card. 2. A computer program that translates and executes one source program instruction before proceeding to the next.

interrupt The process of breaking or stopping the execution of a computer program when a computer's attention is temporarily diverted to another task. Upon completing the task, the computer generally returns to the program which was interrupted.

interval scale A type of measurement in which objects, events, or individuals are assigned to categories of variables in rank order, with equal distances between the units of measure, and with an arbitrary zero point.

in the trade Said of books issued by and obtainable from a commercial publisher.

intralibrary loan A transaction in which one library lends an item from its collection to another library within the same library system upon request.

intramural loan The loan of library materials to individuals or organizations within the normal constituency of a library.

intrinsic value In archives, the inherent value and, in appraisal, the worth in monetary terms of documents, dependent upon some factor such as age, the circumstances regarding creation, signature or the handwriting of a distinguished person, an attached seal, etc.

introduction The part of the front matter of a book which states the subject and discusses the treatment of the subject in the book. Compare with *preface*.

inventory 1. The process of checking the library collection against the shelflist record to identify missing items. 2. The process of checking library equipment, furniture, and other property against an authority list. 3. An authoritative list of library property indicating quantities, descriptions, and original costs. Each item of property may be assigned an inventory number at the time of purchase. 4. In archives, a finding aid for the material in a record group arranged basically in the order in which the material is arranged. It may also include a brief history of the agency or office whose records are being described, and such data as title, inclusive dates, quantity, arrangement, relationship to other series, and description of significant subject content. 5. In records management, a survey of records made before disposition or the development of disposition schedules.

inventory circulation system A circulation system in which a computer-readable record exists for all copies of all items held by a library; when a circulation transaction takes place, an indication is placed in the record that a particular copy of that item is on loan to a particular borrower. In that way there is an automatic record of whether each item in the library is available for circulation or not. Compare with *absence circulation system*.

inversion, principle of In classification, the principle that facets appear in a classification schedule, and hence in a classed catalog, in the reverse of their citation order, with the result that general topics appear before special topics.

inverted file In information retrieval, a file in which records are identified by one or more keywords. The items, numbers, or documents pertinent to the keyword are identified.

inverted heading A heading with the normal order of words transposed to bring a particular word into prominence as the filing element, e.g., Knowledge, Sociology of.

inverted pages see *tête-bêche*

inverted reference A reference from a name, phrase, etc., with a word or words transposed to the form which is to be used as a heading, e.g., Africa, South *see* South Africa.

inverted title A title with words transposed in order to bring a significant word into filing position in the heading of a bibliographic record.

invisible college Groups of collaborators in a research area, linked together through their leaders, who communicate with one another and transmit information on new research findings informally, before publication.

invitation to bid The formal process by which a library or other organization solicits cost quotations from potential suppliers of goods or services prior to awarding a contract. The invitation to bid may include specifications on expected levels of quality where appropriate and may be distributed selectively or to the broadest number of potential bidders.

invoice A document supplied by a vendor indicating the character, quantity, price, terms, and nature of delivery of goods sold or services rendered.

I/O see *input/output*

IOCS see *input/output control system*

iris diaphragm A diaphragm with a central aperture made up of overlapping blades readily adjustable to regulate the amount of light passing through the lens aperture.

ISBD see *International Standard Bibliographic Description*

ISBN see *International Standard Book Number*

isolate In faceted classification, a concept which can be placed in a number of different contexts and which, in isolation, is not considered to be a subject. When placed in the context of a facet of a basic class, the isolate becomes a focus of that facet.

ISR see *information storage and retrieval*

ISSN see *International Standard Serial Number*

issue 1. To produce, or cause to be produced, books or other printed documents for sale or for private distribution. 2. A distinct group of copies of an edition, printed from substantially the same setting of type as the first impression, but usually with a new title page or some addition, deletion, or substitution of printed matter made by the publisher to distinguish them as a consciously planned printed unit, different from other copies of the edition. Issues are frequently termed editions on the title page, e.g., a so-called new edition or large paper edition in which the text of the first impression has been virtually unaltered. Compare with *reissue*. 3. A single uniquely numbered or dated part of a periodical or newspaper.

issuing office The department, bureau, office, division, or other specific government body responsible for the issuing of a government publication.

italic A sloping type based on a cursive rather than a formal humanistic hand. It was introduced and used to print classical texts, but became a secondary type to be used with roman.

item 1. In the bibliographic sense, a *bibliographic item*. 2. In the physical sense, each separate document included in a library collection. 3. In archives, the smallest unit of record material which accumulates to form file units and series, e.g., a letter, photograph, memorandum, abstract, drawing, report, chart, printout, or reel of film or magnetic tape. 4. In data processing, a *data item*.

item-entry system An indexing system in which a card is used for each document and terms representing the subject content of the document are recorded on the card. Synonymous with term on item system. Compare with *term-entry system*.

item on term system see *term-entry system*

ITFS see *instructional television fixed service*

ITV see *instructional television*

J

jack A socket for an electrical plug.

jacket see *book jacket, card jacket, film jacket, sleeve* (1)

jacket cover see *book jacket*

jacketed film see *film jacket*

Japanese paper A thin, tough, extremely absorbent paper of silky texture used in the making of artists' proofs and other proofs of engravings.

Japanese style see *traditional format (Oriental books)*

JCL see *job control language*

job 1. In data processing, a group of operations identified as a unit of work for a computer. 2. In personnel management, a *position*.

job analysis see *position analysis*

job audit see *position analysis*

jobber see *wholesaler*

job classification see *position classification*

job control language (JCL) A programming language designed to describe and control jobs or work for a computer.

job description see *position description*

job information center see *education and job information center*

job lot A group of materials offered at a lower than normal price by a dealer in order to close out or cut down stock. Compare with *remainder.*

job rotation see *position rotation*

job specification see *position specification*

joggle To shake a deck of punched cards in order to align them.

joint Either of the two portions of the covering material that bend at the groove and along the ridge when the covers of a volume are opened or closed. Synonymous with inside strip and hinge.

joint author A person who collaborates with one or more other persons to produce a work in relation to which the collaborators perform the same function. Synonymous with coauthor. (AACR2)

journal A periodical, especially one containing scholarly articles and/or disseminating current information on research and development in a particular subject field. Compare with *magazine* (1).

junior college library/media center A library or media center established, supported, and administered by a junior college or two-year lower division college to meet the information needs of its students, faculty, and staff and to support its instructional and community service programs.

junior department see *children's department*

junior librarian A professional staff member who performs duties of a less difficult nature, requires regular supervision or training, has worked professionally for a relatively short duration, supervises nonprofessional but not professional personnel, or any combination of these criteria. It may be an official or implicit personnel classification in a library system. Compare with *senior librarian.*

justification In printing, equalizing the length of the lines of type by varying the space between the words and thus making them flush at the side margins. Compare with *ragged.*

juvenile department see *children's department*

juveniles Children's books.

k An abbreviation for 1,024 bytes.

Kalvar see *vesicular film*

kb see *kilobit*

keepsake see *giftbook*

kern The part of a type face that extends beyond the body, such as on an f or j.

kettle stitch In binding, the stitch used to secure each section to the preceding one at head and tail. Synonymous with chain stitch and catch stitch.

key In computer science, a character or characters used to identify a group of data elements, a document, or a record.

keyboard A device used to record data by depressing keys, used as a component part of such machines as a typewriter, phototypesetter, keypunch, or computer terminal.

keypunch A manually operated machine which punches patterns of holes representing data in cards. Compare with *card punch.*

keystone effect The effect produced in a projected image when the screen on which the image is projected is not perpendicular to the axis of projection.

key title The unique name assigned to a serial and linked to the International Standard Serial Number by the International Serials Data System (ISDS), an intergovernmental organization under Unesco, with the aim of building a reliable registry of world serial publications containing essential information for their identification and bibliographic control.

keyword   A significant word in the abstract, title, or text of a work which is used as a descriptor.

Keyword and Context Index (KWAC) see *Keyword Out of Context Index (KWOC)*

Keyword in Context Index (KWIC)   A form of permutation indexing, in which the subject content of a work is represented by keywords from its title, derived by a computer from the use of a stop list or go list, or from manual tagging. In the computer printout, the keywords appear alphabetically in a fixed location (usually the center) in an index line of fixed length (usually 60 or 100 characters) and are preceded and followed by such other words of the title as space allows. The keyword, which is the heading of the index entry, and the context, which serves as the modification of the heading, are followed by a serial number or code which is linked to a full identification of the document indexed.

Keyword Out of Context Index (KWOC)   A variation on the *Keyword in Context Index,* in which keywords, removed from the context of the titles that contain them, appear as headings in a separate line index flush with the left margin. Below each keyword heading appear the titles, in full or truncated form, that contain the

keyword. In the titles, the keyword may be replaced by a symbol, or it may be repeated, in which case the index may be referred to as Keyword and Context Index (KWAC).

khz see *kilohertz*

kilobit (Kb)   One thousand binary digits or bits.

kilohertz (khz)   5,000 hertz.

kinescope   A motion picture photographed from a television screen.

kit see *multimedia kit*

knowledge classification   A classification system devised for a branch or branches of knowledge, not specifically for use in classifying books or other documents. Compare with *bibliothecal classification.*

kurtosis   The degree of relative peakedness or flatness of a frequency distribution.

KWAC see *Keyword Out of Context Index (KWOC)*

KWIC see *Keyword in Context Index (KWIC)*

KWOC see *Keyword Out of Context Index (KWOC)*

L

label   1. In binding, a piece of paper or other material, on which the author and title of the book are printed or stamped, which is affixed to a book cover, usually on the spine or the front cover. 2. In computer science, a name or identifier used as a key to identify an instruction in a computer program, data item, field, record, or file. 3. An identifier containing alphanumeric characters, which frequently provides information about the contents of a volume of a machine-readable data file or about the file. 4. A record at the beginning of a volume of a machine-readable data file, or at the beginning or end of a file section, or at the end of a file, that

identifies, characterizes, and/or delimits that volume or file section.

label title   The title and author of a book printed near the top of a separate leaf at the beginning of the book, and occasionally on the verso of the last leaf, in place of or in addition to such title at the front of the book; found in incunables.

laboratory collection   1. A small group of library materials belonging to a college or a university library, kept in a laboratory, a professor's office, or a departmental office as a direct help in teaching or conducting research on a certain subject. 2. A group of library materials in a teacher-preparing institution, a library school, or other similar setting, organized for purposes of demonstration, practice, and project work. Compare with *curriculum materials center.*

laced on Said of boards affixed to a book by passing the cords onto which the sections have been sewn through holes in the boards.

Lacey Luci see *image modifier*

lacuna A gap in a library's collection; usually used when referring to a gap the library wishes to fill.

laid lines see *laid paper* (1)

laid paper 1. Paper handmade on a framed mold of fine wires laid close together and held in place by heavier wires crossing them at right angles. The laid lines, or pattern, made by these wires is visible when the paper is held up to the light. The heavier lines, which run across the short dimension of the mold, are called chain lines, while the finer, more closely spaced lines at right angles are called wire lines. Compare with *wove paper* (1). 2. Machine-made paper upon which chain and wire lines have been impressed by a dandy roll.

lambert A centimeter-gram-second unit of brightness, equal to the uniform brightness of a perfectly diffusing surface emitting or reflecting light at the rate of one lumen per square centimeter.

lamination A method of adhering a special transparent protective film to the image surface of a piece of two-dimensional material. The process usually involves some type of acetate, vinyl, or mylar film which has a transparent adhesive coating on one side. The film, depending on the type being used, may be applied by either a cold process or heat process and by hand or by machine.

laminator A device which passes two-dimensional material through rollers and applies heat and/or pressure to seal a transparent protective film onto the image surface of the material. A dry-mount press can also be used for laminating.

lamp house The section of a projector containing the light source used for illumination.

language The defined set of rules, graphic representations, and conventions used for meaningful communication among people or machines or between people and machines.

lantern slide A 3¼-x-4-inch slide, usually made from a piece of thin glass.

lantern slide projector A slide projector which accepts standard 3¼-x-4-inch lantern slides. Some projectors also accept smaller slides with the provision of special adapters and, usually, a different projection lens.

lap marks The longitudinal impressions on film created by defective rollers during processing.

lap reader see *microform reader*

lap splice see *splice*

large-paper copy or **edition** An impression of a book printed on paper of extra size with wide margins, produced from the same type image as that of the trade or small paper copy or edition, and therefore an issue rather than a true edition.

large print Any type size over 16-point, used in books, periodicals, or other printed publications for the visually handicapped or beginning readers.

laser-beam recorder (LBR) see *computer-output-microfilm recorder*

laser/xerographic printer see *printer* (2)

latent image The invisible image produced by the action of radiant energy on a photosensitive surface, made visible by the developing process.

latent image fade Fading associated with images on undeveloped film. The extent of fading is a function of emulsion type, storage conditions, and intervening time between exposure and developing.

latitude see *tonal range*

law binding A style of plain full-leather binding (usually sheep) in a light color, with two dark labels on the spine, used for law books. Now simulated in buckram.

law super see *crash*

layout The typographical plan of a publication showing general arrangement of text, illustrations, etc., with indication of type styles and sizes.

LBR (laser beam recorder) see *computer-output-microfilm recorder*

leader 1. A blank section of film at the beginning of a reel of motion-picture film, filmstrip, or microfilm for threading into the projector or other equipment and for the protection of the first frames. 2. A blank section of tape at the beginning of a reel of recorded magnetic tape or punched tape to protect the first few inches of the tape. Compare with *trailer* (2).

leaders A line of dots, hyphens, or other characters, used to guide the eye across a space, as in indexes and tables.

leading The spacing between lines of print, obtained by inserting thin metal strips less than type high (leads) between the lines of metal type or by the placement of extra space between lines of type in photosetting. In photosetting, synonymous with line spacing and film advance.

lead-in vocabulary In an index vocabulary, references from synonymous and quasi-synonymous terms to preferred terms, or descriptors, to be used in the indexing and retrieval of documents.

leaf 1. One of the units into which the original sheet or half sheet of paper, parchment, etc., is folded to form part of a book; each leaf consists of two pages, one on each side, either or both of which may be blank. (AACR2) 2. Gold leaf, and, by extension, sheets of metallic foil used in stamping a design or lettering on book covers.

leaf affixing In binding, a general term encompassing the several methods of fastening together the leaves of a book. Includes adhesive binding, mechanical binding, sewing, and stitching. Synonymous with page affixing.

leaf book A book containing an account of an earlier printed book (or occasionally, manuscript) and including an original leaf (or leaves) from that book. The edition size of a leaf book is thus necessarily limited by the number of leaves available from a copy of the original, and, because a single, defective copy of the original is almost always used for this purpose, the edition size is generally quite small, and in any event almost always smaller than the total number of leaves in a complete copy of the original.

leaflet 1. In a limited sense, a publication of two-to-four pages printed on a small sheet folded once, but not stitched or bound, the pages following the same sequence as in a book. 2. In a broader sense, a small thin pamphlet.

learners' advisory service see *education and job information center*

learning package A collection of subject-related materials accompanied by specific directions for learner use and for which there is a list of objectives and test items. (NCES)

learning resources In educational technology, all of the resources (data, people, and things) which may be used by the learner in isolation or in combination, usually in an informal manner, to facilitate learning. Includes resources specifically developed to facilitate purposive, formal learning and resources which have not been designed specifically for instruction but can be applied and used for learning purposes. (AECT)

learning resources center (LRC) see *media center*

learning resources specialist see *media specialist*

leased collection A revolving collection of popular works in high demand provided to a library by a leasing service for a rental fee.

leased line see *private line*

least significant digit see *low-order digit*

least squares method In regression analysis, given a set of observations of a pair of variables, the least-squares method finds that line (or curve) which best fits the observations, in the sense that the sum of the squared deviations of the observed values from that line is smaller than the corresponding sum for any other line. Compare with *line of best fit*.

leather-bound Either fully or partly bound in leather, but always with a leather backstrip.

ledger catalog see *guard book catalog*

ledger weight paper Photographic paper of moderately heavy stock, used when greater body and mechanical durability are desired. (NMA)

LED recorder see *computer output microfilm recorder*

legal deposit A copyright requirement that one or more copies of a publication be received by the copyright office or designated libraries. Synonymous with copyright deposit.

legend 1. A story based on tradition rather than fact, but popularly considered historical. 2. On a map, an explanation of symbols, etc., to aid in the reading. 3. A term for the description or title of an illustration, printed below it.

legislative manual see *state manual*

legislative reference service Assistance given by a library to government agencies and to a legislature, especially in problems of political administration and in connection with proposed or pending legislation. Within library functions at the state level, such assistance sometimes includes the drafting and indexing of bills.

lens A single spherical element or a system of elements, usually constructed of glass, designed to form images through the transmission of radiant energy.

lens aperture The opening, controlled by the diaphragm, which allows light to pass through the lens to form an image on sensitized film.

lensless copying In reprography, any copying process which does not use a lens to form images on photosensitive material. Normally the original is brought into direct contact with photosensitive material and exposed to light. Depending on the specific process and type of material, either a negative or positive can be produced. Synonymous with direct copying. Compare with *optical copying.*

lens speed Specified as an f-number, the lens speed is the measure of the amount of light that can pass through the lens. The f-rating is obtained by dividing the diameter of the lens opening into the focal length when the lens is focused at infinity.

lens stop see *diaphragm* (2)

lens system Two or more lenses arranged to work in conjunction with one another. (NMA)

let-in note see *cut-in heading*

letter 1. A report of research in a primary journal, the usual purpose of which is early, rapid communication of new but perhaps incomplete or not fully substantiated theoretical or experimental findings, or treatment of problems; full papers on the work may be prepared much later, or never. 2. A serial intended to provide the latest information quickly and in unedited form. Compare with *newsletter* (1).

lettera antiqua see *humanistic hand*

letter book 1. A book in which correspondence was copied by writing the original letter with copying ink, placing it against a dampened sheet of thin paper (leaves of which made up the book) and applying pressure. 2. A book of blank or lined pages on which are written letters, either drafts written by the author or fair copies made by the author or by a clerk. 3. A book comprising copies of loose letters which have been bound together, or one into which such copies are pasted onto guards or pages.

letter-by-letter alphabetizing The arrangement of a file alphabetically by the letters in the headings of the records, ignoring the spaces between words. Compare with *word-by-word alphabetizing.*

lettered proof A proof of an engraving with the title and names of the artist, engraver, and printer engraved in the margin.

lettering 1. The activity of applying or inscribing letters and numbers to create text, titles, or captions. A wide assortment of lettering procedures exist involving such aids as lettering guides, mechanical tracing lettering guides, and a variety of letters, including precut and dry-transfer letters. (NCES) 2. In binding, the process or result of marking a cover with the title or other distinguishing characters (and, loosely, accompanying ornamentation).

lettering device, mechanical A device with lettering guides and scriber pens used in the lettering (by hand) of signs, mechanical drawings, and other original artwork. (NCES)

lettering device, photographic A device with master alphabet negative(s) and exposure and processing units which produce photographic copies of selected letters on strips of paper or film. (NCES)

letterpress 1. A printing process using pressure to transfer ink from a raised surface, such as metal type or a photoengraving, to paper or other surface. Synonymous with relief printing. 2. Printed matter produced by such a process. 3. The text of a book, including illustrations within the text but not plates.

letterset see *dry offset*

letter symbols (size notation) see *size letters*

lettre bâtarde see *bastarda*

lettre de forme see *textura*

Levant A high-grade, pronounced-grain, thick goatskin leather used in bookbinding, made from the skin of the Angora goat, especially the large mountain goat of the Cape of Good Hope. French Cape Levant refers to large, high-quality skins.

level of description The degree of bibliographic detail adopted for use in the preparation of bibliographic records for a catalog, determined by the number of data elements chosen for inclusion in the bibliographic description. The *Anglo-American Cataloguing Rules,* 2nd ed., specify three levels. Compare with *bibliographic description.*

level of significance see *significance level*

LIBGIS An acronym for Library General Information Survey, a national library data system with the goal of collecting comparable data for all publicly and privately controlled libraries and for library development activity at the local, state, and federal levels, under the auspices of the National Center for Education Statistics and with the cooperation of state library agencies.

librarian 1. A person responsible for the administration of a library. 2. The chief administrative officer of a library. 3. A class of library personnel with professional responsibilities, including those of management, which require independent judgment, interpretation of rules of procedure, analysis of library problems, and formulation of original and creative solutions, normally utilizing knowledge of library and information science represented by a master's degree. 4. Combined with name of department, type of work, kind of library, or with a personnel rating term, a term used to designate the title of a staff member, such as acquisitions librarian or children's librarian. 5. In computer science, a special computer program that generates, maintains, and controls the set of programs comprising an operating system for a computer.

librarianship The profession concerned with the application of knowledge of media and those principles, theories, techniques, and technologies which contribute to the establishment, preservation, organization, and utilization of collections of library materials and to the dissemination of information through media.

library 1. A collection of materials organized to provide physical, bibliographic, and intellectual access to a target group, with a staff that is trained to provide services and programs related to the information needs of the target group. 2. In computer science, an organized collection of computer programs available to users of the machine.

library administration The process of administration as applied in a library organization, including the planning, direction and execution of operations toward the accomplishment of desired goals.

library associate/associate specialist A class of library personnel who are assigned supportive responsibilities at a high level, normally within the established procedures and techniques, and with some supervision by a librarian or specialist, but requiring judgment and subject knowledge such as is represented by a full, four-year college education culminating in the bachelor's degree. Whether the title is library associate or associate specialist depends upon the nature of the tasks or responsibilities assigned.

library associates see *friends of the library*

library automation The use of computers and other machines by a library to support its systems and services.

library bindery A bindery that specializes in library binding.

library binding Various styles and methods of binding performed for libraries utilizing machine or hand methods, or a combination of each, and executed to provide optimum permanence and/or durability. Included are the first-time hardcover binding of loose periodical issues, case binding of paperbound publications, the rebinding or repair of older volumes, and the prebinding of new publications specifically for high-volume circulation by public libraries (see *pre-library bound*). To be distinguished from *publisher's binding* and *edition binding.*

library board see *board*

library building consultant A library consultant with special expertise in library architecture and the planning of library facilities.

library card see *borrower's identification card*

library classroom An adjacent classroom serving as an instructional area in the school library media center.

library clerk A category of library personnel with general clerical and secretarial proficiencies who perform tasks related to library operations in strict accordance with established rules and procedures.

library club 1. A group of librarians, usually local, organized to meet for discussion and action on professional matters. 2. In a school library media center, see *school library media club.*

library collection The total accumulation of materials provided by a library for its target group. Synonymous with library holdings and library resources.

library-college A union of the library and the teaching program of a college, in which the dominant learning mode is library-centered, independent study, utilizing a full range of media and guided by a bibliographically expert faculty.

library commission see *state library agency*

library consortium A formal association of libraries, usually restricted to a geographical area, number of libraries, type of library, or subject interest, which is established to develop and implement resource sharing among the members and thereby improve the library services and resources available to their respective target groups. Some degree of formalization of administration and procedures is required. Compare with *library network.*

library consultant An external expert commissioned by a library to give professional or technical advice on planning, management, operations, physical facilities, or other area of concern.

library corner A book corner in which the covering material is not cut, the excess being taken up in two diagonal folds, one under each turn-in. Synonymous with Dutch corner; sometimes loosely called *round corner.*

library director see *director* (1)

library discount see *discount*

library district 1. A geographical area in which the citizens have voted to assume a tax to support a library, according to legal provisions. 2. One of the geographical areas into which a state is divided to facilitate the establishment, maintenance, or improvement of libraries in accordance with a state plan.

library edition 1. A publisher's term for an edition of a book in an especially strong binding, though not the equivalent of *library binding.* Sometimes called *special edition.* 2. An edition of a series or set issued in a uniform format.

library extension see *extension library service*

library facilities see *facilities*

Library General Information Survey see *LIBGIS*

library holdings see *library collection*

library materials Materials, of all physical substances and formats, acquired by a library to constitute its library collection. Devices for reading, viewing, or hearing the informational content of materials are excluded.

library network A specialized type of library cooperation for centralized development of cooperative programs and services, including use of computers and telecommunications, and requiring the establishment of a central office and a staff to accomplish network programs rather than merely to coordinate them. Compare with *library consortium.*

Library of Congress card A printed catalog card prepared and distributed by the Library of Congress.

Library of Congress Classification A classification system developed and used at the Library of Congress, beginning in 1897. It is an example of a highly enumerative classification based on literary warrant.

Library of Congress depository catalog A catalog containing a complete set of Library of Congress cards, placed without charge in certain libraries. Maintenance of the catalogs by free distribution of cards was discontinued by the Library of Congress in 1946.

library orientation see *library use presentation*

library pass see *admission record*

library permit see *admission record*

library resources see *library collection*

library school A professional school, department, or division granting a postbaccalaureate degree, which is organized and maintained by an institution of higher education for the purpose of preparing students for professional positions in a library or other information agency.

library science The knowledge and skill by which recorded information is selected, acquired, organized, and utilized in meeting the information demands and needs of a community of users.

library service A generic term for all of the activities performed and programs offered by libraries in meeting the information needs of their target groups. As such, it can encompass a broad range and hierarchy of services (e.g., public services, information services, circulation services) which are determined for a particular library by its goals.

library stamp see *imprint* (*binding*) (1)

library standards see *standards*

library survey 1. A systematic collection of data concerning the management, activities, services, programs, use, and users of a library, singly or in combination and in any or all aspects, in order to determine how well the library is meeting its objectives. A survey may be conducted from within the library (a self-study) or by an outside expert or team of experts. 2. The written report of such a study.

library system 1. A group of independent and autonomous libraries joined together by formal or informal agreements to achieve a specified result, such as a cooperative system and a federated system. 2. A group of commonly administered libraries, such as a consolidated system or a central library and its auxiliary service outlets.

library technical assistant A class of library personnel with specific technical skills who perform tasks in support of library associates or associate specialists and higher ranks, following established rules and procedures, and including, at the top level, supervision of such tasks.

library trustees see *board*

library use presentation An information service to a group designed to introduce potential library users to the facilities, organization, and services of a particular library. Synonymous with library orientation. Distinct from *bibliographic instruction.*

library user A person who uses library materials or services. Preferred to the term reader, since library collections include materials that may be read, viewed, or listened to, and to the term patron, which denotes a library advocate or supporter.

libretto The text of an opera or other work for the musical stage or of an extended choral composition.

license see *cum licentia*

lift A mechanical device for carrying library materials from one floor or stack level to another, operated by hand or by electrical power on the dumbwaiter principle.

ligature Two or three written or printed letters or characters tied together by having one or more strokes in common, such as "ff." Synonymous with double letter and tied letter.

light Luminous energy or radiation of wavelength between infrared and ultraviolet that can be seen by the human eye. The portion of radiation outside this range is termed black light. A major concern in reprography is the extent to which objects transmit, diffuse, or reflect light, and the brightness or luminescence of the light source. The branch of physics concerned with measuring the intensity of light is photometry. Measuring instruments called photometers compare unknown light intensities against that of a standard.

Incandescent light is measured in terms of candle power, and the intensity of cold light is expressed in foot-candles. The international candle, or candela, provides a standard unit of luminous intensity, and brightness is measured in units called lambert.

light board see *light box*

light box A device with a back-illuminated translucent surface which is used for viewing and working with transparent graphics and film. Synonymous with light board.

light-emitting diode (LED) recorder see *computer-output-microfilm recorder*

light filter see *filter*

light meter see *exposure* (1)

light pen 1. A hand-held reader for bar-coded labels or tags. 2. A high-speed photosensitive device that can cause the computer to change or modify the display on the cathode-ray-tube screen.

light-sensitive material Any substance capable of undergoing a physical or chemical change as a result of exposure to light. The term generally refers to the emulsions used on film and paper and photoconductive materials used in xerography.

light-struck film Film damaged by accidental exposure to light. The resulting fog lowers the contrast in desired images, or may produce undesirable latent images.

light trap Any technique or material used to reduce fogging by keeping extraneous light from striking unexposed film, e.g., the use of additional leader around a roll of film.

lignin A major component of wood, removed in the chemical pulping processes. It is unstable and discolors in paper. Because mechanical pulping processes do not remove lignin, groundwood pulp is not desirable in permanent-durable paper.

lilliput edition see *miniature edition*

limited cataloging see *brief cataloging*

limited edition An edition limited to a specifically stated number of copies, which are usually consecutively numbered. Sometimes issued in addition to a regular edition, but with superior paper and binding.

limp binding A style of binding in thin, flexible cloth or leather, without boards.

limp ooze see *ooze leather*

line and staff organization A nebulous distinction between organizational units or positions in an organization, based upon whether the unit or position is directly responsible for the accomplishment of organizational goals (line) or indirectly responsible (staff) through the provision of technical, research, or other assistance to line positions. While some organizational units or positions may be characterized as primarily line

or staff, the distinction is better explained in terms of authority relationships. Compare with *line authority, staff authority, functional authority.*

linear regression In regression analysis, the mathematical linear relationship between two variables, represented by the equation of a straight line.

line art 1. Artwork with no intermediate tones between black and white. Synonymous with line copy. 2. In reprography, a two-tone document or reproduction.

line authority The right conferred upon an administrator or supervisor in an organization by virtue of position to direct the activities of subordinates in the hierarchy. Compare with *functional authority, staff authority.*

line block see *line cut* (1)

linecasting machine see *linotype*

line control The set of operating procedures and control signals used to control channels in a telecommunications system.

line conversion The conversion of continuous tone art into line art by the use of screens through which the artwork is photographed.

line copy see *line art*

line cut 1. A photoengraved plate with an image consisting of lines and solid areas, without tone. Also known as line block, line etching and, when on zinc, zinc etching. 2. A print produced from such a plate.

line density A measure of the opacity of photographic images. Synonymous with image density. Compare with *background density.*

line discipline A means of controlling messages or communications between network stations for an orderly transmission of data.

line division mark A mark, usually a vertical or slanting line or virgule, used in bibliographical transcription to indicate the end of a line of type in the original.

line drawing see *drawing*

line ending The right edge of a line in a manuscript or a printed book. Traditionally printed lines were justified, but recent printing methods allow them to be ragged or unjustified.

line engraving   1. An intaglio process for reproducing drawings, in which the engraving is made by hand with a burin or graver. 2. A print produced from such a plate.

line etching   see *line cut* (1)

line-item budget   A budget which classifies all anticipated expenditures into broad categories (e.g., salaries, wages, materials, binding, supplies, maintenance, and equipment), thus controlling expenditures for the input of resources.

linen   A book cloth made of flax.

linen finish   A linenlike finish given to book cloth, obtained by applying filler and a face coating that includes coloring to undyed cloth and then scraping the face coating so that the white threads of the cloth show partly through.

line noise   Noise originating in a transmission line.

linen paper   Originally a high-quality paper made from linen or cotton rags. Also paper with a finish resembling linen cloth.

line of best fit   A line of regression drawn through all the points that express the relationship of two perfectly correlated variables. In the more frequent case of two variables that are not perfectly correlated and thus will plot as a scattergram whose points do not fall in a straight line, the line of best fit is that line which expresses best the relationship between the variables, using the least-squares method.

line of regression   A straight line on a scattergram which depicts the relationship of the values of two variables; the line of best fit.

line organization   see *line and staff organization*

line printer   A type of computer printer in which an entire line of characters is printed during a single machine cycle. Compare with *character printer*.

linespacing   see *leading*

line spread   see *bleed* (3)

lining papers   see *endpapers*

link   In a term-entry indexing system, and in the case of a document entered under several descriptors, some of which are unrelated, a common symbol added to the document number of related descriptors, in order to avoid false combinations in retrieval. 2. Address of or pointer to the next record in a linked system.

linked books   Separately bound books whose relationship with one another is indicated in various ways, such as a common collective title, mention in contents or other preliminary leaves, continuous pagination, or continuous series of signature marks.

linking entry field   In a machine-readable bibliographic record, a field containing data which relates one bibliographic item to another.

linking references   References which connect two or more variations of a single heading, each of which is filed in accordance with the filing rules of the catalog (i.e., they are in split files).

linocut   1. A linoleum-faced block on which a knife or gouge has been used to recess the nonprinting area and leave the image to be printed in relief. 2. A print made from such a block.

Linotype   The trade name of a once widely used letterpress typesetting machine which casts each line of type onto a single slug of metal. Synonymous with linecasting machine and slugcasting machine. Compare with *Monotype*.

linters   see *cotton linters*

list   1. A simple enumeration of bibliographic items; a *finding list*. 2. In data processing, to print every relevant item of input data. 3. In data processing, an ordered set or group of data items.

listening and viewing area   see *audiovisual area*

listening center   1. An audio distribution device to which headphones are or can be connected to enable one or more learners to hear an audio program at the same time. (LDCH) 2. An area where library or media center users listen to audiorecordings.

listing   A list of instructions or statements of a computer program.

list price   The price at which a publication is made available to the public. It customarily is established by the publisher and is exclusive of any discount. Loosely, the price quoted in a publisher's catalog.

literal mnemonics In classification, the mnemonic device of using the initial letter of a class term as its notation. Similar to *casual mnemonics.*

literary agent One who arranges the sale of authors' works to publishers and negotiates subsidiary rights; also one who acts for publishers in finding special types of works that they need. The author pays for the agent's services on a commission basis.

literary magazine see *little magazine*

literary manuscripts Manuscripts and other documents, including drafts and proofs, of belles lettristic works such as novels, essays, plays, and poetry.

literary property rights see *rights*

literary warrant In classification, the structure of a classification system on the basis of materials to be classified rather than on purely theoretical considerations.

literature search A systematic and exhaustive search for published materials bearing on a specific subject, often the first step in a research project.

lithograph A print produced by lithography.

lithographic film A type of film used in lithography for the production of plates. The film is normally high contrast orthochromatic or panchromatic.

lithography A planographic printing process in which the areas to be printed are grease-receptive and accept the ink, while the nonprinting areas are water-receptive and reject ink. Originally a greasy crayon was used to draw the image onto a specially prepared stone, the stone was treated with acid to make the nonimage area water-receptive, and ink, when applied to the surface, adhered only to the greasy crayon drawing. The commercial form of lithography is called *offset lithography.*

lithophotography see *photolithography*

little magazine A periodical devoted to poetry and avant-garde thinking. Synonymous with literary magazine.

load In computer science, to enter or place data or a computer program into main storage.

loading (paper) see *filling*

loan department see *circulation department*

loan desk see *circulation desk*

loan period The length of time allowed borrowers for the use of items charged from the library collection.

loan record see *charging file*

loan system see *charging system*

local subdivision see *geographic subdivision*

location mark see *location symbol*

location symbol One or more letters, words, or other symbols added to the record of a bibliographic item in a bibliography, bibliographic database, catalog, or list, to indicate the collection, library, etc., in which a copy of the item may be found. Synonymous with location mark.

lock code see *password*

log A record of pertinent facts about activities or transactions that occur in a system.

logical difference Those elements of two sets, A and B, which are members of Set A but not B (A–B). Compare with *logical product, logical sum.*

logical product Those elements of two sets, A and B, which are common members to both A and B (AB). Compare with *logical difference, logical sum.*

logical record In computer science, a record defined on the basis of its content, rather than its physical location or space requirements. Compare with *physical record.*

logical sum Those elements of two sets, A and B, which are members of either A or B or both (A+B). Compare with *logical difference, logical product.*

logic unit see *arithmetic-logic unit*

logo see *printer's mark*

log off To terminate communications with a computer in a time-sharing mode. Compare with *log on*.

log on To initiate communications with a computer in a time-sharing mode. Compare with *log off*.

long shot A picture taken with a lens which tends to reduce depth of field, giving an illusion that space is compressed and that the camera is at a considerable distance from the object being photographed.

long-term film Processed photographic film with a shelf life expectancy of at least 100 years, if stored properly. Compare with *archival film, medium-term film,* and *short-term film.*

loop A sequence of computer instructions which is executed repeatedly until a specified condition is met.

loose-back A type of binding in which the covering material is not glued to the back of the book. Synonymous with hollow back and open back. Compare with *tight back.*

loose in binding A term used to describe the physical condition of a book separated from its case.

loose insert see *insert* (2)

loose-leaf binding A form of mechanical binding which permits the ready withdrawal and insertion of leaves at any desired position. Common forms are ring binding and post binding.

loose-leaf catalog see *sheaf catalog*

loose-leaf service A serial publication which is revised, cumulated, or indexed by means of new or replacement pages inserted in a loose-leaf binder, and used where latest revisions of information are important, as with legal and scientific material. Compare with *serial service.*

loudness The attribute of a sound that determines the magnitude of the auditory sensation produced. The magnitude generally increases as the amplitude of the audio signal is increased. Synonymous with volume.

loudspeaker A device which converts electrical impulses into sounds. Also called speaker.

lowercase letters The minuscule or small letters of a type font, so called because the case which held them historically was below the case for capital letters. Compare with *uppercase letters.*

lower cover see *cover* (2)

low-level language In computer science, a programming language whose instructions usually are on a one-to-one correspondence with those of the computer. Compare with *high-level language.*

low-order digit The least significant or low-weighted digit of a number in a positional notation system. For example, 7 is the low-order digit in the number 8957. Synonymous with least significant digit. Compare with *high-order digit.*

low reduction see *reduction ratio*

low-speed printer A computer printer with a speed usually lower than 500 lines per minute. Compare with *high-speed printer.*

LRC (learning resources center) see *media center*

lumen A unit of measurement of the flow of light, equal to the amount of flow through a unit solid angle from a uniform point source of one candela.

lumen per square centimeter see *lambert*

lumen per square foot see *footcandle*

lumen per square meter see *lux*

lump-sum appropriation A sum of money authorized for a certain purpose without accounting restrictions on how the money is to be dispensed among various funds.

lump-sum budget A budget of a certain dollar amount, without any restriction on its allocation, thereby allowing wide discretion in expenditure on the part of the administrator.

LUMSPECS see *binding specifications*

lux A unit of illuminance equal to one lumen per square meter, or the illumination on a surface that is everywhere one meter from a uniform point source of one candela.

Lyonnaise binding A binding with a large, generally lozenge-shaped, central ornament, and large corner ornaments, the ground generally covered with dots or small ornaments.

machine address see *absolute address*

machine-aided index see *enriched keyword index*

machine binding A category of binding using machines largely or exclusively to perform operations, as opposed to hand, or craft, processes. Used in large measure to perform library binding.

machine code see *computer instruction code*

machine cycle see *cycle* (1)

machine-dependent language see *machine-oriented language*

machine-finish paper 1. In general, any paper with finish obtained on a papermaking machine. 2. Particularly, an uncoated book paper with slight gloss and medium smoothness, not so rough as eggshell but not so smooth as is implied by the term English finish.

machine-independent language A programming language not designed for use with a particular model or class of computers; for example, ALGOL, COBOL, and FORTRAN. Compare with *machine-oriented language.*

machine instruction see *computer instruction*

machine language A language that can be recognized, accepted, and used directly by a machine such as a computer. Synonymous with absolute language and computer language.

machine-oriented language A programming language designed for a specific model or class of computers. Synonymous with computer-dependent language, computer-oriented language, and machine-dependent language. Compare with *machine-independent language.*

machine-readable Pertaining to a format that can be recognized, accepted, and used directly by a machine such as a computer or other data processing device. Synonymous with machine sensible.

Machine-Readable Cataloging see *MARC*

machine-readable data file (MRDF) A body of information coded by methods that require the use of a machine (typically but not always a computer) for processing. Examples include files stored on magnetic tape, punched cards, aperture cards, disk packs, etc. (AACR2)

machine run see *computer run*

machine sensible see *machine-readable*

machine translation The conversion of data or the content of documents in one language into another by a computer. Synonymous with mechanical translation.

machine word see *computer word*

macroform A generic term for any medium, transparent or opaque, bearing images large enough to be easily read or viewed without magnification. Compare with *microform.*

macroinstruction A source language instruction equivalent to several machine language instructions.

macroprogramming Preparation of computer instructions using macroinstructions.

magazine 1. A periodical for general reading, containing articles on various subjects by different authors. Compare with *journal.* 2. In micrographics, a container for processed microfilm which protects the film and is used to load the film into a reader. The term is also applied to storage containers for unprocessed film, or to containers used to transfer film during an intermediate stage of processing.

magazine rack see *rack*

magnetic card A plastic card coated with a magnetic material on which data can be recorded and stored.

magnetic cartridge A phonocartridge that produces electrical voltage by the movement of a magnet or wire coils in a magnetic field by the stylus cantilever. Compare with *piezoelectric cartridge.*

magnetic core A tiny piece of ferromagnetic material, usually ring-shaped, which can be polarized in either direction by passing a current through it and thereby be made capable of storing one binary digit.

magnetic core storage A type of high-speed, direct-access storage consisting of an array of magnetic cores. Each core can store a binary digit or bit of data. Synonymous with core storage.

magnetic disk see *disk*

magnetic drum A rotating metal cylinder coated with a magnetizable material on which data can be recorded and stored as small magnetic spots forming patterns of binary digits or bits.

magnetic film A motion-picture film base with sprocket holes which is coated with a magnetic oxide (similar to that on audiotape) instead of photographic emulsion, upon which sounds may be recorded for playback. (AECT)

magnetic ink character recognition (MICR) The detection, identification, and acceptance by a machine of characters printed with ink containing magnetic particles.

magnetic recording The process of recording audio and video signals on magnetic tape or other magnetic medium.

magnetic sound track see *sound track*

magnetic tape A tape of any material impregnated or coated with magnetic particles, on which audio and video signals and digital data can be recorded as magnetic variations.

magnetic tape base The backing for magnetic tape, usually acetate tape or polyester tape, to which the coating of magnetic particles is applied. Acetate and polyester tapes are available in a variety of thicknesses; in sound recording the choice must be made between thicker base, higher quality sound, and less playing time, or thinner base and longer playing time.

magnetic tape unit A device, usually online to a computer, used for handling data recorded in a machine-readable form on magnetic tape. The machine can be used for input and output of data stored on the tape.

magnification range The extent to which an image can be magnified in a given optical system, as in a microfilm reader, which offers variable enlargement ratios, e.g., 24X through 48X.

main catalog see *central catalog*

main class In classification, one of the principal divisions of knowledge which form the basis for development of a classification system.

main entry 1. The access point to a bibliographic record by which the bibliographic item is to be uniformly identified and cited. Compare with *added entry* (1), *alternative entry.* 2. The complete catalog record of a bibliographic item, presented in the form by which the entity is to be uniformly identified and cited. The main entry may include the tracings of all other headings under which the record is to be represented in the catalog. Compare with *added entry* (2). (AACR2)

main entry heading The access point at the head of the main entry.

mainframe see *central processing unit*

mainframe computer A computer designed for a wide range of applications and with a large capacity for handling mass storage and other peripheral equipment. So called to distinguish it from a *microcomputer, minicomputer,* and *midicomputer.*

main heading The first part of a heading that includes a subheading. (AACR2)

main library see *central library*

main shelf list see *central shelf list*

main storage General-purpose storage which holds computer instructions and data currently being processed by a computer. Main storage is an internal and integral part of a computer system. Synonymous with internal storage, primary storage, and real storage. Compare with *auxiliary storage, mass storage.*

maintenance Work performed on hardware or software to keep it in good working condition.

maintenance department The administrative unit responsible for keeping up the condition of the buildings, physical facilities, and grounds and for making repairs. Synonymous with building department.

maintenance of plant Activities necessary to keep the buildings, grounds, and equipment in operation and in repair.

maintenance personnel Personnel with primary responsibilities and duties related to keeping up the buildings, grounds, and equipment and making necessary repairs. Included are employees such as building engineers, electricians, custodians, and security guards.

majuscule A capital or an uncial letter used in Greek and Latin manuscripts, as distinguished from a *minuscule;* by extension, any capital letter.

make-up In printing, the arranging of text, illustrations, running heads, footnotes, etc., into their relative position on the page.

management 1. A term used variously as a narrower term than administration or synonymously with administration. Management may be defined as the process of coordinating the total resources of an organization toward the accomplishment of the desired goals of that organization through the execution of a group of interrelated functions such as planning, organizing, staffing, directing, and controlling. So defined, management is usually used synonymously with administration in current literature. Administration may be considered to be a broader term, emphasizing the planning function, involving goal setting and major policy formulation, with management variously limited to the process of coordinating certain functions and activities of an organization toward the accomplishment of its goals. 2. Those persons in an organization with primary responsibility for executing the process of management.

management by exception An approach to management based upon clearly delineated policies, procedures, and rules for dealing with all regular activities, thus minimizing supervisory consultation to exceptional situations.

management by objectives (MBO) A total approach to management based upon the participative formulation of goals and performance standards for the organization, its administrative units, and each of its employees. It emphasizes quantitative and measurable goals and standards as a basis for self-monitoring goal accomplishment.

management consultant An expert on management commissioned by a library to study and advise it on management problems.

management information system (MIS) A system designed to supply information necessary to support the management functions, and particularly decision-making, within an organization such as a library, usually with the aid of automatic data processing.

managerial control see *control*

manière criblée see *dotted print* (1)

manual 1. A compact book; a *handbook.* 2. A book of rules for guidance or instructions in how to perform a task, process, etc., or make some physical object.

manual catalog see *card catalog*

manufacturer's catalog see *trade catalog* (2)

manufacturer's number The number, commonly preceded by a prefix of two or three letters, by which an audiodisc or audiotape recording is listed in the trade catalogs. The number appears on the label pasted on each recording and its container.

manufacturing clause In U.S. copyright law, a clause restricting the importation of the nondramatic literary works of an American national or resident alien if the copies were not manufactured in the United States or Canada. The clause expired July 1, 1982 (Public Law 94–553, ch. 6).

manuscript 1. A work written by hand. 2. The handwritten copy of an author's work before it is printed; or, loosely, the author's typescript. 3. In archives, usually used to distinguish nonarchival from archival material; it includes groups of personal papers which have organic unity, collections of documents acquired from various sources, usually according to a plan but without regard to provenance, and individual documents acquired by a repository because of their special importance. (SAA)

manuscript book A handwritten book, as distinguished from a handwritten letter, paper, or other document; particularly, one before or at the time of the introduction of printing.

manuscript group In archives, an organized body of related papers or a collection, comparable to a record group.

map A representation, normally to scale and on a flat medium, of a selection of material or abstract features on, or in relation to, the surface of the earth or of another celestial body. (AACR2)

map index An alphabetical list of geographic names or other features portrayed on a map or maps, giving the location of the features, usually by means of geographic coordinates or grid references. Compare with *index map*.

map profile A scale representation of the intersection of a vertical surface (which may or may not be a plane) with the surface of the ground, or of the intersection of such a vertical surface with that of a conceptual three-dimensional model representing phenomena having a continuous distribution, e.g., rainfall.

map projection In cartography, a systematic drawing of lines on a plane surface to represent the parallels of latitude and the meridians of longitude of the earth or a section of the earth. A map projection may be established by analytical computation or may be constructed geometrically.

map section A scaled representation of a vertical surface (commonly a plane) displaying both the profile where it intersects the surface of the ground of some conceptual model, and the underlying structures along the plane of the intersection, e.g., geological section.

map series A number of related but physically separate and bibliographically distinct cartographic units intended by the producer(s) or issuing body(ies) to form a single group. For bibliographic treatment, the group is collectively identified by any commonly occurring common designation (e.g., collective title, number, or a combination of both); sheet identification system (including successive or chronological numbering systems); scale; publisher; cartographic specifications; uniform format; etc.

map view see *bird's-eye view*

marbled calf Calfskin stained or painted so as to produce a marblelike effect.

marbled paper see *marbling*

marbling The process of transferring designs made by floating inks on a gum solution onto the surface of a sheet of paper or the edges of a book. The process was named marbling because of the resemblance of the original patterns of colors produced to those on marble. Marbled paper is used in hand binding for endpapers and covers. Decorated papers may also be printed to resemble marbled paper.

MARC (Machine-Readable Cataloging) A communications format developed by the Library of Congress for producing and distributing machine-readable bibliographic records on magnetic tape.

margin 1. The blank space around printed or written matter on a page. The four margins are referred to as: the head or top; fore-edge, outer, or outside; foot, tail, or bottom; back, inner, or inside. The combined inside margins of an opening is the gutter. 2. On microfilm, see *frame* (4).

marginalia see *marginal note*

marginal note A written or printed note in the margin of a page, opposite the portion of the text to which it refers. Synonymous with side note and, in the plural, marginalia.

margin-punched card see *edge-notched card*

marker 1. In indexing, a character or other symbol used to separate independent descriptors when more than one is assigned to the same document. 2. In computer science, a special bit pattern or photoreflective strip used to indicate the end of a permissible recording area.

marketing A purposive group of activities which foster constructive and responsive interchange between the providers of library and information services and the actual and potential users of these services. These activities are concerned with the products, costs, methods of delivery, and promotional methods.

market letter A bulletin issued at regular intervals by a brokerage or investment house.

marking 1. The placing of call numbers, location symbols, marks of ownership, etc., on books and other items in a library collection. 2. In serials work, the placing of a mark of ownership and indication of destination on each number or part as it is entered on the check-in record.

mark sense To mark cards or paper with an electrographic pencil, to be read by a mark sensing machine.

mark sensing The sensing by machine of data manually recorded in a fixed location with an electrographic pencil on a nonconductive surface such as paper.

mask 1. To cover portions of a film negative with opaque material in order to define the image area or to create a desired border. 2. In full-color printing, to correct color imbalance and other deficiencies by the use of a set of film negatives made with special filters as masks to control densities in the primary set of color separation negatives.

mass-market paperback A paperback distributed primarily through local news agencies for sale in newsstands, supermarkets, etc., rather than through normal book trade distributors. Compare with *trade paperback.*

mass storage Large-volume auxiliary storage that is readily accessible to the central processing unit of a computer, but not so accessible as main storage. Synonymous with bulk storage. Compare with *auxiliary storage, main storage.*

mass storage device A device, such as a magnetic disk or magnetic drum unit, that provides large-volume auxiliary storage to supplement the main storage of a computer system.

master 1. In copying, the original from which copies are made. 2. In duplicating, a specially prepared, reusable original or exact copy thereof from which multiple copies are made.

master card The first card in a deck of punched cards containing fixed, indicative, or control data for the group. Synonymous with master data card.

master data card see *master card*

master file In computer science, a main file containing relatively permanent data which usually is updated periodically.

master film see *camera microfilm*

master negative film see *camera microfilm*

master network station see *primary network station*

masthead The statement of title, ownership, editors, etc., of a newspaper or periodical; although its location is variable, in the case of newspapers it is commonly found on the editorial page or at the top of page one, and, in the case of periodicals, on the contents page. (AACR2)

mat see *matrix* (1 and 2)

match In computer science, to compare two or more keys, seeking a hit.

matched samples A pair of samples in which sample members are separated into pairs as closely matched as possible with respect to variables other than those under primary investigation; the pairs are then separated at random into two closely matched samples. The object of matching is to lessen the possible effects of unidentified variables.

material bibliography see *historical bibliography*

materials Physical entities of any substance that serve as carriers of information, e.g., books, graphics, audiorecordings, machine-readable data files.

materials conversion The process of converting library materials from one format to another (e.g., microfilming periodicals) for the purpose of preservation.

mathematical data area That area of the bibliographic description of cartographic materials which includes the statement of scale, projection, and/or coordinates and equinox.

matrix 1. A mold from which metal type is cast, or, in photocomposition, the master negative from which the type characters are projected. Also called mat. 2. The papier mâché or plastic mold used to make a stereotype, or a rubber plate used in flexography. Also called mat. 3. In mathematics, a rectangular array of mathematical elements, manipulated in accordance with the rules of matrix algebra. 4. An array resembling a mathematical matrix, especially a rectangular array of elements in rows and columns.

matrix number The alphabetic, numeric, or alphanumeric designator on an audiodisc that identifies the master recording from which duplicates are eventually produced. The designator usually appears on the disc surface between the grooving and the center label and is usually the same as the manufacturer's number.

matrix organization An organizational design built around special projects requiring specialized skills and the coordination of multiple activities, in which the functional divisions of the organization serve the project organizational unit in a supportive relationship and allocate from their resources those that are needed for the achievement of project objectives.

matrix printer A line printer that forms characters on paper by pressing selected wires against an inked ribbon. Wires are arranged in a dot-matrix of 5 x 7, 7 x 9, 9 x 9, or 12 x 9. Synonymous with dot printer and wire printer.

matte A type of finish on photographic prints and other materials which reduces the amount of reflected light. It appears as a flat rather than shiny finish.

maximum density (D-MAX) see *density*

MB see *megabyte*

MBO see *management by objectives*

mean A measure of central tendency obtained by dividing the sum of two or more quantities by the number of those quantities. Synonymous with arithmetic mean.

mean-time-between-failure The average time between failures or malfunctions of a device or machine. Compare with *mean-time-to-failure.*

mean-time-to-failure The average time between the start-up of a device or machine and a failure or malfunction. Compare with *mean-time-between-failure.*

mean-time-to-repair The total time used for preventive and corrective maintenance during a given time period divided by the total number of failures during the period.

mechanical Camera-ready copy of all the elements of a page, adhered to a white board or heavy paper in correct position relative to one another and to the edges of the page, ready to be photographed for making a plate by photomechanical process. Synonymous with paste-up.

mechanical binding A category of leaf affixing in which single leaves and separate front and back covers are mechanically joined through patterns of holes or slots made in their edges. Most mechanical bindings will lie flat when open, but are not strong. They may be loose-leaf and allow the contents to be readily changed, or permanent, such as spiral binding, twin-wire binding, plastic comb binding, and velo-binding.

mechanical dictionary see *automatic dictionary*

mechanical drawing see *technical drawing*

mechanical lettering device see *lettering device, mechanical*

mechanical processing see *physical processing*

mechanical translation see *machine translation*

mechanical wood pulp see *groundwood pulp*

mechanics' library A type of subscription library that flourished in the middle of the 19th century, intended primarily for the use of young artisans and apprentices. Synonymous with apprentices' library.

media Materials in all formats and all channels of communication that serve as carriers of information.

media aide A member of media support personnel who performs clerical and secretarial tasks and assists as needed in the acquisition, maintenance, inventory, production, distribution, and utilization of materials and equipment.

media center An area in a formal educational setting where a collection consisting of a full range of media, associated equipment, and services from the media staff are accessible to students, teachers, and affiliated institutional staff. Synonymous with instructional materials center, learning resources center (LRC).

media management The management of a collection of audiovisual materials and devices to meet the varied needs of users of information. Includes selection, organization, maintenance, storage, retrieval, and distribution of the collection.

mediamobile A truck or van especially designed and operated to distribute print and audiovisual materials. The mediamobile may be used for taking audio and visual programs such as films and puppet plays to outdoor locations and may be large enough to accommodate small audiences inside.

median A measure of central tendency, defined as the value of the middle item of a set arranged according to size or magnitude.

media professional Any media person, certified or not, who qualifies by training and position to make professional judgments and to delineate and maintain media programs as instructional program components. Media professionals may include media specialists, television or film producers, instructional developers, and radio station managers whose duties and responsibilities are professional in nature.

media program An instructional program which assumes responsibility for the deployment of the total resources of instructional technology in the manner that best serves the educational goals of a school, school district, regional education agency, or state education agency, including the purposeful integration of curriculum design and the utilization of educational media.

media specialist A person with appropriate certification under state requirements and broad professional preparation, both in education and media, with competencies to carry out a media program. The media specialist is the basic media professional in the school media program. Synonymous with learning resources specialist.

media support personnel All persons, including technicians and aides, who utilize specific skills and abilities to carry out media program activities as delineated by media professionals.

media technician A member of media support personnel with technical skills in such specialized areas as graphics production and display, information and materials processing, photographic production, operation and maintenance of audiovisual equipment, and installation of instructional program systems components.

mediation The process of involving an intermediary in the resolution of a dispute between the employer and a union or other employee group.

medical library A library serving the information needs of students, practitioners, and researchers in one or more of the health sciences, such as medicine, dentistry, nursing, and pharmacy. It may be maintained and supported by a university; a specialized institution of post-secondary education providing instruction in one or more of the health sciences; a hospital; a medical society; a pharmaceutical firm engaged in research; or a unit of the local, state, or federal government. Synonymous with health sciences library.

medium The physical material or substance upon which data can be recorded or stored; for example, paper, film, magnetic disk, punched tape, and magnetic tape.

medium reduction see *reduction ratio*

medium-term film Processed photographic film with a shelf life expectancy of at least ten years, if stored properly. Compare with *archival film, long-term film, short-term film.*

megabit A million binary digits.

megabyte (MB) One million bytes or characters of data.

megahertz (mhz) One million hertz.

memoir 1. A record of a person's knowledge of, or investigations in, a special limited field, particularly when presented to a learned society. 2. A record of observation and research issued by a learned society or an institution; sometimes, in the plural, synonymous with *transactions.* 3. A memorial biography. 4. In the plural, a book of reminiscences by the author.

memory see *storage*

memory dump see *dump*

mending Minor restoration of a book not involving the replacement of any material or the separation of book from cover. Not so complete a rehabilitation as *repairing.*

mentifact In classification, a mental conception, an abstraction, as opposed to an artifact, or physical object.

menu In a database search, a list of options displayed on the cathode-ray-tube screen.

mercantile library A type of subscription library that flourished in the middle of the 19th century, intended primarily for the use of young merchants' clerks.

merge To combine two or more similarly ordered sets of data into one set that is arranged in the same order. Compare with *collate* (4).

merit rating A periodic performance appraisal of civil service employees for the purpose of determining eligibility for retention, salary adjustment, or promotion on the basis of merit.

merit system A system of selecting civil service employees on the basis of competitive examination and retaining, rewarding, and promoting them on the basis of merit rating.

message 1. A group of characters which are handled together and meant to convey a unit of information. 2. In data transmission, a single transmission in one direction, consisting of a header and data. 3. A unit of information transmitted from one node to another on a network.

message routing The process of selecting a route or circuit path and destination of a message.

message switching see *data switching*

message-switching center see *data-switching center*

methylene blue A chemical dye used to test for residual hypo when determining the archival permanence of processed film. The methylene blue method of testing has largely replaced the Ross-Crabtree method for silver film. If the film has been processed over two weeks, silver densitometric methods are preferred.

mezzotint 1. A method of engraving on copper or steel that reproduces tones through roughening the surface of the plate with a toothed instrument called a rocker or cradle, scraping of the burr thus raised, and burnishing to secure variations of light. 2. A print made by this process.

mhz see *megahertz*

MICR see *magnetic ink character recognition*

microcard A trade name for a 3-x-5-inch microopaque, with microimages arranged in rows and columns on photographic paper.

microcode A number of special routines or instructions built into a computer, which are automatically executed by the hardware when needed. Compare with *firmware*.

microcomputer A small programmable computer with a limited ability to handle mass storage and other peripheral equipment, often designed to handle a restricted number of applications or, in some cases, only one application. A microcomputer often is used as an integral part of other, larger computer systems or other pieces of hardware. Compare with *minicomputer, midicomputer, mainframe computer.*

microcopy see *microimage*

microdensitometer see *densitometer*

microfiche A flat sheet of photographic film, usually 4 x 6 inches or 3 x 5 inches, containing microimages arranged in a grid pattern. Most microfiche contain a title or general descriptive data at the top which can be read without magnification. The top, or microfiche header, may also be color coded. The last frame on a microfiche usually contains an index to the information in the microimages. Microfiche other than the first in a set are termed trailer microfiche. The number of frames on a sheet depends on the reduction ratio and formatting. Microfiche can be produced from strips of microfilm or made directly with a step-and-repeat camera and computer-output-microfilm recorder. Synonymous with fiche.

microfiche catalog A catalog on microfiche produced either by microfilming or as computer output which must be read with the assistance of a microform reader. Compare with *computer-output-microfilm catalog.*

microfiche frame see *frame* (3)

microfiche grid see *microfiche*

microfiche header see *microfiche*

microfiche reader A microform reader for magnifying microimages on microfiche.

microfilm 1. Photographic film containing microimages. The term normally refers to roll film sufficiently long to be placed on reels, cartridges, or cassettes and retrieved by manual or automatic means. Images may be positive or negative and rolls may be 8, 16, 35 or 70mm wide and up to several thousand feet long. Rolls can be cut to produce microfiche, microstrips, or chips to be inserted in jackets or used in other ways. Although the term is used generically to include a variety of microformats, it should be contrasted with *sheet microfilm.* 2. To film originals for the purpose of creating microimages.

microfilm camera see *planetary camera, rotary camera, step-and-repeat camera*

microfilm card A general term used to describe a variety of card formats, such as aperture cards, camera cards, and copy cards.

microfilm catalog A catalog on microfilm in either open reels or cartridges, produced either by microfilming or as computer output, which must be read with the assistance of a microform reader. Compare with *computer-output-microfilm catalog.*

microfilm chip see *chip* (2)

microfilm frame see *frame* (3)

microfilm jacket see *film jacket*

microfilm reader A microform reader for magnifying microimages on microfilm.

microfont A characteristic upper-case font designated for microfilm applications. It was designed by the National Micrographics Association.

microform A general term applied to all forms of microreproduction on film or paper, e.g., microfilm, microfiche, microopaque. Compare with *macroform.*

microform reader A device which magnifies microforms for reading with the unaided eye. The term includes a variety of devices which are generally distinguishable by size and function, but no single device can accommodate all microformats. Hand viewers are small portable devices for viewing single frames on fiche or film and are generally restricted by the quality of the optics and the range of magnification. Lap readers offer greater versatility, are light enough to be used on a lap, and often are designed to fit into a briefcase.

Readers of the next larger size are called desktop or tabletop readers. These can be more expensive but are available with copying capability. For large-volume use by multiple users, desktop models are preferred for their durability. These models also offer semiautomatic or automatic retrieval of specific images and normally can adapt to a variety of formats. Standalone or floor model readers offer high-quality reading and copying capabilities, but can be expensive and cumbersome.

Most microform readers are intended for various formats of microfilm or microfiche. Readers and reader-printers for microopaques are generally more expensive and have not been developed extensively.

microform reader-printer A microform reader which offers the added feature of providing a hard copy of a microimage.

micrographics The science and technology of creating microimages; designing indexing, storage, and retrieval systems for them; or using them in a micrographic system. Micrographics is generally considered a subfield of reprography.

micrographic system An information or management system that incorporates micrographics or microreproduction in some aspect of its operation, notably in archival and records management, document storage, file indexing and integrity, or information storage and retrieval.

microimage A reproduction of an object, such as a source document, that is too small to be read or viewed without magnification. Although the term generally applies to microphotographs, other techniques of reproduction can be used to produce microimages. Synonymous with microcopy and microrecord.

microimaging see *microreproduction*

micromire see *mire*

microopaque A sheet of opaque material bearing one or more microimages. Synonymous with opaque microcopy.

microphone A device capable of transforming sound waves into electric signals, usually for recording or for transmitting and amplifying sound.

microphotography The use of photographic techniques to produce microimages. Compare with *photomacrography, photomicrography.*

microprint A trade name for a 6-x-9-inch microopaque with microimages arranged in rows and columns on photographic paper.

microprocessor The semiconductor central processing unit of a microcomputer.

microprojector   A device designed to enlarge and project microscopic transparencies such as microscope slides for viewing by large audiences. (NCES)

micropublishing   The publishing of documents containing textual or other graphic matter in microform instead of or simultaneously with publication in more conventional formats which do not require magnification for reading or viewing. The term also includes the publication, with substantial alteration of contents, of documents that have been formerly published in some other format. Compare with *microrepublishing*.

microrecord see *microimage*

microrecording see *microreproduction*

microreproduction   The process of reproducing macroform source documents in microform. In unitized microreproduction a single document, such as a technical report, or a sequence of related documents, such as a back file of a periodical, are converted to microform. In collective microreproduction a large number of documents or records, some of which are not related, are converted to microform; an example is a microfilm reel containing microimages of a card catalog, with the microimage of one main entry frequently preceded and followed by main entries of different authorship. Synonymous with microimaging and microrecording.

microrepublishing   The publication in microform of documents containing textual or other graphic matter which have previously been published in a format that does not require magnification for reading or viewing, with little or no alteration of the original. Compare with *micropublishing*.

microscope slide   A slide (usually glass) containing a minute object intended for microscopic inspection through a microscope or by a microprojector.

microscopic edition see *miniature edition*

microsecond   One-millionth of a second.

microslide   A slide containing a single frame of microfilm.

microstrip   A short strip of microfilm which has been cut from a roll. The strips may be attached to a piece of paper, inserted in film jackets, or used to produce microfiche. Synonymous with film strip and strip film.

microthesaurus see *satellite thesaurus*

microwave   A superhigh-frequency electromagnetic wave used in data transmission.

middle management   A somewhat ambiguous term used to designate the group of individuals in an organization who have considerable responsibility in executing and directing the various functions and services which have been differentiated in the organizational structure. In a large library system, the term can be applied to department and division heads and other officers at a comparable level in the organizational structure.

midicomputer   A computer designed for a wide range of applications, with a capacity for handling mass storage and other peripheral equipment that is larger than that of a minicomputer, but smaller than that of a mainframe computer. Compare with *microcomputer, minicomputer, mainframe computer*.

military "D"   The term used for U.S. Department of Defense specifications for aperture cards.

millboard see *binder's board*

millimicrosecond see *nanosecond*

millisecond   One-thousandth of a second.

mimeograph see *stencil duplicator*

miniature   1. A picture painted by hand in an illuminated manuscript. 2. A small, highly detailed painting or portrait, especially on ivory or vellum.

miniature edition   An edition of a book, the copies of which are generally three inches or less at the largest dimension and are usually printed from 6-point, or smaller, type. The tiniest books are often photographically produced. Synonymous with lilliput edition, microscopic edition.

miniature score   A musical score not primarily intended for performance use, with type reduced in size. (AACR2)

minicomputer   A small programmable computer designed for a wide range of applications, but with a limited capability for handling mass storage and other peripheral equipment. Compare with *microcomputer, midicomputer, mainframe computer.*

minicourse see *module* (3)

minidiskette see *diskette*

minimum density (D-MIN) see *density*

minimum wage The hourly wage rate established by law below which an employee cannot be paid.

mint In the same condition as when it came from publisher or printer; new and unhandled, crisp, fresh. The term is used in the antiquarian trade, and is the highest grade which can be accorded to a book's condition.

minuscule A small letter used in Latin manuscripts beginning in the 8th century, developed from the cursive style; by extension, a lower case letter. Compare with *majuscule.*

mire The French word for test charts used to standardize the legibility of microimages. A frequently used international test standard is Mire #1 developed by the International Standards Organization (ISO). An array of 10X ISO Mire #1 legibility test charts is termed micromire.

MIS see *management information system*

mitered corner A book corner in which a triangular piece of the covering material is cut off at the corner so that the turn-ins meet without overlapping.

mixed authorship see *mixed responsibility*

mixed notation In classification, a notation system which uses more than one type of symbol, such as mixture of letters and numerals. Compare with *pure notation.*

mixed responsibility Collaboration between two or more persons or bodies performing different kinds of activities in the creation of the content of a bibliographic item (e.g., adapting or illustrating a work written by another person). Compare with *shared responsibility.* (AACR2, mod.)

mixer A device which permits the user to control and combine two or more audio signals into one composite audio signal, subject to the vari-

ous controls of the mixer. It may be a separate unit or built into a tape recorder.

mixing The activity of controlling and blending two or more separate audio signals into a single composite signal. (AECT)

mnemonic notation In classification, notational symbols designed as aids to memory.

mock-up A representation of a device or process that may be modified for training or analysis to emphasize a particular part or function; it usually has movable parts that can be manipulated. (AACR2)

mode 1. In data processing, a method of hardware or software operation, such as the interpretive mode. 2. With reference to audio equipment, the manner of audio presentation, such as stereophonic, or the operational function, such as the playback mode. 3. In statistics, the value or number in a set of numeric data that occurs most often.

model A three-dimensional representation of a real thing, either of the exact size or to scale. (AACR2)

modem A contraction of modulator-demodulator. A device used to convert digital data from a transmitting terminal to a signal suitable for analog data transmission over a telephone channel and then to reconvert the signal to digital data for acceptance by a receiving terminal. Compare with *acoustic coupler.*

modern-face roman A style of roman type more perpendicular than old-face roman, having more contrast between the weight of the stem and hairline strokes, and having thinner, unslanted serifs. Initiated with the romain du roi of Philippe Grandjean. Compare with *old-face roman.*

modular construction A system of building construction in which the floor area is divided by rectangular modules of equal size between supporting pillars, instead of by permanent or load-bearing walls. Plumbing, electric wiring, and heat and air conditioning vents are accommodated in the pillars and in drop ceilings. Typical of library architecture since the 1940s, such construction allows for maximal flexibility in reassignment of space.

modular programming A technique of developing computer programs in which each is broken into a number of self-contained modules for ease of development and understanding.

modulation The process of varying, altering, or converting a signal to make it compatible with another.

modulator-demodulator see *modem*

module 1. One of the rectangular units of floor space in a building encompassed by an imaginary line connecting the centers of four supporting pillars, which serve as the basis for modular construction. Also called a bay. 2. One logical component of a computer program or a plug-in unit of hardware that is interchangeable with other units. 3. Subject matter organized into short (often self-instructional) units or learning experiences. A module of instruction may be made up of several learning packages. Synonymous with minicourse.

moiré An imperfection in the production of halftones, seen as an unwanted wavy pattern caused by misalignment of a halftone screen with another screen or with dots or lines on the original artwork.

mold 1. A negative impression of a character, line, page, etc., into which material is poured for casting type or plates. 2. A wire screen stretched over a wood frame on which pulp is shaken into a sheet of paper in the manufacture of handmade laid paper and wove paper. (Lee)

mold-made paper A machine-made paper having a deckle edge, with surface and texture resembling those of handmade paper.

monaural The reproduction of sound by an audio device from a single channel with a single amplifier or loudspeaker. Compare with *stereophonic* and *quadraphonic.*

monitor 1. The electronic device or circuit that allows the recordist to see and/or hear an audiorecording or videorecording in progress. 2. A television set designed to accept and reproduce pictures and sounds from videotape or from a closed circuit television system. With the addition of a tuner, it can receive broadcast television programs. 3. To supervise, control, and verify the operation of a system. 4. To check or regulate sound and/or images during audiorecording or videorecording. In so-called source monitoring, the recordist sees and/or hears the program being recorded as it is seen and heard by the recording amplifier. In so-called tape monitor-

ing, the recordist sees and/or hears the program within a fraction of a second of its being recorded, thus permitting instant adjustments in the recording process.

monobath process A process in which film developing and fixing are carried out in a single solution.

monograph 1. In cataloging, a nonserial bibliographic item, i.e., an item either complete in one part or complete, or intended to be completed, in a finite number of separate parts. (AACR2) 2. A systematic and complete treatise on a particular subject.

monographic series A group of monographs, usually related to one another in subject, issued in succession, normally by the same publisher and in uniform style with a collective title applying to the group as a whole. Monographic series may be numbered or unnumbered.

monographic set A monograph issued in two or more physically separate documents.

Monotype The trade name of a letterpress typesetting system that uses paper tape punched on one machine to activate the casting of individual characters on a complementary machine. The letters may be arranged as justified lines of type or as a font for setting by hand. Compare with *Linotype.*

montage 1. The technique of combining several elements from different photographs and printing fragments to form a single picture which gives the illusion that the elements belonged together originally. 2. In the production of films, the superimposition of pictures, fast cutting, and other techniques used in editing to present an idea or set of ideas.

Monte Carlo method In general, any method of estimating by means of sample observations. Usually used in the restricted sense of making sample observations of simulations of some process in which chance plays a part, in order to arrive at an estimate.

monthly A periodical issued once a month, with the possible exception of certain designated months, usually during the summer.

morgue A reference collection in a newspaper office, including back issues, photographs, clippings, and other materials used in the writing or editing of articles or other works. The term originally referred specifically to biographical material collected or to obituaries prepared in advance of the deaths of well-known persons.

morocco Goatskin leather used in binding. Bookbinders tend to use the term goatskin; the antiquarian trade tends to prefer morocco.

mosaic binding see *mozaic binding*

mosaic map see *photomosaic, controlled; photomosaic, uncontrolled*

most significant digit see *high-order digit*

motion picture A length of film with a sequence of consecutive images which create the illusion of natural movement when projected in rapid succession. Some film may have a magnetic or optical sound track. Synonymous with cinefilm.

motion-picture camera A camera which is used to expose motion-picture film. While commercial motion picture companies may use larger cameras and more expensive film, most libraries and media centers use a 16mm or 8mm motion-picture camera to produce films.

motion-picture film A film intended for the production of motion pictures. Most film used in library and media center production is 16mm, 8mm, or super 8mm. The 16mm film has sprocket holes on one edge (called single-perforation film) or on both edges (called double-perforation film). Single-perforation film may have a thin strip of magnetic tape (for sound recording) on the edge opposite the perforations. Regular 8mm film has perforations (similar to those on 16mm film) along one edge. The film may have a magnetic audiorecording stripe. Super 8mm and single 8mm have a single row of sprocket holes. The reduced size and different placement (from regular 8mm) of the sprocket holes allow more image area than regular 8mm film. The film may have a magnetic stripe for audiorecording and is usually packaged in a special cartridge. Super 8mm and single 8mm film are the same size, while the cartridges are different.

motion-picture orientation see *cine orientation*

motion-picture projector A device designed to project motion pictures. It may be equipped to reproduce sound on either magnetic, optical, or both types of sound tracks and may have audiorecording capability.

mottle see *film mottle*

mottled calf, sheep, etc. Leather of calfskin, sheepskin, etc., intended for binding which has been mottled with color or acid dabbed on with sponges or wads of cotton.

mounter The apparatus that cuts, positions, and secures microfilm in aperture cards in a single step. Synonymous with optical mounter.

mounting The activity of attaching graphics or other two-dimensional materials to cloth, cardboard, or other surface. These materials may be attached by paste or glue or by a dry-mounting process in which a heat-sensitive intermediary paper is used and heat and pressure are applied to meld the materials to the surface.

movable location see *relative location*

movable ranges A type of compact shelving consisting of a block of ranges mounted on a track or rail system and with a single-stack aisle. Access to the materials in a given range is gained by opening up an aisle between the two desired ranges.

movable type Type cast as individual, single-character units, which is capable of being combined into words, lines, pages, etc., of text, after the printing of which it is capable of being redistributed and reused. Johann Gutenberg is generally associated with its invention.

mozaic binding Leather bindings decorated with contrasting inlaid, onlaid, or painted colors. The British spelling is mosaic.

MRDF see *machine-readable data file*

mull see *crash*

multicolor printing A color process in which a separate plate is made for each color, and each color is printed separately. The inks used in printing match the colors to be reproduced. Synonymous with flat-color printing. Compare with *full-color printing.*

multicounty library A library system established by joint action of the governing agencies or by vote of the residents of the counties involved, and governed by a single board of trustees.

multifile item A bibliographic entity that consists of more than one machine-readable data file. (AACR2)

multiframe document see *sectioning*

multimedia The combination and integration of more than one format into a program or presentation, such as a program incorporating a filmstrip and audiorecording.

multimedia kit A collection of subject-related materials in more than one medium intended for use as a unit and in which no one medium is identifiable as the predominant constituent.

multipart item A monograph complete, or intended to be completed, in a finite number of separate parts. Synonymous with multivolume monograph. (AACR2)

multiple access A term used to describe a file of bibliographic records which provides various access points (e.g., names, titles, subjects, series) to the records that it contains.

multiple copies see *added copy*

multiple correlation The correlation of three or more variables.

multiple film plane technique A high-reduction microfilming technique for compacting images.

multiplex To transmit two or more messages simultaneously over a single channel.

multiplexer A device which enables two or more messages to be transmitted simultaneously over a single channel.

multiprocessing A technique of handling or executing more than one independent computer program simultaneously by one computer, but with each program having its own storage loca-

tion and interconnected central processing unit. Compare with *concurrent processing, multiprogramming.*

multiprogramming A technique of handling or executing more than one independent computer program simultaneously by one computer. Synonymous with dual programming. Compare with *concurrent processing, multiprocessing.*

multitier stack A permanent self-supporting structure of steel shelving extending upward for several stack levels, or decks, which is independent of the walls of the building. In addition to supporting the total weight of the library materials stored on the shelves, the vertical uprights sometimes support the stack floors at each level. Compare with *single-tier stack.*

multivolume monograph see *multipart item*

municipal library A public library established, maintained, and supported through taxation by a city, town, township, borough, village, or other municipality, whose board of trustees is appointed by municipal authority or elected, or whose library director reports to another office of the municipal government.

municipal reference library A library maintained by a city for the use of city, and sometimes county, employees in their official business. The library is usually administered as a department of the public library supported by the city and is located in the city or city-county building.

municipal reference service Assistance given by a library in problems of city government, particularly in connection with proposed or pending ordinances, often including the drafting of ordinances.

museum library A library maintained by a museum which includes library materials related to its exhibits and areas of specialization.

mutton see *quad*

NACO see *Name Authority Cooperative*

Name Authority Cooperative (NACO) A cooperative name authority file project, administered by the Library of Congress, whereby authority records prepared by cooperating libraries are sent to the Library of Congress, which compares them with its authority file, authenticates them, and integrates them into its Automated Name Authority File.

name authority file   A set of authority records which indicates the authorized forms of personal, corporate, and noncorporate or nonjurisdictional names to be used as headings in a particular set of bibliographic records, cites the sources consulted in establishing the headings, indicates the references to be made to and from the headings, and notes information found in the sources as justification of the chosen forms of headings and the specified references.

name index   An index in which the headings of the index entries are the names of persons and/ or corporate bodies cited or otherwise referred to in the indexed work(s). Compare with *author index*.

name-title entry   1. An access point consisting of the name of a person or corporate body and the title of a bibliographic item or part of a bibliographic item. 2. A bibliographic record with the name of a person or corporate body and the title of a bibliographic item or part of a bibliographic item as the heading.

name-title reference   A reference in which the "refer-from" line, the "refer-to" line, or both, consist of the name of a person or corporate body and the title of a bibliographic item. (AACR2)

nanosecond   One billionth of a second. Synonymous with millimicrosecond.

narrow see *book sizes*

narrow band   A communications channel with a bandwidth narrower than that of a voice-grade channel, and thus capable of a lower speed of data transmission. Compare with *wide band*.

national bibliography   A bibliography of documents published in a particular country and, by extension, documents about the country or written in the language of the country.

national biography   1. The branch of biography that treats of the lives of notable persons living in or associated with a particular country. 2. A collective biography of notable persons living in or associated with a particular country.

National Level Bibliographic Record   A bibliographic record which meets the standards set for all organizations in the United States which create such records with the intent of sharing them with other organizations or for contributing them to a national database. The Library of Congress has published, or plans to publish, rules for various formats, such as books, serials, films, and maps.

national library   A library designated as such by the appropriate national body and funded by the national government. Its functions may include the comprehensive collection of the publication output of the nation (frequently as a copyright depository library), the compilation and maintenance of a national bibliography, the comprehensive collection and organization of publications on an international scale for the scholarly community, the production of bibliographic tools, the coordination of a national library network, the provision of library services to the national government or some of its agencies, and other responsibilities delineated by the national government.

National Library Week   A week in April set aside for special public relations programs and activities promoting support for all types of libraries and library services under the sponsorship of the American Library Association.

National Program for Acquisitions and Cataloging (NPAC)   A Library of Congress program established under the Higher Education Act of 1965, Title II-C, which gave the Librarian of Congress the responsibility of acquiring insofar as possible all publications throughout the world which are of value to scholarship, cataloging them promptly, and distributing bibliographic records through printed catalog cards or other means.

National Serials Data Program (NSDP)   The program at the Library of Congress which registers serial publications and assigns International Standard Serial Numbers to the titles cataloged by the Library of Congress, the National Agricultural Library, and the National Library of Medicine and also to those added to the CONSER database.

natural characteristic   In classification, a quality or complex of qualities common to the things classified and also essential to their being. Compare with *artificial characteristic*.

natural classification A classification in which a quality inherent in and inseparable from the things classified is used as the characteristic of arrangement. Compare with *artificial classification.*

natural finish A soft finish given to book cloth, obtained by first dyeing the cloth and then applying filler to the back only, leaving the face in its natural state.

natural language A human language whose rules have evolved from current usage. Compare with *artificial language.*

natural-language indexing system An indexing system in which no index vocabulary controls are imposed, the indexer being free to use any term considered suitable to represent the subject content of a document. Synonymous with free indexing system. Compare with *controlled-vocabulary indexing system.*

natural-language retrieval system A computer-based information retrieval system that stores and searches the complete text of documents. Subject search is usually conducted on logical combinations of words occurring in the text, and may be further refined by word proximity search. Synonymous with free-text retrieval system and full-text retrieval system.

nautical chart see *hydrographic chart*

navigation chart see *aeronautical chart, hydrographic chart*

NBS (National Bureau of Standards) test chart see *resolution*

near-print publications see *processed publications*

neat line The boundary of cartographic detail on a map.

needle (audiodisc player) see *stylus*

needlework binding see *embroidered binding*

negative-appearing image A photographic image which has tonal characteristics that are the opposite of the original. Normally, the image would appear as light lines and neutral tones on a dark background.

negative paper Photographic paper used to produce paper negatives.

negative-working process see *sign-reversing process*

nest In computer science, to include or embed data or routines within other data or routines.

net assignable space The number of gross square feet of the floor area of a building that is left after the deduction of the nonassignable square feet.

net price In Great Britain, the price fixed from time to time by the publisher and below which a book shall not be sold to the public except as provided by the terms of the Net Book Agreement, 1957. Synonymous with net published price.

net published price see *net price*

network 1. Two or more organizations engaged in a common pattern of information exchange through communications links, for some common objectives. 2. An interconnected or interrelated group of nodes. 3. A *library network.*

network control program see *control program*

network control station A station on a network responsible for controlling transmission, handling problems, and supervising operations such as polling and selecting.

network node see *node*

network operations center A center that controls, manages, and maintains a network and assists its members or nodes in its use.

network redundancy The provision of more communications links than the minimum necessary to connect all nodes of a network.

network security The measures taken to protect a network's equipment, communications, and files from unauthorized access, accidental or willful interference, and damage or destruction.

network station An independent installation of one or more terminal devices and other equipment necessary to establish and maintain communication in a network.

neutral density filter A filter used in optical systems for reducing the intensity of light. It absorbs all colors equally and does not induce chromatic aberration.

Newark charging system A single-entry circulation system, in which charge cards are filed to form a date due record and borrowers' cards are retained by the borrowers. Some variations of the system do not require borrowers' cards.

new edition see *issue* (2)

newsbook 1. A pamphlet of the 16th-17th centuries relating current events. 2. After 1640 in England, a serial, usually issued weekly, consisting of various kinds of news and called *Diurnall, Mercurius, Intelligence,* etc.

newsletter 1. A serial consisting of one or a few printed sheets containing news or information of interest chiefly to a special group. 2. A 16th-17th century manuscript report of the day, written for special subscribers and issued irregularly or weekly. 3. A similar 17th century report for special subscribers, sometimes set in script types and imitating the appearance of the earlier manuscript letter.

newspaper A serial issued at stated, frequent intervals (usually daily, weekly, or semiweekly), containing news, opinions, advertisements, and other items of current, often local, interest.

newspaper rod see *stick*

newspaper shelving Stack shelving of sufficient depth to accommodate bound volumes of newspapers laid flat, usually 16 inches in depth.

newspaper stick see *stick*

newsprint A paper of the kind widely used for newspapers. It has a high proportion of groundwood pulp and hence lignin. It discolors and becomes brittle quickly.

news release see *press release*

Newton's rings Those colored rings seen between the surfaces of two plates of glass due to an intervening thin film of air, named for their discoverer, Sir Isaac Newton.

Niger A superior, soft goatskin leather or morocco used in binding, made from the skin of small, usually wild, goats found in Nigeria and along the Mediterranean coast of Africa, and tending to have a small, pronounced grain and attractive, somewhat unevenly dyed colors.

nihil obstat Literally, nothing hinders, a statement of sanction for publication given by a Roman Catholic book censor, found usually on the verso of the title leaf or following leaf. Compare with *imprimatur.*

Ninety-one Rules A catalog code prepared for use at the British Museum by Sir Anthony Panizzi. Published in 1841, it was the first major code developed for compiling a library catalog.

nitrate film Photographic film with a film base composed principally of cellulose nitrate. Because nitrate film is highly flammable, it has been largely replaced by acetate film.

node A point or junction of communications links in a network, such as a network station, terminal, or communications computer.

no-growth see *steady state*

noise 1. An interfering or unwanted disturbance in the transmission and reception of data over a communications channel. Synonymous with channel noise. Compare with *distortion* (2). 2. Unnecessary and meaningless binary digits in data.

nominal scale A level of measurement in which objects, events, or individuals are assigned to mutually exclusive, collectively exhaustive categories of variables. No order is implied by the classification.

nonassignable space see *assignable space*

nonbook materials see *audiovisual materials*

noncirculating materials Any library materials which are restricted to use within the library.

noncurrent records In archives, records no longer needed in the conduct of current business which can therefore be appraised, transferred to an archival repository, or destroyed. Synonymous with inactive records.

nondestructive read The reading by a computer device of data without erasing or destroying it in the process.

nonerasable storage see *read-only storage*

nonexempt employee An employee whose conditions of employment and compensation are subject to the provisions of the Fair Labor Standards Act of 1938, as amended. Unlike *exempt employees,* nonexempt employees are eligible for overtime payment.

nonfiling element A word or character that does not affect or is not used in filing, e.g., an initial article, or, depending on the filing rules in effect, diacritical marks.

nonimpact printing A printing method in which the ink image is transferred to the paper or other surface without pressure from an inked surface. Compare with *impact printing*.

nonparametric statistics Those statistical procedures intended for use with nominal and ordinal scaling. Compare with *parametric statistics*.

non-Parliamentary papers Government publications prepared by any of the various departments of the British government independently, without direct Parliamentary command, though sometimes presented to Parliament. While many are published by Her Majesty's Stationery Office, many are issued directly by the departments that prepare them. Compare with *Parliamentary Papers*.

nonperforated film Roll film without perforations, or sprocket holes, to aid in transporting and positioning the film in a camera or projector. The elimination of perforations allows for a greater film image area.

nonprint materials see *audiovisual materials*

nonprocessed audiorecording A noncommercial instantaneous audiorecording, generally existing in a unique copy.

nonprofessional personnel see *support staff*

nonrecord material In archives, material not usually thought of as records, including library or museum material intended for exhibition or reference, stocks of publications, etc.

nonresident's card A borrower's identification card issued to a person not residing in the legal service area of a library system, usually upon the payment of a small fee. Synonymous with fee card.

nonreversing film see *direct image film*

normal curve A graphic representation of a normal distribution.

normal distribution A frequency distribution in which the quantities are so distributed that its graphical representation is a continuous, symmetrical, bell-shaped curve, with a high preponderance of frequencies in the vicinity of the mean, median, and mode (which in this distribution coincide) and with low frequencies at both ends. Synonymous with Gaussian distribution.

normal paper Photographic paper used to print negatives of medium contrast. The gradations in the tonal range fall between those used in hard and soft paper.

notation A system of symbols, generally letters and numerals, used separately or in combination, to represent the divisions of a classification system.

notched card see *edge-notched card*

note 1. A statement explaining the text or indicating the basis for an assertion or the source of material quoted (a citation). Notes may appear at the end of a book as endnotes, at the end of a chapter, or at the foot of a page of text as footnotes. 2. In cataloging, a concise statement following the physical description area, in which such information as extended physical description, relationship to other works, or contents may be recorded. 3. A research report in a journal on completed theoretical or experimental work of limited scope or on a substantial stage of progress on a larger project, generally intended to be processed rapidly with far less formal technical review than full-length papers or synoptics.

NPAC see *National Program for Acquisitions and Cataloging*

NSDP see *National Serials Data Program*

null hypothesis The statistical hypothesis that is to be tested (i.e., examined as to its truth or falsity) in an experiment or study. After being tested, the null hypothesis is either rejected or accepted; rejection implies the acceptance of an alternative hypothesis (e.g., the converse of the null hypothesis).

number 1. A single uniquely numbered or dated part of a serial or series. 2. A numbered fascicle.

numbered copy A copy of a book in a limited edition which carries an assigned number.

number system A system for representing numeric values using a predefined set of rules and symbols.

numeric code   A code which uses numbers to represent other data. Compare with *alphabetic code, alphanumeric code.*

numeric register   A union list with entries consisting of Library of Congress card numbers or International Standard Book Numbers in numeric order, with location symbols following each entry.

nut see *quad*

object   An artifact (or replica of an artifact) or a specimen of a naturally occurring entity. Compare with *realia.*

object code   The executable output of an assembler or compiler.

objective   Any lens or lens system used in cameras or projectors to form the image. Synonymous with object lens and projection lens.

object language see *target language*

object lens see *objective*

object program   The computer program, produced from a source program, that is ready to be loaded and executed by a computer.

oblong see *book sizes*

occurrence count   The count of the number of records in a database that are retrievable by a specified search term or statement, included in the index file or calculated at the time of search; used in online database searching to determine whether the search needs to be narrowed by using more specific search terms.

OCR see *optical character recognition*

octal number system   A number system with a radix or base of eight.

octave device see *sector notation*

octavo see *book sizes*

odd-even check see *parity check*

odometer   An indexing device on microfilm readers which counts the number of frames on a roll of microfilm. The odometer count corresponds to an address for images which is given in a separate index or at the beginning of the roll.

offcut   In the signatures of books of a certain size, such as duodecimo, that portion of the sheet that has been cut off, folded separately, and inserted in the middle of the folded signature in order for the leaves to run consecutively.

office collection   A convenient, working collection of library materials for the use of an office within the sponsoring agency of a library, but not owned by the library.

office file   In archives, records or other documents relating or belonging to an office or position, or connected with one holding an office or position.

official catalog   The catalog which members of the library staff rely upon as their authority in the performance of activities which require consultation of the most current and correct record of the library collection. It may also contain, especially in those cases where it is inaccessible to the public, authority records, catalogers' memoranda, etc.

official gazette see *gazette* (3)

official name   The legal name of a governmental agency or other corporate body, which does not necessarily correspond with the form of name used by the body in its publications, or used in cataloging.

offline   Equipment or devices not directly connected to or under control of the central processing unit of a computer. Compare with *online.*

offline processing   Data processing performed away from a main computer system, usually by a separate central processing unit or by another type of data processing equipment. Compare with *online processing.*

offline storage   Storage that is not directly connected to or under control of the central processing unit of a computer. Compare with *online storage*.

offprint   A separately issued article, chapter, or other portion of a larger work, printed from the type or plates of the original, usually at the same time as the original. Synonymous with separate. Compare with *reprint* (3).

offset   A mark or smut on a printed or white sheet caused by contact with a freshly printed sheet on which the ink is wet. Synonymous with setoff.

offset lithography   The commercial form of planographic printing, in which the image and nonimage areas are on a flat surface of the same plane. The inked image is transferred from the photomechanically prepared plate to a rubber blanket and is then offset onto the paper.

offset printing   A printing process in which the type image is transferred from the plate to a rubber-covered cylinder, or blanket, which then offsets the image onto paper. Offset printing may be wet if the image and nonimage areas are on the same plane, as in lithography, or dry if the image is in relief, as in dry offset.

off-site storage collection see *storage collection*

ogive   A graphic representation of a cumulative frequency distribution.

old-face roman   A style of roman type characterized by strokes of relatively uniform weight, with bracketed (that is, curved) and slanted serifs. Used from the late 15th to the mid-18th century by printers ranging from Aldus Manutius to Baskerville. Old-style is a 19th-century adaptation. Compare with *modern-face roman*.

old-style see *old-face roman*

omnibus book   A large one-volume reprint of several novels or other literary works originally published separately. Synonymous with omnibus volume.

omnibus review   A critical article discussing a group of books of a certain type or in a particular field.

omnibus volume see *omnibus book*

on approval   A term used for the arrangement whereby a prospective purchaser has a chance to examine material before buying it. Materials sent on approval must be returned in a specified period of time if not purchased. Compare with *approval plan*.

on-demand publishing   The manufacture of single copies of printed publications in macroform or microform in response to specific orders rather than supplying from inventory. Often relies on reproduction from microform.

one-card charging system see *single-entry charging system*

one-component diazo   A diazo-coated material which does not contain a coupler. The coupler is contained in an alkaline developer. Compare with *two-component diazo*.

one on see *all along*

one sheet on see *all along*

one-sided test   A test of a hypothesis for which the rejection region is wholly located at one end of the sampling distribution of the test statistic.

on-film indicator   Indexing information on roll microfilm which indicates the approximate location of microimages on the roll. The indicators are often so coded as to facilitate visual indexing, such as a flash index.

onlaid   Said of a piece of material attached to the surface of a supporting structure. Compare with *inlaid* (1).

onlay   A decorative panel or shape of paper, leather, or other material, glued to the surface of a book cover. Compare with *inlay* (2).

online   Equipment or devices directly connected to and under control of the central processing unit of a computer. Synonymous with in-line. Compare with *offline*.

online catalog   A catalog of bibliographic records in machine-readable form, maintained in a computer system and permitting interactive access through terminals which are in direct and continuing communication with the computer for the duration of the transaction. Access is typically gained through predetermined procedures, utilizing search keys such as author, title, subject, International Standard Book Number, or a combination of these. Compare with *online public access catalog*. (LDCH)

online cataloging The process by which a cataloger, being in direct contact with a machine-readable bibliographic database, can search, retrieve, and manipulate individual bibliographic records and usually add new records to the database. The user accesses the database by means of an input-output device such as a cathode-ray-tube terminal. The output of the process may be a bibliographic record in one of several possible formats: human-readable hard copy, microform, or machine-readable.

online circulation system see *computer-based circulation system*

online processing Data processing that is directly controlled by the central processing unit of a computer, usually in which individual records or transactions are processed immediately by the central processing unit without batching. Compare with *offline processing*.

online public access catalog (OPAC) A computer-based and supported library catalog (bibliographic database) designed to be accessed via terminals so that library users may directly and effectively search for and retrieve bibliographic records without the assistance of a human intermediary such as a specially trained member of the library staff. Compare with *online catalog*.

online storage Storage that is directly connected to and under control of the central processing unit of a computer. Compare with *offline storage*.

on-order/in-process file An acquisitions file of bibliographic items from the time they are ordered until cataloging and physical processing have been completed.

on-the-job training The process of teaching and counseling new employees in the execution of their assigned duties on-site by their supervisor or a designated fellow employee.

ooze leather Leather made from calfskin by a process which produces on the flesh side a soft, finely granulated finish like velvet or suede. When used in binding without underlying stiff boards, called limp ooze.

OP see *out of print*

OPAC see *online public access catalog*

opaque microcopy see *microopaque*

opaque projector A projector designed to project flat opaque objects such as maps, pictures, or the printed pages of an open book by using a light source that shines directly on the object. Light is reflected from the object onto a reversing mirror, which sends its light through the lens system onto the viewing surface. Synonymous with balopticon. Compare with *overhead projector*.

opaque screen A surface of opaque material on which an image is produced by reflected light from front projection.

open access see *open stack*

open back (binding) see *loose-back*

open back pamphlet file A box enclosed at top, bottom, and three sides, used for holding pamphlets, unbound numbers of periodicals, or other materials unbound or in paper covers.

open bar shelving Shelves made up of a number of hollow bars placed lengthwise at approximately one-inch intervals in lieu of a solid, flat surface. Widely used in early stack construction, they are supported on uprights by various types of fixed brackets and are particularly suitable for heavy and oversized volumes.

open catalog A catalog in which the incorporation of new bibliographic records is unrestricted. Compare with *closed catalog, frozen catalog, integrated catalog*.

opened Said of a book when the folded edges (bolts) of the sheets have been separated by a paper knife. Not to be confused with *cut edges*.

open-ended term list see *free-term list*

open entry A bibliographic record which provides for the addition of information concerning a bibliographic item of which the library does not have a complete set, or about which complete information is lacking.

opening The two facing pages of an open book. Synonymous with spread.

open joint see *French joint*

open-letter proof A proof of an engraving with an inscription engraved in outline letters.

open-office landscaping see *open-office planning*

open-office planning An architectural term used to describe the design concept for office and work areas where movable panels, partitions, and furnishings, usually of a modular character, are used to divide and separate offices, work areas, and activities. Synonymous with open-office landscaping.

open order In acquisition, an order which has not been completely filled, and which remains active.

open reel 1. An unenclosed reel holding audiotape, videotape, or motion-picture film, as distinct from a reel enclosed in a cassette or cartridge. 2. A term used to describe a tape recorder or player or a motion-picture projector which uses a supply reel for holding the tape or film, which is threaded and then fed onto a take-up reel. Synonymous with reel-to-reel.

open reserve A reserve collection in an open stack area to which users have unrestricted access.

open score The score of a musical work for two or more voices, in which each voice part is printed on a separate staff.

open shelves see *open stack*

open stack Any library stack area to which library users have unrestricted access. Synonymous with open access and open shelves. Compare with *closed stack*.

operand The part of a computer instruction which tells the computer where data to be processed or a device to be used is located.

operating expenditures The monies expended for the ongoing provision of library services, including expenditures for personnel, library materials, binding, supplies, and repairs and replacements of existing furnishings and equipment. It may include auxiliary services such as building maintenance, depending upon the accounting system of the parent organization, but does not include capital improvement.

operating system (OS) Software that controls the execution of computer programs and that may provide scheduling, debugging, input-output control, accounting, compilation, storage assignment, data management, and related services. Synonymous with executive program and supervisor computer program.

operation A process or procedure wherein a defined action is executed. Compare with *task*.

operational definition A statement expressing the actual behavior of that which is to constitute or represent a construct or variable.

operation code A machine-readable code which represents a specified operation to a computer. Synonymous with instruction code.

operations research The application of scientific methods and techniques to solving operational problems. A scientific model is developed, incorporating measurement of factors, such as chance and risk, with which to compare the outcomes of alternative decisions, strategies, or controls, with the purpose of helping management determine policy and operational procedures scientifically.

optical character recognition (OCR) The detection, identification, and acceptance by a machine of printed characters using light-sensitive devices.

optical-coincidence indexing system A postcoordinate, term-entry indexing system in which document numbers are posted as holes in standard positions on optical coincidence cards. Holes common to more than one card, which indicate documents with more than one subject in common, are revealed by holding the card set against a light source. A precursor of computer-based information retrieval systems. Synonymous with peek-a-boo indexing system.

optical copying In reprography, any copying process using an optical system to form images on photosensitive material. Compare with *lensless copying*.

optical density see *density* (1)

optical disc see *videodisc*

optical flats see *flats*

optical image An image of an object created when light waves emanating at the point of the object are modified by reflection or refraction by one or more smooth surfaces, such as a lens or mirror, and converge, or appear to converge, at a new point, which is an optical image of the first.

optical mounter see *mounter*

optical path The trajectory of light waves from the point that they enter an optical system until they reach a designated surface, such as a photosensitive material. The path is a function of the optical system, and includes light waves in cameras, microform readers, and various types of projectors.

optical print see *projection print*

optical printer see *projection printer*

optical scanner A device that optically reads or scans handwritten or printed characters and translates them into digital signals for input into a computer or other device.

optical sound track see *sound track*

optical system A combination of lenses, mirrors, or prisms designed for a specific purpose, such as the photography or projection of images. A system may be designed to provide various reduction or enlargement options, to achieve fine resolution, or for uniform brightness, such as a Fresnel lens.

optical viewing system A viewing system in which the photographer views the subject to be photographed through a lens system that is physically separated from the lens system that will take the photograph. Compare with *reflex viewing system.*

opus number In music, a number assigned to a work, or a group of works, of a composer, generally indicating order of composition or of publication.

oral history An aural record, or the transcript of an aural record, originally recorded on a magnetic medium, and the result of a planned oral interview.

order see *purchase order*

order department see *acquisitions department*

order files see *acquisitions files*

order librarian see *acquisitions librarian*

order-number file An acquisitions file of bibliographic items on order, with primary arrangement by order number to facilitate record-keeping when the items are received.

order paper A daily record of the preceding day's votes, proceedings, and other transactions of the British House of Commons, together with an agenda for the current day's proceedings.

ordinal notation In classification, a notation which provides order but does not display hierarchical relationships. Compare with *hierarchical notation.*

ordinal scale A level of measurement in which objects, events, or individuals are assigned to categories of variables in rank order. The categories reflect only the order or sequence; there is no implication of any specific distance or amount of separation between adjacent categories.

ordinary emulsion A film emulsion responding only to the radiation of light waves in the blue range or shorter.

ordinate see *Y-axis*

organizational climate In management, a variety of factors (e.g., leadership style, motivational forces, organizational communications, staff development opportunities) at work in an organization which are perceived positively or negatively by employees and influence their conduct.

organization chart A pictorial presentation of the formal organizational structure which illustrates the hierarchical relationship of administrative units, formal lines of authority, and formal channels for reporting and communication.

organization file 1. In a special library, a collection of material about organizations with the same areas of interest as the library's host organization. 2. In a special library, a collection of material about the library's host organization, including its publications, official documents, and other archival materials.

organization manual A comprehensive compilation of the written documents in effect within an organization, including organization charts; statements of mission, goals, and objectives; administrative policies, rules, and procedures; and other official documents which regulate the activities and operations of the organization. Usually in a loose-leaf format, it is used as a reference source for decision-making and for orientation and training of personnel. Compare with *staff handbook, administrative manual.*

organ-vocal score A score of a work for chorus and/or solo voices and organ, the accompaniment being a reduction of the music originally composed for an instrumental ensemble.

orientation see *image orientation, library use presentation, staff orientation*

original 1. In photography, the object, person, or scene that is the source of an image. 2. The initial photographic record, usually made in a camera. 3. In reprography, the source document or intermediate copy from which copies are produced; thus the original may be a positive or a negative.

original binding The binding that was originally applied to a particular copy of a book at time of issue or at a later date.

original cataloging The preparation of the bibliographic record of a bibliographic item without recourse to an existing record for the identical item.

original film see *camera microfilm*

original parts A term describing the first edition of a bibliographic item in numbered parts with wrappers. Compare with *part-issue.*

original sources see *primary sources*

ornament see *type ornament*

ornamental initial see *initial letter*

orthochromatic film A silver emulsion film sensitive to yellow and green light as well as to blue and violet. Not being sensitive to red, dark red is reproduced the same as black. Compare with *panchromatic film.*

orthophotograph A uniform scale air photograph upon which precise horizontal distance measurements can be made. The central perspective of the original photograph is transformed to an orthogonal projection by a process of differential rectification.

OS see *operating system, out of stock*

OSI see *out of stock indefinitely*

other title information In descriptive cataloging, any title borne by a bibliographic item other than the title proper or parallel titles; also any phrase appearing in conjunction with the title proper, parallel titles, or other titles, indicative of the character, contents, etc., of the item or the motives for, or occasion of, its production or publication. The term includes subtitles, avant titres, etc., but does not include variations on the title proper (e.g., spine titles, sleeve titles). (AACR2)

out of contact An expression used in contact copying to describe noncontact between emulsions. This causes problems with the desired images, such as spreading of images.

out of print (OP) Not obtainable through the regular market, because the publisher's stock is exhausted.

out of stock (OS) A term used to indicate that a publisher does not have an item in stock but will probably have it later.

out of stock indefinitely (OSI) A term used to indicate that a publisher does not have an item in stock and will probably not replenish that stock.

output 1. The results of processing by a data processing or computer system, in contradistinction to the entry or transfer of data into the system for processing *(input).* 2. The signal emanating from an audio or video device, in contradistinction to the signal fed into it *(input).*

output device An electronic or mechanical machine or unit, such as a card punch, printer, or cathode-ray-tube terminal, designed to receive or report the results or output of processing by a computer. Compare with *input device.*

outreach program A library public service program initiated and designed to meet the information needs of an unserved or inadequately served target group, such as the institutionalized, senior citizens, or nonusers. Such programs may emphasize an aggressive publicity effort or extension services to the target group.

outsert One or more folded sheets of four pages, or a multiple of four, wrapped around the outside of a folded signature. The supplemented signature forms a binding unit, or section, of a book. Synonymous with wrap around. Compare with *insert* (1).

outstanding-order file An acquisitions file of bibliographic items on order but not yet received, usually arranged by author and/or title.

overcasting A method of hand binding in which one section is sewn to another by passing the thread through the back edge and diagonally out through the back. When done through holes prepunched by machine, is called oversewing by hand. Compare with *oversewing*. (Rebsamen)

overdevelop To exceed specified parameters during the developing process for photographic materials, resulting in a less-than-desirable image. The parameters can pertain to one or more of the following: time, temperature, developer strength, and agitation. Compare with *under-develop*.

overdue A designation used for an item charged out from the library and not returned on the established due date.

overdue notice A notice sent to a borrower who has failed to return an item charged out from the library on the established due date.

overexpose To exceed recommended parameters during the exposure of photographic materials to light. This generally results in an image that is darker than the original. Less-than-desirable results may be due to an aperture that is too large for the light source being used, excessive exposure time, or a faulty optical system. Compare with *underexpose*.

overflow The portion of a value or quantity that exceeds the capacity of an intended storage device or location.

overhead That amount of expenditures which does not contribute directly to and is not chargeable directly to a particular product or service, such as insurance, maintenance of the physical plant, and general administration.

overhead projector A device designed to project images by a light source shining through a transparency, which is placed on a platform. A mirror changes the direction of the light beam and projects the image through the lens system onto a screen.

overlap see *double document*

overlay 1. A transparency superimposed over a basic transparency and modifying the original projected image. 2. In letterpress printing, the paper used under the tympan to increase or equalize the pressure of the paper against the type and improve ink quality. 3. In computer science, the use of the same area of storage for different data during different stages of processing.

oversewing In binding, a method of side sewing by hand or machine in which sections are sewn to one another near the back edge. Is extensively used in library binding. Compare with *overcasting*.

oversize book A book which is too large to be shelved in its normal place, according to the shelving plan used in a particular library.

over-the-air subscription television see *subscription television*

ownership mark A bookplate, stamp, label, or the like, identifying an item as library property.

ownership stamp A metal or rubber stamp or embosser used to make a library ownership mark somewhere on an item owned by the library.

oxford corners Border rules that cross and project beyond each other, as on title pages and book covers.

P

PABX see *private automatic branch exchange*

pack see *deck (2)*

packet A defined block of data, such as a group of binary digits, which can be handled or processed by a communications system or network.

packet-switched network A network designed to transmit, then reassemble, data or messages broken into independent, small units or packets.

packing density The number of binary digits or characters that can be stored in a designated unit of storage, usually measured in bits per inch or characters per inch.

packing slip A slip accompanying a shipment which lists the items being shipped.

padding see *filler*

page 1. One side of a leaf. 2. A library staff member who delivers needed library materials from a closed stack and performs stack maintenance duties such as reshelving and shelf reading. 3. In computer science, see *paging*.

page affixing see *leaf affixing*

page catalog see *guard book catalog*

page head see *running head*

page proof A proof from type made up into pages after corrections have been made in the galley proof.

pagination 1. A system of marking the pages of a printed or written document, usually with numbers, to indicate their order. The marking of the recto of the leaves rather than the pages is known as foliation. 2. That part of the physical description area which states the number of pages and/or leaves of a bibliographic item.

paging 1. A technique for expanding the capacity of a computer's main storage by dividing data and computer programs into fixed-size segments called pages and placing those pages not needed immediately into auxiliary storage. 2. The action of a computer terminal in displaying data by successive discrete pages (hard copy terminal) or screens (cathode-ray-tube terminal).

paleography The study of the early forms of handwriting, and the deciphering of ancient and medieval manuscripts and other documents, including the study of the various letter forms used at different periods by scribes of different nations and languages, their usual abbreviations, etc. The British spelling is "palaeography."

palimpsest A manuscript written on a surface from which one or more earlier writings have been partially or completely erased.

pam box see *pamphlet file*

pamphlet 1. An independent publication consisting of a few leaves of printed matter fastened together but not bound; usually enclosed in paper covers. 2. As defined by Unesco, a complete, unbound nonperiodical publication of at least 5 but not more than 48 pages, exclusive of the cover. Also called a brochure. 3. A brief controversial treatise on a topic of current interest, usually religious or political, common in England from the 16th to the 18th century.

pamphlet binding A self-cover or paper binding, usually wire stitched, found on pamphlets and periodicals as issued by the publisher. Compare with *pamphlet-style library binding*.

pamphlet boards Plain boards with cloth hinges, and with eyelets in the hinges. A front and back board are laced onto the pamphlet through holes drilled near the inside margin of the pamphlet.

pamphlet box see *pamphlet file*

pamphlet file A box or frame for holding a number of pamphlets, unbound numbers of periodicals, or other materials unbound or in paper covers. Synonymous with pam box and pamphlet box.

pamphlet laws see *session laws*

pamphlet-style library binding A style of binding for a pamphlet or a thin group of pamphlets when use is expected to be infrequent. Its characteristics are side stitching, usually with wire, and covers with cloth hinges, usually of plain boards, heavy paper, paper-covered boards, or thin lightweight cloth, cut flush, without lettering. Synonymous with staple binding. Compare with *pamphlet binding*.

pamphlet volume A volume composed of a number of separate pamphlets bound together either with or without a general title page or table of contents.

panchromatic film A silver emulsion film sensitive to the entire visible color spectrum, and usually to ultraviolet. In black-and-white film, all colors are reproduced in various shades of gray. Compare with *orthochromatic film*.

panel 1. A square or rectangular space on a book cover, enclosed by lines or impressed. 2. A space on the spine of a book, between any two bands or between two parallel lines or sets of lines.

pantograph 1. A device on microfiche readers for positioning specific frames in order to view them on a screen. The device operates by manually sliding a pointer to a specific grid location mounted on the reader which corresponds to an index entry for an image on the microfiche. 2. A device by the aid of which maps, drawings, etc., may be copied mechanically on the same or a different scale.

paper The name for all kinds of matted or felted sheets of fiber (usually vegetable, but sometimes mineral, animal, or synthetic) formed on a fine screen from a water suspension. It can be characterized in a number of ways: the source of the fiber (esparto, rag, wood); the process for making the pulp from which the fibers are extracted (chemical wood, groundwood, mechanical wood); the way the sheet is made (handmade, laid, wove); or its intended use (art, bond, book, cover, newsprint). Its qualities are determined by the purity, length, and fibrilization of the fibers used, its chemical stability, and the finishes achieved.

paperback A book issued in paper covers. Synonymous with paperbound and softcover. Compare with *hardcover book.*

paperback, quality see *trade paperback*

paperback, trade see *trade paperback*

paperboard A general term applied to sheets of fibrous material of the same general composition as paper which are .012 of an inch or more in thickness and certain grades .006 of an inch or more in thickness.

paperbound see *paperback*

paper conservator A conservator trained to employ various physical and chemical procedures and techniques used to preserve objects wholly or partially made of paper. A flat paper conservator specializes in two-dimensional paper objects such as prints and drawings.

paper finishes Properties of surface contour, gloss, and appearance recognized for each category of paper. For uncoated book paper these range from the very smooth supercalendered through the five major finishes: English, machine, vellum, eggshell, and antique. Book paper that is coated is referred to as glossy, semidull, or dull, each with many variations. The main types of finishes for writing papers are supercalendered, vellum, kid, glazed, machine, unglazed, and cockle.

paperless publishing The storage and distribution of information electronically rather than on paper.

papermark see *watermark*

papers 1. In archives, an accumulation of personal and family documents, as distinct from formal records. 2. A general term used to include more than one type of manuscript or typescript material.

paperwork management The application of cost reduction principles and techniques to records creation, use, maintenance, and disposition processes, particularly those involving correspondence, forms, directives, and reports. Sometimes used synonymously with *records management,* though actually a narrower term.

papyrus 1. A writing material of the ancient Egyptians, Greeks, and Romans, made of longitudinal strips of fiber from the papyrus plant, placed in two layers at right angles. 2. A manuscript written on this material.

parallax In photography, an apparent change in relative position or shape of an object being photographed resulting from a change in viewing angle. This phenomenon occurs in cameras where the viewfinder does not focus through the lens.

parallel Pertaining to the simultaneous or concurrent occurrence of two or more related processes, activities, or events. Compare with *serial* (2).

parallel operation Pertaining to the simultaneous or concurrent execution of two or more tasks or operations by providing separate devices for each. Compare with *serial operation.*

parallel title The title proper in another language and/or script. (AACR2)

parallel transmission A method of data transmission in which all bits of a character are transferred simultaneously over separate channels of a communications facility. Compare with *serial transmission.*

parameter In a mathematical expression, a constant or variable that, by taking on various values, serves to distinguish various specific cases. Often used to refer to a quantitative characteristic of a statistical population.

parametric statistics Those statistical procedures intended for use with interval and ratio scaling. Compare with *nonparametric statistics.*

paraprofessional personnel A term used to designate library employees without professional certification or entrance-level educational requirements who are assigned supportive responsibilities at a high level and commonly perform their duties with some supervision by a professional staff member. The term is variously applied to personnel classified as library associates and library technical assistants, and, less precisely, to all members of the support staff. Synonymous with subprofessional personnel.

parchment Usually, the split skin of a lamb, sheep, or occasionally goat or young calf, prepared by scraping and dressing with lime (but not tanned) and intended for use as a writing or binding material. Compare with *vellum,* with which the term is now virtually interchangeable. The distinction favored by collectors of manuscripts tends to be that vellum is a more refined form of skin, and usually made from calf, whereas parchment is a cruder form, usually made from sheep, and thicker, harsher, and less highly polished than vellum.

parish library 1. A library maintained by a parish, i.e., a local division in Louisiana corresponding to a county. 2. One of the libraries sent from England to the American colonies for the clergy and their congregations through the efforts of Rev. Thomas Bray and his associates. Synonymous with Bray library. 3. A library supported by a local church parish.

Paris Principles The "Statement of Principles" adopted by the International Conference on Cataloging Principles held in Paris in 1961, which serve as the basis of the *Anglo-American Cataloguing Rules.*

parity bit A special binary digit or bit added to a pattern of bits to make the sum of the group either odd or even. Compare with *check bit, check digit.*

parity check An automatic error-detection check to determine whether the sum of the 1-bits or 0-bits is odd or even. Synonymous with odd-even check.

Parliamentary Papers In general, any publications ordered to be printed by one or the other of the British Houses of Parliament or required for parliamentary business. Includes three groups of publications: (1) Journals, Debates, and Votes and Proceedings; (2) Bills, Reports, and Papers; (3) Acts of Parliament. In a narrow sense the term includes only the second of the three groups, which is also referred to as *Sessional Papers.* Compare with *non-Parliamentary papers.*

part 1. One of the subordinate units into which a bibliographic item has been divided by the author, publisher, or manufacturer. In the case of printed monographs, generally synonymous with *volume* (1); it is distinguished from a *fascicle* by being a component unit rather than a temporary division of an item. (AACR2, mod.) 2. As used in the physical description area of a bibliographic record, the word *part* designates bibliographic units intended to be bound several to a volume. (AACR2, mod.) 3. The music for one of the participating voices or instruments in a musical work; the written or printed copy of such a part for the use of a performer, designated in the physical description area by the word *part.* (AACR2)

partial contents note A contents note which gives only part of the contents of a bibliographic item.

partial title A part of the title as given on the title page. It may be a catchword title, subtitle, or alternative title.

participative management An approach to management in which managers or supervisors provide employees with the counseling, growth opportunities, and information required to make decisions related to their job responsibilities and encourage their involvement in the decision-making process. Compare with *autocratic management, consultative management.*

part-issue An installment, usually in wrappers, of a bibliographic item published in parts, issued at intervals, and intended to be bound together when the item is complete. Compare with *original parts.*

partition   1. In computer science, a subdivision of available storage into smaller component segments. 2. In a postcoordinate indexing system, to subdivide a work that is indexed in depth and treat each division as a separate work, as a means of linking related descriptors and avoiding the retrieval of false combinations.

part title see *divisional title*

Pascal   A general-purpose, high-level programming language, widely used for teaching programming students and for applications. Named after Blaise Pascal.

pass   1. One complete cycle in processing data, executing a computer program, or operating a device. 2. An *admission record* or *stack permit.*

password   A word or sequence of characters provided by a user of a timesharing system to gain access to files or computer programs. Synonymous with lock code. Compare with *user identification.*

pasteboard   A general term applied to both paperboards and cardboards made by the union of thin layers of paper pulp; popularly used to denote any stiff board of medium thickness.

pasted board   A paperboard used in book covers, made of two or more layers of board or board and paper pasted together.

paste-down endpapers see *endpapers*

paste-in   A revision of, or an addition to, a text, supplied after the original printing and pasted on or opposite the page to which it applies. Synonymous with slip cancel. Compare with *errata.*

paste-up see *mechanical*

patchcord   A coaxial cable used to connect two or more pieces of equipment. Patchcords vary from having plugs or jacks at both ends to having a plug at one end and a jack at the other.

patch panel see *control panel*

patent   1. An official document issued by the United States or another government granting the exclusive right to make, use, and vend an invention for a certain number of years. 2. A publication containing the specifications and drawings of a patented invention, issued by a patent office.

patent document number   The unique numeric or alphanumeric string of characters assigned to a patent document by the patent office that granted and published the patent. (Z39.29)

patent document number, related   The numeric or alphanumeric string of characters identifying other documents to which the referenced patent document is legally related. The legal relationship between a patent document and a related document must be specified, using such terms as: "addition to," "division of," "amendment of," "reissue of," "contribution-in-part of," etc. (Z39.29)

patent file   A file of patents, including specifications and drawings, which may be arranged by country and number, name of patentee, or subject, or an index of such material similarly arranged.

pathfinders see *topical guides*

patients' library   A library maintained by a hospital or other institution with persons in its care because of physical or mental problems, with the purpose of providing recreational, therapeutic, and educational materials to assist in patients' rehabilitation or adjustment to their illness or condition.

patron see *library user*

patronymic   A name derived from the given name of the father, often by the addition of a suffix. (AACR2)

pattern   In binding, a sample volume, sample backstrip, rub-off, or other example used for matching the style.

pattern recognition   The automatic recognition of forms, shapes, or patterns by a machine.

pause control   A control switch on a tape recorder that stops and restarts sound recording or playback.

pawl sprocket   The mechanism in a camera or projector which transports the film forward one frame at a time by engaging the sprocket holes on the film.

PAX see *private automatic exchange*

pay plan see *classification and pay plan*

pay television 1. A system of television programming in which the signals are scrambled and can be rectified only by a special decoding device attached to the television receiver upon payment for each program. Compare with *subscription television (STV)*. 2. A system of television programming in which subscribers pay a fee for access to a special channel.

PBX see *private branch exchange*

Pearson product-moment correlation coefficient A measure of the similarity of behavior of two continuous, Gaussian-distributed variables. Historically the first of the many coefficients of correlation, it was originally called simply the correlation coefficient, by which short name it is still widely known.

pebble-grained morocco Goatskin leather intended for binding whose surface is covered with a tiny, pebblelike grain produced by subjecting it to grained steel plates under pressure; fashionable especially in the 19th century.

peek-a-boo indexing system see *optical coincidence indexing system*

percentile One of the points which divide a frequency distribution into one hundred equal parts.

perfect binding A rapid and comparatively cheap method of adhesive binding used in edition binding. The back of the volume is trimmed to produce a block of separate leaves. The back edges are roughened, adhesive is applied to them, and the case is attached. Its durability depends upon its ability to secure each individual leaf and the continuing flexibility of the adhesive. Hot-melt adhesives are widely used for perfect binding. Compare with *fan adhesive binding*.

perforated film Film with sprocket holes along one or both edges to aid in transporting and positioning the film for successive exposures in a camera and in moving the film through various types of projectors.

perforated tape see *punched tape*

performance appraisal The process of evaluating the performance and behavior of employees individually in their positions for purposes of assessing training needs and determining eligibility for retention, salary adjustments, or pro-

motion. Synonymous with performance evaluation and employee evaluation.

performance budget A budget which groups anticipated expenditures according to activities to be carried out (e.g., reference services, children's services) and establishes cost standards for each set of activities. Emphasis is on efficiency of operations and the control of the quantity rather than on quality of service.

performance evaluation see *performance appraisal*

performance standards see *standards* (2)

period bibliography A bibliography limited to a certain period of time.

periodical A serial appearing or intended to appear indefinitely at regular or stated intervals, generally more frequently than annually, each issue of which is numbered or dated consecutively and normally contains separate articles, stories, or other writings. Newspapers disseminating general news, and the proceedings, papers, or other publications of corporate bodies primarily related to their meetings, are not included in this term.

periodical display shelving Shelving specifically designed to display current, unbound issues of periodicals. The design of such shelving varies but frequently includes a slanted shelf for the latest issue, with a flat shelf for additional unbound issues below.

periodical index 1. A subject index to a group of periodicals. 2. An index to a volume, group of volumes, or complete set of one periodical title.

periodicals collection The library's collection of periodicals and other serials treated like periodicals, bound, unbound, or in microform, which may be kept apart from other materials.

period printing The production or reproduction of a book not on the model of any particular edition, but in the style of the period when the book was first published or with which it is concerned.

period subdivision 1. In classification, the subdivision of a class based on chronological order. 2. The subdivision of a subject heading by a subheading which designates the period treated by the work(s) contained in the bibliographic item or the period during which the item was published. Synonymous with chronological subdivision, time subdivision.

peripheral equipment The equipment used in conjunction with, but which is not a part of, a computer system. Synonymous with auxiliary equipment.

permanent-durable paper A paper made to resist the effects of aging. Durability is reflected by the retention of physical qualities under continual use, while permanence is judged by resistance to chemical action either from impurities in the paper or from environmental conditions. Acid is the most important agent in the breakdown of the cellulose fiber chains and the resultant degeneration of the paper. While a paper with a pH value of 7 may be considered neutral or acid-free, an alkaline-buffered paper or alkaline reserve paper which has a pH value of 8.5 and a 3 to 5 percent alkaline reserve, is preferable for archival materials. Such buffered papers not only are stable, but also resist acid migration and contamination from the environment.

permanent record film see *archival film*

permanent storage see *read-only storage*

permuted index An index in which a string of descriptors assigned to works or the keywords in the titles of works are rearranged to bring each word into filing position in the context of all other words within the string or within the full or truncated title.

personal author The person chiefly responsible for the creation of a work.

personal name entry 1. An access point consisting of a personal name. 2. A bibliographic record with a personal name as the heading. Compare with *author entry, corporate entry.*

personal papers In archives, the private documents and other manuscript materials accumulated by an individual, owned by the individual, and usually subject to the owner's disposition. Synonymous with private papers.

personnel administration see *personnel management*

personnel management All aspects of and activities in the management process concerned with the selection, organization, development, supervision, and control of the human resources within an organization. Synonymous with personnel administration.

PERT see *Program Evaluation and Review Technique*

pH An abbreviation for hydrogen-ion concentration. A measure of the intensity of the acid content of paper, expressed in terms of a logarithmic scale from 0 to 14. The neutral point is 7.0; values above 7 are alkaline; values below are acid.

phase In classification, that portion of a composite subject which has been wholly derived from any one single class.

phase relationship In classification, a relationship between subjects other than the generic, such as one subject influenced by another.

phonocartridge A device that converts the wave forms in audiodisc grooves into electrical impulses which are then sent through the amplifier. The two basic types are the *magnetic cartridge* and the *piezoelectric cartridge.*

phonodisc see *audiodisc*

phonograph see *audiodisc player*

phonograph record see *audiodisc*

phonorecord see *audiodisc*

phonotape see *audiotape*

photocharger A machine used for photographing the record of a circulation transaction using the photocharging method.

photocharging A transaction charging system in which the identification of the item being borrowed, which is on the book pocket, and the borrower's identification card are photographed on 35mm film. A numbered transaction card with the due date is inserted in the borrowed item. The cumulated transaction cards from returned items are arranged numerically, and missing numbers identify overdue items. Information on items not returned is extracted from the film.

photocomposition see *photosetting*

photoconductor A material which conducts electricity only when exposed to light.

photocopy A general term applied to copies produced directly on film or paper by radiant energy. The copies are usually about the same size as the original; thus the term does not normally include microimages. Synonymous with photoduplication, photographic reproduction, photoreproduction.

photoduplication see *photocopy*

photoelectric cell The device in motion-picture projectors with an optical sound system which converts variations of light intensity into electric signals which are then sent through the amplifier.

photoelectrostatic printer see *printer* (2)

photoengraving 1. A photomechanical process for making a metal relief block for letterpress printing. A photographic negative of the image to be printed is exposed against a metal plate with a coating of acid resist. The nonprinting areas are etched to produce the image in relief. Synonymous with process engraving. Compare with *engraving* (1), *photogravure* (1). 2. A print made by this process.

photoflood bulb An electric bulb with a filament designed for low voltage. High intensity is obtained by overloading voltage. It gives an intense light but is short-lived.

photogelatin process see *collotype*

photograph 1. A picture produced by the action of light on a photosensitive material and formed by an optical system using a lens and other optical devices. 2. By extension, any image formed by the action of radiant energy.

photographic film see *film* (1)

photographic lettering device see *lettering device, photographic*

photographic paper An opaque paper base, coated on one side (simplex paper) or both sides (duplex paper) with a light-sensitive emulsion on which images can be recorded by exposure and subsequent processing. Processed photographic paper may have positive or negative images, may be either black and white or color, and is supplied in a number of sizes and types, which include hard, negative, normal, projection, soft, and contrast paper. (NCES)

photographic print see *photoprint* (1)

photographic printing The activity of making an image (usually positive) on film or photographic paper from a piece of processed film (usually negative).

photographic processing The activity of subjecting exposed photographic film or paper to a special process or treatment in order to develop and stabilize the images which have been recorded on them.

photographic reproduction see *photocopy*

photogravure 1. An intaglio platemaking process in which a photographic positive of the image to be printed and a grid similar to a halftone screen are exposed against a metal plate, with the areas to be incised controlled by an acid resist. The printing areas are then etched into the plate to produce the image in recess. Sometimes a distinction is made between photogravure printing from a plate on a sheet-fed press and rotogravure. Synonymous with gravure. Compare with *photoengraving* (1) and *rotogravure* (1). 2. A print produced by this method.

photolithography Lithography using plates prepared by a photomechanical process, as opposed to plates or stone with the image drawn by hand. Synonymous with *lithophotography*.

photomacrography The use of photographic techniques to produce images which are the same size as the original and which can be viewed without magnification. Compare with *microphotography, photomicrography.*

photomap A reproduction of a controlled photomosaic, or of a single rectified air photograph, to which such cartographic detail as names, symbols, gridlines, and marginal information have been added.

photomechanical 1. Any one of the processes of making printing plates by exposing a film negative or positive on the photosensitized plate surface. 2. In composition, the complete assembly of all the elements of a page on a transparent film base, from which proofs can be made by the diazo process and a single-piece negative can be made for the production of an offset printing plate.

photometer see *light*

photometry see *light*

photomicrography The use of photographic techniques to produce enlarged images of very small objects. The objects are usually magnified by using a microscope and then photographed. Compare with *microphotography, photomacrography*.

photomosaic, controlled An assembly of parts of vertical air photographs joined together to leave minimal scale variations. In a controlled photomosaic, the distortions of perspective have been adjusted to ground measurements.

photomosaic, uncontrolled 1. A mosaic composed of uncorrected prints, the detail of which has been matched from print to print without ground control or other orientation. 2. A photograph of an uncontrolled assembly of complete contact prints of vertical air photographs intended to serve as an index or as a map substitute.

photo-offset Offset printing in which the printed image is reproduced from a plate prepared by a photomechanical process.

photoplastic film A heat-developing film with a polyester base and a photoplastic emulsion that is sensitized by an electrostatic change, with the images recorded as deformations in the emulsion. Synonymous with thermal plastic film.

photoprint 1. A reproduction of graphic matter on photographic paper. Synonymous with photographic print. 2. In photosetting, a final proof with all typographic elements in correct position, ready to be pasted into a mechanical.

photoreproduction see *photocopy*

photosensitive Capable of undergoing a physical or chemical change as a result of the absorption of radiant energy, especially light.

photosetting The composition of text, using electronic and photographic methods. Images of type characters are projected from a film or disk onto photosensitive film or paper which is used to produce an offset plate. Some photosetting systems allow the makeup of pages on a cathode-ray-tube terminal. Synonymous with filmsetting and photocomposition.

phototype Type composed on a photosetting machine.

physical description area That part of the bibliographic description which describes the physical item, including the specific material designation; the number of physical units, such as pages of a book or frames of a filmstrip; playing time of audiotape, videotape, etc.; illustrative matter; dimensions; and accompanying material. Formerly called collation.

physical facilities see *facilities*

physical plant see *plant*

physical processing The activities carried out by a library or processing center to prepare items for use. For books, includes jacketing, affixing labels and pockets, stamping ownership marks, and marking, which are sometimes called technical processes. Synonymous with mechanical processing.

physical record In computer science, a record defined in terms of its form or the physical space it requires. Compare with *logical record*.

piano score A reduction of an orchestral score to a version for piano, on two staves. (AACR2)

piano (violin, etc.**) conductor part** In music, the part of an ensemble work for a particular instrument with cues for the other instruments; intended for the use of the person who plays the instrument and also conducts the performance of the work. (AACR2)

piano-vocal score see *vocal score*

pica Originally a type size about 1/6 inch high. Now, the basic unit of the point system of measurement, being equal to 12 points or about 1/6 inch.

pickup tube A form of electron tube used in a television camera whereby an electron image is formed from an optical image and is periodically scanned by an electron beam to produce an electrical video signal.

picosecond One-trillionth of a second or one-thousandth of a nanosecond.

pictograph 1. In ancient or primitive writing, a picture used to represent an idea. 2. A writing composed of pictographs.

picture 1. A representation of an object, person, or scene produced on a flat surface, especially by painting, drawing, or photography. 2. A printed reproduction of any of these.

picture book A children's book, consisting of illustrations and little or no text, such as an alphabet or counting book, generally intended for preschool children.

picture file A collection of pictures, photographs, illustrations, art prints, and clippings. Synonymous with art file.

picture storybook A children's book consisting of a narrative and illustrations that are synchronized with the text, generally requiring a reading ability level of at least third grade and intended to be read to children.

piece 1. In archives, a discrete object or individual member of a class or group, such as a letter. In this sense, synonymous with *item* (3) or *document*. 2. A fragment or part separated from the whole, such as a separated leaf of a longer manuscript or other document.

pie chart A chart of circular shape divided into wedges whose sizes are proportionate to the quantity or percentage being represented. Synonymous with area diagram.

piezoelectric cartridge A phonocartridge of crystal or ceramic that produces electrical voltage by physical pressure. These cartridges are less efficient than *magnetic cartridges*.

pigskin Leather tanned with alum and made from the skin of a pig, and intended for binding; rugged and durable, it is frequently used for large books, or for those expected to receive heavy use.

pilot study A small experimental study conducted prior to a larger or full-scale study, usually with the objective of testing procedures, methodology, or a preliminary hypothesis.

pinfeed form A continuous, fan-fold form that is aligned in a computer printer by pins or sprockets along its margins which also move the paper through the device during printing.

pirated edition An edition issued without the authorization of the copyright holder. Synonymous with pirated reprint. Compare with *unauthorized edition*.

pirated reprint see *pirated edition*

PIRA test A test for acidity in binding leather, first published by the British Leather Manufacturers' Association in conjunction with the Printing Industry Research Association (PIRA) in 1933.

pitch The quality of a sound that is determined by the vibration frequency of the sound waves producing it; the greater the frequency, the higher the pitch.

place subdivision see *geographic subdivision*

Plain Title Edition see *Departmental Edition*

plan 1. A drawing showing relative positions on a horizontal plane, e.g., relative positions of parts of a building or a landscape design; the arrangement of furniture in a room or building; a graphic presentation of a military or naval plan. (AACR2) 2. In cartography, a large-scale, detailed map or chart with a minimum of generalization. (AACR2)

planetary camera A camera used for microfilming large documents or when fine resolution is needed. The document is placed in a horizontal plane and both the film and the document are stationary during exposure. Synonymous with flat-bed camera and stepwise-operated camera.

planning 1. The administrative or managerial function concerned with the formulation and review of goals, objectives, programs, budgets, policies, procedures, and other types of planning within an organization. The planning function establishes the future directions of the organization, and the resulting plans unify the activities toward agreed-upon results. 2. The formal process of setting goals and objectives, determining the extent to which they are being met, considering various courses of action for meeting them, and determining courses of action to take, including what should be done, and how, when, where, and by whom it should be done.

Planning-Programming-Budgeting System (PPBS) A systematic approach to budgeting involving the delineation of programs; the establishment of programmatic goals; the analysis of alternatives, including total cost estimates, for their accomplishment; the allocation of expenditures according to program; and the evaluation of programs based upon the established goals.

planographic printing Printing from a flat surface on which the image area and nonimage area are on the same plane, in contradistinction to letterpress, in which the image area is raised, and to intaglio, in which the image area is recessed.

plant A library's building (or quarters) with mechanical systems (e.g., heat, light, water) and grounds, but not equipment. Compare with *facilities*.

plant publication see *house organ*

plaquette binding see *cameo binding*

plastic comb binding A method of mechanical binding in which the teeth of a specially constructed plastic comb are inserted into slots near the binding edge of the leaves and are allowed to curl back upon themselves and the spine of the comb. Primarily used in offices and information centers for binding reports and other documents issued as separate leaves for short-term retention.

plat In cartography, a diagram drawn to scale showing land boundaries and subdivisions, together with all data essential to the description and identification of the several units shown thereon, and including one or more certificates indicating due approval. A plat differs from a map in that it does not necessarily show additional cultural, drainage, and relief features.

plate 1. Originally a sheet of metal (copper, etc.) used primarily for printing illustrations, maps, music, etc.; now plates of metal, plastic, or rubber are widely used in most processes for printing copy as well as artwork. Some, stereotype and electrotype, are duplicates molded from type and cuts. Other plates are photomechanical and are the original printing surface. 2. In cataloging, a leaf containing illustrative matter, with or without explanatory text, that does not form part of either the preliminary or the main sequences of pages or leaves. (AACR2)

plate line see *plate mark*

plate mark An embossed line around an intaglio print. Caused by the pressure of printing, it shows the edge of the plate. Synonymous with plate line.

platen 1. On a printing press, a flat plate which presses the paper against the inked type. 2. A mechanical device used to position film accurately in the focal plane during exposure.

platen press A printing press on which the type form is held vertically and the paper is fed onto a metal plate that swings up and presses against the type.

plate number A serial number assigned by a music publisher to each publication for purposes of record and identification. It usually appears at the bottom of each page, and may be used as a clue to date of publication. Synonymous with publication number and publisher's number.

plate proof A proof of a printing plate made to check the quality of the plate and to check page corrections.

plating The pasting of bookplates or other labels into books.

play back To perform a playback.

playback The action of reproducing sounds and/or images from an audiorecording or videorecording.

playback deck A magnetic tape deck which will play back the prerecorded tape but will not record on a blank tape and cannot erase.

playback head see *head* (5)

PL 480 Program see *Public Law 480 Program*

PL/1 (Programming Language 1) A flexible, high-level language, developed by IBM, designed for use in programming business and scientific applications.

plotter A peripheral computer device used to generate permanent graphic images on some sort of removable medium, such as paper or film, from digital or analog input signals. If the image is not removable but is displayed for a limited time, as on a cathode-ray-tube screen, the device is called a graphic display.

plug An electrical device with projecting prongs attached to a power cord. When inserted into a jack, electrical contact is made.

plugboard see *control panel*

PMEST The abbreviation for the citation order used in S. R. Ranganathan's *Colon Classification;* represents the five fundamental categories: personality, matter, energy, space, and time.

pneumatic tubes A system of tubes through which cartridges containing call cards, books, etc., are propelled by air pressure or by vacuum.

pocket see *card pocket, cover pocket*

pocket part A supplement intended to be inserted in a pocket on the inside cover of a book. A customary way to update law books.

point 1. A standard unit of type size, about $\frac{1}{72}$ inch in size. Type for miniature books can be as small as 2 or 4 points, while standard book type tends to range in size between 10 and 12 points. 2. In the antiquarian trade, the presence (or its absence) in a book of a peculiarity which serves to distinguish it from other copies, such as a broken letter, uncorrected typographical error; of use in determining, or in seeming to determine, priority of issue.

point-of-use instruction An explanation of how to use a specific reference source which is placed at the location of the source. It may be in print or audiovisual format, or a combination of the two.

Poisson distribution The frequency distribution for the number of random events occurring in a specified time interval; used especially when the probability of occurrence of any one of the events is very small. Named for Siméon D. Poisson.

polarity 1. In reprography, an expression of change in image tone between generations of copies. To change polarity means that tones are reversed from negative to positive, or vice versa. To retain polarity means that there is little change in tone. 2. The positive or negative state of the television picture signal.

polarized light Light waves that vibrate only in one plane with respect to the line of travel. Normal, unpolarized light vibrates in all planes. Normal light can be polarized by passing through crystals or optical devices that transmit only those light waves vibrating in certain planes.

policy An administrative plan or series of guidelines, preferably written, which delineate acceptable practices and actions for a wide range of activities within an organization. A library might have policies covering specific areas of activity, including circulation, information service, gifts, collection development, and cataloging, as well as system-wide policies in such areas as personnel.

policy manual A compilation of written policies in effect within an organization used for staff instruction, consultation, and decision-making. Compare with *procedure manual, staff manual.*

polling A technique by which each terminal in a network is alternately and periodically queried to determine if it has data to submit or transmit. Compare with *selecting.*

polyester tape A plastic tape of polyester used as a magnetic-tape base. Unlike acetate tape, it maintains its flexibility over time and is more dimensionally stable in environments without humidity control. However, it can be easily stretched.

polyglot Said of a book containing several versions of one text in several languages, such as a polyglot Bible.

polyvinyl-acetate adhesive (PVA) A synthetic, water-based adhesive of the resin emulsion type which is applied at room temperature. Dries to a translucent film of great flexibility. Frequently used in adhesive binding.

popular library 1. In a departmentalized library, a collection of materials of general interest and appeal. 2. An obsolete name for a public library.

popular name A shortened, abbreviated, or simplified form of the official name of a government agency or other corporate body, by which it is commonly known.

population In statistics, a collection of objects, events, or individuals having some common characteristic that the researcher is interested in studying. The population may be either finite or infinite. Synonymous with universe.

population parameter see *parameter*

pornography Works depicting sexual conduct in an offensive way, and, in U.S. law, found to appeal to the prurient interest and to be without serious value. Compare with *erotica.*

port That part of a network or central processing unit which provides a channel for receiving or sending data transmitted from or to a remote terminal or other device.

portfolio A case for holding loose papers, engravings, or similar material, consisting of two covers joined together at the spine and usually tied at the fore-edge (and occasionally the top and bottom edges).

portolan chart An early type of map or chart for guiding mariners in coastwise sailing; usually in manuscript. Also (and incorrectly, because it was used before the invention of the compass) called a compass map. In England, portolan charts were known as rutters (from "route").

position The combination of activities, duties, tasks, and responsibilities which are assigned to a given individual in an organization. May be used synonymously with *job*.

positional notation system A method of representing numbers whereby the significance of each digit depends upon its place or position as well as its numeric value.

position analysis The process of examining the characteristics of a position, including the determination of required activities, duties, and tasks, and the identification of the authority-account-ability relationships relevant to the position, as well as the prerequisite education, knowledge, skills, or experience needed for the position holder to perform successfully. It is a necessary step in classifying positions and grades within a classification. Synonymous with job analysis, job audit.

position classification The process of grouping positions within an organization into categories based upon similar activities, duties, tasks, responsibilities, and prerequisite qualifications. Common position classifications within a library include clerks, technical assistants, library associates, and librarians. Within each classification, positions may be assigned grades. Synonymous with job classification.

position description A written and formal statement describing in some detail the activities, duties, tasks, responsibilities, organizational relationships, and prerequisite qualifications of a position. Synonymous with job description.

position rotation The process of systematically transferring employees from one assignment, position, or department to another according to a prescribed time schedule as a method of staff training and development. Synonymous with job rotation.

position specification A description in some detail of the qualities, education, knowledge, skills, training, or other requirements for an individual to perform effectively in a given position. Synonymous with job specification.

position title The name given a position within an organization. It may represent a broad position classification, such as senior librarian, or may be a specific name within a classification, such as reference librarian.

positive-appearing image A photographic image which has the tonal characteristics of the original. Normally, the image would appear as dark or neutral tones on a light background. Synonymous with dark line image.

possible purchase file see *want list*

post In data processing, to enter, place, or transfer a unit of information, a data element, or a descriptor under a heading in a record.

post binding A method of loose-leaf binding using segmented posts of metal, plastic, etc., which are inserted through holes in the edge of the leaves. The basic post consists of two flat-headed pieces which screw one into the other. The binding can be expanded by screwing additional sections between the basic post ends. Post bindings do not open flat.

postcoordinate index An index compiled according to a postcoordinate indexing system.

postcoordinate indexing system 1. An indexing system in which works treating two or more subjects in combination are assigned single-concept descriptors for each subject at the time of indexing, and manipulation (correlation) of the descriptors occurs at the time of search. For example, a work on the automation of library circulation systems might be assigned the descriptors "Automation," "Libraries," "Circulation," and "Systems." At the search stage, using a computer-based, punched card, or optical-coincidence information retrieval system, works entered under each of the search terms are compared to determine which are common to all terms. 2. An indexing system in which the entries in the index of a file are constructed so as to allow their manipulation (correlation) at the time the file is searched. Such entries include access points and headings that lead the searcher to relevant computer records in a bibliographic database. Synonymous with postcorrelative indexing system. Compare with *precoordinate indexing system.*

postcorrelative indexing system see *postcoordinate indexing system*

posting-up see *automatic generic posting*

power amplifier An amplifier designed to increase a preamplified signal.

power bandwidth The frequency range of an amplifier at its rated power output, expressed in number of hertz and watts and percentage of harmonic distortion.

power cord The two- or three-wired electrical connection from the power supply to the electrical device.

power output The amount of electrical signal power which can be produced by an amplifier, usually expressed in watts.

PPBS see *Planning-Programming-Budgeting System*

PQ developer see *developing*

practice work see *practicum*

practicum A specified period of practice work in a library or other information agency with the purpose of relating the study of theory and work experience, both usually being carried on simultaneously. Synonymous with practice work. Compare with *internship.*

preamplifier A special amplifier designed for use with very low input voltages. It usually increases the signal for further amplification by an amplifier (or power amplifier). Preamplifiers are designed for minimum distortion and noise.

prebound see *pre-library bound*

precataloged item A newly purchased bibliographic item which arrived from the dealer accompanied by a set of catalog cards or other form of bibliographic record. Compare with preprocessed item.

precatalog searching The bibliographic searching, usually done before ordering, to verify or provide bibliographic data and to provide an identification number, such as the International Standard Book Number, for obtaining a bibliographic record. Compare with *preorder bibliographic search.*

PRECIS see *Preserved Context Index System*

precision ratio The ratio between the number of works retrieved in a literature search that were judged to be relevant by the person for whom the search was conducted and the number of works retrieved. Compare with *recall ratio.*

precoordinate index An index compiled according to a precoordinate indexing system.

precoordinate indexing system 1. An indexing system in which works treating two or more subjects in combination are assigned descriptors which correlate the subjects insofar as the system allows at the time of indexing, since descriptors cannot be manipulated (correlated) at the time the index is searched. For example, a work on the automation of library circulation systems might be assigned the descriptor "Library automation," modified by the phrase "of circulation systems." 2. An indexing system in which entries in the index of a file are correlated insofar as the system allows at the time of indexing, since they cannot be manipulated (correlated) at the time the file is searched. Such entries include access points and headings that are assigned to lead the searcher to relevant records in a catalog or bibliographic database. Synonymous with precorrelative indexing system. Compare with *postcoordinate indexing system.*

precorrelative indexing system see *precoordinate indexing system*

predicables, five In Aristotelian logic, the five sorts of predicate that can be attributed to a subject, used as a basis for assembling classes in logical order in hierarchical classification systems. They are genus, species, difference, property, and accident.

preface A note preceding the text of a book, which states the origin, purpose, and scope of the work(s) contained in the book and sometimes includes acknowledgments of assistance. When written by someone other than the author, is more properly a *foreword.* To be distinguished from the *introduction,* which deals with the subject of the work(s).

pre-library bound New books having covers imprinted with a design like that on the original publisher's binding which have been bound according to the *Standards for Reinforced (Pre-*

Library Bound) New Books. To be distinguished from publisher's *edition binding, library edition,* or *reinforced binding* not in accordance with that standard. Synonymous with prebound.

preliminaries see *front matter*

preliminary cataloging The preparation of a simplified or partial bibliographic record which serves as the basis for later, complete cataloging.

preliminary edition An edition issued in advance of a final edition, sometimes for criticism of the text before the final edition is published. Synonymous with provisional edition.

preliminary matter see *front matter*

preliminary plans see *architectural drawings*

preorder bibliographic search The process of determining whether a library already has a copy of a requested bibliographic item and gathering or verifying the elements of bibliographic description necessary to place an order. Synonymous with acquisitions searching. Compare with *precatalog searching, verification.*

preparations department see *technical processes department*

prepayment Cash payment accompanying a purchase order.

preprint A portion of a document containing one or more works which is printed and distributed prior to the publication date of the whole, such as an article from a book or periodical.

preprocessed item A newly purchased bibliographic item which arrives from the dealer with its physical processing at least partly completed. Compare with *precataloged item.*

prepublication cataloging see *cataloging in publication (CIP)*

prerecorded materials 1. The same as recorded materials. The implied difference between recorded materials and prerecorded materials is that prerecorded materials have information recorded on them at the time of purchase or acquisition. 2. In broadcasting, materials that were recorded prior to the time of actual broadcast or final production.

prerinse In the processing of silver halide materials, the washing of the exposed materials prior to developing.

presentation copy A copy of a book bearing an inscription of presentation, generally by the author, illustrator, editor, or publisher. Compare with *inscribed copy.*

preservation The activities associated with maintaining library and archival materials for use, either in their original physical form or in some other usable way. Compare with *conservation,* frequently used as a synonym, though distinctions between the two terms seem to be emerging—at least in North America in the library and archive world. Conservation tends to refer to the techniques and procedures relating to the treatment of books and other documents to maintain as much as possible or feasible the original physical integrity of the physical object or artifact. Preservation tends to include conservation, but also comprehends techniques of partial preservation of the physical object (e.g., a new binding), as well as procedures for the substitution of the original artifact by materials conversion, whereby the intellectual content of the original is at least partially preserved.

preservation administrator A person trained in preservation who helps design and administer a library's or other repository's program for maintaining books and other documents for use.

preservation microfilming The microfilming for preservation purposes of books, serials, manuscripts, and other documents, using for this purpose materials and processing methods of maximum permanence, and creating a store of camera microfilm which is housed under controlled conditions and used only to make distribution copies. Compare with *security filming.*

Preserved Context Indexing System (PRECIS) A method of indexing developed for the *British National Bibliography,* in which an initial string of descriptors assigned by an indexer is manipulated by a computer into various combinations according to a system of relational operators.

press see *range*

press braille Braille characters which have been embossed on thin zinc or iron printing plates, from which books for the blind are produced on electrically driven machines similar to a braillewriter. Braillists copy the text directly onto the plates, or a computer program is employed in the conversion of the text to braille and the automatic production of the printing plates.

press release An official or authoritative statement of information for publication in newspapers or other media. Synonymous with news release.

pressure marks Undesirable density in processed film that is the result of pressure on the emulsion prior to exposure and processing.

pressure plate Any device which holds film in the focal plane in photographic equipment.

preventive maintenance Maintenance to prevent problems and malfunctions before they occur, in order to retain hardware and software in good working condition. Compare with *corrective maintenance, scheduled maintenance.*

price index A number used to show the effects of price change, and price change only, on a fixed group of items over a period of time. A price index has a base period of one or more years, and the average price in the base period is assigned the index value of 100; the average price in succeeding years is divided by the base period average and multiplied by 100 to yield the price index for each year.

primary access In information retrieval, direct or immediate access to particular entries or groups of entries in a file or database. Compare with *secondary access.*

primary bibliography An original, extensive or general bibliography dealing with books or other documents related by date or place of publication but unrelated in subject matter. Compare with *secondary bibliography.*

primary journal A journal which has as one of its main purposes the dissemination of the results of basic research.

primary network station A network station which has control of a communications channel at any given time. During this time, the primary station can transmit data to a secondary network station. Synonymous with master network station. Compare with *tributary network station.*

primary sources Fundamental, authoritative documents relating to a subject, used in the preparation of a later work, e.g., original records, contemporary documents, etc. Synonymous with original sources and source material.

primary storage see *main storage*

princeps see *first edition*

princeps edition see *first edition*

Princeton file A box with the back, top, and lower portion of the front unenclosed, used for holding pamphlets, unbound issues of periodicals, and other materials unbound or in paper covers.

print 1. A picture reproduced by any printing process. 2. A photograph made from a film negative or positive on photographic film or photographic paper.

printed as manuscript 1. Printed from a manuscript which has not had final editorial revision. 2. Printed for private circulation; i.e., not to be quoted or sold.

printed but not published Printed, but not offered for sale by the publisher.

printer 1. The person or firm by whom a book or other document is printed, as distinguished from the publisher and bookseller by whom it is issued and sold. 2. A computer-output device which prints characters of data on a medium such as paper.

Direct-impression (impact) printers are characterized by the type of print element or print head they employ. The matrix printer uses fine wires arranged in a dot matrix to form characters; the daisy wheel printer uses single-character spokes radiating from a hub; the thimble printer uses two-character spokes radiating from a hub; the band printer uses a rotating metal or plastic band with embossed characters; the drum printer uses a rotating cylinder with embossed characters; the chain printer uses embossed character slugs which are linked together; the train printer uses embossed character slugs which are not linked together but are pushed along a track.

Nonimpact printers include the ink jet printer, whereby ink droplets are sprayed onto paper in character patterns; the thermal printer, which uses a heated print head to form characters on heat-sensitive paper; the electrostatic printer, which uses static electricity to create latent images on specially coated paper and toner to develop the images; and the photoelectrostatic (laser/xerographic) printer, which uses a laser beam to create latent character images on a photosensitive belt or drum, which are developed with toner and then transferred to paper.

printer's device see *printer's mark*

printer's flower see *flower* (1)

printer's ornament see *type ornament*

printer's or **publisher's mark** An emblem or design used by a printer or a publisher as a trademark. Devices now in use are usually those of publishers rather than printers. Synonymous with printer's device, publisher's device, and logo. Improperly referred to as *colophon.*

print film A fine-grain, high-resolution film used primarily for making contact copies.

printing Any of various means of reproducing identical copies of graphic matter in a fixed form.

printing paper Any paper suitable for printing, such as book paper, newsprint, and writing paper.

printout The printed results of output produced by a computer printer.

print terminal A visual display unit equipped with or accompanied by a printer to provide hard copy output. Compare with *cathode-ray-tube terminal, visual display unit, touch terminal.*

prison library A library maintained by a prison for the use of its staff and inmates. It may include materials of general interest, materials in support of its educational programs, and legal literature.

private automatic branch exchange (PABX) A private telephone exchange using automatic equipment for calls both within an organization and into the public-switched network outside the organization.

private automatic exchange (PAX) A private telephone exchange using automatic equipment for calls within an organization, but with no provision for calls into the public-switched network outside the organization.

private branch exchange (PBX) A private telephone exchange requiring manual switching for calls both within an organization and into the public-switched network outside the organization.

private library A library not supported by taxation, especially a library belonging to an individual.

private line A communications channel and related equipment leased or furnished for the exclusive use of a customer. Synonymous with leased line.

privately illustrated see *extra-illustrated*

privately printed Said of books issued for private distribution only, or issued from a private press and not offered for sale through trade book channels.

private papers see *personal papers*

private press A printing press that issues small editions at the pleasure of the owner. The books often are finely printed, perhaps on a handpress, and while they may be offered for sale to the public, they are rarely distributed through trade book channels.

private publisher A person or firm who assumes the expense of having a book or other document manufactured and the responsibility for distributing it by public sale in order to ensure its issue and/or to oversee the quality of its production. Compare with *vanity publisher, subsidy publishing.*

privilege see *cum privilegio*

proactive library service The development and provision of programs of library service which anticipate the information needs of library users or user groups in the community, as distinct from library service which responds only to demonstrated needs. Synonymous with assertive library service.

probability The likelihood or possibility that a chance event will occur.

probationary period An established period of time during which new employees are trained and their work performance carefully evaluated before they receive permanent status in an organization.

problem-oriented language A programming language such as Statistical Package for the Social Sciences (SPSS), designed to facilitate the writing of computer programs for a specific type of problem. Compare with *procedure-oriented language.*

procedural language see *procedure-oriented language*

procedure An administrative plan, either written or formalized by practice, which establishes the acceptable sequence of steps, actions, and methods for accomplishing a narrowly defined task in an efficient and effective manner.

procedure manual A compilation of written procedures in effect within an organization or one of its administrative units used for staff training and consultation. Synonymous with work manual. Compare with *policy manual, staff manual.*

procedure-oriented language A programming language such as ALGOL or FORTRAN, designed to facilitate the expression of processes in procedural or algorithmic steps. Synonymous with procedural language. Compare with *problem-oriented language.*

proceedings The published record of a meeting of a society or other organization, frequently accompanied by abstracts or reports of papers presented, which are more properly called *transactions.*

process An organized sequence of operations meant to produce specified results.

process camera A camera, usually with special attachments, designed to produce images on an intermediate material from which prints can be made, as in photolithography.

process color printing see *full-color printing*

processed film Film on which images have been developed and stabilized following exposure.

processed publications Publications reproduced by an office duplicating machine from a master rather than by a printing press from metal type or plates. Synonymous with near-print publications.

process engraving see *photoengraving*

process file see *in-process file*

process information file see *in-process file*

processing 1. A term which may include everything that is done to a bibliographic item between its arrival in a library and its storage in the collection or may, in a more restricted sense, refer only to physical processing. 2. The manipulation of data to solve a problem or provide a desired result. 3. In photography, see *photographic processing* and *film processing.*

processing center A library or other central agency in which materials are processed for all libraries of a system or area. Such a center may provide cooperative purchasing as well as cataloging and physical processing.

processing service, commercial see *commercial processing service*

processing unit see *central processing unit*

processor 1. In data processing, a device which can perform operations upon data, e.g., a central processing unit or compiler. 2. In photographic processing, any device which performs the various operations necessary to develop and stabilize the images which have been recorded on photosensitive material.

processor-camera A device which functions both as a camera and a film processor. It is commonly used in the production of camera cards and copy cards.

process slip A card or slip which accompanies a bibliographic item through cataloging and physical processing, acquiring on its way all the information necessary for the preparation of its bibliographic record in card or other format and its physical preparation for use. Synonymous with catalog card copy, catalog slip, cataloger's slip, cataloging process slip, copy slip, guide slip, P-slip, routine slip, search slip, and work slip.

Proctor order The system of arranging incunables developed by Robert Proctor. The arrangement is chronological, based on the earliest date of printing, under the following groupings: by country, by place under the country, and by printer under the place.

producer (motion picture) The person with final responsibility for the making of a motion picture, including business aspects, management of the production, and the commercial success of the film. (AACR2)

production company (motion picture) The company or other organization that determines the content and form of a motion picture and is responsible for its manufacture or production. If there is, in addition, a sponsor, the production company is normally responsible only for the manufacture or production of the motion picture. (AACR2)

professional personnel Those staff members holding professional positions in a library.

professional positions Those positions in a library which entail responsibilities, including those of administration, that require independent judgment, interpretation of rules and procedures, analysis of library problems, and formulation of original and creative solutions for them. Such positions require professional training and skill in the theoretical or sciencific aspects of work in libraries, as distinct from its mechanical or clerical aspects. The normal educational requirement is a master's degree (or its historical antecedent) in library or information science or in another acceptable field, such as educational communications and technology, management, public administration, or foreign language and literature. Examples of professional positions are librarian, media specialist, and subject specialist.

profile 1. An outline drawing representing a vertical section of land, water, underlying strata, etc., generally with the vertical scale exaggerated. 2. A biographical sketch.

pro forma invoice An invoice sent to a customer before the order is sent and usually paid before the order is received.

program budget A budget which groups anticipated expenditures according to the activities (programs) to be performed, with costs such as salaries and wages, materials, and supplies and equipment allocated to each program.

Program Evaluation and Review Technique (PERT) A sophisticated and systematic approach to planning and implementing a complex program which includes precise scheduling, allocation of resources, and monitoring of progress. Presented in graphic format as a PERT diagram, it is usually a computer-assisted approach employing mathematical models, but can be modified and applied to simpler programming problems. Commonly referred to as PERT, it is similar to the *Critical Path Method (CPM)*.

program library see *library* (2)

program maintenance Making changes and correcting errors in a computer program in order to keep it in a usable, working condition.

programmed instructional materials An individualized educational method consisting of a planned sequential presentation of material. Each separate presentation of a small basic unit of material requires a response from the student, who is then given immediate feedback about the correctness of the answer.

programmed text A book format of programmed instructional materials.

programmer A person who designs, writes, and tests computer programs. Synonymous with coder.

programming The process of designing, writing, and testing computer programs.

programming flowchart A flowchart used to depict the logic of a computer program.

programming language An artificial language used to prepare sets of instructions or programs which direct a computer in processing data.

Programming Language 1 see *PL/1*

program records Records created or received and maintained by an office or agency in the conduct of the substantive functions for which it is responsible. Compare with *housekeeping records.*

progressive proofs Proofs used in full-color printing which show each color alone and in combination with the other colors, including a final proof in which all colors appear.

projected books Microfilmed books which can be read by projection onto a flat surface such as a wall or ceiling. The books are intended primarily as an aid for the physically handicapped.

project file see *case file*

projection 1. The reproduction of an image on a viewing screen or other surface by means of an optical system. 2. In cartography, see *map projection.*

projection distance The distance between a lens or lens system and the surface on which an image has been clearly projected, through the lens. Synonymous with throw.

projection lamp The device used in a projector to illuminate and project the image upon the screen or other surface.

projection lens see *objective*

projection paper A fast photographic paper used in a projection printer to produce prints.

projection print A photoprint produced by a projection printer. Synonymous with optical print.

projection printer An optical device containing a light source and lens system, used to project film positive or negative or an original onto a photosensitive material (usually paper) which, when processed, produces a print or copy. Although called an enlarger, it is often used to produce reduced as well as enlarged images. Synonymous with optical printer. Compare with *contact printer.*

projection ratio A measure of the degree to which images on film are magnified when projected on a screen or other surface.

projector An optical device consisting of a light source, lens system, and image holder for projecting an image on a screen or other surface.

prompt A message from the computer in an online system indicating to a terminal operator what data to enter next or what task to perform next.

promptbook The copy of a play used by the prompter, showing action of the play, cues, movements of actors, properties, costume, and the scene and light plots. Synonymous with prompt copy.

prompt copy see *promptbook*

pronounceable notation see *syllabic notation*

proof see *binding proof*

proof before letters A proof of an engraving without any inscription; i.e., before title and names of artist and engraver are supplied.

proof copy In micropublishing, a distribution copy for comparison with the original.

proof impression see *proof print*

proof in slips see *galley proofs*

proof print An impression of an illustration taken from a finished plate before the regular impression is published and usually before the title or other inscription is added. Also called proof impression.

proofs Trial impressions made from metal type, plates, photographic film, magnetic tape, or magnetic disk for inspection and correction at various stages of composition. Proof sheets is a general term for proofs of textual matter. During the printing of a book there may be several kinds and stages of proofs that are designated according to their form (galley proofs, page proofs) and according to their destination or purpose (author's proof, artist's proof, engraver's proof, book club proof, foundry proof, plate proof, reproduction proof). When a book is printed by a photomechanical process, proofs may be contact prints made by the diazo process from photographic film, called whiteprints (a positive print from a positive film); blues or bluelines; or brownlines or vandykes (a brown print instead of a blue). Typesetting machines that transform text on tape or disk into tape composition on paper or film produce a printout for use in proofreading prior to composition.

proof sheets see *proofs*

property In classification theory, an attribute which is common to a class but not essential to the definition of that class.

property map see *cadastral map*

proprietary information Information of a confidential nature generated or purchased by an organization which receives protection against unauthorized disclosure.

proprietary library A library with its capital held in a common fund as joint stock, and owned by stockholders in shares which each may sell or transfer independently. It early became the practice for proprietary libraries to subject proprietors to annual assessments on their shares and to permit others to use the library by paying an annual stipulated fee. Synonymous with shareholders' library. Compare with *subscription library.*

prospectus An advertisement separately printed and distributed by a publisher to describe and solicit orders for a recent or forth-coming publication. In the case of a book, it may include sample pages.

protocol A formal set of conventions for the orderly exchange of data between network stations. Includes rules governing format and the control of data input, transmission, and output.

provenance 1. Information concerning the transmission or ownership, as of a book or manuscript. 2. In archives, the principle that the archives of a given records creator must not be intermingled with those of another origin; this principle is frequently referred to by the French expression, "respect des fonds." 3. In archives, the originating entity which created or accumulated the records; or the source of personal papers.

provisional edition see *preliminary edition*

pseudonym A name assumed by an author to conceal or obscure his or her identity. (AACR2)

pseudo-random number A number whose digits are obtained through a defined process, usually generated by a computer. Pseudo-random numbers can, for most purposes, be used as *random numbers.*

P-slip see *process slip*

public access channel A channel in a cable communication system on which any member of the general public may distribute programming. Allocation of time and selection of programming is controlled by an agency or organization designated by the holder of the cable system franchise.

publication 1. According to the 1976 Copyright Act of the United States, the act or process of distributing copies of a work to the public by sale or other transfer of ownership, or by rental, lease, or lending. The offering to distribute copies to a group of persons for purposes of further distribution, public performance, or public display also constitutes publication. 2. A published document.

publication date 1. The year in which a document is published. In a book, generally the date given at the bottom of the title page, in distinction from copyright and other dates. Synonymous with date of publication. 2. The day of the month or week on which a periodical is issued. Synonymous with publication day. 3. The

month and day when a new publication is placed on sale by a publisher, generally announced in advance. Synonymous with publication day and date of publication.

publication day see *publication date* (2), (3)

publication exchange see *exchange* (1)

publication number (music) see *plate number*

publication state see *state* (2)

public catalog A catalog for use by the public, as distinct from an *official catalog.*

public document see *government publication*

public domain A work which is not protected by copyright is said to be in the public domain.

Public Law 480 Program A Library of Congress acquisition program, established under the Agricultural Trade Development and Assistance Act of 1954 (P. L. 83–480), which, as amended, authorized the Librarian of Congress to use U.S.-owned currencies in foreign countries to procure books and other library materials in those countries, to distribute such materials to libraries and other research centers in the United States, and to carry on, in the foreign countries in which such currencies are available, such related activities as cataloging, photocopying, and binding.

public library 1. Any library which provides general library services without charge to all residents of a given community, district, or region. Supported by public or private funds, the public library makes its basic collections and basic services available to the population of its legal service area without charges to individual users, but may impose charges on users outside its legal service area. Products and services beyond the library's basic services may or may not be provided to the public at large and may or may not be provided without individual charges. 2. Earlier, a library accessible to all residents of a given community, but not generally free, as distinguished from a private library.

public records 1. Records open to public inspection by law or custom. 2. Records made and accumulated by government agencies, which may or may not be open to the public.

public relations Purposive activities on the part of a library or other information agency to inform users and potential users about its programs and services and to improve the public's value judgment of those programs and services.

public service area   That portion of the user area allocated to public service desks (e.g., circulation desk and information desk), the public catalog, and exhibits and displays.

public services   Those library activities and operations which entail regular, direct contact between library personnel and library users, including circulation services, information services, reprographic services, and others with similar characteristics. The term is, in practice, sometimes broadened to include collection development and evaluation activities.

public-switched network   A network that provides circuit-switching services to the public.

public television   Collectively, the television broadcast stations and the institutional entities creating and managing programming for the stations which provide cultural, educational, and instructional programs for the public. Programming is usually financed by profit-making organizations and by donations from viewers, although some stations accept commercial advertising. Compare with *commercial television.*

publish   To have a document manufactured and made available to the public.

published   Said of a document that has been made available to the public.

publisher   The firm or other corporate body or the person responsible for the manufacture and distribution of a document to the public.

publisher's binding   The binding of a book as it is issued by its publisher, usually in a hardcover, fabric, case binding. Synonymous with trade binding.

publisher's device see *printer's* or *publisher's mark*

publisher's mark see *printer's* or *publisher's mark*

publisher's number (music) see *plate number*

publisher's series   Reprinted books, not necessarily related in subject or treatment, issued by a publisher in uniform style and usually with a common series title, such as Cambridge Edition,

Everyman's Library. Sometimes known as trade series and reprint series. Compare with *subject series.*

publishing   A process which includes negotiations with the persons or corporate bodies responsible for the intellectual or artistic content of documents, the overall activity of controlling their production, and their distribution to the public.

puff see *blurb*

pull-down see *film advance* (1)

pulp   The chemically or mechanically prepared fibrous material from which paper is made. Pulp may be designated by the source of the fiber (wood, rag, esparto, recycled paper, etc.) as well as by the treatment used to release the cellulose from the raw materials. Often mixtures of pulp are used.

pulp magazine   A cheap, 20th-century magazine printed on newsprint and devoted to stories of adventure, love, and mystery. Synonymous with pulp-paper magazine, pulp sheet, and wood-pulp magazine.

pulp-paper magazine see *pulp magazine*

pulp sheet see *pulp magazine*

pulse see *synchronizing signal*

punched card   A card in which holes are or may be punched in standardized patterns representing characters of data. Once called Hollerith card for Herman Hollerith, who invented a method for representing data as holes in punched cards.

punched-card charging   A charging system using a computer-readable punched card as a charge card and a borrower's identification card to create a computer-readable charging file record for an item borrowed from the library. The charge card is also used to remove the record from the charging file upon the return of the item.

punched tape   A paper or plastic tape in which holes are punched in standardized patterns representing characters of data. Synonymous with perforated tape.

punched-tape reader An input device used to transfer data stored in punched tape into a computer for processing.

purchase order An official order record authorizing a dealer or vendor to deliver materials or services at a set price. This becomes a contract upon acceptance by the dealer or vendor. The basic components standard to most purchase orders include: unique purchase order number, dealer or vendor name and address, description of items ordered, quantity ordered, price per item and totals, fund to be charged, delivery address and instructions, time frame to complete order, shipping terms, discount or credit terms, and name and address of the ordering agency.

purchasing agent see *agent*

pure notation In classification, a notation which uses only one type of symbol. Compare with *mixed notation.*

pure research see *basic research*

PVA see *polyvinyl acetate adhesive*

pyroxylin Cellulose nitrate material that may be used for coating or impregnating book cloth.

quad A space used in setting type, measured in ems. Originally, a blank square block of metal, lower than the height of metal type, and used for indention, spacing, and blank lines. An em quad is a quad whose height (point size) and width (set) are the same or nearly the same; colloquially called a mutton. An en quad is half the width of the em quad; colloquially called a nut.

quadraphonic The reproduction of sound by an audio device from four channels separately and simultaneously. Also used to denote any related recordings, equipment, and techniques. The four-channel system more closely reproduces the original sound sources and their spatial distribution than *monaural* or *stereophonic* sound reproductions.

qualified heading A subject heading or descriptor which contains a qualifier, usually enclosed in parentheses, such as "Composition (Art)," "Bit (Drill)."

qualifier A term that modifies or limits the meaning of another term.

quality paperback see *trade paperback*

quarter binding A style of book cover in which the spine is of a material different from that of the sides. The spine should extend onto the sides up to one-eighth of the width of the boards.

quarterly A periodical published at regular intervals four times a year.

quarter track An audiotape on which each of four recorded tracks occupies slightly less than one-fourth of the width of the tape.

quartile In statistics, one of the three points dividing a frequency distribution into four equal parts.

quarto see *book sizes*

quasi-experimental research Research in which the conditions of an experiment are approximated and the variables are not completely controlled or manipulated.

query To ask for data from a system.

question negotiation see *reference interview*

queue A line of items or people waiting to be processed or served in a system. Synonymous with waiting line.

queueing theory A type of probability theory dealing with queues and their behavior, involving the time of arrivals, time of service, and queuing discipline, such as the number of queues and the method of selecting items for service.

quire 1. In the paper trade, of a ream; 25 sheets of fine-quality paper or 24 sheets of coarse paper in the same size and stock. 2. A *signature.*

quota sampling A type of sampling often used in public opinion, advertising, and market surveys, in which an investigator is instructed to collect information from an assigned number of persons. Usually the investigator is also instruct-

ed to include a certain number of persons having a common characteristic, such as level of income.

rack A framework or stand for displaying library materials. Sometimes distinguished according to use, such as bookrack or magazine rack.

rack and tank A method of film processing in which lengths of film are attached to racks or frames and immersed in processing solutions.

radial stack A stack in which the ranges are arranged as radii of a semicircle. Synonymous with radiating stack.

radiant dryer A device for evaporating water from processed photographic material through the use of infrared energy.

radiating stack see *radial stack*

radio receiver An electronic device which intercepts the signal of a radio broadcasting station, amplifies it, and converts it to audible sounds. It combines the functions of a tuner, preamplifier, and power amplifier. A receiver may be frequency modulation (FM), amplitude modulation (AM), or both.

rag-content paper A paper with a minimum of 25 percent rag or cotton fibers, usually used when permanence is a primary requirement. Generally made in grades containing 25, 50, 75, or 100 percent rag fibers. Rag, especially linen, has long cellulose fibers; hence rag-content paper can be very strong.

ragged Said of a type page having lines of varying lengths. Synonymous with unjustified. Compare with *justification.*

raised bands 1. Bands that appear as ridges running across the spine of a book when they protrude from the back. Compare with *sunk*

bands. 2. False bands, made to imitate real raised bands.

raised-letter printing see *thermography* (1)

RAM (random-access memory) see *direct-access storage*

R&D see *research and development*

random access see *direct access*

random-access memory (RAM) see *direct-access storage*

random-access storage see *direct-access storage*

random number A number whose digits are obtained by chance, using a process whereby each digit is equally likely to be any one of a specified set. A random number can be considered free from statistical bias. Compare with *pseudo-random number.*

random processing see *direct-access processing*

random sample A sample obtained as a result of selecting items from a population, with each item in the population having an equal chance of being selected.

range 1. A row of several sections of single- or double-faced shelving with common uprights or shelf supports between each section; a component of a stack. Called a press in British usage. 2. In statistics, a measure of the difference between the largest value and the smallest in a set of data.

range aisle A narrow passageway between ranges in a stack area. Synonymous with stack aisle. Compare with *cross aisle.*

range end The part of a range which faces a cross aisle. Synonymous with range front and stack end. Compare with *end panel.*

range-finder camera A camera in which the viewing system includes some means of semiautomatically determining the distance from the camera to the subject.

range front see *range end*

range guide A label located on one or both range ends or end panels to indicate the contents of the range.

range number A number assigned to a range to assist library users in the location of library materials.

rank order The placement of objects, events, or individuals on an ordinal scale.

rare book A desirable book, sufficiently difficult to find that it seldom, or at least only occasionally, appears in the antiquarian trade. Among rare books are traditionally included such categories as incunables, American imprints before 1800, first editions of important literary and other texts, books in fine bindings, unique copies, books of interest for their associations; but the degrees of rarity are as infinite as the needs of the antiquarian trade, and the term is decreasingly used in libraries and other repositories, many of which prefer the terms *special* or *research collection* to *rare book collection.*

rare book collection A special collection of library materials separated from the general collection because of their rarity and, frequently, because of their fragility or their intrinsic, monetary, or research value. The term is decreasingly used by libraries and other repositories, many of which prefer the term *special collection,* or, if the collection is of sufficient depth to support extensive research in one or more subject fields, the term *research collection.*

rare book room The room or rooms in a library or other repository set aside for the use, exhibition, or the housing of rare books and other special collections of books, manuscripts, and other documents which need special handling because of their intrinsic or monetary value, size, fragility, or other reason.

ratio scale A level of measurement in which objects, events, or individuals are assigned to categories of variables in rank order, with equal distances between the units of measure, and with an absolute zero point.

raw data Data that have not been processed or reduced.

raw stock Any photosensitive material that has not undergone exposure.

read In computer science, to sense data in a storage medium or device. Compare with *scan.*

readable negative A negative-appearing image on which only the tones, and not the image itself, are reversed from the original. Thus textual materials are still readable, even though the text appears as white on a dark background.

reader 1. A person employed by a printer to compare proofs with the copy for fidelity. 2. A person employed by a publisher to evaluate and report upon manuscripts received. 3. A *library user.* 4. A *microform reader.*

reader area see *user area*

reader-printer see *microform reader-printer*

readers' adviser A librarian concerned specifically with the reading problems of adults, who recommends books, compiles lists of selected titles, instructs adult readers in the use of the library and its resources, and maintains relations with adult education agencies. Synonymous with readers' consultant and readers' counselor.

readers' consultant see *readers' adviser*

readers' counselor see *readers' adviser*

read-in To enter data into a computer via an input device such as a card reader or magnetic tape unit.

reading file In archives, a file containing copies of documents arranged in chronological order. Sometimes known as a chronological or day file (and in Canadian usage, a continuity file).

reading room 1. A room in a library used primarily for reading and study, sometimes provided with library materials. 2. In archives, see *research room.*

reading shelves see *shelf reading*

read-only memory (ROM) A synonym for read-only storage, the term in use today.

read-only storage Storage from which data can be read but not altered or erased. Synonymous with fixed storage, nonerasable storage, permanent storage, and read-only memory (ROM).

read-write head A small magnetic device used to record, sense, or erase the magnetic spots or dots representing characters of data on such media as magnetic tape and magnetic disk.

ready reference collection Standard reference tools, set aside from the general reference collection for the purpose of providing rapid access to information of a factual nature. Examples of reference sources typically located in ready reference are almanacs, dictionaries, and directories. (LDCH)

realia Actual objects (artifacts, specimens) as opposed to *replicas.* Compare with *object.*

real image In optics, an image of an object formed by converging light rays, which exists where it appears to be. Compare with *virtual image.*

real storage see *main storage*

real time Pertaining to the execution of a computation or routine by a computer quickly enough to affect a related physical process taking place simultaneously.

ream A number of sheets of paper, either 480 or 500, depending on the grade. (The U.S. government specifies 1,000-sheet reams.)

rear illumination see *back lighting*

rear projection The projection of images onto the back of a translucent screen, the images being viewed from the front. Synonymous with back projection and rear screen projection. Compare with *front projection.*

rear screen projection see *rear projection*

reback To put a new backstrip on a book without doing any other rebinding.

rebind 1. A volume that has been rebound. 2. To subject a volume to rebinding.

rebinding The thorough rehabilitation of a worn book, the minimum of work done being resewing and putting on a new cover.

recall 1. A request by a library to a borrower for the return of a borrowed item before the due date. 2. To request a borrower to return a borrowed item before the due date.

recall ratio The ratio between the number of relevant works retrieved in a literature search and the number contained in the bibliographic

sources used in the search; a measure of the completeness of a literature search. Compare with *precision ratio.*

recasing 1. The resetting of a book into its original cover; sometimes with resewing. 2. The replacing of a book's case or cover.

recataloging The substantial revision of catalog records for selected items in a library collection in order to meet the needs of the library more effectively.

receiver see *radio receiver, television receiver*

receiving room see *shipping room*

recension A textual revision of a work, based on critical study of earlier texts and sources.

reciprocal borrowing privilege The granting of borrowing privileges to the members of each other's user groups by cooperating libraries.

reciprocity law In photography, a law which states that the optical density of an exposed photographic emulsion is equal to the intensity of radiant energy multiplied by the time of exposure. Deviations from this law are termed reciprocity law failures.

reclassification 1. The revision, according to a defined classification system, of classification numbers assigned to selected items in a library collection in order to better relate the items to other items in the collection. 2. The process of converting an entire library collection from one classification system to another.

recon see *retrospective conversion*

reconditioning (film) see *conditioning* (2)

record 1. A named collection of data items or fields, standardized in format and content, and treated as a unit. 2. In archives, a document made or received and maintained by an organization or institution in pursuance of its legal obligations or in the transaction of its business. 3. An *audiodisc.* 4. To use an audiorecording device to store audio signals for the purpose of later reproduction.

recorded materials In instructional technology, materials on which information has been recorded. The term is usually used with those materials which can be erased and reused, such as an audiotape or videotape.

recorder see *audiorecorder, videotape recorder*

record group In archives, a single organized and identified body of records established on the basis of provenance and constituting the archives (or the part thereof in the custody of a repository) of an autonomous record-keeping corporate body.

record head see *head* (5)

recording see *magnetic recording*

recording area see *frame* (4)

record layout In computer science, the format or arrangement of data items in a record.

record length In computer science, the physical size of a record, usually expressed in terms of a number of characters or bytes.

record mark A special machine character used to designate the end of a record in a machine-readable file. Synonymous with record terminator.

record office In British usage, an office in which contemporary official records concerning local government (and also earlier records of all kinds, especially those relating to the respective area) are preserved and made available.

record player see *audiodisc player*

records center A facility for the efficient storage and retrieval of semicurrent or noncurrent records, pending their ultimate disposition, sometimes especially designed and constructed for this purpose.

records control schedule see *disposition schedule*

records disposition see *disposition*

record series In archives, a group of records maintained as a unit because they relate to a particular subject or function, result from the same activity, have a particular form, or because of some other relationship arising out of their creation, receipt, or use; and intended to be kept together in a definite arrangement.

records management The area of management concerned with achieving economy and efficiency in the creation, use, handling, control, maintenance, and disposition of records. Compare with *paperwork management.*

records manager The person responsible for or engaged in a records management program.

records retention plan A two-part plan used by the U.S. government for identifying the records of an agency or office which will form a permanent part of its archives; the first part designates categories of records deserving of preservation (or those functions and activities for which the documentation should be preserved); the second part designates the location and titles of particular record series or subseries in which the documentation can be found. Compare with *comprehensive records plan.*

records retention schedule see *disposition schedule*

records schedule see *disposition schedule*

record subgroup In archives, a body of related records within a record group, usually consisting of the records of an important subordinate administrative unit. Subgroups may also be established for related bodies of records within a record group that can best be defined in terms of chronological, functional, or geographical relationships. Subgroups may be divided into as many further levels as are necessary to reflect the hierarchical organizational units within the subordinate administrative unit, or that will assist in grouping record series entries in terms of their relationships.

record subseries In archives, the file units within a record series readily separable from one another by subject, form, type, class, or filing arrangement.

record terminator see *record mark*

recovered Said of a volume which has had a new cover attached, usually without resewing.

recto 1. The right-hand page of a book, usually bearing an odd page number. (AACR2) 2. The side of a printed sheet intended to be read first. (AACR2) Compare with *verso.*

recycled paper Paper made in a range of qualities from reclaimed or recovered wastepaper, mechanically disintegrated into pulp and variously processed to remove unwanted materials such as ink. Unless made from carefully selected, long-fibered stock, is of poor color and strength.

red board   A thin, tough board used in flexible binding.

redox blemish see *blemish*

red-tape operations see *housekeeping operations*

reducer   In developing, a chemical agent for reducing the density of images on materials sensitized with silver halide.

reduction ratio   An expression of the number of times a document or other object has been reduced to form a photographic image. For example, 18X means that the image is 18 times smaller than the linear dimensions of the original. Reduction ratios can be classified as low reduction (up to 15X), medium reduction (up to 30X), high reduction (up to 60X), very high reduction (up to 90X), and ultrahigh reduction (above 90X). Compare with *enlargement ratio.*

redundancy reduction see *data compression*

red under gold edges   The edges of a book, colored red and then gilded.

reel   1. A flanged spool for holding recorded or processed audiotape, videotape, motion picture film, or roll microfilm. 2. The tape or film wound on such a spool.

reel-to-reel see *open reel*

refereed   Said of a periodical or other serial when manuscripts are evaluated by at least one subject specialist in addition to the editor before being accepted for publication.

reference   1. A set of bibliographic elements that refers to a work and is complete enough to provide unique identification of that work for a particular bibliographic function. (Z39.29) 2. In cataloging and indexing, a direction from one heading to another.

reference book   1. A book designed by the arrangement and treatment of its subject matter to be consulted for definite items of information rather than to be read consecutively. 2. A book whose use is restricted to the library building.

reference card   A catalog card containing a reference.

reference center   1. The reference department or other administrative unit of a library or the administrative unit of a system office which provides centralized auxiliary information service to the members of a library system of independent and autonomous libraries. 2. The reference department in the central library of a commonly administered library system which provides centralized auxiliary information service to branch libraries and other service outlets of the system.

reference collection   A collection of reference books and other materials in a library, useful for supplying authoritative information or identifying sources, kept together for convenience in providing information service, and generally not allowed to circulate.

reference department   The department of a library which supplies information requested by library users and assists users in locating needed information, using all available reference sources, and performs other information services. The department usually supervises and maintains the collection of reference materials which are not for circulation, but for consultation in the library only.

reference interview   The interpersonal communication between a reference staff member and a library user to determine the precise information needs of the user. Synonymous with question negotiation.

reference librarian   1. A librarian employed in a reference department or responsible for providing information service. 2. The librarian in charge of a reference department.

reference library   1. A library with either a general collection or a collection limited to a special field, organized for consultation and research, and generally noncirculating. 2. A library whose materials may not be taken from the library building or quarters.

reference mark   A symbol, letter, or figure used in printing to refer to material in another place, as in a note. Symbols in order of use are: * (asterisk), † (dagger), ‡ (double dagger), § (section mark), ‖ (parallels), ¶ (paragraph mark).

reference matter see *back matter*

reference question   Any request by a library user for information or assistance in locating information which involves an encounter in person, by mail, by telephone, or by other means between the user and a member of the reference staff. Compare with *reference transaction.*

references A list of publications and other information sources cited in a work, placed at the end of the work or divisions of it, as at the end of the chapters of a book.

reference service see *information service*

reference source Any source used to obtain authoritative information in a reference transaction. Reference sources include printed materials, audiovisual materials, machine-readable databases, library bibliographic records, other libraries and institutions, and persons both inside and outside the library.

reference staff All library staff members whose assigned duties include the provision of information service. Synonymous with information staff.

reference transaction An information contact which involves the use, recommendation, interpretation, or instruction in the use of one or more reference sources, or knowledge of such sources, by a reference staff member. Compare with *directional transaction,* from which it is to be distinguished by characteristics other than its duration, and with *reference question.*

"refer from" reference The indication in a subject heading list, authority file, etc., of those headings from which "see" and "see also" references have been or may be made to a given heading.

referral center An information agency which directs or refers requests for documents or information to appropriate sources, such as libraries or other information agencies, which can fill the requests.

reflectance A measure of the intensity of light reflected from a surface, as compared with the intensity of light incident upon the surface. Reflectance is a property of opaque materials, such as paper. Reflectance is measured with a reflection densitometer. The values are compared with those on a reflectance test target to arrive at a relative measure of reflectance. Synonymous with coefficient of reflection.

reflectance test target see *reflectance*

reflection copying see *reflex copying*

reflection densitometer see *densitometer, reflectance*

reflection density see *density* (1)

reflex camera A camera in which a mirror placed at an angle between the lens and the film reflects the image formed by the lens to a ground-glass focusing screen on top of the camera. There are two types of reflex cameras: (1) a single-lens reflex camera, in which the same lens is used to form the image on the focusing screen and to expose the film, and (2) a twin-lens reflex camera, in which one lens is used to form the image on the focusing screen and the other, of the same focal length, to expose the film.

reflex copying A contact copying method used for originals which are opaque or contain text or other graphic matter on both sides. With the original and the photosensitive material in direct contact, transmitted light is passed through the photosensitive material and reflected back from the original, producing a negative copy, which is then used to produce a positive copy. By using the diffusion transfer process, it is possible to produce the negative and positive copies in a single operation. Synonymous with reflection copying. Compare with *transmission copying.*

reflex viewing system A viewing system in which the viewfinder lens and the lens that takes the photograph are one and the same; the lens system of the single-lens reflex camera. Compare with *optical viewing system.*

refraction The deviation in the course of a ray of light when it passes through the surface of a transparent medium, such as a prism. The power of a transparent medium to refract a ray of light is expressed by a number called its index of refraction, which varies with the wavelength (color) of the ray. In general, the shorter the wavelength, the greater the index of refraction.

regional branch A branch library which acts as a reference and administrative center for a group of smaller branches in a public library system.

regional catalog A union catalog of the collections of a group of independent libraries in a particular geographical area, such as a metropolitan area, a state, or a group of states. Synonymous with regional union catalog.

regional depository library A depository library designated by law to receive and retain at least one copy of all U.S. government publications distributed by the Superintendent of Documents to depository libraries and to provide interlibrary loan and reference service from its documents collection to other libraries of a state or a region of a state.

regional libraries for the blind   Those libraries, located throughout the United States, that have been selected by the Library of Congress to serve as distributing agencies for the resources provided by its Division for the Blind and Physically Handicapped. These libraries are located in agencies serving the blind, in public libraries, or are connected with state library agencies.

regional library   A public library serving a group of communities, or several counties, and supported in whole or in part by public funds from the governmental units served.

regional media program   The media program conducted by a region. In some instances this is an intermediate unit between the state department of education and the local education agency. In others it is a consortium of local education agencies.

regional union catalog see *regional catalog*

region of rejection see *rejection region*

register   1. A list of symbols by which the leaves of the signatures are marked to indicate their order to the folder and binder, and/or to indicate the order and location of plates, maps, or other illustrative material; found especially in early printed books, where they are sometimes printed on a separate page. 2. In archives, the list of events, letters sent and received, actions taken, etc., usually in simple sequence, as by date or number, and often serving as a finding aid to the records, such as a register of letters sent, or a register of visitors. 3. Adjustment of printing so that lines or columns of print on both sides of a leaf exactly correspond, or, in multicolor work, so that the successive impressions are in precise relation to one another. 4. In a computer system, a device in the central processing unit used for temporary storage of a small amount of data, usually one computer word.

registration   1. The process by which persons receive authorization to borrow materials for use outside the library. 2. An accurate positioning or alignment relative to a specified reference.

registration card see *application card*

registration file   A file of records identifying authorized library borrowers and including such

information as name, address, telephone number, and borrower's identification number. A registration card file is usually arranged numerically by borrower's identification number and may consist of application cards to which that number has been added. Synonymous with borrowers' file.

registrum   A register for the binder.

regression analysis   A statistical technique for predicting that value of one variable (the predicted variable) which is most likely to occur with another variable (the predictor variable).

regression line see *line of regression*

reinforced binding   A special publisher's edition binding in which cloth is pasted to the back edges of the endpapers and, sometimes, the first and last sections. Other methods of strengthening bindings can be used, and portions of an edition may be specially handled and issued as a library edition. These edition bindings do not match the standards established for pre-library bound books.

reissue   A second or subsequent impression of an edition involving a new title page and changes in the front and back matter, but leaving the main text substantially unaltered. Compare with *issue* (2).

rejection region   In a test of a statistical hypothesis, the proportion of the area in the sampling distribution which is equal to the significance level and which represents those sample values that are highly improbable if the null hypothesis is true. For example, if a hypothesis is tested at the .05 level, 5 percent of the area will be in the rejection region and 95 percent will be in the retention area.

related body   A corporate body that has a relation to another body other than that of hierarchical subordination; e.g., one that is founded but not controlled by another body; one that receives only financial support from another body; one that provides financial and/or other types of assistance to another body, such as "friends" groups; one whose members have also membership in or an association with another body, such as employees' associations and alumni associations. (AACR2)

related work see *dependent work*

relational operators see *role operators*

relative index An alphabetical index to a classification system which brings together the various aspects of all subjects and shows their dispersion throughout the classification schedule.

relative location A method of arranging materials in a library collection according to their relations to one another, usually according to a classification system or an alphabetical arrangement. As acquired, items are inserted into their proper places in the order. Synonymous with movable location. Compare with *fixed location* and *sequential location*.

release see *press release*

releasing agent The agent or agency responsible for the initial distribution of a motion picture. (AACR2)

relevance ratio see *precision ratio*

reliability An expression of the precision with which a test measures whatever it measures. Compare with *validity*.

relief map A map showing land or submarine bottom relief in terms of height above, or below, a datum by any method, such as contours, hachures, shading, or tinting. Synonymous with hypsographic map, hypsometric map.

relief model A scale representation in three dimensions of a section of the surface of the earth or other celestial body. A relief model designed to display both physical and cultural features on the surface of the earth is sometimes known as a topographic model.

relief printing see *letterpress* (1)

remainder The unsold copies of a book which the publisher disposes of as a lot to a distributor who will offer them for sale at a reduced price. Compare with *job lot*.

remarque proof see *artist's proof*

remedial maintenance see *corrective maintenance*

remote access Communication by one or more users, devices, or stations with a distant computer system.

remote batch A method of submitting jobs into a computer from a remote terminal.

remote job entry (RJE) The submission of jobs to a computer via a remote terminal, such as a card reader, and the receipt of output via another remote terminal, such as a printer or card punch.

remote processing The processing of data received by a computer system from remote locations or remote terminals.

remote sensing The gathering and recording of information on natural phenomena, such as the features on the surface of the earth or other celestial body, from a distance, generally conducted by means of sensors in aircraft or spacecraft.

remote-sensing image An image produced by a remote-sensing device located in an aircraft (aerial remote-sensing image), in a spacecraft (space remote-sensing image), or on the earth (terrestrial remote-sensing image).

remote station see *tributary network station*

remote terminal A terminal, usually attached to a communications link, for transmitting data and messages to and from a distant computer.

renewal transaction The act of extending a circulation transaction for a period of time beyond that of the original loan period. Compare with *circulation transaction*.

rental collection A group of selected books in high current demand that are circulated by a public library for a small fee.

rental library A group of selected books in high current demand owned by a commercial agency which charges a small loan fee.

repair department The administrative unit of a library which does mending, repairing, and pamphlet-style library binding.

repairing The partial rehabilitation of a worn book, the amount of work done being less than the minimum involved in rebinding and more than the maximum involved in mending. Includes such operations as restoring the cover and reinforcing at joints. Not to be confused with *mending*.

replacement 1. The substitution of another copy of an item for one no longer in a library. 2. The copy of an item substituted, or to be substituted, for another copy no longer in a library.

replenisher A chemical solution used to recycle used developer.

replevin 1. In archives, the recovery of property such as records and manuscripts by an institution or organization claiming ownership. 2. The writ and legal act by which a person or institution takes over such property.

replica A copy or reproduction of an object, especially of a work of art produced by the artist of the original or under the supervision of the artist.

report 1. An official or formal record, as of some special investigation, of the activities of a corporate body, or of the proceedings of a legislative assembly. 2. A separately issued record of research results, research in progress, or other technical studies. In addition to its unique, issuer-supplied report number, it may also bear a grant number and accession or acquisition number supplied by a central report agency. 3. In the plural, publications giving judicial opinions or decisions.

report generation A technique of producing complete reports by a machine such as a computer when given information describing the content and format of the report wanted and about the machine-readable file to be used for input.

report literature Scientific and technical information contained in reports not made available to the general public at the time of issue and therefore not formally published.

report program generator (RPG) A popular and easy-to-learn programming language designed for writing reports from machine-readable files.

repository A place where archives, manuscripts, books, or other documents are stored. Frequently used as synonymous with depository.

repository collection The total holdings, including both accessions and deposits, of a repository.

representative fraction The scale of a map as represented by the ratio between distance measured on a map and the corresponding distance on the ground. Thus a map on the scale of 1 inch to 1 mile has a representative fraction of 1:63,360, there being 63,360 inches in a mile.

representative sample A sample that is judged, or claimed, to have the same characteristics as, or to represent accurately, the population from which it came; an informally used term that should not be confused with random sample.

reprint 1. A new impression of an edition. 2. A new edition from a new setting of type, for which an impression of a previous edition has been used as copy. 3. A separately issued article, chapter, or other portion of a previously published larger work, usually a reproduction of the original, but sometimes made from a new setting of type. Compare with *offprint*.

reprint series see *publisher's series*

reproduce In data processing, to prepare a duplicate of data stored in punched cards, magnetic tape, magnetic disk, or other similar medium. Compare with *copy* (5).

reproducer An offline device that reproduces decks of punched cards. Also called card reproducer.

reproduction proof A proof of a page on coated paper, bearing the most nearly perfect image of text and illustrations possible for use as camera-ready copy in the production of a printing plate by photomechanical process.

reprography The science, technology, and practice of document reproduction. It encompasses virtually all processes for copying or reproduction using light, heat, or electrical radiation, including microreproduction. Reprography is often characterized by its economy of scale, generally excluding large-scale, professional printing operations. Synonymous with document copying and documentary reproduction.

repro typing Any distinctively clear, well-formatted typewriting which is well suited for purposes of reproduction by a reprographic process.

republication 1. A reissuing of a bibliographic item by a different publisher without change in text; sometimes applied to reprinting in another country. Also an item thus reissued. 2. In a very broad sense, a reissuing of an item, with or without change in text, or as a new edition; an item thus reissued.

request for proposal (RFP) A document used to solicit proposals from bidders to design or supply a system or perform work of some kind. Compare with *request for quotation.*

request for quotation (RFQ) A request to a company, organization, or individual for a price quotation for a system, equipment, or work to be performed. Compare with *request for proposal.*

requisition A written request, usually submitted on a standardized form, for the acquisition of books and other library materials, supplies, equipment, or services.

rerecording The process of reproducing the signals of a recorded audiotape or videotape onto a blank audiotape or videotape for the purpose of editing or otherwise modifying.

research Systematic, exhaustive, and intensive investigation and study, usually through hypothesis and experiment, to discover new knowledge, facts, theories, and laws.

research and development (R&D) Basic research and applied research directed toward the design and development of products and processes.

research book In motion-picture research libraries, a scrapbook made up of abstracts and reference material relating to the setting, architecture, costume, etc., collected for a particular picture in advance, or in the course of production.

research collection A separate collection of specialized materials, of sufficient depth to support extensive research in one or more subject fields.

research library 1. A library which contains an in-depth collection in a particular subject field (such as a technical library) or in-depth collections in several subject fields (such as a university library or a large private or public library). The collections include primary sources and provide extensive chronological and/or geographical coverage. 2. A *reference library.*

research room In archives, that area in a repository, generally enclosed, where records, manuscripts, or other documents are consulted

by researchers under the supervision of the repository staff. Sometimes referred to as a reading room or search room.

reserve collection Especially in an academic library or school library media center, a collection of materials segregated, usually temporarily, from the general collection and assigned restrictive loan periods so as to assure greater availability to certain user groups, such as students in a particular course, who will have need of the materials within a limited time period.

reserved item An item from a library collection that is held, upon its return by one borrower, for a prescribed length of time for another borrower by request. Synonymous with hold.

reservoir library see *storage center*

residence library see *dormitory library*

residual dye-back Black particles or dark streaks remaining on microfilm after processing, caused by incomplete removal of the backing.

residual hypo Hypo remaining on processed photographic film or paper after washing, which, if excessive in amount, reduces its permanence. Synonymous with residual thiosulfate.

residual hypo test A chemical test for the amount of hypo remaining on photographic film or paper after washing. Testing methods include methylene blue, silver densitometric, and the largely superseded Ross-Crabtree.

residual thiosulfate see *residual hypo*

resist see *acid resist*

resolution The measure of the ability of a lens or photographic material to render sharp images. Sharpness of images is formally measured in lines per mm (millimeter). Acceptable resolution for microfilming can range from 90 to 180 lines per mm. A more subjectively derived expression of resolution is termed *definition*. To test for resolution, images are compared with patterns on a resolution test chart, such as an NBS test chart (National Bureau of Standards). Synonymous with sharpness and resolving power.

resolution test chart see *resolution*

resolving power see *resolution*

resource sharing A term covering a variety of organizations and activities engaged in jointly by a group of libraries for the purposes of improving services and/or cutting costs. Resource sharing may be established by informal or formal agreement or by contract and may operate locally, regionally, nationally, or internationally. The resources shared may be collections, bibliographic data, personnel, planning activities, etc. Formal organizations for resource sharing may be called bibliographic utilities, cooperative systems, consortia, networks, bibliographic service centers, etc.

respect des fonds see *provenance*

response time The elapsed time between the submission of a query, command, or work to a computer and the return of the results by the system.

responsibility In an organization, the obligation of an employee to perform a set of assigned tasks and duties. Compare with *accountability.*

restricted access In archives, limitation or limitations on the use of all books, manuscripts, records, or other documents, or on those containing information of a certain kind or form. The restriction may limit the use for a time to a particular person or persons, or may exclude all use. Such restrictions are usually imposed by officials of transferring agencies or by donors, and are enforced by the repository.

restricted circulation The charging of certain library materials with some limitation, such as a restricted period of loan or restriction to in-house use.

restricted funds Funds restricted as to use in accordance with legal restrictions and donor stipulations.

retcon see *retrospective conversion*

retention plan see *records retention plan*

retention schedule see *disposition schedule*

retrieval coding A system for retrieving particular data or images recorded on microform.

retrospective bibliography A bibliography which lists documents or parts of documents, such as articles, published in previous years, as distinct from a current bibliography, which records recently published documents. Retrospective bibliographies are frequently divided into two types: research-oriented, which are intended as jumping-off points for those doing research in the topic covered; and didactic, which list reasonably accessible publications and are intended for persons with little knowledge of the topic covered.

retrospective conversion The process of converting to a machine-readable form the records in a manual or non-machine-readable file that are not converted through day-to-day processing. Sometimes abbreviated "recon" and "retcon."

revenue In governmental accounting, one part of income, being the receivables and receipts from taxes, customs, and other sources, but excluding appropriations and allotments.

reversal film Film, usually silver, used to produce a positive original directly in the camera by means of a reversal process. Synonymous with direct-reversal film.

reversal paper Sensitized paper used in a reversal process.

reversal process A special developing process by which a negative image formed on an image-reversing photosensitive material is converted to a positive image, with the result that a positive is produced from a positive. By the same process a negative may be produced from a negative.

reverse reading A reproduction which is a mirror image of the original. Textual images would be seen backward, making reading extremely difficult. Compare with *right reading.*

reversing film see *image-reversing film*

review 1. An evaluation of a literary work, concert, play, etc., published in a periodical or newspaper. 2. A periodical devoted primarily to articles of criticism and appraisal, such as a literary review.

review copies Copies of a newly published book sent free by a publisher for review, notice, or record. Synonymous with editorial copies. Compare with *advance copies.*

revised edition A new edition with the main text of the original edition changed and corrected, and sometimes with additions that supplement it or bring it up to date.

reviser One who checks and corrects the work of another, usually less experienced, staff member.

revolving case A compact kind of bookcase having four faces with one or more shelves built around a central cylinder that turns on a spindle.

rewind 1. To transfer film from one reel to another, usually to reposition the images for subsequent viewing. 2. A device consisting of two sets of spindles and cranks, used to transfer film between reels. The device can be used to rewind film that has been removed from the projector.

RFP see *request for proposal*

RFQ see *request for quotation*

ribbon marker see *bookmark*

Rider's Classification see *International Classification*

ridge In binding, the projection or flange formed along the edges of the back by rounding and backing. It should be the thickness of the board. Synonymous with flange and shoulder.

right reading An image which is positioned and oriented for normal reading, although magnification may be required. Compare with *reverse reading*.

rights 1. Statutory rights to a literary property include the following: prepublication serial (first serial rights); book publication, including book club; magazine second serial; newspaper second serial; book reprint; dramatization; dramatization for stock; musical comedy; amateur leasing; motion picture (commercial and noncommercial); radio; television; mechanical, electronic, or xerographic reproduction, or other kinds covered in the inclusive term "reprographic reproduction"; condensation and abridgment; anthology; translation; quotation; commercial exploitation rights. Most of these are also commonly referred to as *subsidiary rights*. (Bookman's Glossary) 2. The common-law right under which the author of letters or manuscripts or the author's heirs retain the right of first publication of the documents, regardless of the ownership or location of the originals. Unlike statutory copyright, common-law literary property rights are perpetual and are terminated only by general publication or positive dedication. (SAA)

ring In the antiquarian trade, a group of dealers or other persons who agree to refrain from bidding against one another on certain lots of books or other items at auction, in order subsequently to reauction the material so acquired among themselves and divide the savings effected by the elimination of competition. Rings are generally illegal in North America and in the United Kingdom; opinion varies as to their prevalence.

ring binding A loose-leaf binding using a number of metal rings fixed in a metal spine. The rings open (usually at the center) for removal or addition of prepunched leaves.

ring network A network in which each node is linked or connected with each adjacent node. Compare with *fully connected network, distributed network, star network*.

rinsing see *washing*

RIs see *Rule Interpretations*

RJE see *remote job entry*

roan Sheepskin dyed a dark color and having an irregular surface, used as a cheap substitute for morocco in the binding of books.

role operators In indexing, symbols which represent the relationship, such as agent, action, cause, effect, or product, between descriptors arranged in a string. Synonymous with relational operators.

roll 1. An early form of book, written on a strip of papyrus or other material, and rolled on a rod or rods. Also called a scroll. 2. In binding, a tool consisting of a brass wheel about three inches in diameter fastened to a long handle. The edge of the wheel is engraved so as to impress a continuous, repeating pattern when it is heated and made to revolve on the cover under pressure. Compare with *fillet* (2), with which it is frequently confused. 3. The design impressed by a roll.

rolled edges The edges of a book cover decorated with a roll, a finishing tool having a brass wheel with a design on its rim.

roller shelves Deep shelves for storing oversize books, such as elephant folios, fitted with a series of small rollers to facilitate the removal and handling of the books and to protect the bindings. Compare with *sliding shelves*.

roll microfilm see *microfilm* (1)

roll-to-card printer A device used to produce duplicate card-mounted microfilm from roll microfilm by a contact copying process.

roll-to-roll printer A device used to produce duplicate rolls of microfilm by a contact copying process.

ROM see *read-only memory*

Roman Index see *Index Librorum Prohibitorum*

romanization Conversion of names or text not written in the roman alphabet to roman-alphabet form. Compare with *transliteration*. (AACR2)

roman type An early Italian type, the capitals based on Latin inscriptions and the small letters on humanistic book hand. Is commonly used as text type for books, periodicals, and newspapers. The three main families are 15th-century, old-face roman, and modern-face roman.

Ross-Crabtree method The use of mercuric chloride and potassium bromide to test for residual hypo when determining the archival permanence of processed film. Now largely superseded by the methylene blue method.

rotary camera A relatively inexpensive microfilm camera designed to rapidly film single-sheet documents, such as bank checks. A transport mechanism moves the film and the document during exposure; so there is no relative movement between the film and the image of the document. Both sides of the document can be filmed. Synonymous with flow camera and continuous-flow camera.

rotary card file A filing device consisting of cardholders attached to a revolving drum or wheel.

rotary press A printing press that prints from curved plates clamped to a cylinder which revolves against a cylinder on which the paper is carried. Inked rollers revolve against the plate cylinder on the other side.

rotogravure 1. Photogravure printing on a rotary press. Synonymous with gravure. 2. A print made by this process.

rotunda The 15th-century Italian form of formal gothic or black-letter type which became standard for theological, legal, and scholastic texts. It is rounder than textura and lacks the fere-humanistica tendency to roman.

rough edges A generic term including uncut, untrimmed, and deckle edges of paper.

round back 1. The back of a thin booklet of which the folded sheets have been inserted one inside another and stitched through the fold to the cover. 2. Said of a book which has been rounded and backed.

round corner 1. A book cover in which the board is rounded at the corner before the covering material is added; usually confined to leather bindings. Synonymous with rounded corner. 2. Sometimes loosely used for *library corner.*

rounded corner see *round corner*

rounding and backing Rounding is the process by which the back of the book is hammered or molded into a convex shape. Rounding protects the fore-edge of a book. In backing, each section of the binding edge, working from the center out, is bent over the section next to it. This preserves the round, improves flexibility in opening, and provides a ridge and groove allowing a better cover joint.

routine A sequence or set of instructions which will cause a computer to execute a special operation or task as a part of a computer program.

routine maintenance see *scheduled maintenance*

routing 1. The systematic routing of new publications, particularly current issues of journals, to library staff members (automatic routing). 2. In a special library, the circulation of new publications to the staff members of the host organization on a list, in accordance with their fields of specialization, or circulation to selected staff members in accordance with their known individual interests (selective routing).

Roxburghe binding A style of binding with a plain dark leather back, paper-covered board sides, gilt top, and other edges untrimmed. The style was used for the publications of the Roxburghe Club, a private book collectors' club, founded in London after the Duke of Roxburghe's sale in 1812.

RPG see *report program generator*

rub see *rub-off*

rubbing see *rub-off*

rub-off An impression of the lettering on the spine of a volume, made by placing a piece of strong, thin paper over the spine, and rubbing it with the lead of a heavy pencil or something similar; used for matching bindings. Synonymous with rub and rubbing.

rubricated Having initials, catchwords, titles, or other parts of a work written or printed in red, and sometimes blue or other colors, as in ancient manuscripts and early printed books.

rule A strip of type-high metal designed to print a plain or decorated line.

Rule Interpretations (RIs) Expansions, interpretations, clarifications, and/or individual policy on procedural decisions or application of a catalog code such as the *Anglo-American Cataloguing Rules.* Although any cataloging agency may issue rule interpretations for its own use, the Rule Interpretations are generally promulgated by national cataloging agencies.

rumble An undesirable low-frequency sound generated in audiodisc systems by the turntable motor, vibrations in the turntable platter, or a faulty audiodisc.

runes Letters or characters of the early alphabet used by the Teutonic or German peoples.

run-in head A subheading set on the same line as a line of text.

running foot The line of type, of uniform content and style, at the foot of each page, below the text, of a book or periodical. The content is the same as that of a running head. Synonymous with footline.

running head The line of type, of uniform content and style, at the head of each page, above the text, of a book or periodical. In a book, the head may contain the book title, division or section title, chapter title, or the subject of a page; in a periodical, the periodical title, issue number, article title, or section title. Synonymous with headline and page head.

running title The title, or abbreviated title, of the book repeated at the head of each page or at the head of the versos. (AACR2)

rush A term indicating the requirement of special speed in preparation, process, or action; used to indicate, for example, that a purchase order so designated be given special handling by the dealer or that a bibliographic item be given cataloging priority.

russia A specially tanned calf used in binding, finished with birch oil, which gives it a characteristic spicy odor.

rustic capitals 1. Lighter and less formal capital letters than the square capitals used in early manuscripts during the 2nd–6th centuries. 2. Letters from upper case display type with an appearance meant to suggest that lengths of (usually bark-covered) logs or sticks were used in their formation, and commonly employed by typographers to suggest a woodsy or folksy mood in display and other advertising.

rutter see *portolan chart*

sabbatical leave A leave of absence for a specified period of time with full or partial salary, provided at periodic intervals (usually every seven years) for the pursuit of independent study or research related to professional expertise.

saddle stitching In binding, a method of leaf affixing in which thread or wire is passed through the fold of a booklet composed of a single section. So called because the section is laid on the saddle of the stitching machine.

safelight A light source used in a darkroom which gives a subdued illumination of a color to which the emulsion on exposed unprocessed photographic film and paper is relatively insensitive.

safety film A film with a relatively noninflammable base, such as cellulose acetate.

salary range   1. The lowest and highest possible salary paid to incumbents within a given position classification. 2. The lowest and highest possible salary available for a given position, dependent upon the qualifications and experience of the candidates.

sample   In statistics, some part of a particular population, chosen by some method and examined in order to provide information about the population as a whole.

sample issue   A single issue of a periodical, commonly the first, sent by the publisher to the library as a potential subscriber.

sample size   The number of elements or observations in a sample, usually designated as "n".

sampling   1. Measuring the value of a variable at regular or random intervals. 2. Selecting individual items from a population.

sampling distribution   A theoretical frequency distribution, based on a mathematical model, that represents the distribution of values of a statistic that would be obtained from an infinite number of random samples of a given size.

sampling error   An estimate of the deviation, due to chance, of a sample statistic from the true value of the population parameter.

sans-serif   Type faces without serifs and with strokes of equal width and boldness. Synonymous with block letter.

satellite, communication see *communication satellite*

satellite thesaurus   A thesaurus for a specific or specialized field or discipline using a general thesaurus as a base. Synonymous with microthesaurus.

saw-kerf binding   A form of side stitching in which thread is laid across the entire thickness of a book in slits which have been cut at a slant into the back in a dovetail pattern. Compare with *cleat binding*.

SBN see *International Standard Book Number*

scale   In cartography, the ratio of a distance on a photograph, map, or other graphic to its corresponding distance on the ground, or to another graphic. Scales are named by the type of graphic on which they appear, and the manner in which they are expressed, e.g., a bar scale.

scan   In computer science, to examine data systematically for some specific purpose or intent. Compare with *read*.

scanning   The process by which an electron beam in the television pickup tube moves, in a definite pattern, across and down the photosensitive surface on which the picture to be transmitted appears as an electron image, dissecting the picture into minute elements of light values, which are sent through the tube sequentially for subsequent reconstruction of the picture by the television receiver.

scanning device   On microform readers, a device which permits a portion of an image to be centered on the screen by moving the microform or the optical system. This is especially useful when the entire image cannot appear on the screen at one time.

scanning lines   In the scanning process, the lines of successive elements of light values into which the picture to be televised is dissected.

scattergram   A graph illustrating values jointly taken on by two variables.

scattering see *Bradford's law of scattering*

schedule   1. A *classification schedule*. 2. In information retrieval, the list of terms or descriptors used to construct a file. 3. In (especially British) archives, a document attached to another document, for purposes of amplification.

scheduled maintenance   Maintenance performed on hardware or software according to a regular and planned schedule. Synonymous with routine maintenance. Compare with *corrective maintenance* and *preventive maintenance*.

schematic plans see *architectural drawings*

school branch library   A library in a school building administered by a public library and/or a board of education for the use of students and teachers and frequently for adults of the neighborhood.

school district   A local basic administrative unit existing primarily to operate schools, public or nonpublic, or to contract for school services. A district may or may not be coterminous with the county, city, or town boundaries and may be identified by such terms as school system, basic administrative unit, local school system, or local education agency.

school district library 1. Earlier, a tax-supported library established in a school district for use of schools and free to all residents of the district. 2. A free public library established and financially supported by action of a school district for the use of all residents of the district and supervised by a local board of education or by a separate library board appointed by a board of education. 3. A collection of professional materials within a school district for use by the professional staff and administrators of that district; a component of the school district media program.

school district media program The media program that is conducted at the school district level through an administrative subunit.

school learning resources specialist see *media specialist*

school library media center An area or system of areas in an elementary, secondary, or combined school where a collection consisting of a full range of media, associated equipment, and services from the media staff are accessible to students, teachers, and affiliated school staff.

school library media club In a school library media center, a club which assists in the work of the library and may or may not follow a reading program.

school media program The media program for a school, conducted through an administrative subunit.

school media specialist see *media specialist*

school television Television programming that pertains to the operation and purposes of school systems, including programming for direct instruction, school administrative purposes, teacher in-service training, and community information and education.

Schrotblatt see *dotted print* (1)

Schwabacher A popular gothic or black-letter type used in early German-language books, which gradually became a secondary type (like italic) and was superseded by Fraktur. Was revived mid-20th century.

scientific method An organized and systematic approach to problems or experiments in which the problem is defined, data are collected and analyzed, one or more solutions are derived on the basis of the available data, and applications of the solutions are proposed.

scintillation On microform readers, a defect which occurs with some translucent screens. The phenomenon appears in the form of small points of light and spectra.

scope note A note that explains how a term in a subject heading list, thesaurus, or classification system is used, usually referring to a related or overlapping term.

score 1. A series of staves on which all the different instrumental and/or vocal parts of a musical work are written, one under the other in vertical alignment, so that the parts may be read simultaneously. Synonymous with full score. (AACR2) 2. In library binding, to make a crease near the edge of a section or leaf, in the case of moderately stiff paper, in order to facilitate opening of the volume.

scrambled book A text form of programmed instruction which utilizes branching through the book rather than the sequential pattern of the programmed text. A multiple-choice question follows each information presentation, and the answer selected refers the student backward or forward to a particular page for confirmation or correction.

scratch A film defect generally caused during processing or subsequent use. It appears as a clear or dark line across the image area and may penetrate to the base. Scratches are particularly troublesome in microforms as the reduction ratios become higher. Compare with *abrasion.*

screen 1. A prepared surface on which images are projected. The surface of the screen may be glass beaded, matte, beaded and matte, or frosted. The type of surface affects the brightness of the image and the angle of viewing. Screens may be portable or fixed, rigid or flexible, and may be designed for front or rear projection. 2. The front surface of a cathode-ray tube, where images are displayed. 3. In computer science, to examine data for an initial selection of those items which meet specific conditions or criteria. 4. To interview persons requesting the use of fragile, valuable, or sensitive materials, especially of rare books and materials in special and research collections, to determine if they have a suitable or sufficient reason to use them. 5. In archives, to examine records to determine the presence of restricted material, and to remove such material from the files.

screen image An image that appears on a screen through either front or rear projection.

screen printing A stencil printing process in which the nonprinting area of a screen of silk, plastic, or woven metal is masked, and ink or paint is forced through the unmasked area. Much used for posters and for printing on glass, plastics, and textured surfaces.

scribal copy A written manuscript, produced by a copyist, as opposed to the original manuscript produced by the author, or from the author's dictation.

scrinium A cylinder-shaped receptacle with movable top used by the Romans to hold a number of scrolls.

script 1. A typescript; specifically of a play, motion picture, or the text of the spoken part of a television program, etc. Sometimes called "the book." Compare with *acting edition*. 2. A typeface based on everyday handwriting rather than on a cursive book hand.

scriptorium Literally, a writing room. A place in a medieval monastery or abbey set apart for the preparation of manuscripts, and for writing and studying generally.

scroll 1. The movement of images on microform readers or cathode-ray-tube screens, such that images disappear at one edge as new images appear at the opposite edge. 2. As a book form, see *roll* (1).

scroll fiche Uncut microfiche rolls, generally viewed on special readers.

SDI see *selective dissemination of information (SDI)*

seal print A 15th-century woodcut which has received blind embossing of the paper after the print has been made. Synonymous with gypsographic print.

sealskin A binding leather derived from the Greenland or Newfoundland seal; often used for limp bindings.

search A systematic examination of records in a file for the purpose of locating specific data or records.

searcher One who verifies or supplies bibliographic data.

search key In computer science, a character or characters to be compared with specified data in records during a file search. Compare with *file key*.

search mechanics The means provided in a specific information retrieval system to access, search, and display/print the results of a database search within that system. Search mechanics are the command capabilities and operations provided in the design of a system to enable its functional use. Common operations such as truncation or Boolean intersection may vary in their actual implementation in different retrieval systems.

search record A record in a special library which shows the publications, individuals, and organizations consulted in an extended search for information.

search room see *research room*

search service A business which looks for out-of-print or rare materials that are specifically requested by customers.

search statement The expression of an information need or query in the language and format acceptable to a specific information retrieval system. The construction, use, and development of the expression are largely dependent on the search and operational (command) mechanics provided by the system.

search strategy A plan for part or all of a search which guides the selection of search terms and statements in the formulation of the search of a file. Such a plan incorporates logical approaches to information retrieval which are independent of specific retrieval systems and their databases or other files. However, the vocabulary and search mechanics of a specific retrieval system must be utilized when formulating a search according to one strategy or another.

search term In an information retrieval system, a term expressing an information need or query in the language and format acceptable to the specific system. Search terms may be combined to form a search statement. Compare with *approach term.*

search thesaurus   A thesaurus used to identify terms for a search strategy and locate other related terms when necessary.

search time   The average time required to locate specified information in a file or database, measured from the time the search is initiated until the information is located, all entries in the file or database have been searched, or a search strategy is completed.

secondary access   In information retrieval, access from particular entries to related entries in a file or database. Compare with *primary access.*

secondary bibliography   A bibliography dealing with books or other documents relating to one subject. Compare with *primary bibliography.*

secondary network station   A network station that has been selected to receive a transmission from a primary network station.

secondary sources   Any material other than primary sources used in the preparation of a written work.

secondary storage   see *auxiliary storage*

second generation microfilm   see *first reproduction microfilm*

second reproduction microfilm   A third generation microfilm copy made from first reproduction microfilm. Synonymous with third generation microfilm.

section   1. A separately published part of a serial, usually representing a particular subject category within the larger serial and identified by a designation that may be a topic, or an alphabetical or numerical designation, or a combination of these. (AACR2) 2. A folded printed sheet, together with any plates and inserts, assembled and arranged as a binding unit of a book. Sometimes used synonymously with quire, signature, and gathering. Compare with *signature.* 3. The basic vertical division which is enclosed by two uprights or vertical supports within a range of single- or double-faced shelving. A standardized section in the United States is 3 feet wide and 7½ feet high. Called a tier in British usage. 4. A subdivision of a larger administration unit in a library. 5. In classification, see *hierarchical classification system.*

sectioning   The microfilming of only a portion of a one-page document on a film frame, usually because the document is too large to fit on one frame for a desired reduction ratio. The remaining sections of the document are filmed on subsequent frames. The product is referred to as a multiframe document.

section title   see *divisional title*

sectorizing device   see *sector notation*

sector notation   In classification, a notation which reserves the final digit of a set (such as a 9 or z) as a repeater to extend the representation of coordinate classes and thereby increase its expressiveness. For example, classes with notation a, b, c, . . . za, zb, zc . . . etc. would all be considered coordinate. Originally called an octave device and also known as a sectorizing device. Compare with *group notation.*

security filming   The microfilming of source documents as a safeguard against destruction of the originals. The film is generally stored in a remote location under archival conditions. Compare with *preservation microfilming.*

security system, electronic   see *electronic security system*

"see also" cross reference   see *"see also" reference*

"see also" reference   A reference from a name, term, etc., used as a heading to one or more related names, terms, etc., which are also used as headings. Synonymous with "see also" cross reference. Compare with *"see" reference.*

"see" cross reference   see *"see" reference*

"see" reference   A reference to a name, term, etc., used as a heading from another form of the name, term, etc., which is not used as a heading. Synonymous with "see" cross reference. Compare with *"see also" reference.*

segmentation   In classification systems, the device used to indicate the logical places to shorten notation, when that is considered desirable in a smaller collection.

selecting In data communications, the process of inviting another network station or node to receive data. Compare with *polling*.

selection The process of deciding which specific documents should be added to a library collection.

selection officer The staff member of a library who is responsible for the coordination of materials selection activities and who has final responsibility for materials selection, in conformity with the library's collection development policy.

selective cataloging The practice of varying the fullness of bibliographic description depending on the type of bibliographic item being cataloged. Compare with *brief cataloging, full cataloging.*

selective dissemination of information (SDI) A service provided by a library or other information agency whereby its users are periodically notified of new publications, report literature, or other sources of information in subjects in which they have specified an interest. Synonymous with current awareness service.

selective routing see *routing*

selector 1. In information storage and retrieval, a device for identifying data in a file. 2. In data communications, a device for automatic telephone switching.

self-charging system Any charging system in which the borrower creates or assists in creating the charge record.

self-cover A pamphlet cover made of the same paper as the body of the pamphlet. Compare with *self-wrapper.*

self-instructional materials Programmed instructional materials, learning packages, and audiotutorial systems which include stimuli, provision for responses, feedback, and testing, so that students learn with minimum of teacher guidance.

self-lining The first and last pages of text paper pasted to the cover of a book without endpapers.

self-paced instruction A form of instruction which permits the learner to proceed toward objectives at a pace which is self-determined.

self-positive see *direct positive*

self-study see *library survey*

self-wrapper The paper cover of a pamphlet which is part of a signature, and not a binder's addition. Compare with *self-cover.*

semiannual A serial publication frequency of every six months or twice a year.

semiconductor A material that conducts an electrical current less easily than a metal but more easily than an insulator such as glass or ceramic.

semicurrent records In archives, infrequently needed records which can be moved to a holding area or directly to a records center.

semidry process A diazotype process that uses a separate liquid developer.

semimonthly A serial publication frequency of every two weeks. Synonymous with biweekly and fortnightly.

seminar room 1. A small room in a college or a university library in which selected material on a subject is placed temporarily for the use of a group engaged in special research. 2. A room in a college or a university library in which a large part of the library collection in a particular field is shelved for the convenience of advanced students and faculty. 3. A small classroom located in a college or university library where classes with library-intensive requirements are held.

semis A binding decoration of small figures, such as sprays, flowers, and leaves, repeated frequently at regular intervals, over the greater portion of the binding, thus producing a powdered or sprinkled effect.

semiweekly A serial publication frequency of twice a week.

senior librarian A class of library personnel with superior knowledge of some aspect of librarianship based on relevant experience and education beyond the master's degree, who are assigned top-level responsibilities, including but not limited to administration. Compare with *junior librarian.*

senior specialist A class of library personnel with a superior knowledge of a subject field relevant to librarianship, such as personnel management, based on relevant experience and education beyond the master's degree, who are assigned top-level responsibilities including, but not limited to, administration.

sensing mark A periodic mark on a roll of film or paper, sensed by an electronic device, which actuates a cutting mechanism, as in the production of microfiche.

sensitivity An expression or measure of the responsiveness of photographic materials or chemical substances to various forms of radiation, such as those emitted by heat or light. As the material is exposed to radiation, a corresponding change occurs, such as the formation of latent images on photographic film. These changes are generally a function of time, intensity of radiation, and type of material. Given specified conditions of exposure and development, film sensitivity is usually expressed in terms of ASA (American Standards Association) film speed. The higher the ASA number, the faster or more sensitive the film emulsion to light. Sensitivity of a material affects the contrast of the images. Synonymous with speed of film.

sensitize To coat or treat a material such as film or tape so as to make it sensitive to radiant energy.

sensitometric curve see *contrast*

sensitometry The science of measurement of the response of photographic materials upon exposure to light or other forms of radiant energy.

separate see *offprint*

separate registration A method of recording authorized borrowers in which each branch maintains its own registration file and no union registration file is maintained in the central library. Synonymous with branch registration. Compare with *central registration.*

separator see *delimiter*

sequel A literary or other imaginative work that is complete in itself but continues an earlier work. Compare with *supplement.* (AACR2)

sequence The arrangement of data items, data elements, or records according to a defined set of rules.

sequential access see *serial access*

sequential camera see *step-and-repeat camera*

sequential indexer A device which automatically stamps numbers on documents during microfilming.

sequential location A method of arranging items in a library collection, in an order (such as accession order) which does not allow insertion of later acquisitions within the sequence. Compare with *fixed location, relative location.*

sequential processing A technique of processing data only after it has been grouped or batched and sorted into a predefined sequence. Compare with *direct-access processing.*

sequential search An item-by-item search of a file or database until a specified record is located.

sequential storage Storage in which data can be accessed only by reading through all data preceding that which is desired. Synonymous with serial storage. Compare with *direct-access storage.*

serial 1. A publication in any medium issued in successive parts bearing numerical or chronological designations and intended to be continued indefinitely. Serials include periodicals; newspapers; annuals (reports, yearbooks, etc.); the journals, memoirs, proceedings, transactions, etc., of societies; and numbered monographic series. (AACR2) 2. In computer science, the sequential execution of tasks or operations or the sequential handling of data. Compare with *parallel.*

serial access In computer science, a method of referring to records arranged in a sequential or serial order in a file. Access time to records is dependent upon examining all those preceding a desired one in the file. Synonymous with sequential access. Compare with *direct access.*

serial catalog A public or an official catalog of serials in a library, with a record of the library's holdings.

serial number 1. The number which identifies the order of a publication in a series. 2. A unique identifying number assigned to a serial and used as a code in lieu of title in records and communications, such as the International Standard Serial Number and CODEN. 3. One of the consecutive numbers assigned to a volume of the *United States Serial Set.*

serial operation In data processing, pertaining to the sequential execution of tasks or operations or the sequential handling of data. Compare with *parallel operation.*

serial record One or more files identifying the serials represented in a library collection, including for each title such data as holdings, the beginning date of the subscription, publisher, source from which ordered, payment record, and binding record. A single file containing complete data for each serial title is called a central serial record.

serials department The administrative unit of a library which has charge of serials; may be responsible for ordering, checking in, cataloging, preparing for binding, etc.

serial service A periodical publication which revises, cumulates, abstracts, or indexes information in a specific field on a regular basis by means of new or replacement issues, pages, or cards to provide information otherwise not readily available. Compare with *loose-leaf service.* (Z39.20)

Serial Set see *United States Serial Set*

serial storage see *sequential storage*

serial transmission A method of data transmission in which the bits of a character are transferred sequentially, one after another, over one channel of a communications facility. Compare with *parallel transmission.*

series 1. A group of separate bibliographic items related to one another by the fact that each item bears, in addition to its own title proper, a collective title applying to the group as a whole. The individual items may or may not be numbered. (AACR2) 2. Each of two or more volumes of essays, lectures, articles, or other writings similar in character and issued in sequence, e.g., Lowell's *Among my books,* second series. (AACR2) 3. A separately numbered sequence of volumes within a series or serial, e.g., *Notes and queries,* 1st series, 2nd series, etc. (AACR2) 4. In archives, a *record series.*

series authority file A set of records indicating the authorized forms of series entries used in a particular set of bibliographic records; the references made to and from the authorized forms; the information, and its sources, used in the establishment of the headings and the determi-

nation of references to be made; and series treatment.

series entry 1. An access point to a bibliographic record which consists of the name of the author or issuing corporate body and/or the title of a series, together with any other identifying element, such as number or name of subseries. 2. A bibliographic record with an access point as described above as the heading.

series statement That area of the bibliographic record consisting of data elements relating to the series to which the bibliographic item belongs. In addition to the title proper of the series, it may include the parallel title, other title information, statement of responsibility, International Standard Serial Number, the numbering of the item within the series, and the name and details of a subseries.

series treatment The manner of creating the bibliographic record of a series consisting of separate bibliographic items. A separate record may be created for each item, with an access point for the series if it provides a useful collocation, or a record may be created for the series, with the separate items analyzed or listed in a contents note.

serif A short line crossing or projecting from the main stroke of a letter as a finish.

service area A public library term applying to the geographic area, and the residents thereof, for which the library has been established to offer services and from which (or on behalf of which) the library derives income. Typically, this area corresponds to that from which the library derives its legal identity.

service-based subscription see *service basis*

service basis A method of scaling prices for a publication, determined by such criteria as total library income, book fund, circulation, and potential value of the publication to a subscriber; for periodical indexes, based on number of indexed periodicals in a library. Synonymous with service-based subscription.

service bureau see *data-processing center*

service center see *bibliographic service center*

service charge In acquisitions work, the charge added by a wholesaler on an item with little or no discount from the publisher.

service copy see *distribution copy*

service course A course offered by a library school primarily for the benefit of other parts of the parent institution.

service outlet Any location where library materials and services are made available to the library's target group and other potential users.

service point A specific location within a service outlet, at which library users are provided with a particular service or set of services.

Sessional Papers see *Parliamentary Papers*

session laws Publications containing collections of laws passed by a state legislature or, formerly, of laws passed during particular sessions of the U.S. Congress. The federal session laws, which were slip laws collected and reprinted with different page numbers, were also known as pamphlet laws. With their discontinuation, the statutes at large began to be published at the end of each session of Congress instead of, as formerly, at the end of each Congress.

set 1. Two or more documents in any physical form, published, issued, or treated as an entity, and as such forming the basis for a single bibliographic description. 2. In printing, see *body size*.

setoff see *offset*

set solid Said of type set without leading or spacing between the lines.

sewing In binding, a method of leaf affixing in which sections are fastened to each other by thread or wire passed through the center fold or the side near the back edge. The major kinds of sewing are sewing through the fold, known as bench sewing when done by hand, and side sewing, which includes overcasting, oversewing, and cleat binding. Compare with *stitching*.

sewing frame see *frame* (2)

sewing through the fold In binding, a method of leaf affixing in which thread or wire is passed through the center of the section. May be done by machine or as bench sewing. When the volume is a one-section booklet, the method is called *saddle stitching*. Synonymous with fold sewing.

shaken Said of a book which has weak or torn inner joints, but which is not yet loose in binding.

shank see *body*

shared authorship see *shared responsibility*

shared cataloging 1. A specific type of cooperative cataloging, arranged by the Library of Congress with other national library agencies under the National Program for Acquisitions and Cataloging for the exchange of bibliographic records. 2. Loosely used synonymously with *cooperative cataloging*. Compare with *centralized cataloging*.

shared responsibility Collaboration between two or more persons or bodies performing the same kind of activity in the creation of the content of a bibliographic item. The contribution of each may form a separate and distinct part of the item, or the contribution of each may not be separable from that of the others. Compare with *mixed responsibility*. (AACR2)

shareholders' library see *proprietary library*

sharpness see *resolution*

shaved Said of a book trimmed so closely that letters of text have been touched but not mutilated. Compare with *cropped*.

sheaf catalog A catalog made up of sets of slips of a standard size (most typical is 7¾ x 4 inches) fastened together in a loose-leaf binder; used at one time, chiefly in British libraries. Synonymous with loose-leaf catalog.

sheep Leather made from sheepskin, used in binding (usually in cheaper ones).

sheet 1. A single rectangular piece of paper, either printed or blank. 2. A unit of handmade paper the size of the paper mold, either printed or blank. 3. In cataloging, a single piece of paper other than a broadside, with manuscript or printed matter on one or both sides. (AACR2)

sheet-fed press A printing press that is fed paper in sheets rather than in rolls.

sheet microfilm Microfilm used in sheets rather than rolls. Generally the term applies to microfiche, although the distinction is lost when roll microfilm from which microfiche are produced remains uncut. Although the microfiche format is retained for the placement of the frames, microform readers are available for viewing uncut roll microfiche.

shelf capacity see *shelving capacity*

shelf height   The distance between shelves adopted arbitrarily in a library to accommodate materials of different height.

shelf label   A small label or device which fits on the edge of an individual shelf to indicate its contents.

shelf life   The period of time a material may be stored before natural deterioration renders it unusable. Compare with *use life*.

shelflist   A catalog of the bibliographic items in a library collection, arranged by call number, with each item represented by one record. It frequently contains the most up-to-date information on copy and volume holdings.

shelf mark see *call number*

shelf notation see *shelf number*

shelf number   1. The notation by which a document is shelved or otherwise stored. In this sense, synonymous with *call number*. 2. The number assigned to a shelf and incorporated into a document's individual shelf number in a fixed location system. Synonymous with shelf notation.

shelf order   The order in which materials in a library collection are shelved or otherwise stored.

shelf reading   The activity of examining the arrangement of books and other library materials in a stack or other storage area to assure that all items are in proper call number sequence. Synonymous with *reading shelves*.

shelf support   The frame or vertical part of a stack structure which holds the shelves either directly, in the case of standard shelving, or indirectly, in the case of bracket shelving. Compare with *uprights*.

shelving   1. Collectively, the shelves upon which books and other library materials are stored. 2. The act of placing materials on library shelves in proper order.

shelving base   The flat surface at the bottom of a bookcase or section of shelving which may serve as the bottom shelf and contribute to the stability and aesthetics of the shelving unit.

shelving capacity   The capacity of a library for storing the various materials in its collection, expressed by the total number of feet of shelving available for storing materials, the total number of assignable square feet of shelving, or the number of volumes and other material units that can be accommodated on the shelves, derived from various formulas, such as the number of volumes per section or linear foot of shelving. Also called book capacity, shelf capacity, volume capacity. Compare with *stack capacity*.

shipping room   The area in a library where postal deliveries and other shipments of materials are received, sorted, and sent on to other units in the library, and to which the various units send materials to be shipped out. Synonymous with receiving room.

short discount see *discount*

shorts   Books to be sent later because they were not in the dealer's stock when the order was received.

short score   A sketch made by a composer for an ensemble work, with the main features of the composition set out on a few staves. (AACR2)

short stop see *stop* (1)

short-term film   Processed photographic film with a shelf life expectancy of less than ten years. Compare with *archival film, long-term film,* and *medium-term film*.

shoulder see *ridge*

shoulder head   A subheading printed on a separate line flush with the left margin of the text. Compare with *shoulder note*.

shoulder note   A marginal note printed at the upper and outer corner of a page. Compare with *shoulder head*.

show through see *bleed through*

shutter   An automatic mechanism designed to allow light to pass through the lens aperture of a camera to the light-sensitive film or paper for a definite length of time to make an exposure.

shutter speed The length of time in which light-sensitive film or paper is exposed to light when the shutter is opened and closed.

side The front or back board of a book cover.

sidehead A run-in head or a shoulder head.

side note see *marginal note*

side sewing In binding, a method of leaf affixing in which the book is built up by sewing successive sections to one another near the back edge. Includes overcasting and oversewing. Compare with *side stitching.*

side stitching In binding, a method of leaf affixing in which single leaves or sections are stitched together near their back edge by passing thread or wire through the thickness of the entire book. Compare with *side sewing.*

side title A title impressed on the front cover of a bound book. Compare with *binder's title, cover title.*

sign A conventional mark or device having a recognized particular meaning and used in place of words; an ideographic mark, figure, or picture conventionally used in writing or printing to represent a technical term or conception.

signal An electrical impulse transmitted or received, which serves as a carrier of data, sound, or scene over a circuit or channel.

signature A printed sheet, folded or ready for folding to form a section, with the addition of any plates or inserts, to which a signature mark has been given. Sometimes called quire, section, or gathering. Compare with *section* (2).

signature mark A distinguishing mark, letter, or number, or some combination of these, printed on a sheet at the foot of the first page, and sometimes on subsequent leaves, of each signature of a book or pamphlet to indicate the order in which sheets are to be arranged for folding and gathering. When other sheets or portions of a sheet are to be inserted, they also are signed to indicate their order.

signature title An abbreviated form of the author and/or title of a book, given on the same line as the signature mark, but toward the inner margin of the first page of each signature of a lengthy book.

significance In a test of a statistical hypothesis, the probability that the null hypothesis will be judged false, when it is actually true, as a result of chance factors in the selection of the sample. One strives to design the test so as to have a low significance level (e.g., 5 or 1 percent), so that one may have a high degree of confidence in the judgment as to the truth of the null hypothesis.

significance level In a test of a statistical hypothesis, the amount of significance that the researcher chooses to use, designing the test to provide it.

significant letter code In information retrieval, a code consisting of the important or significant letters or characters of words.

sign-reversing process In reprography, a copying process in which the normal development of latent images reverses the polarity of the original. Synonymous with negative-working process.

silent filmstrip see *filmstrip*

silking A process for repairing or preserving paper by the application of silk chiffon or another transparent material to one or both sides of the sheets or leaves.

silk screen printing see *screen printing*

silver densitometric testing method A method of measuring residual hypo on processed film.

silver film A film which is sensitized with silver halide. The term includes nongelatin dry silver film as well as silver halide film, which is coated with silver halide suspended in gelatin and is developed by a wet process. Silver film is considered by many to be the only film suitable for archival permanence.

silver halide The combination of silver and a member of the halogen family to form silver chloride, silver bromide, silver iodide, or silver fluoride.

silver halide film see *silver film*

silver recovery The recovery of silver from the fixing solution. The silver may be precipitated by addition of sodium sulfide or zinc dust, or electrolytically deposited on cathodes suspended in the fixing solution. Upward of 90 percent of the silver in the solution can be recovered.

simplex A microfilm format in which only one image is photographed across the width of the film. The orientation can be either comic or cine.

simplex paper see *photographic paper*

simplex transmission Data transmission over a channel in one direction only. Compare with *duplex transmission, half-duplex transmission.*

simplified cataloging see *brief cataloging*

simulate 1. To represent certain features of the behavior of a physical or abstract system by the behavior of another system. 2. To represent the functioning of a device, system, or computer program by another; for example, to represent the functioning of one computer by another, to represent the behavior of a physical system by the execution of a computer program, to represent a biological system by a mathematical model.

simultaneous processing see *concurrent processing*

single-concept film A short motion picture spliced in a continuous loop and encased in a cartridge. This film is designed to explain a process, idea, or concept, or to develop a skill.

single-copy order plan A plan devised by the American Booksellers Association to allow dealers ordering single copies of books according to prescribed regulations a full trade discount.

single-entry charging system A charging system in which one record identifying the item borrowed and the borrower is kept in a file usually arranged by call number. Synonymous with one-card charging system. Compare with *double-entry charging system.*

single-faced shelving A bookcase, section, or range with accessible shelving on only one side and frequently positioned against a wall.

single-frame filmstrip see *filmstrip*

single-lens reflex camera see *reflex camera*

single-perforation film see *motion-picture film*

single-tier stack A stack of single-story height, usually 7½ feet, with the weight of the stack structure and the library materials stored on the shelves carried by a load-bearing floor. Compare with *multitier stack.*

sink see *data sink*

sinking funds Sums of money set aside or temporarily invested which are pledged for a future expenditure of a specified nature, such as the replacement of equipment, or new or expanded physical facilities. Sinking funds are part of the unexpended balance of a library's budget.

site visit see *field visit*

sixteenmo see *book sizes*

sixtyfourmo see *book sizes*

sized paper Paper treated with gelatin, starch, or, more modernly, with rosin to control its acceptance of ink and other aqueous solutions.

size letters A set of abbreviations (F=folio; Q=quarto, etc.) formerly used to indicate the size of books.

size notation The indication of the height and/or width of a book, as by fold symbol, size letter, or measurement in centimeters.

size of books see *book sizes*

size of film see *film size*

size of type see *type size*

size rule A ruler 30 centimeters long on which size letters and corresponding fold symbols are given at proper intervals; used for measuring books.

skeleton abstract see *telegraphic abstract*

skewness The lack of symmetry in a frequency distribution.

skiver The hair side of split sheepskin, frequently finished in imitation of other and more expensive skins used in binding. The term is sometimes used to describe binding leathers other than sheepskin.

slanted abstract An abstract which is slanted toward the interests of the group of subject specialists for whom it is intended. Synonymous with special-purpose abstract.

sleeper A term used in the book trade to describe a trade book for which low initial demand gradually grows into a steady market and also to describe a rare book whose true value is not recognized by the dealer currently owning it.

sleeve 1. A protective envelope for an audiodisc, made of cardboard or paper. Sometimes called jacket. 2. For film, see *film jacket.*

slick A high-circulation consumer magazine printed on slick paper; usually refers to a magazine containing fiction, for which authors are paid more than is paid by pulp magazines.

slide A transparent positive image (usually photographic) on film or glass, intended for projection on a slide viewer or slide projector. Actual image area may vary from microimage to 3¼ x 4 inches (called a lantern slide). Most slides other than 3¼ x 4 inches and 2¼ x 2¼ inches are mounted in a cardboard or plastic frame whose outside dimensions are 2 x 2 inches. The predominantly used slide is a transparency of 35mm color film mounted in a 2-x-2-inch frame.

slide/audiotape A set of slides accompanied by an audiotape containing a sound track and sometimes a synchronizing signal to project the next slide in the sequence.

slide mount A 2-x-2-inch cardboard or plastic frame in which a film slide is placed for storage and projection.

slide projector A projector for slides or transparencies mounted in small frames, usually 2 x 2 inches. Some models have provision for playing accompanying audiorecordings and may have automatic slide advance cued by a signal on the audiotape. (NCES)

slide/tape see *slide/audiotape*

slide viewer A device equipped with a small built-in viewing glass or translucent screen for viewing slides by rear-screen projection. Models are available with provision for playing accompanying audiorecordings. Some models have automatic advance mechanisms keyed to the audiorecording.

sliding shelves Deep shelves for the storage of oversize books, such as elephant folios, slot-designed so that they may be pulled out in order to facilitate handling of the books and to preserve bindings. Compare with *roller shelves.*

slip 1. A form or small piece of paper used for making a note or record, usually preceded by a modifier, such as call slip or date due slip. 2. To

discharge an item charged from the library collection by taking the charge card from the charging file and replacing it in the item.

slip cancel see *paste-in*

slipcase A box designed to protect a book, covering it so that its spine only is exposed.

slip law A law in its first printed form after its passage in the U.S. Congress.

slippage In continuous printing, a defect which results in blurred images. It occurs when one film surface slips while in direct contact with the other.

slip proofs see *galley proofs*

slipsheets 1. Waste or rough paper used to interleave freshly printed sheets, to prevent them from offsetting onto each other. 2. Sheets of translucent or nearly transparent tissue paper, laid or tipped into books in front of engravings or other illustrations, to prevent them from offsetting.

sloping shelves The lower shelves of a bookcase or section of shelving, arranged in a tilted position so that titles and call numbers of books or other materials can be read more easily. Synonymous with tilted shelves.

slotted shelving A type of metal standard shelving with solid vertical panels the full depth of the shelves, having precut slots into which the shelves are inserted. The precut slots are placed at regular intervals to permit the shelves to be adjusted.

slow emulsion A photographic emulsion with a low sensitivity to light.

slow motion A sequence in a motion picture or videotape photographed or taped at a higher-than-normal speed so that when the picture is played back at normal speed the action appears to be slower than in nature. The same effect occurs if the projector is slowed to project a relatively smaller number of frames per second.

slow-scan television (SSTV) A device which compresses the video signal to a bandwidth suitable for transmission over telephone lines. Slow-scan television usually cannot reproduce moving images, since it takes many seconds to recreate one picture.

slug-casting machine see *linotype*

small capital A capital letter of approximately the x-height of the same type size. Frequently referred to as "small cap" or abbreviated "s.c.," and indicated in copy by underlining the appropriate letter(s) with two lines.

small letter Any letter that is not a capital; a lower case letter, indicated in copy by the abbreviation "l.c."

small-paper edition An impression of a book printed on paper of a smaller size than that of a large-paper edition produced from the same type image.

smart terminal see *intelligent terminal*

SMD see *specific material designation*

snapshot dump A dump at various times during a computer run in order to evaluate the contents of a storage device.

sobriquet A fanciful or humorous appellation given by others; a nickname.

social library Generically, a voluntary association of individuals who contribute money toward a common fund to be used for the purchase of library materials. Though every member has the right to use the materials, title to all is retained by the group. The term is used loosely for a whole group of subscription and association libraries, including athenaeums, lyceums, mechanics' libraries, and mercantile libraries.

society A corporate body consisting of a group of associated persons who usually meet periodically because of common interests, objectives, or profession. Synonymous with association.

society library 1. A library established and maintained by a society primarily for the use of its members, but sometimes available to others on the payment of fees. 2. A library of specialized materials organized by a society for the use of members interested in a particular subject or field of knowledge.

society publication A publication issued by, or under the auspices of, a society or institution, including proceedings, transactions, and memoirs. Occasionally called association publication.

soft copy An image viewed on the screen of a cathode-ray tube, or a microimage viewed on a microform reader screen. Compare with *hard copy.*

softcover see *paperback*

soft-ground etching 1. A method of etching that produces the effect of a pencil or crayon drawing, made by applying a soft wax coating to the plate and covering it with thin transfer paper, on which the drawing is done with a pencil. When the paper is removed, it retains bits of the coating, leaving a flecked line. 2. An etching produced by this method.

soft paper Photographic paper used to print negatives when low contrast is desired. The gradations in tonal range exceed those used in normal and hard paper; thus the change in tone is less perceptible.

software 1. The computer programs, routines, procedures, and other documentation associated with operating a computer system. 2. Audiovisual materials, such as motion picture films, slides, and videorecordings, that require the use of audiovisual equipment for projection or playback. Compare with *hardware.*

Solander case A book-shaped box for holding a book, pamphlets, or other material, named for its inventor, D. C. Solander. It may open on side or front with hinges, or have two separate parts, one fitting over the other. Its most developed form has a rounded back and projecting squares, like a book.

solid (type) see *set solid*

solid-state device A device made of a semiconducting material, used to control the flow of electrons or to generate, amplify, or detect electromagnetic waves. Diodes, transistors, and integrated circuits are examples of solid-state devices.

solidus see *virgule*

sort In typesetting, any character or piece of type in a font.

sorter A machine or device which can arrange or rearrange punched cards into a desired sequence.

sound cartridge see *audiocartridge*

sound cassette see *audiocassette*

sound disc see *audiodisc*

sound filmstrip see *filmstrip*

sound-on-slide see *audioslide*

sound page see *audiopage*

sound-recorded book see *talking book*

sound recording 1. The activity of using an audiotape recorder and related audio equipment, such as mixers, amplifiers, and sound sources, to record sounds on an audiotape or magnetic film (or in special cases on motion picture film). Includes placement of microphones, mixing sounds. (NCES) 2. An *audiorecording.*

sound sheet see *audiopage*

sound slide see *audioslide*

sound tape reel see *audioreel*

sound synchronizer A device linking an audiotape player or recorder and an automatic slide or filmstrip projector, which causes the projector to advance at a signal on the audiotape. (AECT)

sound track The sound portion of a motion-picture film or a videotape. On film, the sound track may be a photographic image of sound produced by a beam of light (optical sound track) or a magnetic coating on one or both edges of the film for recording sound (magnetic sound track). The term is sometimes used to distinguish between the audiotape track containing the sound presentation and the track containing the synchronizing signal.

source citation In authority work, the listing of the place or document where information relevant to the heading or reference was found, or where it was sought and not found. The citation usually contains both the identification of the source consulted and the information found.

source document 1. In reprography, the original document from which copies are produced, normally containing text or other graphic matter that can be read or viewed without magnification. 2. In data processing, an original document used to generate or prepare input into a data processing system.

source index A card index to sources of unusual and elusive information, which, in addition to listing publications, may refer to individuals and organizations. It is frequently the cumulative product of dealing with difficult reference inquiries.

source language In computer science, the language from which data are translated.

source material see *primary sources*

source monitoring see *monitor* (4)

source program A computer program, usually written in a symbolic language, to be translated into an object program.

source record A bibliographic record originating with a national cataloging agency, such as the Library of Congress; assumed to be a record of the highest quality and bibliographic accuracy.

space character see *blank character*

space remote-sensing image see *remote-sensing image*

span of control In an organizational structure, the number of employees, usually with similar degrees of authority, who report to and are supervised by the same superior.

speaker see *loudspeaker*

special character In data processing, a graphic character other than a letter, digit, or space; for example, a dollar sign, a comma, an asterisk, a plus sign.

special classification system A classification system which covers a limited area of knowledge.

special collection A collection of library materials separated from the general collection because they are of a certain form, on a certain subject, of a certain period or geographical area, rare, fragile, or valuable. Examples are collections of audiovisual materials, women's history, East Asian materials, and rare books.

special collections department The administrative unit of a library system responsible for the organization, maintenance, and servicing of one or more special collections.

special edition 1. An issue of a standard work or the works of a standard author, generally with a distinctive name and sometimes with added introduction, notes, appendix, and illustrations. 2. An issue that differs from the original edition by some distinctive feature, such as better paper and binding, or the addition of illustrations. 3. A special number of a newspaper, usually devoted to a particular subject, such as an anniversary number. Synonymous with special number. 4. A *library edition.*

special issue see *special number*

specialist A class of library personnel with professional responsibilities, including those of management, which require independent judgment, interpretation of rules and procedures, analysis of library problems, and the formulation of original and creative solutions for them, normally utilizing knowledge of a subject field relevant to librarianship represented by a master's degree.

special library A library established, supported, and administered by a business firm, private corporation, association, government agency, or other special-interest group or agency to meet the information needs of its members or staff in pursuing the goals of the organization. Scope of collections and services is limited to the subject interests of the host or parent organization.

special number A single issue or a supplementary section of a serial or a newspaper devoted to a special subject, with or without serial numbering, such as a number of a periodical containing proceedings of a convention, or an anniversary number of a newspaper. Also called special issue, and if celebrating an anniversary, anniversary issue. A special number of a newspaper is sometimes called *special edition.*

special-purpose abstract see *slanted abstract*

special-purpose computer A computer designed to solve or handle only one or a few selected types of problems. Compare with *dedicated computer, general-purpose computer.*

species In classification, one of the classes of things into which a genus is divided on the basis of a characteristic added to the genus; the species may in turn become a genus when divided into subspecies.

specification A formal, detailed description of an item or items to be purchased, provided, or built; usually associated with bids, purchase orders, and construction contracts.

specification slip see *binding slip*

specific classification see *close classification*

specific entry The representation of a work or bibliographic item in a catalog or index under a subject heading or descriptor that is coextensive with its subject content. Compare with *class entry.*

specific material designation (SMD) In descriptive cataloging, a term indicating the special class of material (usually the class of physical object) to which a bibliographic item belongs, such as videocassette. Compare with *general material designation.* (AACR2, mod.)

speckled calf see *sprinkled calf*

spectrophotometer A photosensitive instrument used to measure the relative intensity of transmitted or reflected light in different parts of a spectrum.

speech compressor An electronic device, usually involving an audiotape, capable of compression and expansion of an audio signal (usually human speech) with respect to its speed without a corresponding increase or decrease in pitch.

speed of film see *sensitivity*

spherical aberration An optical defect in a lens which appears in the form of blurred images. It occurs when light rays that pass through the edges of the lens and those that pass through the center do not focus at the same point.

spindle The shaft onto which film reels are mounted during viewing or rewinding.

spine The part of the binding that connects the front and back covers and conceals the back or bound edge of a book. Usually bears the title and frequently the name of the author. Synonymous with backbone. Compare with *backstrip,* which is sometimes used synonymously, and with *back.*

spine title The title that appears on the spine of a volume. Synonymous with back title.

spiral binding A form of mechanical binding in which a wire or plastic coil is drawn through holes punched in the edges of the separate leaves. The volume will lie open flat, but the open pages will not remain aligned horizontally.

Synonymous with coil binding. Compare with *twin-wire binding*.

spirit duplication The activity of duplicating which employs a master copy made by placing a sheet of direct-process dye material behind the paper master and writing, typing, or drawing on the face of the master. The dye adheres to the back of the master. The master is placed (usually on a rotary drum) on a spirit duplicator with the dye side out. The master is then brought into contact with a sheet of paper wetted with duplication fluid. The dye mixes with the fluid and is pressed onto the paper. Synonymous with ditto. (NCES)

spirit duplicator A duplicating machine which prints on paper from a paper master on which there is a dye image. Paper passing through the machine is dampened slightly with a special fluid to receive and retain the dye image. (NCES)

splice A joining of two pieces of film or magnetic tape by cementing, taping, or welding, using a splicer. Cemented splices overlap and are called lap splices. Splices made by welding (heat splices) or with adhesive splicing tape butt together without overlapping and are called butt splices. Magnetic tape is spliced with adhesive tape on the uncoated side.

splicer A device for joining two strips of film or magnetic tape so they will function as a single piece when passing through a projector, audiotape or videotape player, or other equipment.

split files The result of adopting a new form of heading and incorporating bibliographic records with the new heading into a catalog, while leaving records using the old form of heading unrevised. Old and new forms are filed in accordance with the filing rules of the catalog (i.e., they are not interfiled). The two files may or may not be connected with linking references. Compare with *interfiling* (1).

split leather Leather that has been divided into two or more thicknesses, for use in binding.

spoking Distortion of film on a reel due to excessive curl.

sponsor A person or corporate body subsidizing or otherwise encouraging the production of a book.

sponsored book see *subsidy publishing*

spool A flanged holder onto which unprocessed roll film is wound, designed to be inserted into cameras and film processors.

spooling The process of temporarily storing data on magnetic disk or magnetic tape for later processing.

spread see *opening*

spring back A strong type of binding used on account books, characterized by a clamping action that causes the book to snap open and shut.

sprinkled calf Calf given a speckled appearance by sprinkling with coloring matter or by an acid treatment. Synonymous with speckled calf.

sprinkled edges Book edges on which color has been irregularly sprinkled or sprayed.

sprocket In cameras and projectors that use perforated film, a wheel with teeth that engage with the film perforations, or sprocket holes, and aid in transporting and positioning the film.

SPSS see *Statistical Package for the Social Sciences*

spurious imprint see *fictitious imprint*

square see *book sizes*

square capitals Letters similar to the forms of the letters used in monumental inscriptions, used in early Latin manuscripts.

square corner A book corner in which a piece of the covering material is cut at the corner so that one turn-in considerably overlaps the other without additional folding.

squares 1. The portions of the edges of a book cover that project beyond the paper body of the book and protect it. 2. That part of the turn-in on a book cover not covered by the endpaper.

SSN see *International Standard Serial Number*

SSTV see *slow-scan television*

stabilization A photographic quick-processing technique in which chemical treatment of the exposed and developed film image renders the silver halides in the nonimage area inert, thereby eliminating the step of washing out the silver halides. Prints produced on stablization paper have a life span of only a few weeks.

stab stitching In binding, to stitch with wire or thread, with long stitches near the back fold and through the entire book.

stack 1. Frequently used in the plural (stacks), a series of bookcases or sections of shelving, arranged in rows or ranges, freestanding or multi-tiered, for the storage of the library's principal collection. 2. The space in a library designated and equipped for the storage of its collections.

stack aisle see *range aisle*

stack capacity The capacity of a stack area for storing books and other library materials, expressed as the total number of feet of shelving provided, the total number of square feet of shelving, or the number of volumes and other material units that can be accommodated on the shelves. Stack capacity may be determined by the use of various formulas, such as the number of volumes per square foot or cubic foot. Compare with *shelving capacity.*

stack end see *range end*

stack level see *deck* (1)

stack permit A special borrower's identification card authorizing access to a closed stack.

stack supervisor The library staff member with overall responsibility for maintaining the order of the stacks, including such duties as shelving and reshelving library materials, shelf reading, and, sometimes, delivering requested items to the circulation desk.

staff The entire group of persons who together execute the activities necessary for accomplishing the goals of an organization or any of its administrative units.

staff association An association of members of the professional and/or the support staff of a library, formed for specified work-related purposes.

staff authority The right conferred upon an administrator or other individual in an organization to advise or assist one or more managers or supervisors in the performance of their duties, usually in specified areas of expertise. Compare with *line authority* and *functional authority.*

staff card A specially designated borrower's identification card issued to a library staff member.

staff development A purposive effort to improve the overall effectiveness of personnel in the performance of their duties and their contribution to the goals of the organization by providing and encouraging participation in a continuum of internal and external in-service training and continuing education opportunities.

staff handbook A compilation of selected written documents in effect within an organization, including policies, rules, procedures, and other official documents. Usually in loose-leaf format, it is designed for the staff as a reference source on accepted practices. Synonymous with employee handbook. Compare with *organization manual, administrative manual.*

staff manual A handbook for staff of an organization, consisting of general policies, rules, and procedures, as well as those of the various administrative units, and usually containing samples of forms and lists of supplies. Compare with *policy manual, procedure manual.*

staff organization see *line and staff organization*

staff orientation An initial training process designed to acquaint new employees with various aspects of the organization, including established goals, policies, and procedures; the physical environment; other personnel and working relationships; job duties and responsibilities; and fringe benefits.

staff room A room set aside for staff members to use for work breaks, meals, staff socials, and other recreational activities.

staff turnover The number of resignations or terminations on the staff of an organization during a given period of time, sometimes stated as a percentage ratio.

stained calf see *calf*

stained edges Book edges that have been stained with color.

stained label A colored panel printed or painted directly on the spine or front cover of a book as a background for lettering and simulating a label of leather.

stamping The impressing of a design, including decoration and lettering, on a book cover by means of a stamping die, or plate. Cold stamping is done in ink on a platen press similar to those used for printing. Hot stamping is used for applying leaf, for blind stamping, and for embossing, heat being necessary to transfer the leaf to the cover and, in blind stamping and embossing, to mold the covering material and boards. In British usage, called *blocking,* to distinguish stamping with a single block containing the complete binding design. Compare with *tooling.*

stand-alone reader see *microform reader*

stand-alone system A computer system which operates independently of other computer systems.

standard binding A category of library binding roughly equivalent to the Library Binding Institute Standard for Library Binding in construction and materials; however, the bindery does not collate the material, binding it as received, and offers uniform lettering and colors for specific periodicals. Also called standardized binding.

Standard Book Number see *International Standard Book Number (ISBN)*

standard book numbering agency The agency in each participating country which assigns International Standard Book Numbers to the books published by publishers participating in the program in that country.

standard deviation A widely used measure of variation in a set of data, obtained by computing the square root of the sum of the squared deviations of the data about the mean, divided by the number of items in a population, or, for a sample, divided by one less than the number of items.

Standard English Braille The braille system as adopted and authorized for use in the United States and England in 1932 and modified in 1956. In the United States the system is designated as English Braille, American Edition, since, although the symbols are the same in American and British usage, the governing rules of usage differ.

standard error The standard deviation of a sampling distribution.

standardized binding see *standard binding*

standards 1. Criteria by which library services and programs may be measured or assessed. Established by professional organizations, accrediting bodies, or government agencies, the criteria may variously reflect a minimum or ideal, a model procedure or process, a quantitative measure, or a qualitative assessment. 2. Criteria of expected performance or achievement established within a library for the purpose of evaluating the performance of individual staff members and organizational units. Synonymous with performance standards. 3. A set or code of rules established by national and international organizations for the purpose of bibliographic control, including those providing for the unique identification of bibliographic items, such as the International Standard Book Number and International Serial Number; the uniform description of items, such as the International Standard Bibliographic Description; and the exchange of bibliographic records by means of a bibliographic information interchange format, such as the MARC (Machine-Readable Cataloging) format.

Standard Serial Number see *International Standard Serial Number (ISSN)*

standard shelving Any type of shelving with solid vertical panels the full depth of the shelves which allow the ends of the shelves to be supported across their total depth or in the front and rear. Standard shelving may have fixed shelves or adjustable shelves. Compare with *bracket shelving.*

standard-size card The size of card generally used in library catalogs: 12.5 x 7 centimeters.

Standard Technical Report Number (STRN) The complete, formatted, alphanumeric designation that is usually the primary means of identifying a specific technical report. It consists of two essential parts: a report code, which designates an issuing agency or corporate entity without subdivision, and a sequential code, giving the year of publication, subdivision of the issuing agency or corporate entity, and local suffix. The maximum number of characters for the STRN is twenty-two, including the group separator and any subdividers.

standard title see *uniform title*

standing committee A committee with specific charges and responsibilities within an organization which meets on a regular basis to fulfill its charge. In a library system, such groups frequently perform a coordination and communication role and may be involved in decision-making and policy formulation.

standing order A general order to a dealer to supply the volumes or parts of a particular title or type of publication as they appear, until notified otherwise. Compare with *continuation order* and *'til forbid.*

staple binding see *pamphlet-style library binding*

star map see *celestial map*

star network A network in which all nodes are connected to a central node or network control station. Compare with *fully connected network, distributed network, ring network.*

start 1. In binding, a section of leaves that has not been properly secured in the back of a book and thus projects beyond the rest. 2. A break between the sections of a book, frequently caused by forcing the volume open while the leaves are held tightly.

start-stop data transmission see *asynchronous data transmission*

state 1. A copy or a group of copies of a bibliographic item which differs from other copies within the same impression or issue, but which the publisher does not wish to call attention to as representing a consciously planned printed unit. Compare with *issue* (1). 2. An impression of an engraving, taken from a plate at any stage in the process of perfecting or modifying. An early impression is one made while the finished plate is still comparatively new and unworn. The finished state is called the publication state.

state document see *state publication*

state document center A library that assumes the responsibility of collecting, organizing, and preserving as complete a file as possible of the government publications of the state in which it is located.

state documents depository see *depository library* (2)

state library A library maintained by state funds for the use of state officials and employees, and usually for the use of all citizens of the state.

state library agency An independent agency or a unit of the state library or other state governmental unit, such as the state department of education, created or authorized by a state to extend and develop library services in the state through the direct provision of certain services statewide and through the organization and coordination of library services to be provided by other libraries of one or more types. Also called library commission, state library commission, and state library extension agency.

state library commission see *state library agency*

state library extension agency see *state library agency*

state manual A publication issued by a state, usually annually or biennially, giving an outline of the state government, lists of officials, and other data. Sometimes called legislative manual and blue book.

state media program The media program conducted by a state education agency and prescribed by state legislation. State boards of education generate policies and recommend legislative action, while the education agency provides leadership for local and regional media programs.

statement In computer science, an instruction or expression for a computer to execute.

statement of responsibility A statement, transcribed from the bibliographic item being described, relating to persons responsible for the intellectual or artistic content of the item, to corporate bodies from which the content emanates, or to persons or corporate bodies responsible for the performance of the content of the item. (AACR2)

state-of-the-art see *annual review*

state publication Any document originating in, or issued with the imprint of, or at the expense and by the authority of, any office of a state government. Synonymous with *state document.*

static eliminator see *static marks*

static marks Undesirable marks on paper or film created by static electricity during photographic processing or photocopying. The problem is minimized by various chemicals or devices termed static eliminators.

station see *network station, deposit station*

statistic In inferential statistics, a quantitative characteristic of a sample that is used to estimate the value of a corresponding population parameter; also a *test statistic.*

statistical bibliography see *bibliometrics*

statistical hypothesis A statement that (1) specifies the value of a population parameter, or (2) asserts that a specific relationship exists between population parameters, or (3) asserts that a variable has a specified distribution.

Statistical Package for the Social Sciences (SPSS) A prewritten statistical computer program for manipulating, transforming, and modifying existing data, intended for use in social science research.

statutes at large Statutes in their original full form; particularly, publications containing laws passed during a single session of the U. S. Congress, together with other documents, such as resolutions, treaties, and presidential proclamations; prior to the law of 1938, issued after each Congress as a consolidation of the session laws.

steady state Said of a library collection where withdrawals equal accessions. Synonymous with no-growth, zero growth.

steel engraving An engraving made from a steel, as opposed to a copper, plate, a process which became common in the 1820s and which enjoyed a considerable popularity through the middle years of the 19th century because of the ability of the plates to endure the printing of large editions. Steel engravings tend to have a sharp, silvery look, and can thus be distinguished from the more mellow look of copper engravings. Long in disfavor as an artistic medium, 19th-century steel engravings are now being eagerly collected.

stem The vertical stroke(s) of a letter.

stencil duplication The activity of duplicating by writing, drawing, typing, or otherwise perforating the face of a special master (stencil). The pressure of the writing or typing makes tiny holes in the stencil which is then placed (usually on a rotary drum) on a rotary stencil duplicator. Ink is then forced through the holes and onto the blank paper which comes into contact with the stencil. Produces images of different colors, depending on the ink used. (NCES)

stencil duplicator A machine for making copies of written matter or drawings by means of a stencil fastened to a rotating drum. Ink is squeezed through the stencil, thereby making a copy on the paper fed through the machine. Synonymous with mimeograph.

stencil printing A printing process in which the image to be printed is reproduced on a thin sheet of porous material, either coated or uncoated. If coated, the coating is removed from the printing area; if uncoated, coating is applied to the nonprinting area. Ink or paint is then forced through the porous printing area.

step-and-repeat camera A microfilm camera which produces a series of separate images according to a predetermined sequence, usually in orderly rows and columns on 105mm microfilm, which is cut after processing to create microfiche. Synonymous with sequential camera.

step printer A contact or projection printer which exposes one frame at a time by means of an intermittent advance mechanism and a shutter.

stepwise-operated camera see *planetary camera*

stereograph A pair of opaque or transparent images (usually photographic) intended to produce a three-dimensional effect when viewed with stereoscopic equipment. (NCES)

stereograph slide see *stereoscope slide*

stereophonic The reproduction of sound by an audio device from two channels separately and simultaneously. Also used to denote any related recordings, equipment, and techniques. Compare with *monaural, quadraphonic.*

stereoscope An optical device with two lenses, enabling each eye to see a separate image of essentially the same scene. The combined image seen by the two eyes gives the effect of three dimensions, as in normal binocular vision. (NCES)

stereoscope slide Paired slides made from negatives taken from two slightly different viewpoints, designed to produce a three-dimensional effect when viewed through a stereoscope. Synonymous with stereograph slide.

stereotype A duplicate letterpress plate made by pouring molten metal into a papier mâché or plastic mold, or matrix, made from the face of set metal type and cuts.

stick A device for holding together the pages of a current issue, or several current issues, of a newspaper, for the convenience of readers. Sticks are frequently stored in specially designed racks.

still camera A camera in which there is no movement of the film during exposure. Still cameras are intended primarily for the production of single photographs, as distinct from cameras used to produce motion pictures.

stipple engraving 1. A method of engraving in which the design is both etched and cut. The outline of the design is etched; then fine dots and dashes are cut with a graver to give effects of light and shade that resemble pencil shading. 2. A print made by this method.

stitching In binding, a method of leaf affixing in which the leaves of the entire book are fastened together as a single unit, often with wire, rather than as a sequence of sections sewn to one another. Includes stab stitching, side stitching, and saddle stitching. Compare with *sewing.*

stop 1. In the photographic processing of silver halide materials, the process of bathing photographic film or paper in a mildly acidic solution to neutralize the alkaline developer with which the materials are saturated upon removal from the developing bath and arrest development beyond a desired point. Synonymous with short stop and stop bath. 2. The marking of a series of diaphragm settings, calibrated by f-numbers. 3. A *diaphragm.*

stop bath see *stop* (1)

stop list A list of common or insignificant words that are not to be used as keywords and are therefore to be excluded in automatic indexing. Compare with *go list.*

stop motion A device on some motion-picture projectors which allows the operator to hold the projector on a single film frame.

storage Pertaining to a device or unit of a computer into which data can be placed for either temporary or permanent retention and later retrieval. Synonymous with memory.

storage area 1. That portion of a library building or some other building in which a library stores little-used materials, which are available upon request. 2. That portion of a library building used to store supplies and equipment not in immediate use.

storage buffer see *buffer*

storage capacity The maximum amount of data which a particular storage device can contain at a given time, defined usually in terms of bytes, characters, or computer words.

storage center A facility in which cooperating libraries store little-used items from their collections, which are then available upon request. Each library retains the ownership of the materials it stores cooperatively. Synonymous with deposit library and reservoir library. Compare with *cooperative collection resource facility.*

storage collection A collection which is infrequently used by the library's user group and is therefore housed separately from the remainder of the library collection. The collection is typically in a building away from the library's main facilities.

storage device A device having the capability of storing data, usually in a machine-readable form.

store-and-forward switching see *data-switching*

stored-program computer A computer whose actions are controlled by sets of instructions or computer programs stored internally in the machine.

story board A series of sketches or pictures and any accompanying text which visualize each topic or item in a work to be produced in audiovisual format.

story hour A period devoted regularly to the telling or reading of stories to children in the children's department of a public library or in a school library media center.

straight-grain morocco Goatskin leather intended for binding whose surface is covered with parallel crinkles produced by subjecting it to grained steel plates under pressure.

stratified sampling A type of sampling in which the population is divided into parts, or strata, for the purpose of drawing a sample; an assigned proportion of the sample is then selected from each stratum.

strawboard A paperboard made from straw which is treated chemically and then passed through the customary papermaking process.

streak A film defect occurring during processing that results in light or dark areas running parallel to the film edge.

stretch A film defect in which the images exhibit a longitudinal blur. It is a result of poor synchronization between the film and the original in rotary cameras or between the two film surfaces in continuous printing.

strike-on printing see *impact printing*

string In computer science, a group of characters, items, or bits arranged in a predetermined sequence.

stripe The magnetic coating applied to one or both edges of a motion picture film for recording sound.

strip film see *microstrip*

strip in see *strip up* (2)

strip up 1. To cut roll microfilm into strips for insertion into film jackets or for producing microfiche. 2. In photocomposition, to perform the makeup process by arranging positive film on a sheet of transparent film. Synonymous with strip in.

STRN see *Standard Technical Report Number*

stroke generator see *character generator*

struck-image printing see *impact printing*

strut bracing The crosswise stabilization of stacks by affixing ranges to one another with channels, or metal bars, running across the tops of the ranges.

stub 1. The portion that remains when a leaf is cut out of a volume. It may be used to tip in a replacement leaf. 2. A narrow strip of paper or fabric sewn between sections of a book for attaching a folded map or other material of extra bulk. 3. A narrow strip or strips of paper or fabric bound into the front or back of a volume to permit the addition of a pocket.

student assistant A part-time employee of an academic library or a school library or media center who is simultaneously enrolled on a regu-

lar basis in the institution of which the library is a part. A student assistant typically performs clerical duties and is paid an hourly wage.

student's card 1. In some public libraries, a distinguishable borrower's identification card issued to elementary and secondary school students. 2. In some public library systems, a distinguishable borrower's identification card issued for a limited period of time to nonresident students attending schools or colleges in the legal service area of the library.

Student's t-distribution see *t-distribution*

study carrel see *carrel*

study print A picture, generally with accompanying text, prepared specifically for instructional purposes.

STV see *subscription television*

stylus 1. The point or needle on a shaft, or cantilever, attached to the phonocartridge of an audiodisc player. The stylus sends the mechanical vibrations from the audiodisc grooves to the phonocartridge to be converted into electrical impulses and sent to the amplifier. Synonymous with needle. 2. A hard-pointed instrument used by the ancients to write on clay or wax.

subbing A clear coating that facilitates adhesion between an emulsion and a film base.

subdivision see *hierarchical classification system, subject subdivision*

subfield code A content designator used to identify a subfield in a machine-readable record.

subgroup (archives) see *record subgroup*

subhead see *subheading* (3)

subheading 1. A secondary heading added to a subject heading to divide the entries under the subject. Compare with *subject subdivision.* 2. The name of a subordinate body added to the heading for a corporate body. 3. In composition, any type of heading making a subdivision of the text, usually set in smaller type than a main heading. Also called subhead.

subject The primary theme or topic on which a work is focused, or a tangential concept that introduces, justifies, proves, or amplifies the primary theme or topic.

subject authority file A set of records indicating the authorized forms of terms used as subject headings in a particular set of bibliographic records; the references made to and from the authorized forms; and the information used, and its sources, in the establishment of the headings and the determination of the references to be made. Compare with *subject heading list.*

subject bibliographer see *subject specialist*

subject bibliography A bibliography of works about a given subject.

subject catalog A catalog consisting of subject entries only.

subject cataloging The process of determining the subject of the work(s) contained in a bibliographic item for the purpose of classifying the item and of determining the appropriate subject or form heading(s) under which the item is to be represented in a catalog.

Subject Classification A classification system, published by James Duff Brown in 1906, with four main classes (Matter and Force, Life, Mind, and Record) and mixed notation. It is the most prominent general classification scheme developed in Great Britain.

subject cross reference see *subject reference*

subject department In a large general library, the subdivision of the library collection and services into administrative units according to subject specialization, as, for example, a science/technology division or department in a public library.

subject entry 1. An access point consisting of a subject heading. 2. A bibliographic record with a subject heading at the head of the record.

subject heading An access point to a bibliographic record, consisting of a word or phrase which designates the subject of the work(s) contained in the bibliographic item. Compare with *form heading.*

subject heading list A standard list of terms to be used as subject headings, either for the whole field of knowledge (such as the *Library of Congress Subject Headings*) or for a limited subject area, including references made to and from each term, notes explaining the scope or usage of certain headings, and occasionally corresponding class numbers. Compare with *subject authority file.*

subject reference A reference from one subject heading to another; may be upward, downward, or collateral. Synonymous with *subject cross reference.*

subject series A number of books treating different phases of one subject and issued by a single publisher in uniform format and layout. The books usually are not reprints and each is by a different author. Compare with *publisher's series.*

subject specialist A library staff member with superior knowledge of a subject or discipline, with responsibilities for the selection and evaluation of the library's materials in the subject area and sometimes with the added responsibilities of information service in the subject area and the bibliographic organization of the materials. Sometimes called subject bibliographer.

subject subdivision The method of extending a subject heading by indicating the form of the subject matter (form subdivision), the place to which it is limited (geographic subdivision), the period of time treated or the time of publication (period subdivision), or the aspect or phase of the subject treated (topical subdivision). Compare with *subheading* (1).

subordinate body A corporate body that forms an integral part of a larger body in relation to which it holds an inferior hierarchical rank. (AACR2)

subprofessional personnel see *paraprofessional personnel*

subscription The arrangement by which, in return for a sum paid in advance, a periodical, newspaper, or other serial is provided for a specified number of issues.

subscription agent An agent who, for a fee, handles the placing and renewing of subscriptions for a library.

subscription book 1. A book for which subscriptions by individuals are obtained prior to publication. 2. A book or a set of books, such as an encyclopedia, which is sold to individuals by the publisher by mail or by a publisher's representative.

subscription library A library whose members pay annual dues or subscriptions which entitle them to library services. Title to the property is held by the members acting as a single person, in the manner of a common-law corporation, not by members individually. Compare with *proprietary library.*

subscription television (STV) A system of broadcast television programming in which the signals are scrambled and can be rectified only by a special decoding device attached to the television receiver for a fee. Compare with *pay television* (1).

subsection (classification) see *hierarchical classification system*

subseries 1. A series within a series; that is, a series which always appears in conjunction with another, usually more comprehensive, series of which it forms a section. Its title may or may not be dependent on the title of the main series. (AACR2) 2. In archives, a *record subseries.*

subsidiaries see *back matter*

subsidiary rights Statutory rights to publication in other than the original form of a work, such as serialization, paperback, motion picture, public performance.

subsidy publishing The publication of scholarly or other specialized works (such as a company or local history) of interest to a small group and not expected to be a commercial success, with the costs met wholly or in part by the author, a foundation, or other sponsor. Such a work may be called a sponsored book, especially if the sponsoring organization or person has guaranteed to purchase a significant quantity of the edition. Compare with *private publisher, vanity publisher.*

substance number The weight in pounds of a ream (usually 500 sheets, but may be 1,000 for U.S. federal agencies) of 17-x-22-inch paper suitable for writing or printing. Abbreviated "sub." Compare with *basis weight.*

subsurface illuminator A light box used to eliminate shadows caused by incident light during optical copying. Compare with *top lighting.*

subtitle A secondary title, usually an explanatory phrase, added to the main title of a bibliographic item or work.

subvoice-grade channel A channel with a bandwidth narrower than that of a voice-grade channel, i.e., under 300 hertz.

summary A brief, recapitulative statement within a written work.

summary guide In archives, an abbreviated, often preliminary, guide to the holdings of a repository, usually lacking in descriptive detail regarding the informational content of record and manuscript groups, subgroups, etc.

summer reading program A formal program organized by a public library to foster reading by children during the summer months, sometimes supplemented by audiovisual materials. Synonymous with vacation reading program.

sunk bands Bands that have been laid into grooves sawed across the back of the sections of a book to effect a smooth back or spine. Compare with *raised bands* (1).

super see *crash*

supercalender A calender separate from the papermaking machine which gives a high gloss to paper by means of a burnishing action.

supercalendered paper The glossiest of uncoated book papers, produced by putting the paper under pressure between the rolls of a supercalender.

superfiche Microfiche containing images with a reduction ratio of 75X.

superimposition 1. The policy of adopting a new catalog code while leaving headings derived from an earlier code unrevised. Compare with *desuperimposition.* 2. In a faceted classification, the notational device used to specify composite subjects which arise from a combination of foci occurring in the same facet.

Superintendent of Documents Classification see *Documents Office Classification*

supervision The function of coordinating, directing, and guiding the activities of designated personnel within an organization toward the desired goals established for the organization.

supervisor A staff member who plans, organizes, and directs the work of a given department or a group of individuals.

supervisor computer program see *operating system*

supplement 1. A complementary part of a written work which brings up to date or otherwise continues the original text and is sometimes issued with it, in which case it is more extensive than an addendum, though usually issued separately. The supplement has a formal relationship to the original as expressed by common authorship, a common title or subtitle, and/or a stated intention to continue or supplement the original. Synonymous with continuation. Compare with *appendix, sequel.* 2. An extra sheet, section, or number accompanying the regular issue of a periodical or newspaper.

supplied title In the case of a bibliographic item that has no title proper on the chief source of information or its substitute, the title provided by the cataloger. It may be taken from elsewhere in the item itself or from a reference source, or it may be composed by the cataloger. (AACR2)

supplies A term used to encompass all material items of an expendable nature that are consumed, worn out, or deteriorate in use. For budgetary and accounting purposes, the parameter of the term is frequently expanded to include nonexpendable equipment items costing less than an established minimal amount. Compare with *equipment.*

supply reel That reel on a tape recorder or motion-picture projector from which tape or film is fed through the equipment and onto the take-up reel.

support services see *administrative and support services*

support staff A general term frequently used in personnel classification to designate all non-professional library personnel, including clerks, library technical assistants, and library associates.

supposed author An author to whom is attributed, by some authoritative source, the authorship of a work published anonymously or of doubtful authorship. Synonymous with attributed author.

suppressed 1. Said of a work withheld or withdrawn from publication or circulation by action of the author, publisher, governmental or ecclesiastical authority, or court decision. Synonymous with banned. 2. Of a leaf, canceled from a book because of some imperfection or objectionable feature. 3. Said of data in a machine-readable record whose public display is prevented under certain specified conditions. For example, a "see" reference that leads from a heading which is used on a bibliographic record may be automatically excluded from public display.

surface development A method of photographic processing in which only one side of the photosensitive material comes in contact with the developing solution.

survey A scientifically conducted study through which data are gathered according to a definite schedule and are presented in a statistical, tabulated, or summarized form.

survey research Research based upon contemporary data measured directly through interviews or questionnaires or upon data taken from other experiments and studies.

sustained silent reading see *free reading period*

swash letter An early italic capital having tails and flourishes. Also, any letter, though usually a capital, elaborated with flourishes.

sway bracing The stabilization of stacks lengthwise by using heavy crossrods forming an X to connect the two sides of single- or double-faced sections.

swinging-case shelving A type of compact shelving in which each fixed double-faced section of shelving has an additional case of double-faced shelving attached to each face by hinges. Either of the attached cases can be swung out to permit access to the materials stored on the fixed section or on the inner side of the case.

switched line A communications link in which a connection is made as a result of manual dialing.

switching center see *data-switching center*

swivel head A projection head found on some microform readers which rotates to permit normal viewing of film with images of different orientations.

syllabic notation In classification, an alphabetic notation which combines vowels and consonants in such a way that class numbers can be

pronounced. Synonymous with pronounceable notation.

symbol An arbitrary or conventional sign used in writing or printing relating to a particular field (such as mathematics or music) to represent operations, quantities, spatial position, sounds, or other ideas or qualities.

symbolic language Any programming language such as ALGOL, COBOL, and FORTRAN in which computer instructions can be written by a programmer using symbols easily understood by humans.

synch pulse see *synchronizing signal*

synchronize To cause two or more devices to move or operate at the same rate or at the same time; e.g., to cause a film advance and an odometer to move together on a microfilm reader.

synchronizing signal On an audiotape or audiodisc accompanying a set of slides or a filmstrip, a signal, audible or inaudible, that synchronizes the playback of the tape or disc and the advance of the slides or filmstrip in a projector. When the player is linked with a projector with an automatic advance mechanism, the projector advances at the signal. If the projector is not automatic, an operator advances the projector at the audible signal. Synonymous with pulse and synch pulse.

synchronous data transmission A mode of data transmission achieved in a steady flow by synchronizing or timing the transfer of characters at the beginning of a message. Compare with *asynchronous data transmission.*

syndetic catalog A catalog which includes the references that provide a syndetic structure. Synonymous with connective catalog. Compare with *asyndetic catalog.*

syndetic index An index in which relationships between entries or headings are shown through the use of subheadings and cross references.

syndetic structure In a catalog or index, the network of "see" and "see also" references that shows the generic and specific relationships among the headings or descriptors used.

synopsis A condensed, orderly abridgment of a written work, such as the skeletal plot of a novel and the main points of a periodical article, often prepared by someone other than the author of the original. Sometimes used synonymously with *abstract, compendium* (2), and *epitome* (2).

synoptic A concise (usually two-page) first publication in a periodical of those key ideas and results of research considered to be most important and directly useful to others, prepared by the author of a larger work reporting the research, and including an abstract.

synthetic classification An analytico-synthetic classification or an enumerative classification which by its notation joins class numbers to denote composite subjects.

synthetic language see *artificial language*

system A group or set of methods, procedures, and techniques organized to achieve a specified end result or function.

systematic bibliography see *enumerative bibliography*

systematic catalog see *classed catalog*

systematic mnemonics In classification, the mnemonic device of using in notation the same digits to denote a particular aspect of a topic or a particular subdivision, such as form, wherever it occurs in the classification schedule. Compare with *casual mnemonics, variable mnemonics.*

system flowchart A flowchart which depicts a system as a whole and includes only its subsystems or major elements.

systems analysis The process of studying an activity (e.g., a procedure, method, technique, or business), typically by mathematical means, to determine the goals or objectives of the activity and the most efficient and effective ways of accomplishing them.

systems theory A theory or set of hypotheses concerning the nature and behavior of systems.

T

tabcard A lightweight card of exact dimensions on which data may be represented by a pattern of punched holes or other means which can be sensed mechanically, optically, or electrically. Short for tabulating card.

table of contents In a book, a number of a periodical, etc., a list of its parts, such as chapter titles and periodical articles, with references by page number or other location symbol to the place they begin, and in the sequence in which they appear.

tablet A piece of clay, or a thin piece of wood or other material covered with wax, on which in ancient times records were written.

tablet book An ancient writing book, consisting of wax-covered tablets of wood, ivory, or metal fastened together at the back by rings or thongs of leather, on which writing was done with a stylus. Compare with *codex* (1).

tabletop reader see *microform reader*

tabs In binding, small pieces of paper, card, or fabric attached along the fore-edge of a book, with printed or stamped letters, words, or other characters showing the alphabetical, subject, or other arrangement of the text to provide quick reference. Compare with *thumb index.*

tabulating card see *tabcard*

tachistoscope A device similar to a slide projector which has a special shutter allowing the operator to project pictures, words, numbers, and sentences rapidly, as an aid in increasing reading speed or testing learning abilities, such as memory and attention.

tacking iron In dry mounting, a small wedge-shaped device used to heat and melt dry-mount tissue which has been placed between the back of the two-dimensional material to be mounted and the mounting surface.

tag A label of one or more characters or binary digits that identifies or describes a computer instruction, data item, data element, or field. Compare with *flag* (1).

tagging The process or activity of selecting and adding tags to data items or data fields.

tail see *foot*

tailpiece A type ornament decorating the end of a chapter or the bottom of a printed page.

take-up reel The reel on a tape recorder or motion-picture projector which receives the tape or film which has been fed from the supply reel through the equipment.

talking book A spoken text recorded either on audiotape or on an audiodisc (generally at 16⅔ rpm, but also at 33⅓ rpm) intended particularly for use by the visually handicapped. Synonymous with sound-recorded book. (NCES)

talking-book machine A machine similar to an audiodisc player, manufactured for playing talking-book audiodiscs.

tall copy A copy of an impression with head and foot margins little trimmed in binding. Not to be confused with *large-paper copy.*

tall organization A formal organizational structure in which supervisors at each level of the hierarchy have a small number of subordinates reporting to them, or a narrow span of control. Compare with *flat organization.*

tape deck see *audiotape deck, videotape deck*

tape drive see *tape transport*

tape monitoring see *monitor* (4)

tape recorder see *audiotape recorder, videotape recorder*

tape recording see *audiotape, videotape*

tapes Lengths of tape, or strips of cloth, to which sections are sewn in bookbinding. Compare with *cords* (1).

tape speed The speed at which magnetic tape moves past a fixed point in an audiotape or videotape recorder, usually measured in inches per second. Recorder speeds range from 1⅞ to 15 inches per second; the faster the speed, the better the quality of the recording.

tape transport The head assembly, motor(s) and control mechanisms in a tape recorder or computer which move the magnetic tape past the heads. Synonymous with tape drive.

tape unit see *magnetic tape unit*

target 1. A graphic set of patterns or images on a chart which serve to identify or assess an attribute of a document reproduction, such as a reflectance target or a resolution test chart. 2. Coded information placed on roll microfilm to facilitate the rapid location of document images, such as a flash index.

target group Those persons whom the library or other information agency by its mission is intended to serve.

target language In computer science, the language into which another language is to be translated. Synonymous with object language.

tariff The published rate for leasing or using a device, communications facility, or type of service offered by a communications common carrier.

task A unit of work, usually the smallest possible, in a system. Compare with *operation.*

task force An organizational unit established to accomplish a particular task or purpose. Synonymous with action group, working group. Compare with *ad hoc committee.*

t-distribution A sampling distribution based on the t-statistic, developed for the construction of confidence intervals for small samples (typically of fewer than 30 cases). Derived by William S. Gossett, who first published the mathematical expression of the distribution under the pseudonym "Student." Synonymous with Student's t-distribution.

tear sheet A sheet torn from a publication. When used in the plural, a clipped article.

technical assistant see *library technical assistant*

technical drawing A cross section, detail, diagram, elevation, perspective, plan, working plan, etc., made for use in an engineering or other technical context. (AACR2)

technical information center An information center which selects, acquires, organizes, processes, stores, retrieves, and disseminates technical information.

technical library A library primarily containing materials relevant to one or more of the applied sciences or the industrial or mechanical arts. It may be a separate administrative unit of a public or academic library or a special library.

technical processes A term which is sometimes used synonymously with *technical services* and at other times synonymously with *physical processing.*

technical processes department The administrative unit of a library which carries out technical processes, however the term is interpreted in that library. Sometimes used synonymously with preparations department.

technical report A report giving details and results of a specific investigation of a scientific or technical problem.

Technical Report Number see *Standard Technical Report Number*

technical services The area of library operations that includes acquisition of materials, organization and bibliographic control of materials, physical processing, and collection maintenance. Sometimes called technical processes.

telecommunications The long-distance transmission of signals over communication links or channels.

teleconferencing The use of telecommunication systems, such as telephone lines, computer networks, and two-way closed-circuit television, frequently by communication satellite, for personal communication among widely dispersed groups of people.

telefacsimile The transmission of a facsimile reproduction by means of electrical signals over telephone lines.

telegraphic abstract An abbreviated abstract consisting of keywords, role indicators, and other symbols, suitable for machine processing and storage. Synonymous with *skeleton abstract.*

telephone service Specific type of information service geared to efficiently and quickly conducting reference transactions by telephone.

teleprinter A typewriterlike printer used in data communications, teleprocessing, or timesharing.

teleprocessing A technique of data processing in which data is transferred to a remote computer system over communications links, processed, then transmitted back to the originating point.

telereference A means of consulting library materials from a remote location, usually by means of a cable television channel. The library user may request information by telephone or by means of a small transmitter. The reference staff member transmits the requested information from an online database or by placing the material, such as a map or graph, under a television camera for display on the user's television screen. Synonymous with video reference service.

telescope box see *double slipcase*

teletext A semi-interactive data communication system transmitting information through regular or cable television broadcast signals. The television viewer with a properly modified television receiver uses a small transmitter to instruct the receiver to display certain "pages" of alphanumeric or graphic information from a continuously updated database, the contents of which are determined by the television station. Compare with *videotex.*

teletype A form of telegraphy in which the transmitting station operates the keys of a receiving typewriter by means of a keyboard or a punched tape.

teletype code see *baudot code*

television camera A camera with a pickup tube that receives the image of the scene being televised and converts it into electrical impulses which are sent to receivers and converted back into pictures on the screen of a television receiver or monitor.

television monitor see *monitor* (2)

television projector An electronic device that projects television images onto a screen, usually for viewing in large areas and/or by groups of people.

television receiver An electronic device which intercepts the electrical signal of a television broadcast or (with adaption) television signals from other sources, and amplifies and converts the signals into image and sound.

television receiver/monitor An electronic device that combines the functions of both the television monitor and the television receiver but not simultaneously.

temporary cataloging The preparation of a temporary catalog record, consisting normally of a main entry heading, brief bibliographic description, and location symbol, made for a bibliographic item for which complete cataloging is deferred. Synonymous with brieflisting, deferred cataloging.

temporary storage see *working storage*

tenure 1. The period of time that an employee has been employed by an organization, held a given position within an organization, or may expect to hold a position within an organization. 2. Guaranteed permanence of employment granted to an employee based upon meeting established criteria and after a specified number of years.

term A word or phrase used in a definite or precise sense.

term classification see *automatic term classification*

term-entry system An indexing system in which each card represents a subject term and documents pertaining to the subject are posted to the card by assigned number. Synonymous with item on term system. Compare with *item-entry system.*

terminal 1. Any point in a system where data can enter or leave. 2. A device such as a cathode-ray tube or optical scanner used to enter data into or receive data from a computer system or data transmission system.

term on item system see *item-entry system*

terrestrial remote-sensing image see *remote-sensing image*

test of hypothesis A decision procedure, including the following steps: statement of the null hypothesis, specification of the significance level, calculation of the test statistic of each sample, acceptance or rejection of the null hypothesis, and, if the null hypothesis is rejected, acceptance of an alternative hypothesis.

test-retest method In statistics, a technique of testing the reliability of a statistical test or measure by applying it twice to the same sample or population.

test routine A routine to test for malfunctions in a computer. Synonymous with checkout routine.

test statistic A number that is calculated from a sample of observations made in order to test a statistical hypothesis and whose value, when compared with a criterion, leads to the decision on acceptance or rejection of the hypothesis.

test target see *target* (1)

tête-bêche A form of binding in which the text of one work begins at the "front" and the text of another at the "back," head to tail, with the texts being inverted with respect to one another. Such a volume usually includes two or more separate works or versions of the same work(s). Synonymous with inverted pages. Compare with *dos-à-dos*.

text 1. The words of the author, or the signs and symbols used in place of words by the author, in a written or printed work. 2. The body of a book, exclusive of the headlines, notes, illustrations, and other elements of a page. 3. A term used as a general material designation to designate printed material accessible to the naked eye (e.g., a book, a pamphlet, or a broadside). (AACR2) 4. The words of a song, song cycle, or, in the plural, a collection of songs. (AACR2) 5. In data transmission, the body of a message.

textbook edition An edition published for the use of students, as distinguished from the trade edition of the same work. It may be an issue rather than a true edition.

textile binding An ornate style of binding using fine fabric covers, typically satin and velvet, popular in England and France during the Renaissance. The covers were frequently embellished with many-colored silks and with gold and silver threads.

text paper Originally a book paper; now also a quality paper available in a variety of finishes and colors, frequently with laid lines, used for brochures, advertising booklets, programs, announcements, and the like.

text type Type used for reading matter, as in the body of a book, as distinguished from display type, used in headings, display lines in advertise-

ments, etc.; usually 12-point or smaller. Synonymous with body type.

textual bibliography The study of the relationship between the printed text and the text as conceived by the author. Synonymous with textual criticism.

textual criticism see *textual bibliography*

textura The most formal of the gothic or black-letter types, used for early Bibles and church service books. Synonymous with lettre de forme.

thematic index A list of a composer's works, usually arranged in chronological order or by categories, with the theme given for each composition or for each section of large compositions. (AACR2)

Theory X A term coined by Douglas McGregor, a management scholar, to describe a set of assumptions held by administrators about individuals or employees (namely, that they dislike work, have little ambition, and seek security) which influences how they deal with employees (namely, by coercion, manipulation, and threat). Compare with *Theory Y*.

Theory Y A term coined by Douglas McGregor, a management scholar, to describe a set of assumptions made by administrators about individuals or employees (namely, that they like work, respond to positive reinforcement, seek responsibility and growth) which influences how they deal with employees (namely, by encouraging self-direction and initiative). Compare with *Theory X*.

thermal copying see *thermal process*

thermally processed silver (TPS) see *dry silver film*

thermal plastic film see *photoplastic film*

thermal printer see *printer* (2)

thermal process A nonreversing copying process which uses thermal energy for document reproduction. Exposure takes place through infrared radiation; the dark parts of the original document reflect heat, which darkens the corresponding parts of the heat-sensitive copy paper or film. Synonymous with heat copying, thermal copying, and thermography in the general sense.

thermography 1. Any printing process involving the use of heat. Synonymous with *thermal process.* 2. Specifically, a raised-printing process in which an impression taken from letterpress is sprinkled while still wet with a special powder and heated, causing the powder particles to adhere to the printed surface and fuse to give the printing a raised effect. Also called raised-letter printing and imitation embossing.

thesaurus 1. A compilation of terms showing synonymous, hierarchical, and other relationships and dependencies, the function of which is to provide a standardized, controlled vocabulary for information storage and retrieval. Its component parts are an index vocabulary and a lead-in vocabulary. 2. A lexicon, especially of synonyms and antonyms in classified order.

thimble printer see *printer* (2)

third generation microfilm see *second reproduction microfilm*

thirtytwomo see *book sizes*

thread sealing A method of binding that combines leaf affixing by sewing and adhesive binding.

three-color process see *full-color printing*

three decker A term applied to the three-volume novels published in England in the latter half of the 19th century. The format was discontinued in the late 1890s.

three-quarter binding A style of book cover in which the spine and traditionally the corners are of one material and the sides of another. The same as half binding, except that the spine material extends farther on the sides (theoretically to three-quarters of half the width of the sides), with proportionately large corners.

threshold In photography, the minimum exposure needed to produce density on an emulsion.

throat In rotary cameras, the section where documents are loaded into the camera for microfilming.

throughput A measure of the total amount of work performed by a system within a specified period of time.

throw see *projection distance*

throw-in see *insert* (2)

throwout A leaf bearing a map, table, diagram, or similar material, mounted at the end of a volume on a guard the full size of the leaf, so that the leaf, when opened out, may be consulted easily as the book is read.

thumb index A series of rounded notches cut out along the fore-edge of a book, with printed or stamped letters, words, or other characters showing the alphabetical, subject, or other arrangement of the text to provide quick reference. Synonymous with cut-in index and gouge index. Compare with *tabs.*

tickler file A memorandum file of matters (inquiries, requests, forthcoming publications, etc.) which should be followed up at a definite date in the future. Synonymous with follow-up file.

tied letter see *ligature*

tier see *section* (3)

ties Cords, ribbons, or narrow strips of leather, attached to the edges of book covers, designed to hold the front and back covers together.

tight back A type of binding in which the covering material has been glued to the back of the book. Usually confined to leather-backed books, paperbacks, and books in LUMSPECS binding. Compare with *loose back.*

tight joint see *closed joint*

'til forbid A type of standing order usually given to a serials subscription agent, meaning that the agent should renew the order for a particular title or group of titles until notified to the contrary. Synonymous with until forbid. Compare with *continuation order, standing order.*

tilted shelves see *sloping shelves*

time and motion study A systematic analysis of the time spent and the motions employed in the performance of a specific work operation or task in order to establish the most effective and efficient method of performance and to provide a means of work measurement, or the standard time required to perform a specific task.

time-lapse photography A method of slow-motion photography in which film is exposed "stop motion" frame by frame at regular intervals over a long period of time to record motion, growth, or construction. When the film is projected, an event which takes a long time in reality appears in an extremely accelerated form.

timesharing The simultaneous use of a computer by a number of users from separate terminal devices.

time subdivision see *period subdivision*

tinted stock A film with its base tinted with a light-absorbing color for the prevention of halation.

tip in To use a thin strip of adhesive to affix a leaf or leaves to a page of a book. Synonymous with tip on.

tip on see *tip in*

tissued plate A plate protected by a thin sheet of tissue pasted to its back margin or left loose.

title 1. The distinguishing name of a work or a subdivision of it, such as the chapter of a book. 2. In cataloging, a word, phrase, character, or group of characters, normally appearing in a bibliographic item, naming the item, a work contained in it, a document which is part of the item, or the series to which the item belongs. 3. A *bibliographic item.*

title-a-line catalog A printed catalog consisting of records that take only a single line of type.

title entry 1. An access point consisting of the name of a bibliographic item, a work contained in it, a document which is part of the item, or the series to which the item belongs. 2. A bibliographic record with a title as the heading.

title leaf The leaf on which the title page is printed.

title letter see *work mark*

title mark see *work mark*

title page A page at the beginning of a bibliographic item bearing the title proper and usually, though not necessarily, the statement of responsibility and the data relating to the publication. The leaf bearing the title page is commonly called the *title page,* although properly it should be the *title leaf.* (AACR2)

title proper The chief name of a bibliographic item, including any alternative title but exclud-

ing parallel titles and other title information. (AACR2)

title reference A reference to a uniform title from a variant title or from one uniform title to another that is related to it.

title sheet The first signature of a book, often without a signature mark, containing the title leaf and other front matter. Synonymous with title signature.

title signature see *title sheet*

title vignette see *vignette* (3)

tonal range The variations in tone between light and dark that a photosensitive material is capable of reproducing. Synonymous with latitude.

tone The shadings between light and dark in a photographic or printed image.

tone arm The device on an audiodisc player into which the phonocartridge is fitted. Mounted above the turntable, the tone arm swings across the surface of the audiodisc.

toner A dry resinous powder employed in xerography or other materials present in solutions used to develop latent images on photosensitive materials.

tooling The impressing of a design, including decoration and lettering, on a book cover by means of hand tools. Synonymous with hand tooling. Compare with *stamping.*

top-edge gilt Having only the top edge of a book cut smooth and gilded.

topical guides Bibliographic guides that arrange in search-strategy order the various types of library resources available for doing a literature search on particular topics. Synonymous with pathfinders. An example of such a guide is the Library of Congress-produced *Tracer Bullets.*

topical subdivision The subdivision of a subject heading which represents an aspect or phase of the main subject of the work(s) contained in a bibliographic item.

top lighting The illumination of documents from above during optical copying. Compare with *subsurface illuminator.*

top management A term used to designate the group of individuals in an organization who have ultimate responsibility for the determination and accomplishment of organizational goals. In a library system, top management would normally encompass the head librarian or library director and those officers at the next organizational level, such as assistant or associate directors or librarians.

topographic map A map whose principal purpose is to portray and identify the features of the earth's surface as precisely as possible within the limitations of scale.

topographic model see *relief model*

total systems concept The concept of integrating all major systems of an organization into one comprehensive and coordinated system.

touch terminal A computer terminal equipped with a cathode-ray-tube screen that is sensitive to touch. For example, a computer may be programmed so that a user may respond to the display of a menu (a list of options) by touching that part of the screen where the chosen option appears. The touch alters the state of the electrical charge on that part of the screen, and the charge is transmitted to the computer as input.

township library A free public library maintained by a township.

toy, educational A play item which has value in developing physical or mental capacities and manipulative and motor skills, in addition to its value for pleasure and recreation. (NCES)

toy library A collection of toys available for loan in a library.

TPS (thermally processed silver) see *dry silver film*

tracings 1. The record of the headings under which a bibliographic item is represented in a catalog or bibliographic database. 2. In an authority file, the record of references made to and from headings to be used in a particular set of bibliographic records.

track 1. That discrete area of a film, videotape, or, more usually, of an audiotape on which are recorded electrical signals which can be converted to reproduce sound. An audiotape may have a number of tracks (usually 1, 2, 4, or 8) recorded upon it, depending on the number and/or configuration of the record heads used to record the signals on the tape. Tracks are parallel to the long dimension of the film or tape. (AECT) 2. The portion of a computer storage medium such as magnetic tape, magnetic disk, or magnetic drum directly beneath one read-write head and thus accessible for reading or writing data.

tract 1. A pamphlet made from a single sheet imposed in pages. 2. A pamphlet issued as propaganda, particularly on a topic of religious, political, or social interest.

trade bibliography 1. A list of books in print or for sale, compiled by a book publisher, a bookseller, or a group of such agencies. 2. Collectively, the mass of such bibliographies.

trade binding see *publisher's binding*

trade book 1. A book produced by a commercial publisher for sale to the general public primarily through bookstores, as distinguished from a textbook edition, subscription book, or a book meant for a limited public because of its technical nature, specialized appeal, or high price. 2. Any high-discount (more than 40 percent) book, regardless of subject matter or type of publisher.

trade catalog 1. A catalog designed to present a line of products or various sizes and models of a product, and to supply sufficient technical information to facilitate the purchasing process. (Z39.6) 2. A catalog issued by a manufacturer, a dealer, or a group of manufacturers, describing (and sometimes illustrating) their products, and sometimes including or accompanied by a price list. Synonymous with *manufacturer's catalog, trade list.*

trade discount see *discount*

trade edition An edition supplied by the publisher to bookstores at the wholesale discount and intended for retail to the general public.

trade journal A periodical devoted to the interests of a trade or industry and its allied fields. Synonymous with trade paper.

trade list see *trade catalog*

trade literature Catalogs and other advertising or promotional material distributed by business firms, usually free of charge.

trade paper see *trade journal*

trade paperback A paperback usually published by a trade publisher or university press and sold primarily in general and college bookstores. Synonymous with quality paperback. Compare with *mass-market paperback.* (Z39.20)

trade publisher A publisher of books intended primarily for sale through retail bookstores.

trade series see *publisher's series*

traditional format (Oriental books) Format of books consisting of double leaves with folds at the fore-edge and with free edges sewn together to make a fascicle. Usually several fascicles are contained in a cloth-covered case. Synonymous with Chinese style and Japanese style. Compare with *folded book.* (AACR2)

trailer 1. A blank section of tape at the end of a reel of motion-picture film, filmstrip, or microfilm for threading through the projector or other equipment and for the protection of the last frames. 2. A blank section at the end of a reel of magnetic tape or punched tape to protect the last few inches of the tape. Compare with *leader.* (2). 3. A short motion-picture film consisting of selected scenes from a film to be shown at a future date, to advertise that film. (AACR2)

trailer microfiche see *microfiche*

training The process of developing the knowledge, skills, and attitudes needed by employees to perform their duties effectively and to meet the expectations and goals of the organization. This diverse process, which may be performed by supervisors, fellow employees, and personnel officers, involves planning, preparation, execution, and evaluation.

train printer see *printer* (2)

transactional analysis The systematic analysis of a communication transaction between individuals.

transaction card A card bearing a sequential number and the due date which is inserted in an item at the time it is charged out when using the transaction charging system.

transaction charging system A charging system in which the records of circulation transactions are kept in the order in which they are made, transactions being given numbers in con-

secutive order. At the time of recording the loan a numbered "transaction card" is inserted in the borrowed item and remains there until the item is returned to the library, when it is withdrawn. Transaction cards for all returned items are then put into numerical order, and missing cards identify overdue items.

transaction file (computer science) see *detail file*

transactions The published papers and abstracts of papers presented at a meeting of a society or other organization, frequently accompanied by a record of the meeting called the proceedings. Sometimes used synonymously with *memoir* (2).

transceiver A terminal which can both send and receive data.

transcript A transcribed copy, usually written or typewritten, made from an original; particularly, a copy of a legal document.

transcription (music) see *adaptation, arrangement (music)*

transfer electrostatic process see *electrostatic process*

transfer process A contact copying method for reproducing documents which involves the transfer of images from a master. In a gelatin transfer process, images are transferred mechanically. The diffusion transfer process uses chemical transference.

transfer type Clear sheets of letters with adhesive back or press-on letters which may be applied to a master or an original.

transistor A small semiconductor device which is basically an amplifier, but which can also perform other tasks, such as high-speed switching, which enables a transistor-type computer to perform thousands of operations per second.

translate In computer science, to convert data from one programming language or form to another without loss of meaning.

translator 1. One who renders from one language into another, or from an older form of a language into a modern form, more or less closely following the original. (AACR2) 2. A special computer program such as a compiler or assembler that converts other computer programs from one programming language to another. Also, a device that converts data in one form or representation to another.

transliteration   A representation of the characters of one alphabet by those of another. Compare with *romanization.*

translucent screen   A surface of translucent glass or plastic on which an image may be produced by rear projection.

transmission block see *block* (3)

transmission copying   A contact copying method used for one-sided, translucent originals in which transmitted light passes through the original to form an image on photosensitive material. The resulting negative may then be used to produce a positive copy by the same process. Compare with *reflex copying.*

transmission densitometer see *densitometer*

transmission density see *density* (1)

transmission frame see *block* (3)

transmission line   A path for moving or transferring data from one point or location to another along a channel.

transmission rate see *data transfer rate*

transmitted light   Light passing through transparent or translucent material, such as a translucent screen.

transparency   1. A transparent sheet of acetate or other material with printed, pictorial, or other graphic matter which can be displayed by means of transmitted rather than reflected light. 2. In reprography, material with a transparent base on which images are recorded for viewing or to produce additional copies.

traveling library   A small collection of selected library materials sent by a central library agency for the use of a branch, group, or community for a limited period.

treatment   1. An experimental condition to which a sample is subjected in order to observe and compare its effects with those of other treatments or the absence thereof. A "treatment" may refer to a physical substance, a procedure, or any stimulus which is capable of controlled application according to the requirements of the

experiment. 2. The presentation of subject matter in a particular manner or style, or by a particular method.

treatment of correspondence see *correspondence management*

treble   The upper end of the audible frequency range, from about 3,000 to 20,000 hertz.

tree calf   In binding, calf that has been treated with acid so as to produce a design on the cover resembling a cross section of the burl or roots of a pronounced-grained wood.

trial proof see *engraver's proof*

tributary network station   Any network station that is not a network control station. A tributary network station can transmit only with the network control station. Synonymous with remote station. Compare with *primary network station.*

trimmed edges   Sometimes distinguished from cut edges in that the head may or may not be cut or even opened, while the other edges are only roughly made even. Compare with *cut edges.*

trimmed flush see *cut flush*

trimming   In binding, the act of making all pages of a book uniform in size by smoothly cutting the leaves along the head, fore-edge, and foot with a guillotine.

tripper   A device which actuates camera functions, such as the film advance.

triptych   An ancient hinged writing tablet consisting of three panels of wood, metal, or ivory, covered with wax on the inside surfaces, on which writing was done with a stylus.

troubleshoot see *debug*

truncate   1. In data processing, to drop or terminate data at a specified place or point. 2. In database searching, to cut the search term short at any point in order, for example, to retrieve all terms with a common root or both the singular and plural forms of a word.

trunk circuit   A circuit or channel between two data-switching centers.

t-statistic   The ratio of the difference between a sample mean and a hypothesized mean to the standard error of the mean, or the ratio of the difference between two sample means to the standard error of the difference between means. The t-statistic is especially important and useful in hypothesis testing with small samples. The significance of the t-statistic is a function of both its magnitude and its number of degrees of freedom.

t-test A test of significance which makes use of the t-distribution and the t-statistic to compare a sample mean with the hypothesized population mean, or to compare two sample means to determine whether they may be judged to have come either from the same population or from two populations whose means are equal.

tubular back A type of binding in which a tubular piece of fabric is glued to the back of the book and to the spine of the cover. The spine is thereby fastened to the back of the book, but can curve outward when the book is opened, as in a hollow-back binding.

tuner A device in a radio or television receiver which produces amplitude or frequency modulation suitable for selecting a desired signal.

turnaround time 1. In data processing, the amount of time between the initiation of a task, operation, or job in a system and its completion. 2. In data communications, the time required to reverse direction during half-duplex transmission of data.

turn-in The portion of the covering material that folds over onto the three inside edges of the front and back boards of a binding.

turnkey system A system that has been designed and developed by a company or other organization and then offered for sale or lease. The purchaser or lessee must only "turn the key" to begin using the system.

turnover see *staff turnover*

turntable The components of an audiodisc player which include the tone arm, the phono-cartridge, the turntable platter, and the motor to drive the platter.

turntable platter The rotating disc of an audiodisc player on which the audiodisc rests.

tweeter That component of a loudspeaker system which reproduces the treble range of the audible frequency range.

twelvemo see *book sizes*

twentyfourmo see *book sizes*

twin-lens reflex camera see *reflex camera*

twin-wire binding A style of mechanical binding using a double wire coil passed through slots or holes in the edge of the single leaves. It opens flat and, unlike *spiral binding*, the open pages remain aligned horizontally.

two along In binding, a style of hand-sewing in which two sections are treated as one unit by sewing each to alternate cords or tapes in the progress from the head to the tail kettle stitch. Generally used to reduce the thickness in the back of a book comprised of many thin sections, by reducing the amount of thread added in sewing. Synonymous with two on and two sheets on. Compare with *all along*.

two-card charging system see *double-entry charging system*

two-color process see *duotone*

two-component diazo A diazo-coated material containing both the coupler and diazonium salts in the base. Development is achieved by using an ammonia process. Compare with *one-component diazo*.

two on see *two along*

two sheets on see *two along*

two-way alternate transmission see *half-duplex transmission*

two-way paging The system of page numbering used for a book with texts in two languages, one of which reads from left to right (English, etc.) and the other from right to left (Arabic, Hebrew, etc.). The texts are in two distinct sections with page sequence from opposite ends to the center of the book.

two-way simultaneous transmission see *duplex transmission*

tympan The paper covering the platen, or paper-bearing cylinder, of a printing press to serve as a cushion behind the paper being pressed against the type and to equalize the pressure of paper to type.

type 1. A rectangular block, usually of metal, its face being a raised character or design that, in letterpress printing, is inked and pressed against the paper or other surface to be printed, to transfer the image to it. 2. The characters produced by direct-impression printing or nonimpact printing.

typeface 1. The printing surface of type. 2. The general design or style of the characters of a font of type, such as gothic, roman, and italic.

type-facsimile A reprint from a new setting of type in which the type and general appearance of the original are followed as closely as possible. Synonymous with *facsimile reprint*. Compare with *facsimile edition.*

type high see *body size*

type ornament In printing, a general term for decorative designs, not usually part of a type font, but available separately. May be used for a headpiece or tailpiece or combined to form a border. Synonymous with *printer's ornament.*

type page The area of the printed page produced from copy, exclusive of margins, headlines, footlines, and page numbers.

typescript A copy of a work in typewritten form, as distinguished from one in printed or handwritten form.

typesetting The setting of type from copy by hand; by the casting of hot metal type by machine; by direct impression, as with a typewriter; or by photosetting.

type size The measure in points of the dimensions of type, taken from the body rather than from the type face.

UDC see *Universal Decimal Classification*

UHF see *ultrahigh frequency*

ultrafiche Microfiche containing images with a reduction ratio of 90X or more.

ultrahigh frequency (UHF) In radio and television, a frequency band of 300 to 3,000 megahertz.

ultrahigh reduction see *reduction ratio*

ultraviolet light (UV) Light waves beyond the violet portion of the visible spectrum, shorter than those of visible violet light and longer than those of X rays.

unauthorized edition An edition issued without the consent of the author or the representative to whom the author may have delegated literary rights and privileges, but not in violation of copyright. Compare with *pirated edition.*

unbound 1. Said of issues of periodicals, parts, or fascicles intended to be bound several to a volume. 2. Said of a printed publication having leaves or signatures that have not been joined and bound to form a single volume. 3. Said of a printed publication issued without a cover, or with its cover removed.

uncial A style of handwriting used from the 4th through the 8th century, consisting of large, rounded majuscule letters that were a modification of capital letters and give an indication of the beginnings of our small, or lower-case, letters.

uncut Said of a book which has not had its edges cut smooth by the binder's machine. Not the same as *untrimmed.*

underdevelop To allow insufficient developing time for photosensitive materials. This generally results in a poor tonal quality, although it may be done intentionally to achieve a desired effect. It can also be caused by a weak developer, insufficient temperature during developing, and age of the material. Compare with *overdevelop.*

underexpose To allow insufficient light to reach photosensitive materials during exposure to take full advantage of the materials' properties. Underexposure may be a result of poor judgment or equipment failure, or it may be done intentionally in order to achieve a desired effect. It is a function of exposure time, lens aperture, and age of material. Underexposure usually results in poor contrast. Compare with *overexpose.*

undergraduate library A library service outlet established, supported, and administered by a university, usually as a branch of the university library, for the purpose of taking primary responsibility for meeting the library needs of its undergraduate students and instructional programs.

underground films Films covering controversial political, sexual, or social topics. Independently produced in the 1950s and 1960s, these films were not shown in theaters at that time. However, they revolutionized filmmaking and may be owned by and shown in libraries today.

underground publications 1. Printed publications issued secretly by a group or movement organized usually to overthrow or undermine a governing authority or, in time of war, the power in authority. Synonymous with clandestine publications. 2. Sometimes used synonymously with *alternative publications.*

unexpended balance That portion of the monies appropriated for each fund and the total budget which has not been expended or encumbered at any given time of accounting during the fiscal year or at the end of the fiscal year. Depending upon the established fiscal procedure for the organization, the unexpended monies in any fund may revert to the appropriating agency at the end of the fiscal period or become part of the expendable funds for the succeeding fiscal period.

unexpurgated edition An edition including material deleted in some editions as offensive.

uniform edition see *author's edition* (1), *collected edition*

uniform title 1. The particular title by which a work that has appeared under varying titles is to be identified for cataloging purposes. (AACR2) 2. A conventional collective title used to collocate publications of an author, composer, or corporate body containing several works or extracts, etc., from several works, e.g., complete works, several works in a particular literary or musical form. Synonymous with conventional title, filing title, standard title. (AACR2)

UNIMARC (Universal MARC Format) A project sponsored by the International Federa-

tion of Library Associations and published in 1977; intended to serve as a common denominator for the international exchange of bibliographic data in MARC format.

union catalog A catalog of the collections of all the libraries of a library system (a central catalog) or of a group of independent libraries cooperating for this purpose, with indication by means of location marks of the libraries in which a given bibliographic item may be found.

union finding list see *union list*

union list A list of bibliographic items of a given type, in a certain field, or on a particular subject, in the collections of a given group of libraries, with indication of the libraries in which a given bibliographic item may be found. Synonymous with union finding list.

union shelflist see *central shelflist*

union trade catalog see *consolidated trade catalog*

unit card system A data-processing system using one card, such as a punched card, for each record and an electromechanical machine such as a sorter or collator to manipulate the cards.

unit cost 1. The cost of a single item of library materials, supplies, or equipment usually purchased in larger quantities. 2. In cost accounting, the total cost of a single unit of production or service, such as the unit cost of cataloging or circulating an item. It is determined by dividing the total units of production or service into the total of all of the related costs.

unit entry system In a multiple-access catalog or list, the representation of each bibliographic item by a separate record for each access point provided to it. In a card catalog, the main entry is usually duplicated for each secondary access point to be provided, and the access point is added in filing position at its head.

United States Serial Set A special edition of publications of the United States House and Senate and such other publications as Congress orders to be printed in it. They are designated as reports or documents of the House or Senate and are assigned numbers within each Congress and category. However, the volumes of the set are numbered serially. Also known as Congressional Edition, Congressional Set, and Serial Set.

unitize To separate a roll of microfilm into individual frames or groups of related frames for insertion into a film jacket or other carrier.

unitized microreproduction see *microreproduction*

unit record A storage medium such as a punched card which can contain one complete and separate record.

unity of command The management concept that each employee in an organization should report to and receive orders from only one superior.

universal bibliographic control An international proposal for each national cataloging agency to take the responsibility for acquiring all new publications of that country, preparing cataloging data for them, and distributing these bibliographic records to other countries.

Universal Copyright Convention An international copyright convention formulated under Unesco sponsorship in 1952 and since ratified by more than sixty countries, including the United States. Under it, each signatory country extends to foreign works covered by the Convention the same protection extended to works of its own nationals published within its own borders.

Universal Decimal Classification (UDC) A general bibliographic classification system based on the *Dewey Decimal Classification*, but with much more elaboration of detail and more synthetic features. Developed under the leadership of Henri La Fontaine and Paul Otlet, it was first published in a French edition in 1905 with German and English editions following later, and updated by an international group of experts. Synonymous with Brussels Classification and Classification Décimale Universelle.

Universal MARC Format see *UNIMARC*

universe (statistics) see *population*

university library A library, or system of libraries, established, supported, and administered by a university to meet the information needs of its students and faculty and support its instructional, research, and service programs.

university press A nonprofit publishing house attached to a university (or serving a group of universities and other scholarly institutions),

and specializing in the publication of scholarly books. (Bookman's Glossary)

unjustified see *ragged*

unopened see *untrimmed*

unprecedented heading A heading on a bibliographic record which has not been used before in a given catalog. Automated authority control systems may include a means of giving notification, suppressing input, etc., when a heading is used for the first time, usually as an indication that authority work is or may be necessary.

unscheduled maintenance see *corrective maintenance*

unscheduled records In archives, records for which no final disposition has been made.

unsought link In classification, the unwanted term which may occur in a chain index because the notational hierarchy has unnecessary steps or because of faulty subordination in the classification system. Such links are unlikely to be used by a searcher.

until forbid see *'til forbid*

untrimmed Said of a book when the folded edges (bolts) have not been cut, but are to be separated by hand, and the uneven edges of projecting leaves have not been pruned square by a cutting machine. Synonymous with unopened. Compare with *uncut*.

updateable microform see *electrophotographic film*

upgrading The process of raising the grade level of particular positions within a position classification to reflect an increased level of complexity, responsibility, etc. Compare with *downgrading* (2).

uppercase letters Capital or majuscule letters of a font, so called because the case which held the capital letters of metal type historically was above the case for small letters. Compare with *lowercase letters*.

up-posting see *automatic generic posting*

uprights The vertical steel standards which support the shelves and separate the stack or ranges into sections. In a multitier stack they extend through several decks and support the load on the decks above. Compare with *shelf support*.

up time The time during which a computer or other machine is working or available for productive use. Compare with *down time*.

upward reference A reference from a term used as a subject heading or descriptor to a term that is more general. Compare with *downward reference*.

use life The period of time or number of times a material may be used, under normal conditions, before it becomes unusable. Compare with *shelf life*.

user area That portion of a library's assignable floor space that is intended primarily for library users, such as a reading room or audiovisual area.

user education A term which encompasses all types of activities designed to teach users about library services, facilities, and organization, library resources, and search strategy. It includes instruction in the use of one or more reference

sources as a part of reference transactions, library use presentation, and bibliographic instruction.

user group The members of the library target group and others who actually use the collection or services of the library. Synonymous with clientele.

user identification A group of characters which identifies a user of a computer system. Compare with *password*.

user profile see *interest profile*

U-shaped distribution A frequency distribution having the majority of the frequencies at the two extremes of the distribution, in the general shape of the letter U.

utility, bibliographic see *bibliographic utility*

utility program Special software used to perform routine or housekeeping operations in a computer system.

UV see *ultraviolet light*

vacation reading program see *summer reading program*

vacuum-back camera A camera in which the film is held in place by vacuum.

vacuum tube An evacuated glass tube enclosing two or more metallic elements for controlling the flow of electrons and for other purposes, such as the amplification or detection of electromagnetic waves.

validity An expression of the extent to which a test actually measures what it is intended to measure. Compare with *reliability*.

value-added network A network which leases services from a communications common carrier, adds special services or features to the sys-

tem, and sells the improved services to customers.

vandyke see *diazotype process, proofs*

vanity press see *vanity publisher*

vanity publisher A publisher who specializes in producing books entirely at the author's expense. Synonymous with vanity press. Compare with *private publisher, subsidy publishing*.

variable In statistics, observable and measurable traits, characteristics, or other phenomena of objects, events, or individuals that have no fixed value and can assume any of the values of a specified set.

variable budget A budget based upon varying levels of output or activity for a budget period, with expenditures stated in ranges to reflect the varying levels. Synonymous with flexible budget.

variable contrast paper A photographic paper on which contrast characteristics can vary between those associated with hard and soft paper.

The contrast is controlled by the color of the light used for exposure, normally through a series of filters.

variable costs Those expenses which vary in a direct relationship to the level of activity or production.

variable field In data processing, a field whose length may vary within predefined limits according to the amount of data to be recorded. Compare with *fixed field, free field.*

variable-length record In data processing, a record whose length is not limited to a defined number of characters, thus enabling data of varying lengths to be stored or recorded. Compare with *fixed-length record.*

variable mnemonics In classification, the mnemonic device of using generally in notation the same digits to denote a particular aspect of a topic or a particular subdivision, such as form, but with some deviations. Compare with *casual mnemonics, systematic mnemonics.*

variance In statistics, the square of the standard deviation.

variance-ratio distribution see *F-distribution*

variorum edition An edition recording variant versions of the text or notes by several editors or commentators.

VCR see *videotape recorder*

VDT (video display terminal) see *cathode-ray-tube terminal*

VDU see *visual display unit*

vellum A thin sheet of calf (or sometimes of lamb, kid, or pigskin) dressed with alum and polished; used for writing or binding. Frequently used as synonymous with *parchment.*

vellum finish 1. A smooth finish given to book cloth by first dyeing the cloth and then applying filler to both sides and a coating that includes the coloring to the face. 2. A paper finish similar to eggshell, but with a smoother surface texture.

velo-binding A method of mechanical binding in which the projecting pins of a plastic strip are inserted through holes along the binding edge of the leaves and into matching holes in another plastic strip. A special machine compresses the leaves, cuts the pins to the proper length, and fuses the pins to the strips. This binding is fairly strong and permanent, but will not open flat.

vendor file see *dealer file*

verification In acquisitions work, the process of determining that a requested bibliographic item has actually been published and that the supplied bibliographic data are correct and adequate for use as order information. Compare with *preorder bibliographic search.*

verifier 1. A device similar to a keypunch used to detect errors in the punching of data into punched cards. 2. A staff member who checks the accuracy of bibliographic data, machine coding, etc.

version 1. A particular translation of the Bible or any of its parts. 2. An adaptation, or modification of a work for a purpose, use, or medium other than that for which the original was intended. 3. One of the variant forms of a legend, fairy tale, or other work of unknown or doubtful authorship.

verso 1. The left-hand page in an open book, usually bearing an even page number. 2. The side of a printed sheet intended to be read second. Compare with *recto.*

vertical file 1. A collection of materials such as pamphlets, clippings, and pictures, which, because of their shape and often their ephemeral nature, are filed vertically in drawers for easy reference. 2. A case of drawers in which materials may be filed vertically.

very high frequency (VHF) In radio and television, a frequency band of 30 to 300 megahertz. This band is stronger than *ultrahigh frequency* and can cover a larger broadcast area.

very high reduction see *reduction ratio*

vesicular film A duplicating film, usually sign-reversing, which uses heat alone to develop latent images after exposure to ultraviolet light. The images become permanent upon cooling, although some care should be taken in storage, as heat may affect images on poorly developed film. It is not generally considered to be of archival quality. At one time the film was referred to as Kalvar, after the company that originally produced it.

vesicular process A dry developing and fixing process which uses heat to develop latent images on exposed vesicular film. Nitrogen is released during exposure, and heating creates tiny vesicles which then produce images.

VHF see *very high frequency*

videocartridge A single reel of recorded videotape, permanently encased in a plastic container, with the videotape ends joined to form a continuous loop. Synonymous with cartridge videotape and videotape cartridge.

videocartridge player see *videotape player, videoplayer*

videocartridge recorder see *videotape recorder*

videocassette A recorded videotape permanently encased in a plastic container with two reels, a supply reel and a take-up reel. Synonymous with videotape cassette.

videocassette player see *videotape player, videoplayer*

videocassette recorder see *videotape recorder*

videodisc A videorecording on a disc, usually plastic. The videodisc can be played back to reproduce pictures and sound, using a television receiver or monitor and a playback device similar to an audiodisc player. Synonymous with optical disc.

video display terminal (VDT) see *cathode-ray-tube terminal*

video head The head in a videotape recorder or player which records and/or plays back the video signals on the magnetic tape.

videoplayer An electronic device which can play back images and sound from a videorecording, either a videotape or videodisc. It has no capability for recording. The player must be compatible with the videorecording to be played. (AECT)

videorecording 1. A generic term for material on which both pictures and sound are recorded and which can be played back electronically to reproduce both pictures and sounds using a television receiver or monitor. Includes both videotapes and videodiscs. (AECT) 2. The activity of operating a videotape recorder to elec-

tronically record pictures and sounds on videotape. (AECT)

videoreel A reel holding recorded videotape.

video reference service see *telereference*

videotape A magnetic tape on which video and audio signals may be or are recorded for television use. The tape varies from ¼ to 2 inches in width and from 0.5 to 1.5 mils in thickness. The most common sizes for instructional and educational use are ½, ¾, and 1 inch wide.

videotape cartridge see *videocartridge*

videotape cassette see *videocassette*

videotape deck A device equipped with a tape transport and electronic components for recording and playing back images and sounds on videotape, but not with amplifiers, loudspeakers, or a monitor.

videotape monitor see *monitor* (1)

videotape player An electronic device which can play back, but cannot record, videotapes on open reels, in cartridges, or in cassettes. The player must be compatible with the particular type of cartridge or cassette to be played.

videotape recorder A device which can record television images and sound on videotape and which can play back the videotape for viewing on a television monitor or special television receiver. The videotape recorder may use reels, cartridges, or cassettes. Abbreviated VTR and, in the case of videocassette and videocartridge recording, VCR.

videotex An interactive data communication system linking computer databases to television receivers through telephone or cable television lines. The television viewer with a properly modified television receiver uses a small control panel to request the display of "pages" of information from any one of a number of continuously updated databases. Search instructions are displayed also on the screen, telling users how to proceed from the general to the specific in a step-by-step search for information. Synonymous with viewdata. Compare with *teletext.*

vidicon A photoconductive television pickup tube, in which light from the scene being televised falls upon a transparent target, whose electric conductivity varies with the intensity of the radiation. A low-velocity electron beam scans the reverse side of the target, and the circuit is completed by a transparent signal plate.

viewdata see *videotex*

viewfinder A device on a camera which shows the area of the subject to be included in the photograph.

viewing system The part of a camera in which the photographer views the scene or subject to be photographed. Two basic systems exist: the optical viewing system and the reflex viewing system.

vignette 1. In manuscripts, a design of vine tendrils decorating an initial. 2. An engraving or other picture, without a definite border and with its edges shading off gradually. 3. Loosely, any ornamental design before a title page, on a title page, or at the beginning or the end of a chapter. A vignette on a title page is called a title vignette.

virgule An oblique stroke, / , used in bibliographic descriptions to indicate line endings. Sometimes called a solidus.

virtual image In optics, an image of an object formed by an extension of light rays, which does not exist where it appears to be, such as an image in a plane mirror. Compare with *real image.*

virtual memory see *virtual storage*

virtual storage In computer science, a conceptual form of main storage which does not actually exist. Main storage is made to appear larger than it really is through the use of an extremely fast auxiliary storage device located close to the central processing unit. Synonymous with virtual memory.

visible file see *visible index* (1)

visible index 1. A filing unit containing a series of metal frames, panels, or flat trays fitted with pockets for holding card records. The pockets are so arranged that approximately one-fourth inch of each card, which contains the index entry, is exposed. The units come in a variety of designs and configurations. Synonymous with visible file. 2. The collective records kept in such a file, mostly serial records and holdings information.

visible joint see *exposed joint*

visitor's card A temporary borrower's identification card issued to a transient borrower, sometimes upon the payment of a fee. When free, also called courtesy card.

visual aids see *audiovisual materials*

visual display unit (VDU) A computer terminal which usually contains an input device, such as a keyboard or light pen, and a cathode-ray-tube for output and indication of the input. Compare with *cathode-ray-tube terminal, printer terminal, touch terminal.*

visual range That portion of light spectrum of wavelength between the infrared and the ultraviolet which can be seen by the human eye.

vocabulary The limited number of words, terms, or codes under command of, or available to, a person, machine, or system.

vocal score In music, a score showing all vocal parts, with accompaniment, if any, arranged for keyboard instrument. (AACR2)

voice-grade channel A communications channel capable of transmitting ordinary speech, usually within a bandwidth of 300–3,000 hertz.

voice response unit In computer science, an output device which uses a prerecorded vocabulary to provide spoken responses to an input of digital data, usually over telephone lines. Synonymous with audio response unit.

volume 1. In the bibliographic sense, a major division of a bibliographic item, regardless of its designation by the publisher, distinguished from other major divisions of the same item by having its own inclusive title page, half title, cover title, or portfolio title, and usually independent pagination, foliation, or signatures. This major bibliographic unit may include various title pages and/or paginations. (AACR2, mod.) 2. In the material sense, all that is contained in one binding, portfolio, etc., whether as originally issued or as bound after issue. The volume as a material unit may not coincide with the volume as a bibliographic unit. (AACR2) 3. The collective issues of a periodical that constitute the whole or a consecutive part of a definite publishing period, either bound or unbound. 4. Of a machine-readable data file, a physical unit of external storage such as a disk, a reel of magnetic tape. (AACR2) 5. In acoustics, see *loudness.*

volume capacity see *shelving capacity, stack capacity*

volume number 1. A number assigned to a volume of a serial, a set, or a series. 2. A number added to a book number to distinguish one volume from another volume of the same work.

volume signature The number of the volume, or a letter indicating its sequence (such as "a," "b," etc.) given on the same line as the signature mark, but toward the inner margin of the first page of each signature.

volunteer services see *contributed services* (1)

voucher In fund disbursement, the form to which invoices and receipts are attached, indicating authority to pay.

VTR see *videotape recorder*

waiting line see *queue*

waiting list see *want list*

wallet edge The edge of a limp leather binding in which the back cover is extended to overlap the front edge of the volume, terminating in a tongue to be inserted through slots in the front cover when the book is closed.

wall shelving Single-faced cases or sections of shelving placed against a wall and sometimes secured to the wall.

want list A file recording documents which are to be purchased by a library when funds are available or when the documents become available. Synonymous with desiderata, possible purchase file, waiting list.

wash bath see *washing*

washboard A film defect normally associated with rotary-camera microfilming. Varying illumination or faulty document or film advance creates bands of varying densities perpendicular to the film edge.

wash drawing In book illustration, a drawing in black, white, and gray only, done with a brush.

washing In the photographic processing of silver halide materials, the process of bathing photographic film or paper in water to remove fixing chemicals which, if left on the materials, cause deterioration of the image. Synonymous with wash bath and rinsing.

watermark A design usually worked in the center of one half of a paper mold or on a dandy roll. It appears as an increased translucence in the paper and sometimes includes letters and numerals. Variations in design over time and place allow it to be used in dating and localizing paper production. Synonymous with papermark. Compare with *countermark*.

water spot A film defect caused by water drops deforming portions of a photographic emulsion during processing. The defect appears also on prints made from a water-spotted negative. The problem is usually alleviated through the use of a chemical wetting agent which reduces the surface tension of the water.

waxed tablet An ancient tablet, usually of wood or ivory, with slightly raised borders, the depression being covered with blackened wax, on which writing was done with a stylus.

web-fed press A printing press that is fed paper from a roll instead of separate sheets.

weed To select items from a library collection for withdrawal or for transfer to a storage area.

weekly A periodical or newspaper published once a week.

weighted-term retrieval system A method of computer-based information retrieval in which numeric weights are assigned to each search term, and only documents bearing terms with combined values exceeding a predetermined numerical value are retrieved.

wet carrel see *carrel*

wet process Any method of producing a copy from a film positive or negative or from an original which requires the use of water solutions, as for conventional silver halide materials. Compare with *dry process.*

wetting agent see *water spot*

white light Radiated light, containing all the visible rays of the spectrum, which produces the same color sensation to the average human eye as average noon sunlight.

white-line method see *wood engraving* (1)

white paper 1. An official government report on any subject. 2. A popular name for a relatively short British government publication, derived originally from its white paper cover, which distinguished it from the lengthier blue book, but now used mainly to denote important policy statements published as *Parliamentary Papers* or, sometimes, as non-Parliamentary papers.

whiteprint see *diazotype process, proofs*

whiteprint process see *diazotype process*

whole binding see *full binding*

whole number The single unique number assigned by a publisher to each part of a serial or series, counting from the beginning of the publication, in distinction from two numbers: one for volume or series and another for the part.

wholesaler A book dealer who buys from publishers and sells to libraries and bookstores. Synonymous with jobber. Compare with *agent, dealer.*

who's who file see *biography file*

wide band A communications channel with a bandwidth wider than that of a voice-grade channel, and thus capable of a higher speed of data transmission. Synonymous with broad band. Compare with *narrow band.*

wire binding Any method of leaf affixing which uses wire.

wireless headphone A headphone capable of receiving a low-power-signal broadcast, such as that in an audio induction system.

wire lines see *laid paper* (1)

wire printer see *matrix printer*

wire side The side of a sheet of paper which has rested on the wire or screen of the mold or papermaking machine. It bears the indentations from the screen. The other side, which in handmade paper has been turned onto the felts for drying, and in machine-made paper comes into contact with the felt blanket of the papermaking machine, is called the felt side.

withdrawal 1. The process of removing an item no longer in the library collection from the library's records of holdings. 2. An item ready to be withdrawn.

withdrawal record A record of all items officially withdrawn from a library collection.

with the grain Said of paper which has been folded or cut parallel to the grain.

wood block A type-high block of wood on which an image for letterpress printing has been cut.

woodcut 1. A wood block on which a knife or gouge has been used along the grain to recess the nonprinting area and leave the image to be printed in relief. Also called black-line method because the printed image appears as black lines on a white background. Compare with *wood engraving* (1). 2. A print made from such a block.

wooden boards The covers of bound books of wood over which leather is stretched. The use of pasteboard for binding was not introduced into the West until about the 15th century and at first was used only on books of small size.

wood engraving 1. A wood block on which a graver or burin has been used across the grain to define the image with a recessed line. Also called white-line method, because in this relief printing process the printed image appears in white outline against a dark background. Compare with *woodcut* (1). 2. A print made from such a block.

wood pulp Paper pulp prepared from various kinds of trees by either mechanical or chemical means.

wood-pulp magazine see *pulp magazine*

woofer That component of a loudspeaker system which reproduces the bass range of the audible frequency range.

word-by-word alphabetizing The arrangement of an alphabetical file using words rather than letters as filing units. In this system, spaces between words and sometimes marks of punctuation are treated as filing elements. Compare with *letter-by-letter alphabetizing.*

word-frequency analysis In automatic indexing, an analysis of a document whereby the frequency with which significant words occur in the text is counted and words most frequently used are selected to represent the subject content.

word indexing see *derived indexing*

word length see *computer word length*

word processing A management approach or technique in which people, procedures, and equipment are systematically organized for effective and efficient handling and transformation of verbal information into a readable form of communication. Word-processing units commonly use sophisticated strike-on typewriter equipment, a microcomputer, and a cathode-ray-tube video display of text; and some allow the interface of the unit with a photosetting machine.

word processing-output microfilm (WPOM) The procedures and equipment which provide a direct means of digitally transmitting from word processing equipment to a computer-output-microfilm recorder via data communications or magnetic medium (tape, disk) without using a computer main frame. (NMA)

word-proximity search In a natural-language retrieval system, a searching technique for retrieving documents in which two particular words are immediately adjacent or appear at specified intervals apart.

word-truncation search In an information retrieval system, a search conducted on words containing the same string of characters, such as words beginning with the form "ferro-."

work Bibliographically defined, a specific body of recorded information in the form of words, numerals, sounds, images, or any other symbols, as distinct from the substance on which it is recorded.

work area The portion of a library's total floor space allocated for use by library staff members for performance of their duties. It includes space for desks, furniture, and any needed equipment, as well as space for sorting and packing materials.

workbook A learning guide, which may contain exercises, problems, practice materials, space for recording answers, and, frequently, means of evaluating work done.

working drawings see *architectural drawings*

working group see *task force*

working papers Documents such as notes, calculations, or rough drafts assembled or created and used in the preparation or analysis of other documents.

working storage A part of the main storage of a computer reserved for data being processed or awaiting output. Synonymous with temporary storage.

work manual see *procedure manual*

work mark One or more symbols added to the author mark to provide subarrangement by title and to arrange editions of the same title in order. Synonymous with title letter and title mark. Compare with *author mark.*

workmen's compensation insurance Insurance that reimburses an employer for damages paid to an employee or the dependents of an employee who is injured, disabled, or killed during the course of regular employment. The amount for various claims is stipulated by law.

worm bore see *wormhole*

wormhole A hole or series of holes bored into or through a book's covers and/or leaves, made by a bookworm. Synonymous with worm bore.

wove paper 1. Paper handmade on a framed mold of fine wires woven like cloth, with the wires interlacing one another closely and evenly. A fine mesh pattern made by the wires is visible when the paper is held up to the light. Compare with *laid paper* (1). 2. Machine-made paper upon which a mesh pattern has been impressed by a dandy roll.

wow Distortion, usually mechanical, in the form of a slow fluctuation in pitch, caused by a variation in the speed of a component in the sound-producing system of audiotape recorders and audiodisc players.

WPOM see *word processing-output microfilm* (*WPOM*)

wrap around see *outsert*

wraparound plate   A plate that is normally flat but is flexible enough to be wrapped around the cylinder of a rotary press.

wrapper   1. The original paper cover of a book or pamphlet, to which it is attached as an inte-

gral part of the volume. 2. Sometimes used synonymously with *book jacket.*

write   In computer science, to transfer data into a storage device or record data on a recording medium.

write time   The time between the beginning and completion of the recording of data in a storage device or on a recording medium such as magnetic tape or magnetic disk.

writing paper   Paper with a surface suitable for pencil, pen, typewriter, or printing press. It is made in a range of qualities and from various pulps and mixtures which can include groundwood pulp.

X-axis   A horizontal line or axis on a map, chart, or graph using rectangular coordinates. Usually referred to as the abscissa. Compare with *Y-axis.*

xerography   A generic term for an electrostatic copying process. In particular, one which involves the transfer of a dry toner from an elec-

trostatically charged plate to ordinary paper. Sometimes referred to as dust development.

x-height   Of a type face, the distance between a line that would connect the top of the lower-case letters that do not have ascenders and a line that would connect the base of the lower-case letters that do not have descenders, as x, z, o, m.

X Theory see *Theory X*

xylographic book see *block book*

Yapp edges see *divinity-circuit edges*

Y-axis   A vertical line or axis on a map, chart, or graph using rectangular coordinates. Usually referred to as the *ordinate.* Compare with *X-axis.*

yearbook   An annual compendium of facts and statistics of the preceding year, frequently limited to a special subject. Compare with *almanac* (1).

yellowback   A popular, cheap novel bound in yellow board or paper covers with a picture on the front. Yellowbacks originated in England in

the 1850s and were popular there into the late 19th century.

young adult book   A book intended for adults which is of particular interest to young adults between 14 and 18 and in the ninth through twelfth grades.

young adult department   1. The part of a library devoted to collections and services for users between the ages of 14 and 18 and in the ninth through twelfth grades. 2. The administrative unit of a public library system that has charge of work with young adults in the central library and all other service outlets offering services to young adults.

young adult librarian A librarian responsible for developing and providing services and collections for young adults. The librarian may be a staff member of the adult services department or of a separate young adult department.

young adult room A room in the central library or in a branch of a public library set aside for services and collections for young adults.

Y Theory see *Theory Y*

Z

zero-based budgeting A budgeting system in which every program, whether new or continuing, must be justified in terms of its merit and in comparison to others for each new budget period.

zero growth see *steady state*

zinc etching see *line cut*

zinc oxide paper Paper coated with a zinc oxide emulsion used in the electrostatic copying process.

Zipfian distribution The characteristic hyperbolic distribution of words used in a large collection of text, displayed by the plotting of the cumulative percentage of total word usage against the cumulative percentage of words contributing to this usage. Derived from the analysis of G. K. Zipf, who found that a comparatively small number of words occur frequently and account for a large proportion of all the word occurrences in the text.

zirconium lamp A special high-intensity lamp used as a source of radiant energy in photocopying.

zoom lens A lens with a focal length that is continuously variable between certain limits. It permits the optical image to be varied in size without altering the focus.

z-score The value of a score in a collection of scores expressed as so many standard deviations above or below the mean. The conversion of a collection of raw scores to z-scores produces a score distribution with a mean of zero and a standard deviation of one.